Operations Management in Practice

Operations Management in Practice

Edited by
C D LEWIS
University of Aston

NAPIER COLLEGE
THE QUEEN'S LIBRARY
SIGHTHILL

Philip Allan

First published 1981 by
PHILIP ALLAN PUBLISHERS LIMITED
MARKET PLACE
DEDDINGTON
OXFORD OX5 4SE

© PHILIP ALLAN PUBLISHERS 1981
All rights reserved.

British Library Cataloguing in Publication Data

Operations management in practice.
1. Production management
I. Lewis, Colin David
658.5 TS155

ISBN 0-86003-511-5
ISBN 0-86003-611-1 Pbk

Set by MHL Typesetting Limited, Coventry
Printed in Great Britain at The Camelot Press Limited, Southampton

Contents

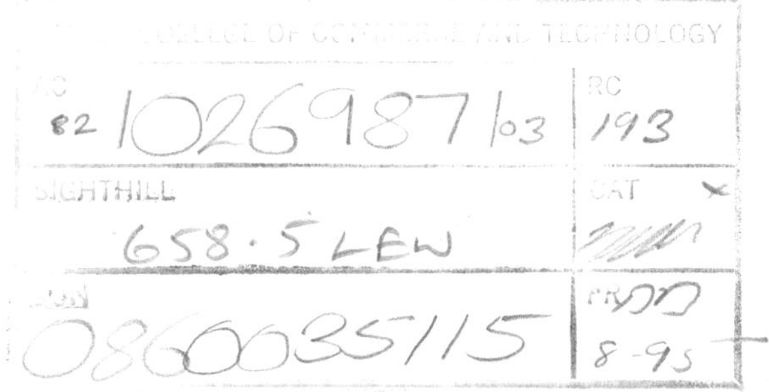

Foreword

The subject covered by the relatively new term '*Operations Management*' is increasingly appearing before the general public linked particularly with job opportunities in national newspapers, and also in the educational world by the establishment of chairs at Universities throughout the USA and the UK. What, however, is Operations Management?

To some extent the term has the same antecedents as Operational Research (UK) or Operations Research (USA), whereby the emphasis came to be laid on the 'operation' for which functional activities acted as co-ordinated contributors, rather than as strictly divisionalised company functions. Thus, in theory, a manager appointed to supervise an operation such as the flow line production of TV sets would have available to him a supporting team made up of members of the company's functional activities of accounts, personnel, planning and control, organisation and methods (O & M), operational research (OR), design and development etc. These would all be able to continue their specialised knowledge (and that of their supporting functional department) to the efficient management of the operation of producing TV sets, to which they as individuals were specifically committed. This concept replaced the traditional role of a line manager working beneath a Production Manager who raised problems relating to the operation with managers of other functional departments – who then delegated responsibility on the basis of who was free, rather than who was particularly knowledgeable about the TV production process.

Another reason for the use of the term Operations Management is the increasing realisation that many of the techniques and skills traditionally referred to as Production Management have applications in the production of services as well as in the production of goods. Thus the provision of a service through the issue and administration of a complex system of forms and related paperwork (such as that provided by national and local government agencies) can be viewed as being essentially very similar in organisational terms to the production of TV sets. Obviously emphases do differ between the two, but increasingly similarities are being found.

Since there are already several excellent books on Operations Management, what role does *Operations Management in Practice* have to play? Essentially its aim is to bridge the gap between the non-technical appreciation of the manager and intelligent layman, and the lengthy specialised texts on the subject. Thus our book is aimed not only at student and practising Operations and Production Managers, but also at the numerous engineers, economists, accountants and those involved in other management service functions. Such readers may never actually become Operations Managers, but are more than likely to work with them at some time or other and may wish to gain an insight into the techniques and practice of Operations Management.

The book centres around the many contributions made in the OM area by the University of Aston Management Centre's large MBA programme and the increasing OM context of the undergraduate Managerial and Administrative Studies course. In both these courses, lectures by members of the academic staff of the Centre are supplemented by guest speakers from industry and the public sector, together with visits to sites within Britain's most diversified industrial community – the Midlands conurbation.

Because both the courses from which the book derives and the subject of Operations Management itself have a unifying theme of 'getting the job done', the majority of the chapters are accompanied by illustrative case studies from practising managers, indicating that the material of the preceding chapter has, in fact, been successfully used in a real-life situation.

C D Lewis
November 1980

1
An Introduction to Operations Management

D J BENNETT

Senior Lecturer in Operations Management,
The University of Aston

1 Introduction – What is Operations Management?

Operations Management is a subject which has quickly grown from relative obscurity to become a major subject for study in most management and business schools. Moreover, in the world of business itself, the importance of Operations Management has emerged and is recognised as an area of management which requires special skills and training. What is the reason therefore for this acceptance that 'operations' may be regarded as an area which has a common body of knowledge and which may be reduced to a single set of concepts and techniques?

To answer this question it is appropriate to examine the development of the various ideas which have given rise to Operations Management. It is probably true to say that, traditionally, manufacturing industries have tended to dominate management thinking and the function that dealt with the organisation of resources has been termed 'production management'.

Since the industrial revolution, the constant drive has been to improve the efficiency of production systems and to this end successive generations of engineers and managers have examined a series of problem areas in their attempt to maximise the return from their investment.

The solution to these problems can be broadly categorised within the various 'schools' which together form the basis of production management thinking as shown in figure 1.1.

The Process School
The Scientific Management School → Production
The Operational Research School → Management
The Human Factors School

Figure 1.1 *The Basis of Production Management Thinking*

The Process School

The Process School, by far the oldest, concentrates on the technical aspects of production. The origins of this school can be traced back to the eighteenth century when the progress of industrial production was dependent on the inventiveness of a relatively small handful of individuals.

The problem of motive power, for instance, was tackled by James Watt, who in 1769 developed the first viable steam engine. John Wilkinson invented the first of a generation of machine tools in 1774, while in 1798 the American Eli Whitney employed the concept of standardisation together with the use of jigs and tools to manufacture large volumes of muskets with interchangeable parts using largely unskilled labour.

The Scientific Management School

The Scientific Management approach recognised that improvements in efficiency were also possible by looking at work methods, motivation and organisation. In 1895 Frederick Taylor devised what he called a 'piece rate system' by which operatives could be remunerated on the basis of their output. Coupled with this, Frank Gilbreth developed Motion Study in 1911 which sought improvements in the way jobs were carried out, and more effective control of production was the goal when, in 1917, Henry Gantt devised a charting procedure which would become a standard tool of management.

The Operational Research School

Operational Research differs in its origins, in that it was initially non-industrial. Multi-disciplinary research teams working on wartime operations between 1939 and 1945 were involved in solving problems relating to civilian defence, bombing strategies, early warning radar systems, etc. The benefits to industry were a spin-off from the work done by these teams and included various problem solving techniques used in the areas of stock control, scheduling, forecasting, reliability, etc. Although large public and private corporations do still employ separate OR teams, most organisations rely on the adoption of standard established OR techniques by the functional disciplines, particularly the production function.

The Human Factors School

Until the 1960s the process, scientific management and operational research schools encompassed most production management thinking and formed the basis of the education and training of managers destined for careers in the production function. The human element, perhaps the most important resource of all, had been virtually ignored in preference to those resources which could be more readily understood. It is true that scientific management examines work rather than processes, but it is criticised by many for assuming that operators are merely extensions of their machines and ignoring anything more than basic motivational factors.

A series of experiments carried out between 1927 and 1932 at the Western Electric Company's Hawthorne plant in Chicago indicated, however, that even in a simple controlled environment the behaviour of workers had a profound effect on production.

Work carried out in Britain by researchers from the Tavistock Institute of Human Relations in the 1950s also supported the argument that group behaviour is an important factor when designing production systems. The impact of this new dimension to industrial production theory has now become so significant that entire productive units are being built based on concepts which have been developed as a result of behavioural as well as technological considerations. The impact of this will be discussed later in this chapter.

2 Manufacturing and Service Industries

Manufacturing industries have been important in shaping the social and economic pattern of virtually every developed country. As an employer of people, however, and even as a generator of wealth, the service sector has now assumed equal, and in some cases even greater, importance. From being a relatively small sector, more than 60% of the working population of the USA and more than 50% of that in the UK and other major European countries now work in the service industries. There is no reason to believe that this trend will not continue and some forecasters believe that by the year 2000 as few as 2% of the working population of post-industrial economies could be employed in manufacturing. As productive processes become more and more automated, there will be a shift towards the (currently) more labour intensive service industries. Trade in 'invisible' goods produced by banking and insurance etc. will continue to strengthen, while entertainment, health, travel and sport will provide a greater contribution to the quality of life.

We may see, therefore, that a management discipline which concentrates solely on the production of physical goods has already become an anachronism. Operations Management therefore seeks to extend beyond the bounds of manufacturing and to embrace the activities of all organisations, whatever the nature of their output.

A definition of Operations Management will now be appropriate, together with a discussion on the scope of the subject and its treatment in this text.

3 Definition and Scope of Operations Management

Operations Management is that function of an organisation which is concerned with the design, planning and control of resources for the production of goods and the provision of services.

From the above definition it is apparent that one of the main objectives of Operations Management is the most efficient use of resources, these resources being physical (materials and facilities), human (labour and administration) and financial. There may also be a number of intangible resources employed in an operations system. Knowledge and skills for instance are becoming an important consideration when making operations management decisions.

The second point to note from the definition is that Operations Management is concerned with the design, planning and control of these resources. We are, therefore, interested in the complete product or service 'life-cycle' from the original conception stage right through to that point where output is discontinued, facilities are written off or salvaged and the cycle starts again.

In this respect the approach taken in presenting the material in this book has been to start with those aspects of Operations Management relevant to the 'design of production systems'.

The chapters on new product decisions and product design and development form the basis of this section, while the chapter on facility decisions looks at the equipment decisions which have to be made in order that goods may be produced and services provided.

The chapter on incentive schemes takes a critical look at the controversial subject of remuneration and the design of schemes for rewarding work, while cost control of operations is covered in costing for operations and production management.

The remainder of this book then deals with the 'planning and control' aspects of Operations Management starting with operations planning and control which sets the scene for the following material which is concerned with the running of the operations system. The chapter on forecasting concentrates on the need to make accurate estimates of future demand, while inventory control methods and material requirements planning both consider the management of materials. Scheduling and monitoring procedures include techniques for the day-to-day planning of operations and measurement and control of output and the chapter on quality and reliability deals with an aspect of operations which is becoming increasingly important at a time when organisations need to compete not only on price and delivery, but also on long-term performance and ownership costs. To illustrate the application of the material in these chapters, each is accompanied by a chapter comprising an illustrative case or example.

4 Types of Operations System

The nature of production and service operations varies considerably. Manufacturing can include such diverse activities as the production of ships, electricity, clothing, domestic appliances and chemicals. Likewise, service industries can include banks, hospitals, railways, theatres and restaurants. It would be unreasonable therefore to imagine that there could be a single theory able to embrace every production or service situation.

Nevertheless, it is possible to classify operations systems according to one or more of their characteristics and thereby develop a set of problem areas and solution procedures which are appropriate to a particular case.

5 Classification of Operations Systems

Numerous writers in the area of Production and Operations Management have formulated different classifications for operations systems. The reason that so many classifications exist is in part due to the purpose for which they have been derived. For instance some classifications are conceptual and one such example (Wild)[1] identifies four basic functions (i.e.

manufacture, transport, supply, and service), each of which has a different configuration or structure. Another writer on the other hand (Woodward),[2] in looking only at manufacturing, identified as many as eleven production systems in a study of industrial 'organisation' in south Essex. These varied from 'production of units to customers' requirements' to 'continuous flow production of liquids, gases and crystalline substances'.

However, for the purpose of analysing the design of production systems and the planning and control of operations, perhaps the most simple yet useful classification is that based on the concept of job, batch and flow. Although such a system uses traditional means of describing manufacturing, this view of operations systems can in many cases be applied to services and also, in the context of this book, can be taken as the basis of the ideas which are pursued throughout. Each system type may be described as follows.

The *Job* system is where a complete product or service is completed by a group of workers and facilities. In this way a variety of different products or services can be completed in parallel. This is the most general and versatile type of system. However, it does not usually make the most efficient use of resources and is, therefore, often regarded as the most costly alternative. Custom-built items made entirely to customer specification are typically made using such a system; for example power stations, large passenger ships and certain special one-off factories and office buildings. Within the service sector the 'personal' assistance offered by a small grocery store, an insurance broker or à la carte restaurant, is analogous to the manufacturing situation just described.

The *Batch* system is where a number of products or customers are processed in batches or lots in order that some of the recurring fixed items of expenditure may be shared between each individual in the batch. This lacks some of the versatility of the job system and, because of variations in production and consumption rates, inevitably leads to storage or queuing of materials or customers at some stage within the system. Examples of products which would probably be batch produced include machine tools, furniture and glassware. Services which might use batch processing within their operations would be fast food outlets, transport operators and hospital out-patients departments.

Lastly, the *Flow* system is where products or customers are processed continuously, being passed successively through the required sequence of facilities. Flow systems are the least flexible and least versatile of all three types, changes in the product or service being made infrequently. Continuity of demand is necessary in order that the rate of production can match that of consumption. Obvious examples of goods which are flow produced include household items such as washing machines, radios, light bulbs, etc. In the service sector flow processes are less common, although the economies of scale offered by such systems have meant that operations managers in service industries are constantly seeking ways in which the benefits of flow may be derived. A few examples may be found in, for example, self-service restaurants, and banks (Reed).[3]

6 Features of Different Types of Operations Systems

Having briefly described the three types of operations system it will be helpful now to discuss in more detail some of their specific features.

The characteristics of each system will therefore be analysed under the following headings:

Physical Factors i.e. layout of facilities, type of machine and tools, materials handling

Planning and Control Factors i.e. routing of work, queues and work-in-progress, time spent in system

Labour and Organisational Factors i.e. ratio of managers to other grades, number of management levels, ratio of skilled to semi-skilled workers.

Some of the issues relating to the physical factors will be discussed in the chapter on facility decisions (Chapter 6).

However, it is appropriate at this time to introduce the three basic types of facility layout which are: fixed position layout (where the material or major component remains fixed while equipment, labour, tools, etc. are brought to this one place of work); functional layout (where equipment or processes of the same type are grouped together and 'products' move between them, usually in batches); and product layout (where 'products' are moved continuously within one area or along a flowline so that operations may be performed sequentially).

As a general rule, fixed position layout is associated with job systems, functional layout with batch systems, and product layout with flow systems. Although such arrangements of facilities are generally regarded as 'accepted practice' for the systems described, numerous problems are encountered particularly in the case of batch and flow systems. We shall, therefore, return to this issue later in the chapter.

Machines, tools and material handling equipment may broadly be described as: general purpose; specially adapted general purpose; and special purpose. Although general purpose items are flexible, relatively inexpensive and available 'off the shelf', they have the disadvantage of being comparatively inefficient and requiring a higher degree of operator skill. Adapting such items (by for example fitting automatic feeding or control devices) overcomes some of these disadvantages, but obviously reduces the flexibility and increases the expense. Therefore, although general purpose equipment may be found in all types of operations system, adapted variants are a feature of large batch or flow systems where they can be justified by higher volume levels or continuity of demand. Special purpose items of equipment are purpose built and, consequently, least flexible and most expensive. They are, therefore, almost exclusively used in flow systems where economies of scale can justify the heavy investment involved.

The planning and control factors are to a large extent determined by the layout of the facilities. Starting with routing of work, we may readily see that job systems using fixed position layout involve very little movement since most of the facilities and labour are brought to the workplace. By comparison, functional layout involves extensive movement of materials (usually in batches) between each facility where an operation is carried out. In the case of product layout, this inter-facility movement is minimised due to the close proximity of each of the machines or work stations.

This naturally has an effect on the amount of queuing that takes place and the amount of work in progress generated. With fixed position layout, queues and work-in-progress are dependent on the overall time scale for the project. Functional layout, however, involves extensive queuing due to the more or less random arrival rate of jobs at facilities and considerable amounts of work-in-progress are generated as a result. The queuing and work-in-progress occurring in product layout situations are very much reduced due to the minimum of partly finished work being held between processes.

The time that work spends in the system is dependent on queuing and work-in-progress, so it follows that when functional layout is used this time could be of a high order compared with the sum of the individual operation times. Planning is sometimes even done on the basis of 'one week per operation' making a throughput time of several weeks (or even months) quite common. Conversely, where a product layout is used, the time a job spends in the system may be little more than the sum of the operation times, a matter of only hours for even the most complex of products.

In looking finally at labour and organisational factors it is helpful to describe some of the findings of the south Essex study. Firstly, looking at the ratio of managers and supervisory staff to total personnel, it was found that in unit and small batch firms this averaged 1:23, while in large batch and mass it was 1:16, and in process 1:8. Since these categories are broadly equivalent to our job, batch and flow classifications, we may see that as the system moves from one type to another so the labour structure changes. In particular, flow systems require additional managerial and supervisory skills since there is a need to manage and maintain the fixed assets.

This pattern was also reflected in the number of management levels in direct production departments. The median for unit and small batch firms was found to be three levels, for large batch and mass it was four, while for process it was six. Moreover, where firms used more than one system there was a tendency to organise each system independently along the lines of the single process firms.

Lastly, looking at the ratio of skilled to semi-skilled workers, it is interesting to compare shipbuilding (an example of a job system) with domestic appliance manufacture (an example of a flow system). While shipbuilding employs 67% skilled and 14% semi-skilled, the comparable figures for domestic appliance manufacture are 18% and 55%. This clearly illustrates the dependency of job systems on large amounts of skilled labour compared with flow systems. Although flow systems employ a smaller percentage of skilled labour, it should, however, still be stressed that the skills in this type of system are used in the 'critical' areas of machine setting, maintenance, etc.

So, if we now assess the costs of each of our three types of operations system we will find that they are, in theory, highly volume dependent as shown in figure 1.2.

On the basis of this simple economic analysis therefore, job systems are theoretically suitable for low volumes due to the small fixed cost element. The high variable costs, however, normally render them unsuitable for large volumes. Flow systems on the other hand seem most appropriate where volumes are large, since their variable costs are low and the fixed costs may be more easily absorbed; for intermediate

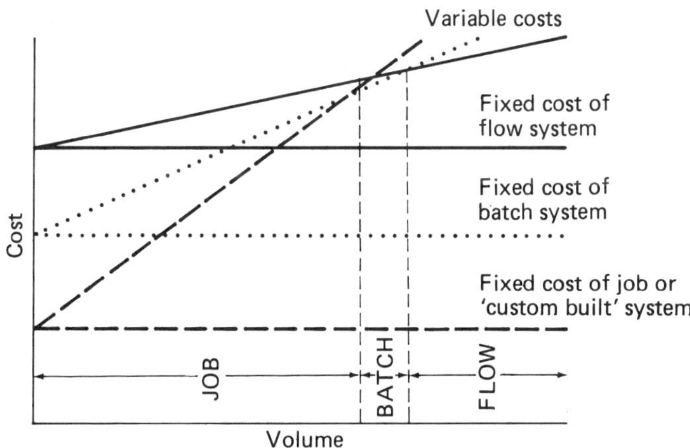

Figure 1.2 *Relative Costs of Operations Systems*

levels of activity, however, batch systems are in theory most suitable.

7 The Changing Profile of Operations Systems

The simple cost justification described above has tended to determine an approach to the design of operations systems which over the years has become widely accepted.

Therefore, many of the problems and inefficiencies associated with each system stem from the acceptance that the 'features' described previously are fixed and incapable of being improved by management.

In recent years, however, there has emerged an awareness that some of these problems, in particular those associated with batch and flow situations, may be solved by system redesign rather than by seeking to introduce merely minor improvements to the planning and control of the existing system.

Of all the changes that have been made in this respect, perhaps the most significant and important are the use of 'Group Technology' for the production of items in batches and the use of 'Autonomous Work Groups' for continuous production.

Group Technology (Gallagher and Knight)[4] recognises that many of the problems associated with batch situations (i.e. relatively long set-up times, high work-in-progress levels, long throughput times, etc.) are due to system design, and in particular the assumption that functional layout is necessary to preserve the flexibility normally required with batch production. In Group Technology components and products are grouped into 'families' and machines or process are grouped into 'cells' or 'lines' in order that some of the benefits normally only associated with flow systems may be achieved.

Autonomous Group Working (Gyllenhammar)[5] on the other hand recognises that flow systems suffer from technical deficiencies (e.g. balancing problems, line unreliability, etc.) as well as behavioural problems (e.g. high labour turnover, absenteeism, etc.). The approach here, therefore, is to break down the long line, with its associated short cycle times, into parallel work systems (short lines or even completely self-contained work areas of the type normally only associated with job situations). The effect of such system redesign has been found in most cases to be of considerable benefit in solving many of the traditional problems found in flow lines to the extent that the benefits justify the higher investment needed and the consequent reduction in economy of scale.

8 Conclusion

Although such new forms of work organisation will not be described in detail in this particular book, it is important that operations managers are aware of changes which are being made worldwide (ILO)[6] in the area of operations system design. Such changes, along with the improvement in information processing which is bound to occur with the widespread use of microcomputers, are likely to make the future of operations management even more varied and exciting than the past. There will therefore no longer be a place for the operations manager who relies solely on past experience and intuition, since future operations managers will require forethought, imagination and the ability to call upon an armoury of tools and skills to cope with an ever-changing environment.

References and Further Reading

1 Wild, R., *Concepts for Operations Managment*, Wiley 1977.
2 Woodward, J., *Industrial Organisation Theory and Practice*, Oxford University Press 1965.
3 Reed, J., 'Sure it's a bank but I think of it as a factory', *Innovation*, No. 23, 1971.
4 Gallagher, C.C. & Knight, W.A., *Group Technology*, Butterworths 1973.
5 Gyllenhammar, P.G., *People at Work*, Addison-Wesley 1977.
6 ILO, *New Forms of Work Organisation*, International Labour Office, Geneva, 1979.

2
New Product Decisions

M H OAKLEY

Lecturer in Product Design,
The University of Aston

1 Introduction

Of all the decisions taken by operations managers, those concerning new products often have the most dramatic effect on the general success of the enterprise. A new idea for a product which is soundly conceived, expertly designed and efficiently introduced into the production system will enhance the profitability and growth prospects of the firm. On the other hand, decisions about new products which are adopted without enthusiasm or commitment, followed by a mis-directed design programme and a bungled transfer to production, are the all-too-common hallmarks of the badly managed company.

Control of the tasks associated with new products is an essential part of operations management. But in many respects the nature of these tasks is quite different from those of the main production or operations process. For example, production managers aim to achieve continuity of output by using fairly precise methods of scheduling and control. Product development programmes cannot be organised in the same manner. The predictability and standardisation found in well planned production systems are not present in new product programmes where often the predominant features are uncertainty and diversity.

Perhaps because of these problems, many firms attempt a

complete separation of production and design operations. This is rarely successful unless communications are exceptionally good and there is a well developed procedure for the smooth handover of new products from design to production. For the majority of firms, new product activities must be an integral part of the general operations system. Operations managers and production managers should expect new product decisions and responsibilities to be a normal part of their activities. This chapter examines the nature of these decisions and responsibilities.

2 Realising the Need for New Products

(a) The Need in Established Firms

All firms need new products where the objective is growth, or even just stability of profits and turnover. In established firms, products which are successful now might be struggling in their markets in a few years time. Unless replacements or improvements have been planned and developed, crisis action might be the result. Crash programmes to provide new products or services do not stand very good chances of success – money is short, time is very short and tempers tend to be extremely short.

Managers need to be aware of the threats which may undermine their existing products. Early identification of danger signals gives the best chance of planning to meet the impending challenge. Broadly, these threats may be classified under five headings.

(i) Competition from within the industry This is relatively easy to monitor. Employees change firms and constitute a flow of information and expertise. Trade journals report on new developments and manufacturers' associations publish data on trends in member companies.

(ii) Competition from outside the industry This is much more of a problem than threats from within the industry. Issues of new technology are frequently involved which only

companies with wide resources can hope to counteract. Sometimes whole industries are jeopardised by failure to detect and react to outside advances. In recent times, probably the most famous example is the failure of the mechanical watch industry to meet the challenge of the electronics industry. The world's major supplier of mechanical watches, Switzerland, was lulled by decades of market domination and completely failed to match the challenge of the new technology because warning signs were not detected early enough.[1]

A less dramatic example was the introduction some years ago by the Moulton Company of the small wheeled bicycle which featured a number of innovations including rubber suspension.[2] The traditional manufacturers found themselves with obsolete designs and had to move quickly to follow the new trend imposed on their business from outside.

(iii) Changes of attitude, fashion and taste These may occur gradually – as with the trend to lower consumption of some dairy products in the UK – or abruptly – such as with styles and types of clothing. In either case, managers need to consider the implications for their firms and to develop new products accordingly.

(iv) Legal changes and political trends Changes of this nature are usually evident long before they actually happen. For example, tobacco manufacturers have had plenty of time to diversify into new product areas ahead of restrictions on the sale of their traditional products.

(v) Diminishing natural resources This is the subject of much discussion and speculation but there is ample evidence that many products will need to change considerably.[3] Vehicles will be redesigned to consume less fuel and will be constructed using smaller quantities of steel and other materials. New forms of packaging for goods will be introduced as some materials become scarce. Many traditional products will disappear. The challenges for product designers may be considerable, but there will be many opportunities as well as threats. Already we see new scope for the manufacturers of

insulation products and considerable attention is being devoted to solar heating systems.

(b) Need for New Products in New Firms

Sooner or later, all firms experience influences which may be categorised under one or more of the five headings. Established products have to be redesigned or replaced as a result. In new firms the same problems are likely to be encountered, but there are two special features of such firms which reinforce the need for new products.

(i) Many new firms are based on a single product idea. This implies vulnerability to competitive threats and for security additional products must be developed as quickly as possible.

(ii) Frequently, new firms are under-capitalised and in order to survive must build up income levels swiftly. Additional new products which can be accommodated in the existing operations system can generate this income.

3 The Product Life-Cycle Concept

No firm can expect to escape for ever the need to modify or replace its products or services. It is true that there are many products and services which have always been necessary and which will be sought indefinitely, for example bread, shoes and medical attention. But within these broad classifications, major and minor variations are always occurring. So particular forms of products have finite lives in terms of their value to the company as part of its operations. The example of men's shoes illustrates this point. For many years, the standard construction consisted of leather for both the upper and the sole. The introduction of rubber soles caused a decline in the demand for all-leather products because of the better wearing properties of rubber. Later, polyurethane and other plastic materials became available and another switch in demand resulted. These changes in materials were accompanied by important changes in methods of manufacture, such as assembly with adhesives rather than traditional stitching. Individual firms in the industry found they had to change product designs and manufacturing processes – or go out of business.

This concept of limited product life is well known to marketing specialists but, sometimes, is less well appreciated by production and operations managers. The plotting of *life-cycle curves* helps to demonstrate several important points:

(i) The life of product designs is never infinite;
(ii) Adequate indication is available that revised or new designs are needed;
(iii) Failure to develop and launch new products in time may result in a temporary decline in profitability or even the death of the enterprise.

A typical life-cycle plot is shown in figure 2.1. It is usual to relate sales volume to time, but records of production output against time can provide similar information assuming that any additional supplies of the product obtained by the company from elsewhere are included in the calculations.

The form of the life-cycle curve will be different for every product. Some products have a rapid growth in sales and then decline almost immediately. Other products continue to exhibit a rising trend even during the 'mature' period followed by a gradual or sudden decline. Often, a decline in sales can be

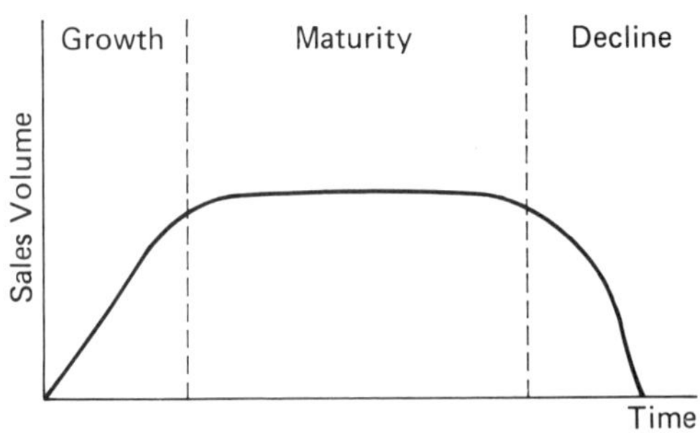

Figure 2.1 *Typical Form of Product Life-Cycle Curve*

reversed by redesigning the product; a technique (Value Analysis) for doing this will be described in Chapter 4. However, sometimes it is necessary to introduce a totally new product. It is important that this should be done before the decline in sales of the original product has advanced too far. This is particularly important in firms which are based on a small number of products or services. Firms which provide a broad range of different products are less vulnerable, but still need to ensure that sufficient new products are being developed to provide continuity.

The basic problem associated with the design and development of new products is that the process, in addition to money and management commitment, requires considerable periods of time, which can usually be reckoned in months and often in years. Unless the need for new products is perceived well in advance, sufficient time may not be available to enable a competent development programme to be undertaken. Life-cycle data, knowledge of customer attitudes, information about technical advances and an awareness of competitors' actions are all elements which managers need to consider in making decisions about the timing of new products.

Recognising the forthcoming need for a new product or service is vitally important, but it is only the first step. At this stage, the nature of the new product may be known only vaguely if at all. Before a final decision can be taken about the type of product which needs to be designed and developed, managers must analyse a variety of features in their companies and outside. The effectiveness of this planning activity will greatly influence eventual success and what this analysis should consider will now be examined.

4 Planning for New Products

Between the realisation that new products are needed and the actual setting up of design and development projects come three important stages of analysis and decision. These stages

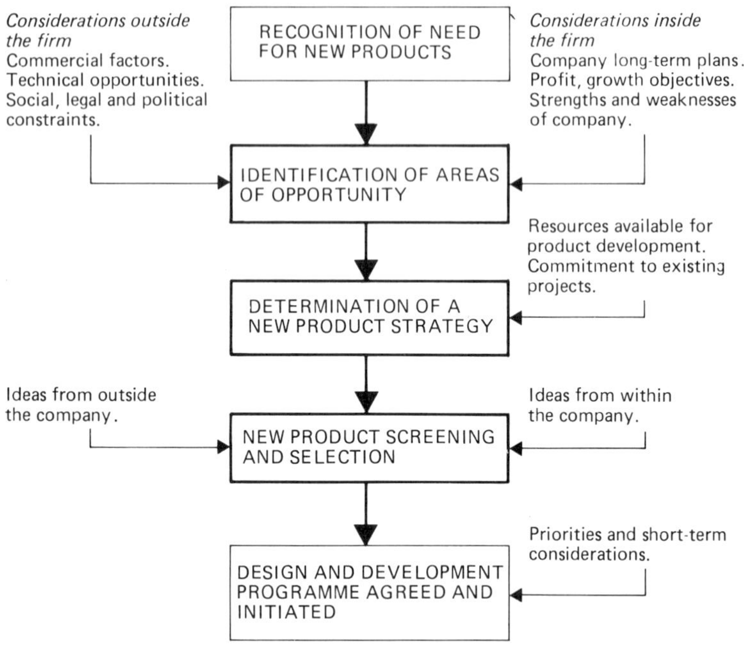

Figure 2.2 *A Decision Plan for New Products*

are represented in figure 2.2 together with some of the main points of consideration and constraint.

(a) First Stage: Identifying Areas of Opportunity for New Products

In order to decide which areas offer the best prospects for growth, a careful analysis must be made of:

(i) The firm's resources, limitations, objectives and plans. This 'corporate audit' should examine every part of the enterprise with the aim of identifying not only those aspects in which the firm has particular competence, but also those where there is weakness.

(ii) Factors outside the firm, as they exist at present, together with projections of future conditions. This analysis may need to cover not only market features and the activities of competitors, but also wider issues of social and technological change.

Only when the firm and its environment have been analysed in this way can decisions be made with any confidence about new products. In large companies, where issues may be complex and diverse, specialist staff should be employed to seek and present the information to top management. In smaller companies it is usually a part of the general responsibility of management to do this work. The strengths and limitations of small companies may be all too apparent to their managers, but external issues require investigation in just the same way as they do by larger companies.

(i) The 'corporate audit'

This should be a *systematic* investigation of all activities in the company. Each department in turn should be reviewed, and a clear description made of it in terms of:

(a) type of operations carried out
(b) number of personnel employed
(c) skills and attitudes of personnel
(d) nature of management structure and control
(e) efficiency of tasks
(f) relationships with other departments
(g) relationships outside the company etc.

All departments can be analysed in this way. For example, in the Marketing section of a company, under 'type of operations', a note might be made of activities such as market research, product promotions planning, advertising and after-sales service. Sufficient quantitative detail needs to be provided to give an idea of the scale of different activities. Market research activity, for instance, could involve anything from occasional analysis of published statistics to full-blown field research exercises.

By making an 'audit' in this way, a good picture can be built up of the company's capabilities. Particular strengths and weaknesses will be highlighted which may have a significant effect on the choice of new products and their eventual success or lack of success. Even in small companies where managers feel that they already have clear knowledge of all activities, unexpected but important information will often emerge.

In large companies, top management may find as a result of a critical analysis that long-held beliefs are no longer true. Functions like Research and Development for example often acquire a reputation for certain expertise on the basis of past achievements. Not until a disinterested assessment is made is it realised that most members of the staff possessing the expertise have retired or moved to other jobs and that new skills now predominate.

For production managers and operations managers the concept of a corporate audit may be viewed with some reservation. Surveys suggest[4] that these managers tend to see their problems within a relatively short time scale – the production manager often feels he is judged by his ability to meet target output this *week* or this *month*, say. The need for production to be involved in product planning decisions is often accepted only with reluctance. It is a common view in companies that the production or operations system should readily adapt to whatever demands are made upon it by new products. While all departments need to be able to adjust to necessary changes, there is no reason why new products should not be designed to capitalise on the strengths of the existing production system, rather than to compound its weaknesses. So the analysis of the production department should identify:

(a) The manufacturing processes where greatest expertise lies;
(b) those processes which are fully utilised and those which offer spare capacity;
(c) the aptitudes and flexibility of workforce and management;
(d) the capabilities and strengths of particular production functions such as production control, quality control, stock control, etc.;
(e) the nature of current products, the degree of standardisation of components and quantities manufactured;
(f) the scope and competence of production and industrial engineering functions.

All this information is needed before sound decisions can be made about new products. The information will also help managers to understand better the nature of their own departments and the way they relate to other functions in the company. Once the audit has been completed and its findings accepted as accurate, it is necessary to ensure that the information remains up to date. Circumstances change in firms, sometimes very quickly, and frequent revisions will probably be necessary. Even after a new product development programme has been initiated, regular progress reviews should be made in the light of the latest information available (including that about the firm itself) and decisions taken whether to continue to the next review point or not.

(ii) Analysis of external factors

Companies need to investigate the environment in which they operate in order to identify competitive threats to existing products and market opportunities for new products. As in the case of the internal review of the firm which has just been considered, the extent of involvement of operations or production managers in the external analysis will depend on the nature and structure of the firm. However, it is important that in all firms these managers have at least an understanding of the way threats and opportunities can be identified. This enables them to make a more informed contribution to new product decisions. What follows is an introduction to some means of investigating current market conditions and how predictions about future trends might be made. This latter is important because product development programmes, once initiated, may not generate new products for several months or even years, by which time the nature of the market might be quite different.

In analysing the current situation, information can be derived from two sources – from within the company and from outside.

Sources of information within the company

1. Quantitative sources With increasingly widespread use of computers there can be large amounts of valuable information readily available in companies. In any case, in most firms the following data should be fairly easily obtainable:

(a) *Sales figures* These can indicate areas of growth or decline – but may tell little about *overall* trends in the market unless the results of other companies are known as well. Sales figures can highlight the relative success of the firm's different products.
(b) *Financial data* This should enable product areas of greatest profitability to be identified.
(c) *Purchasing trends* Records may be available on recent price trends and aspects of suppliers' quotations – for example delivery dates, the length of which may be a good indication of demand and activity.
(d) *Marketing data* Depending on the type of company and the nature of its products, this may be a source of information about such things as advertising response rates, effects of promotional offers, results of recent market analysis.

2. Qualitative sources There are many possibilities here; the problem is usually that of deciding which sources to tap and what mechanism to use to actually gather the information. Typical sources of qualitative information include:

(a) *Sales force reports* Some companies require representatives to provide periodic commentaries on events in their areas. In this way, current information may be available on customers' actions and comments, competitors' activities (e.g. test-marketing of new products, changes in prices) and general business trends (e.g. news of short-time working, opening of new factories).
(b) *Other sources of 'informed opinion'* Employees at all levels may have valuable information. Senior managers who are involved with outside activities may make contacts at high level during participation in meetings of professional bodies, employers' associations or at conferences. Less senior employees, whose work involves an awareness of current activities outside the company (for example, research scientists and personnel officers) should be encouraged to contribute as well.

(c) *Divisional and departmental reports* Especially in large multi-centre companies, reports produced in one division may be of great value to other sections. Very large companies have full library and abstracting services to assist this flow of information.

Sources of information outside the company

Again, two types of information are available – statistical data and descriptive data.

1. Statistical sources A large quantity of published statistical data is available to assist managers in understanding their business environments. Highly important in the UK are *UK Government statistics* which are available in many forms covering a vast range of topics. They are generally considered to be reliable and most can be purchased easily by companies or examined in libraries. The Central Statistical Office publishes several excellent guides[5,6,7] to help non-specialist managers use Government statistics to maximum advantage. Some of the best known are:

(a) *Business Monitor Statistics:* UK sales figures on more than 5,000 product lines, published every three months.
(b) *Family Expenditure Survey:* regional breakdown of household expenditure, published annually.
(c) *Census of Production:* information about total purchases, sales, stocks, work in progress and other aspects of industrial production. Published annually in separate parts for each industry.

As well as Government statistics, there are statistics published by bodies such as:

(a) Trade associations (but frequently only available to member companies).
(b) Productivity councils and similar bodies.
(c) Commercial Market Research Bureaux which often sell generalised data derived from market investigations commissioned by clients.

Although all these sources of statistical data can be extremely helpful to managers, it must be remembered that they all provide only 'secondary data'. In other words, information which has not been collected specifically for their particular needs. Consequently it may require some 'interpretation' or 'adjustment', in which case managers need to understand the assumptions which may be being made.

When satisfactory data cannot be obtained from published sources, 'primary' or 'field' research may be considered. This involves direct investigation perhaps utilising questionnaires or interviews; it can be very expensive and is often not feasible for small companies.

2. Qualitative sources Important indicators of present conditions and trends may be seen by regular inspection of items such as:

(a) *Trade journals*, particularly those relating to relevant areas of business;
(b) *Annual reports* of companies which are engaged in similar types of operations to those of the manager's own firm;
(c) *Newspapers*, for example the *Financial Times* and others with strong industrial and commercial sections;
(d) *TV and radio programmes* which give a serious coverage of business and technological issues;
(e) *Conferences and exhibitions* where new ideas and techniques may be presented thus giving an idea of relative progress between firms.

On their own, none of these information sources can tell managers enough about market trends and opportunities to enable new product strategies to be developed. But they are valuable sources of background information which can be coupled with the more rigorous data from other sources. This will allow managers in even small firms to build a comprehensive picture of their business environment and reduce the chances of missing opportunities.

(b) Second Stage: Determining a Strategy for New Products

At this point, a number of areas may be seen where strengths within the company coincide with apparent opportunities in markets and the development of new products seems desirable.

In other cases, for example where there are weaknesses in the company in functions like product design or production, it may be concluded that the best course is the acquisition of another company to obtain new products, or a merger with another firm or perhaps a re-direction of the firm's activities, say, from manufacturing into distribution of products made elsewhere.

Where the decision *is* to develop new products, a strategy for doing this must be decided upon. In determining this strategy the basic considerations are what skills and resources the company has available (or can easily obtain), and which market opportunities will be exploited. Then four steps of refinement are needed:

(a) forecasting future trends
(b) confirming areas of product interest
(c) calculating resources available for product development
(d) underwriting commitments to existing projects.

Each of these will now be considered in turn.

(i) Step one: forecasting future trends

This needs to be done in respect of both the market and the products. For the market, this means taking the information obtained about present and historical conditions and making estimates about conditions in the future when the results of product development in the firm will be ready for exploitation. Fundamental questions are:

(a) what will be the size of the total market?
(b) what will be the share of the market held by competitors?
(c) what share of the market can *we* expect to gain?

Simply projecting sales figures into the future and analysing individual company performance can give rise to falsely optimistic expectations. Just because total annual sales of a certain type of product have risen steadily for the last four years, say, there may be no guarantee that they will continue to do so for the next four years. Customer tastes, actions by home and foreign competition, social and political trends, availability of credit, are just a few of the factors that may have to be encompassed in the predictive process. The longer the anticipated product development period, the more uncertainty there will be. For further discussion on the complexities of market forecasting, reference should be made elsewhere.[8,9,10]

As far as products are concerned, predictions also need to be made. What will be the nature of products in the future? What level of performance will be the norm? What size? What fuel consumption? What speed of operation?

Information about technical aspects may be revealed by the use of various techniques of 'Technological Forecasting' (TF). Again appropriate references[11,12] should be consulted for fuller discussion, but two techniques can be mentioned here:

Trend extrapolation In the same way that historical market data (e.g. sales figures) can be plotted and projected to give future estimates, then so can data on measurable technical features of products. As an example, consider the results that might be obtained if the feature 'speed of operation' for electric kettles was examined; data as shown in figure 2.3 might be obtained.

It will be noticed that for each technical system, refinement occurs until the boiling speed reaches a level where little further improvement is obtainable, and the plot flattens. Not until a new technical system is achieved (in this case the placing

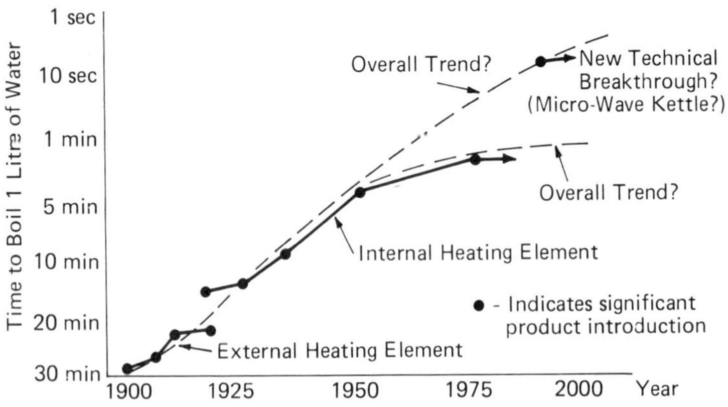

Figure 2.3 *Possible Representation of Speed of Operation of Electric Kettles*

of the element inside the kettle instead of strapping it below the base) does improvement continue until a further plateau is reached. This feature of technical progress is sometimes referred to as the 'S-curve phenomenon' because of the shape of the plots obtained. The problem for forecasters is to decide the nature of the overall trend. In this case, has the ultimate level of performance been achieved – or is a major technical breakthrough about to occur? If so, what will be the effect on product development plans? Wills[11] gives further examples concerning features of computers, hovercraft and aircraft.

Delphi Forecasting Method This is a method of assembling the expert opinion which is necessary to interpret the sort of quantitative data that is involved in extrapolating trends – for example, in the case just examined, to decide which of the alternatives is the overall trend.

Typically, a Delphi exercise is carried out by asking experts (in the areas being explored) to consider a list of possible future events and to say when, if ever, they expect each to occur, with explanations. The answers are correlated and extreme replies investigated. Eventually a 'scenario' is constructed of generally expected events together with probable dates of occurrence. See Twiss.[12]

Delphi-type exercises may seem appropriate only to large companies with extensive resources, but there is no reason why smaller companies should not attempt limited exercises perhaps using knowledgeable employees as sources of information.

(ii) Step two: confirming areas of product interest

When future trends have been evaluated, it will be possible to confirm the areas in which new products must be developed. It is important that a clear statement should be made so that all concerned with product development will know where their efforts should be directed. Nothing is more likely to contribute to the failure of new products, and consequently to the failure of the company, than an ambiguous, inconsistent new product policy. This does not mean that no change of direction should ever occur; as circumstances alter, firms must be ready to curtail some development projects and to start new ones. But such action must be based on sound information and not the intuition or faint-heartedness of managers.

(iii) Step three: calculating resources available for product development

Developing new products can be highly expensive. The company needs to decide how much it can afford to allocate to new products, bearing in mind that a continuing commitment is required. Individual projects may last for several years and there is little point in starting unless funds will be available for the whole period.

In calculating funds the company must look at the financial reserves it has available including its ability to raise loans from banks and cash from shareholders. It must also predict future levels of costs, sales and profits. Projects must then be devised which are well within the financial scope available, always remembering that many new products are eventually unsuccessful. In framing its commitment to development work, it is desirable that the firm should allocate a fixed percentage of annual turnover. This is better than relating allocations to profit since in many companies this will mean some years with adequate funds interspersed by others where little or no cash is available. A low level of steady support is better than widely fluctuating support even if this involves a high *average* level.

Not all the resources needed for product development are financial. Adequate managerial competence must be available together with specific skills and experience. Workshops and test equipment may be needed, together with the co-operation of various departments; for example, the production department in providing access to normal manufacturing equipment for test purposes.

(iv) Step four: underwriting commitments to existing projects

Amidst enthusiasm for a new product programme it is vital that any existing projects are not forgotten. Before a final decision is taken to allocate time and money to the programme, the continuing needs must be assessed of any new products already under development. It is particularly important to reinforce the morale of those working on existing projects by a restatement of commitment. Enthusiasm by senior managers for new ventures may cause unease and uncertainty amongst staff unless consistent support is given to their projects as well. Too often managers allow their fascination with latest ideas to undermine their responsibilities for other projects which are still important, but happen to have reached the mundane stage in development concerned with repetitive testing and improvement.

(c) Third Stage: Screening and Selection of Specific New Product Ideas

So far new product decisions will have been considered in the general sense of product types and market areas. Now it is time to decide about the adoption of specific ideas for new products. Companies need first to investigate the sources of ideas available to them, then to evaluate ideas in a way that will enable them to choose those with the greatest potential.

(i) Sources of ideas for new products

Within most companies, there will be individuals with a talent for producing ideas for new products. Such people are likely to be working in research or design departments, where they will be encouraged to explain and develop their ideas. However, creativity is not necessarily confined to these areas of the company and many useful ideas can be obtained from production, marketing, or other departments if the opportunity exists for information to flow. Some companies use suggestion schemes for this purpose or make a point of having 'open door' policies so that product ideas (and other topics) can be freely discussed with managers. In addition, some firms arrange seminars or conferences so that employees (particularly sales representatives and supervisory staff) can meet and discuss points of interest including means by which present products and services can be improved or new ones developed.

The problem with ideas generated internally though, is that they tend to reflect company needs rather than customer needs. For this reason, ideas originating outside the company may hold much better prospects for success. Customers' ideas and needs, if they can be defined directly, should lead to commercially attractive products. Market research techniques may be used to identify the needs of both consumer and industrial markets,[13] although in some industries it is common for customers to make direct requests for new products (e.g. defence equipment) which, when developed, join the company's range of standard products. Regular meetings with customers encourage this type of request, a principle which also applies to organisations providing services, for example local authorities meeting residents' associations to define the services needed.

Sometimes, private inventors or other companies may offer to sell ideas or proposals which they are unable to develop themselves. These *may* be useful and worth considering, but it is important to consider the reasons why the invention is being sold. Are there serious weaknesses in the idea? Is expensive development required? Also, unpleasant misunderstandings may arise if such proposals are not handled carefully. If a proposal is declined because the company is already working on similar lines, eventual launching of the product may bring accusations of plagiarism from the inventor. As a general rule, managers should insist that an outside inventor always files an application for a patent (see Chapter 4) before disclosing his idea.

Companies may actively seek out such ideas by advertising for them, or by having 'new products competitions' or by sponsoring research in universities, research establishments, etc. Some companies subscribe to research associations (e.g. the Battelle Institute in Geneva) which give members the option to take over promising lines of research. Large companies may have a 'scanning department' whose job it is to check publications for news of ideas. Journals, reports, newspapers etc. should be monitored as well as specialist publications such as the bulletins of inventions which are published by the National Research Development Corporation, a body which helps to bring together inventors and companies.

(ii) Screening and selection of ideas for new products

It is easy to be either unduly euphoric or pessimistic about individual ideas. To avoid this, a screening or evaluation procedure should be carried out which examines each proposal against a set of basic criteria. For most companies a two stage procedure is sufficient; a quick screening to eliminate the weakest ideas, followed by a more thorough investigation of the survivors.

The quick screening should be conducted using a checklist of essential parameters; failure at any point means rejection of the idea. Factors which may be specified might include:

(a) market characteristics (e.g. at least 15% market share attainable, growth rate of 5% p.a. required)
(b) profit on investment (e.g. 25%)
(c) production facilities (e.g. must not require new equipment to produce)
(d) competitive advantages
(e) service facilities, etc., etc.

Skinner[8] (Chapter 3, p. 31) gives a specimen checklist with ten factors.

The nature of the parameters will depend on a company's individual requirements and should be set by top management. However, the screening against the parameters can then be carried out by less senior personnel.

This initial screening may eliminate up to 90% of the original ideas. The remainder should then be analysed in detail starting with those ideas which the initial screening indicated as being most attractive. Basically, the detailed evaluation will cover the same ground as the quick screening but in much greater depth. This is necessary to identify as far as possible the extent of the risks involved in the proposed new project – and to confirm that the company is able to carry these risks.

In general the evaluation should examine:

(a) Product (or service) characteristics. A full definition of the idea with details of size, features, selling price, etc. This is essential to allow accurate estimates of effects of competition, costs involved, manufacturing problems etc.
(b) Marketing aspects i.e. customers' requirements, competitors' activities.
(c) Manufacturing aspects i.e. plant requirements, storage, handling, skills etc.

(d) Financial aspects i.e. cost of the development programme, sales needed to recover overheads etc.
(e) Social, political and legal aspects. Considerations here might be those of pollution (caused by the new product itself or during its manufacture), or possibly problems associated with the supply of raw materials from a politically unstable country. From the legal point of view, there may be features of the new product proposal which require attention, such as patent infringement or statutory regulations concerning design features.

Several publications are available to help managers carry out effective evaluation. Particularly useful are two checklists published by the British Institute of Management.[14] For further information also see Skinner,[8] Holt[15] and White.[16]

5 Organising for Design and Development Work

Efficiency in recognising the need for new products and then carefully screening and selecting ideas will all be in vain if the organisation of the company is not suited to the special requirements of new product work. The nature of these requirements can be understood if features of design and development departments are compared with those of other operating departments, particularly production with which design is often closely linked, since both are considered to be 'technical' parts of the business. Table 2.1 summarises the main features of difference.

In the light of these differences, managers need to consider both the organisation of the new product unit itself, and its relationship to the rest of the company.

(a) Organisation of Product Design and Development Units

Several years ago Burns and Stalker[17] analysed the organisational aspects of a sample of firms involved with new products and their work is still worth study today. They noted that

Table 2.1 Comparison of Organisational Features of Production with Product Design

Features of Production	*Features of Design and Development*
1. Rational, standardised, predictable	1. Irrational, novel, unpredictable
2. Operations accurately timed	2. Accurate timing of activities usually impossible
3. Long runs of identical products	3. Activities frequently changing
4. Creativity and initiative not developed in workforce	4. Highly creative personnel essential
5. Work closely controlled – essential for profitability. Risk eliminated	5. Profitability related to skill, chance, judgment, intuition, risk-taking, etc.

within these companies there were organisational styles ranging from what they termed 'mechanistic' (very formal, hierarchial, bureaucratic and inflexible) to styles which they termed 'organic' and that were informal, based on teams and highly adaptable.

They concluded that mechanistic systems work satisfactorily only where conditions are stable – flow line production departments for example, or other situations where close control of highly specialised work is essential. Mechanistic forms of organisation are not likely to prove satisfactory when applied to new product units, which need flexibility in many respects. Organic systems are much more appropriate and, as Burns and Stalker observed, such systems gave much better prospects of success with new products or services.

Table 2.2 lists some of the features that will be found in organic systems. Operations managers responsible for product design and development departments need to consider how they can promote 'organic features'. This may be a delicate matter, especially within those firms which are otherwise organised along precise and inflexible lines. Without attempting to impose any particular working system, managers here must be aware of the actions they can take to assist creative work so that organisationally desirable features predominate

Table 2.2 Typical Features of Organic Systems

1. Unifying theme is the 'common task' – each individual contributes special knowledge and skills – individual's tasks are constantly re-defined as the total situation changes.
2. Hierarchy does not predominate – problems are not referred up or down, but are tackled on a team basis.
3. Flexibility – jobs not precisely defined.
4. Control is through the 'common goal' rather than by institutions, rules and regulations.
5. Expertise and knowledge located throughout the organisation not just at the top.
6. Communications consist of information and advice rather than instructions and decisions.

rather than undesirable ones. Whitfield[2] discusses a range of problems associated with creativity and innovation.

Apart from these considerations of management style and attitude, there are a number of more mundane points that firms need to consider when committing themselves to work on new products:

(a) *Accommodation* Are workshop or laboratory facilities available? Is the environment satisfactory for creative work? (A corner of a noisy factory may not be the best place.)
(b) *Technical back-up* Is there a competent drawing office? Is there a company 'library' of technical specifications? Can production equipment be 'borrowed' for test purposes?
(c) *Customer information* Is there a system for checking requirements directly with customers? Is the marketing department able to provide information?
(d) *Links with production* What will happen when new products are ready for production? Is production participating in development? Will the existing production unit take up new products or will extra production facilities be needed?

These questions lead to consideration of the organisational problems which arise out of the relationship of the design and development department with the rest of the firm.

(b) Location of Design and Development Work in the Firm

It is not always easy to decide who should be responsible for new product work within the firm. As already suggested, product development is often considered to be a technical activity of a kind similar to production. However, because of the fundamentally different natures of the two functions, giving control of product development to production may result in failure. This may happen either because organisational conditions inappropriate to product development are imposed or simply because production has resistance to new products (because of the disruption involved). This resistance may take the form of constant rejections of new designs, refusal to supply information and help, or simply general obstruction – all while paying lip-service to the need for new products. These attitudes may be particularly acute in long-established firms where design work has been limited previously to improvements and modifications.

These problems have been investigated by a number of researchers,[17,18,19,20] but no universal solution has been proposed. If the development department is made an independent part of the company away from the production or any other department, problems may still exist. Its manager may have to bargain with other departmental bosses for cash and resources. Because product development is a long-term activity, it may seem to senior managers in other functions that it is just a wasteful consumer of the income which they create. Some companies try to overcome this problem by directing new product operations through a steering committee which represents all major functions. Others appoint 'product champions' whose job it is to push the new product through all barriers and solve any problems which may arise.

Another approach which has been reported is the 'venture' method. Here, no attempt is made to develop new products within existing operations but a design and development group is set up separately to carry through a new project all the way from first idea to manufacture and distribution. A number of accounts are available of successful examples in British[21,22,23] and US[24] companies.

6 Conclusion

Planning for new products is a complex process which should involve all sections of the company. The operations or production system is a major consideration and its managers should expect to be involved in decisions about new products as a matter of course. The aim of this chapter has been to show operations and production managers the problems involved in product planning and how they can bc dealt with; this information is especially important where these managers find that they have direct responsibility for new product work.

References and Further Reading

1 Uytenhoeven, H.E.R., Ackerman, R.W. and Rosenblum, V.W., *Strategy and Organization: Text and Cases in General Management*, Irwin 1977.
2 Whitfield, P.R. *Creativity in Industry*, Pelican 1975.
3 Meadows, D. *et al.*, *Limits to Growth*, Pan 1972.
4 Prabhu, V. and Russell, J., The truth about production, *Management Today*, June 1979.
5 *Government Statistics – a brief guide to sources*, HMSO (published anually).
6 *Profit from Facts*, HMSO (updated periodically).
7 *Guide to Official Statistics*, HMSO 1977.
8 Skinner, R.N., *Launching New Products in Competitive Markets*, Associated Business Programmes 1974.
9 Midgley, D.M., *Innovation and New Product Marketing*, Croom-Helm 1977.
10 Freeman, C., *The Economics of Industrial Innovation*, Penguin 1974.
11 Wills, G. *et al.*, *Technological Forecasting*, Penguin 1972.
12 Twiss, B.C., *Managing Technological Innovation*, Longman 1974.
13 Wilson, A., *The Assessment of Industrial Markets*, Cassell Associated Business Programmes 1973.
14 British Institute of Management, *Management Checklist Nos 29 & 30 – Launching New Products*, BIM London, 1977/79.
15 Holt, K., *Production Innovation: A Workbook for Management and Industry*, Newnes-Butterworth 1977.
16 White, R., *Consumer Product Development*, Longman 1973.
17 Burns, T., and Stalker, G.M., *The Management of Innovation*, 2nd edn, Tavistock Publications 1966.

18 Basil, D.C. and Cook, C.W., *The Management of Change*, McGraw-Hill 1974.
19 Mueller, R.K., *The Innovation Ethic*, American Management Association 1971.
20 Jones, W.H. and Oakley, M.H., A case study in venture management, *International Journal of Management Science*, Vol 7, No 1, 1979.
21 Gardner, J.B., Innovation through new ventures: a new venture concept in BOC, *R & D Management*, Vol 3, No 2, 1973.
22 Vernon, A., A new business venture, *R & D Management*, Vol 4, No 2, 1974.
23 Oakley, M.H., *The Torque Hose Actuator: A Study of the Development of a New Product*, unpublished Ph.D. thesis, The University of Aston in Birmingham, 1978.
24 Hill, R.M., and Hlavacek, J.D., The venture team: a new concept in marketing organisation, *Journal of Marketing*, Vol 36, 1972.

3
British Super Products Limited

M H OAKLEY

Lecturer in Product Design,
The University of Aston

1 Introduction*

This company has plants in several parts of the UK and employs about 14,000 people. Its business might be described as 'general engineering'. Functionally, it is organised into several sections, each of which produces a family of products. These sections are operated independently of each other with separated functions such as production, marketing, sales etc. Until recently, this organisation has seemed to work well. Each section has enjoyed a steady level of activity, supplying long runs of products to a small number of industrial customers. As a consequence, the company in general has become very strong in manufacturing skills and organisation, but has weak marketing and sales operations.

A few years ago, senior managers in the company recognised that dependence on a few customers and product lines could be dangerous. Indeed, during a ten year period up to 1978 the turnover of BSP decreased by over 20% in *real* terms, although ever increasing *money* turnovers disguised the problem. The need was seen for diversification into new areas

* All names and some other details have been disguised to preserve the anonymity of the real company to which this case study relates.

and also for a general infusion of new products. Product development work was already carried out in each section, but it was limited in scope – mainly concerned with modifications to existing product designs. The Board decided to create a central 'Product Development Department' (PDD) which would develop product ideas to the point where they would be handed over to one of the manufacturing sections. It was thought that this department would stand a better chance of yielding viable new products than would expanded Design and Development groups within the individual sections. It was accepted that these were so strongly production-oriented that creativity and innovation were effectively suppressed. Furthermore, it was agreed that ideas for new products were needed from outside the traditional areas of business. Again, preoccupation with manufacturing aspects meant that existing sections were ill-equipped to undertake the generation and subsequent evaluation of ideas.

Thus PDD was set up in a self-contained building on one of the company's sites in the south of England. Its chief, Mr W.R. Page, was appointed to the Board as a director of the company. So in theory, as figure 3.1 shows, PDD was an operating unit of similar status to each of the manufacturing sections which were also represented by their respective directors on the Board.

Mr Page was given a free hand to organise and run PDD. His brief was simply 'to develop new products'. He responded by building up a group of engineers and designers, and also established a well equipped workshop. Within a short time he

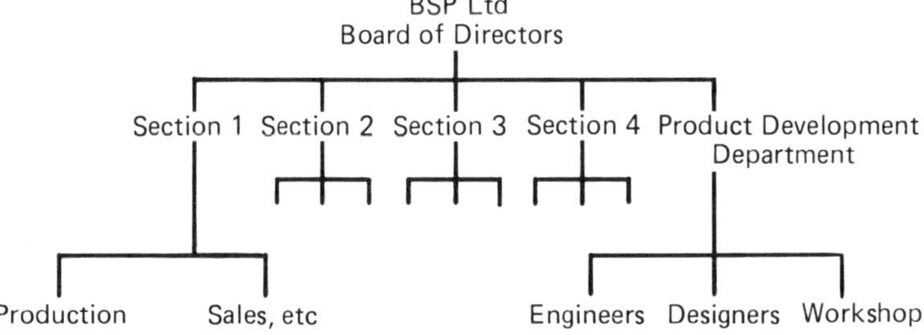

Figure 3.1 *Simplified Organisation of BSP Limited*

had identified several promising ideas for new products and work proceeded on their development. However, after several years of work on these and further ideas, considerable sums of money had been spent, but no commercially successful products had evolved; the department was closed amidst disillusionment and anxiety.

Looking back over the operation of PDD a number of valuable lessons emerge for other companies contemplating setting up this kind of new product unit:

2 Need for a 'New Product Policy'

The top management of BSP did not analyse the existing business to see what type of new products would seem logical. Instead of seeking to build on existing strengths in the company, it was left to Mr Page to decide what avenues to pursue. His suggestions were usually supported to start with, but after a period of expenditure on development work it was often the case that the Board would begin to question the relevance of the work. This led to a reduction of resources and effort on that particular line of development until it was finally scrapped.

This lack of guidelines for new product work made life difficult for Mr Page. On the one hand he had the advantage of freedom of approach to his work, on the other hand he had the disadvantage of an unlimited choice of areas in which to try to find new opportunities. This gave rise to a bewildering mixture of different development projects without any common theme or relevance (except accidental) to features of the existing business, such as distribution channels, or manufacturing techniques. None of this would have mattered had the organisation been sufficiently flexible to be able to absorb and exploit these new products. In fact, it was highly rigid (as production-dominated industries tend to be) and new products were usually rejected outright at handover time from PDD. Had there been an agreed policy for new product activities, these problems might not have appeared.

A further consequence of this lack of a policy was the

effect on sources of new product ideas. If a limited field of investigation had been defined, many sources of ideas could have been analysed with thoroughness. With an unlimited field so many ideas were available that few received, at best, more than just cursory examination. The main criterion for the further examination of an idea tended to be the inherent interest it had to Mr Page, rather than a more rational alignment against a previously formulated guideline.

3 Need for a Balanced Approach to New Product Work

The Product Development Department had a staff of engineers, designers, and workshop technicians. At no time did it recruit any marketing or financial personnel. As a result of this technical bias, it was not surprising to find that new product ideas were assessed mainly in terms of engineering feasibility – the only non-technical assessment being carried out by Mr Page, himself an engineering specialist. In this respect, the organisation of PDD reflected the rest of BSP which, as already noted, was strong technically but weak in marketing skills.

The fact that ideas were selected for development mainly on their technical potential inevitably led to a high percentage of product failures. The markets which it had been assumed 'must exist for technically superior products', were usually found *not* to be there when the new idea was presented to the world.

Another result of this imbalance between engineering and marketing skills was that even when ideas with real all-round potential *were* selected, the wrong kinds of features were built into the products. So, for example, PDD found that one new product which boasted a very compact design, but was rather noisy in operation, did not sell very well. Eventually, it was discovered that customers did not care about the size of the product, but did demand silent operation.

The lesson here is that companies *must* find out what the customer really wants and then design the product to suit. Most readers will say that there is nothing new about this statement (which is true), but the fact remains that many companies *do* spend money on the development of products that no one wants. Particularly in traditional companies producing industrial goods, there is a mistrust of 'marketing' ('alright for toothpaste but not for trolley-jacks', the writer was told recently by one company boss). The misconception persists that the subject is exclusively about pressure selling, advertising and complicated mathematical modelling beyond the comprehension of ordinary managers. This is a pity, since a few elementary techniques of market research could greatly assist many companies to improve their product success rates.

4 Need for Consistent Top Management Support

The Board of BSP set up PDD with the expectation that it would quickly generate new products. As months passed without the completion of many of the development projects, the directors began to question whether money was being spent wisely. Because product ideas were only briefly evaluated when selected for development, there was plenty of scope for subsequent doubts. So when the company went through a bad financial patch, funds were hastily withdrawn from PDD. At other times, when cash was easier, Mr Page was urged to 'speed up' the work on his most promising projects. Invariably, as these things happen, when Mr Page needed money for some important line of work, cash was tight and he had to modify his plans.

The effect of this 'stop–go' policy was seriously to damage the efficiency of the development work. To the people working in PDD it seemed that one month top managers were desperate for results, the next month they wished the department didn't exist. The engineers and designers became frustrated and insecure, which in turn affected the quality of their work.

Once again, the problem could be traced back to the setting up of PDD. As well as failing to ask 'what do we expect to achieve?', the Board also failed to ask 'what expenditure can we *consistently* afford, over what period?'. All companies need to provide consistent management support for new product ventures reflected in consistent allocations of funds.

5 Need for Inter-Functional Participation

PDD was designed to be independent of the other sections of the company. It had been envisaged that as the development of each product was completed, it would be handed over to one of the manufacturing sections and then work would start on the next project. By being able to concentrate on development without getting side-tracked into day-to-day production problems, it was expected that a specialist PDD would be more successful than if it was attached to one or more of the sections.

In fact, the managers of the manufacturing sections resented being presented with new products by what they saw as an outside unit. Although they needed new business, it hurt their pride to have new ideas forced upon them – a classic example of the frequently quoted 'Not Invented Here' syndrome.

The mistake lay in the concept of isolating PDD. It is true that design and development work needs some protection from the crises and distractions of production operations. But this does not rule out the need for co-operation. In many cases production managers may have had good reasons for resisting new products – perhaps they did not have the right machinery, capacity or skills available. With interaction from the start of each development project between the manufacturing sections and PDD (and customers, perhaps) there would have been a much better chance of new products emerging that had general acceptability.

4
Product Design and Development

M H OAKLEY

Lecturer in Product Design,
The University of Aston

1 Introduction

In Chapter 2, attention was directed to some of the preliminary decisions and investigations which are required before serious work can begin on new products. The discussion was concerned with the examination of market opportunities for new products and services, and also the state of resources within the firm that could be used to create them. In particular, the nature of design and development departments was explored, with attention given to the facilities needed by them and the special organisational problems which can arise.

This chapter continues the examination by reviewing the main aspects of design and development work and then by attempting to evaluate the extent of designers' responsibilities for features such as cost, quality and compatibility. Finally, attention is moved from new products to the question of re-designing existing products and the case for planned programmes to accomplish this. The valuable, but often ignored, technique of Value Analysis is outlined, together with a discussion of the benefits and results which it can produce.

2 The Nature of Design and Development Work 

(a) The Specification

The starting point for a new project is always some kind of 'specification'. Depending on the complexity or scale of the project, the specification may be little more than a rough sketch and a few notes. At the other extreme, for a new product such as a motor vehicle, the specification may run to many volumes and describe in precise terms the multitude of parameters which must be observed. Such a document might take several months, or even years, to prepare and will be based on extensive market investigations and internal policy deliberations. Generally though, specifications should be as brief as possible and should be presented in such a way that designers are allowed as much discretion as possible. There is little point in employing creative design staff if freedom of action is then restricted by excessive direction.

The essential information which ought to be provided by the specification may be summarised as follows:

(i) *Exact type of product to be designed* – described in terms of existing alternative products if available, or in terms of the *functions required* if the product is a totally new concept.

(ii) *Major technical requirements* – such as speed of operation, maximum and minimum dimensions that can be allowed, performance levels required, etc.

(iii) *Styling requirements* – general nature of appearance, shapes and colours preferred, carrying capacity, arrangement of major features, etc.

(iv) *Operational requirements* – size of controls, forces required to operate, safety features, compatibility with operator's dimensions or other items of equipment, etc.

(v) *Cost constraints* – target selling prices or production costs of the product, requirements regarding maintenance and service cost levels if relevant, and operating costs, etc.

(vi) *Special requirements* – for example, 'need for product to be safe for use by small children'.

Exactly where the responsibility lies for drawing-up the specification will vary from company to company. Frequently, it is put together by representatives of the major functions perhaps through the mechanism of a 'new product committee'. Sometimes the specification is compiled by a senior executive or by a specialist consultant. However it is put together, the final version should be understood, approved and supported by top management. The specification for a new product determines – at least in part – the company's future achievements and prospects; for this reason its importance should not be undermined by indifferent management attitudes.

(b) The Design Operation

The designer's task is to seek workable solutions which satisfy the requirements of the specification. Typically this entails the sketching of basic ideas followed by modifications and insertion of more and more detail until a complete solution to the problem is achieved. It is far outside the scope of this chapter to analyse in detail the whole subject of design. However, although the reader is directed for further information to the wide literature on the topic – a sample of which forms part of the list of references[1,2,3] – there are a number of points which can be usefully made here.

For example, it is interesting to consider the general nature of design work. In most projects there is both a *technical* content and an *artistic* content. Cursory examination of household products will confirm this. Electrical appliances, tools, items of furniture, fabrics, cutlery, floor coverings – all have involved technical design work in some measure to achieve performance, rigidity, durability, safety etc. Similarly, an artistic input will have been involved, particularly in the case of furnishings and other products which are purchased largely on the basis of appearance. For many products, technical features are well understood and the job of the designer is to apply the most suitable technology to his particular problem. To do this efficiently, he needs to receive appropriate technical training, but equally important, he must have access to up-to-date information. The responsibility of the operations manager is to ensure that both these requirements are met, the first by training and staff development, the second by the provision of technical information systems within the firm and by encouraging designers to explore new technological developments outside the firm.

Similar comments can be made about the artistic aspects of design. Perhaps the most important point that operations managers need to grasp is that artistic aspects of product design are *not* necessarily of minor importance. It is true that in the past, some products have competed on technical strengths with little interest given to appearance or other artistic features – for example engineering machine tools, commercial vehicles and many consumer products. Now, with competing manufacturers able to achieve similar high levels of technical quality and performance, it is often the artistic features of products which determine success in the market place.

The artistic features of products need to be considered throughout the design process – not just at the final stage. Where projects are of such a small scale that only individual designers are involved, they have to pay regard to both technical and artistic considerations. In larger companies, with more extensive design operations, there will be some designers who will be technical specialists (the 'design engineers' perhaps) and others who will concentrate on artistic aspects (the 'stylists'). Projects must be tackled by both on a collaborative basis from the beginning. A sequential approach of first tackling the technical problems and then handing over to the stylists to 'finish the job' does not lead to consistently good results.

In addition to these aspects of design work, there are two other areas of importance. These may be called the *ergonomic* and *economic* considerations of design. They are often seen as minor components in the overall design process, but increasingly they are developing as specialisms.

A 'good' ergonomic design is one which is totally satisfactory to the user in terms of the way it 'suits' the human body. For example, a motor car with excellent visibility, well positioned controls and easily adjustable seats is ergonomically good.

However, paper roll dispensers which easily trap fingers and ironing boards which cause backache are examples of ergonomically bad designs. For many products it is a straightforward matter to ensure that the design will be convenient in use; all that is required is an awareness that dimensions, material choice, layout etc. must all be appropriate for normal conditions of use. Where there is doubt or when the design area is an unfamiliar one, satisfactory ergonomic design can be achieved only by studying directly the requirements of users. This may involve the firm in a programme of tests and measurements using a sample of subjects selected to represent the range of characteristics relevant to the design problem in hand. Such work may best be left to specialists if ergonomic considerations are especially important or if sensitive issues need to be investigated. However, in many cases a few simple checks by the design department is all that is required to determine whether, say, a range of four products rather than three is necessary to satisfy all likely users, or whether a particular layout of controls is readily understandable. It is much better that a little time and expense should be devoted to the direct examination of users' characteristics at the design stage, than to allow problems to be identified by the customer after purchase, possibly leading to early re-design or even total failure of the product.

For many firms, economic considerations in design work are confined to ensuring that eventual costs of manufacture will be sufficiently low to enable the product to be sold at a price which will allow a reasonable operating profit. It is clearly one of the designer's main responsibilities to avoid any unnecessary costs in his work and this will be considered in greater detail later. However, it is often imperative that adequate consideration is given to other economic aspects of products apart from just production cost and selling price.

Products which consume fuel may need to be designed to be as efficient as possible. In the wake of the recent escalation in the price of all kinds of fuel, many customers are anxious about the running costs of the products they are buying. So it is found that even products like televisions and refrigerators – which previously might have been considered 'negligible' consumers of power – are now judged by their efficiency. To achieve high efficiency, the designer may have to restrict the number of features that can be incorporated in the product. Or he may have to propose some other kinds of compromise, perhaps affecting quality or performance.

Another 'economic' concern of customers is the level of maintenance expenditure that may be required. This expenditure can be greatly affected by actions at the design stage. If components are designed so that they can be easily replaced by the customer without specialist knowledge or equipment then the product will be much cheaper to maintain than if expert attention is required. Maintenance costs will be even less if parts are designed so that they last for the life of the product. But this often involves higher standards of quality and consequently higher selling prices for the product. Thus a balance may have to be sought between purchase price, maintenance expenditure and running costs in order to offer the customer an attractive 'overall deal'. A good designer or design team will be able to explore these problems and devise good solutions. However, ultimately it is a matter of company policy to decide how the economic considerations of products should be resolved. If the aim is to achieve the lowest possible selling price in the market for example, the design of the product may reflect this by using cheap materials and production methods, which may then dictate a subsequent high level of maintenance expenditure.

(c) The Value Engineering Concept

The real skill in design lies in the ability to satisfy simultaneously all the demands of both the firm which manufactures the product and the customer who buys it. The needs of the firm are minimum cost of production coupled with maximum profit – which depends very largely on the attractiveness of the product to the customer. In competitive, capitalist markets, the customer's decision to purchase one firm's product rather than another is based on 'value'. Not just 'value for money' or 'economic value', but a concept of 'total value' comprising an adequate measure of all the attributes that the customer feels he requires. Broadly speaking these attributes include those aspects of design already mentioned – the technical, artistic, ergonomic and economic aspects.

The term 'Value Engineering' is sometimes used to describe a philosophy of design where the aim is to provide maximum value for the customer at minimum cost to the producer.[4] Value Engineering emphasises the need to understand exactly what the customer requires and to preserve this from the beginning to the end of the design process. But Value Engineering also emphasises the need for minimum cost and in order to achieve this advocates the use of certain techniques of critical appraisal, particularly at the later stages of the design process. These techniques are described in Section 4 which is concerned with the need for periodical re-design of existing products to improve the maximum value/minimum cost relationship. The final stage in the design of a *new* product should be to view it as an *existing* product and to apply these techniques (of 'Value Analysis') to ensure that the best possible design has indeed been achieved given the circumstances prevailing. As will be seen later, the Value Engineering/ Value Analysis approach introduces several special features into the design operation including the direct involvement of non-designers, the encouragement of multi-disciplinary teamwork and the thorough examination of *every* component of the design to ensure both that its function is necessary and that it is being achieved in the most cost-effective manner.

(d) The Development Operation

It has been stated that the designer's task is to seek solutions which satisfy the requirements of the specifications. Usually a final design cannot be achieved without a good deal of testing of ideas and experimental comparisons of alternative solutions. Hence, design units are often supported by some kind of 'development' facility – basically a workshop or laboratory where test-pieces can be made and subjected to whatever examination may be required.

Design and development proceeds hand in hand. During the early stages of the design programme, the demand on development may be for information about material strengths or corrosion resistance, for example. Later, when this information has been used and the design of the product has proceeded to the point where a general layout has been achieved, individual components may be built by the development section and tested to assess properties or performance. In the light of the results obtained, the design can be changed as necessary to meet the standards demanded by the specification. Eventually, a final version of the new product will be built and tested, typically to examine features like reliability, durability, safety and general performance.

Depending on the scale of the product being designed, the development effort may be concerned with scale-models or full-size models. Where possible, full-size tests should always be encouraged because 'scaled-up' results usually involve some error; obviously this is not always feasible when dealing with products like aircraft, ships or similar objects. Similarly, it should be remembered that full-sized models (sometimes called 'prototypes') which have been made using 'one-off' techniques rather than mass production methods may exhibit features different from those of the finished product. Consequently, the final activity of the design and development operation should be to examine the product as soon as the production process has been set up. Some unexpected features may be discovered which must be rectified before large scale production continues.

Sometimes, quite major problems are encountered at this stage, the cause is often lack of co-operation between production and design during earlier stages of the project. In Chapter 2 it was noted that relationships between the departments may be difficult because of the differences in organisational styles and objectives. Nevertheless, it is essential that production (and other functions) is involved in design decisions as they are made. Failure to do so is a recipe for disaster – years of design effort may be wasted if assumptions are made about production matters without checking the true facts. The co-operation of production managers is also needed to enable realistic development trials to be carried out. Often actual production equipment has to be used to test ideas or to form components for prototype trials; few firms can afford to duplicate highly specialised production equipment, so time has to be set aside for experimental work. This can be acutely irritating to production managers who are judged by their ability to reach output targets and they may well resist or obstruct development projects. The answer lies in ensuring that capacity lost during development exercises is properly 'credited' to the production department. Once again, it can be seen that what is needed is a proper understanding of the nature of new product work by top management, together with a firm commitment once a project is underway.

(e) Legal Aspects of Design

This is an appropriate point to mention briefly some legal considerations which are of concern to designers. Two broad areas need to be considered – aspects of the law which are to do with the rights of those involved in creating new products, and aspects of the law concerning the rights of those who buy and use these products.

(i) Rights of Designers and Inventors In order to encourage innovation, the State provides various forms of legal protection of ownership and exploitation to the originators of new products.[5] Most managers are familiar with the concept of *patent* protection – in effect a monopoly of manufacture and trade granted (for up to 20 years in the UK) in respect of a particular novelty of function. The procedure for obtaining a patent is not particularly complex or expensive in terms of the fees charged by the Patent Office. However, the degree of protection which the patent will provide ultimately depends upon the thoroughness with which the 'claims' are presented. To ensure that no 'loopholes' are overlooked that might be used by competitors, most companies use specialist lawyer-engineers (sometimes called patent agents) to manage patent applications. Large companies may employ their own specialists, but most will use independent consultants. Either may involve considerable expense, even more so if patents are being sought in a number of countries when translations and foreign agents will have to be engaged.

In view of this, and the fact that around three years normally elapses between the initial application and eventual granting of a patent (during which time no protection exists), the number of occasions where a patent is appropriate is relatively small – only in those cases where a long and lucrative life-cycle for the product is envisaged. Unfortunately, in the same way that academics are judged by the number of publications they achieve, designers and their companies often see the accumulation of a large number of patents as a measure of achievement. In fact, the granting of patents in no way guarantees any commercial success and may even detract from it if the pursuit of patents becomes an end rather than a means.[6] However, there are circumstances where patents may be highly beneficial, but apart from the initial application,[7] all stages in the procedure should be handled by a competent specialist.

While a patent protects the function of an object, it does not usually give any protection to appearance. Yet distinctive appearance is often a major factor in the success of a product. The law recognises ownership of product designs in the same way that it recognises ownership of other artistic creations such as music, paintings, books and plays. *Copyright* automatically protects the distinctive appearance of a firm's products; legal action to prevent infringement and to recover damages may be brought if copying or imitation occurs. Such action may be difficult where the source of the infringement is overseas, or where there is difficulty in proving ownership of the original design. The latter problem may be avoided by *registration* of the design, as soon as it is conceived, with the Designs Registry of the Patent Office. The procedure for doing this is simple although, as in the case of patent procedures, reference to an appropriate specialist, or at least an authoritative text,[8] is strongly advised.

(ii) Rights of users of products There has been a considerable increase in the scope of consumer legislation in recent years, both in the UK and elsewhere. Many of these laws directly affect the actions of designers, for example where minimum standards of performance are specified or where levels of quality are described. Of particular importance is the question of *product liability*[9] – the trend in many countries is towards the view that consumers should be entitled to compensation for losses caused as a result of the defective design of products. In some cases, individual designers and managers as well as their companies may be held responsible if negligence or wilful malpractice is proven.

Consumer law is complex and is changing rapidly and no

attempt can be made here to present even a summary. All that can safely be said is that it is important for design managers and operations managers to be aware that such legislation exists and that they should obtain qualified advice about the extent to which their activities may be affected by it.

3 Designing for Production

In carrying out their work, designers have many responsibilities both within the firm and outside. The need to comply with the requirements of consumer legislation has just been discussed. Designers must also ensure that their work satisfies customers' needs – that products work well, are attractive, have acceptable dimensions, do not make too much noise, are easy to maintain, and so on. Within the company, designers must aim to satisfy the requirements of many different functions. Finance will demand a product that will enable an acceptable return on investment to be achieved. Marketing will expect a product that will complement the existing range and will allow the fulfilment of operational plans. Production will be concerned with cost, time and quality considerations, and also with ensuring that the new product will be compatible with existing systems.

Good design practice means accommodating all these demands – in fact, this is the basis of the 'Value Engineering concept' discussed earlier in this chapter. It cannot be stressed too strongly how dangerous it is to aim consistently to satisfy only certain demands – say, those of the production department – whilst ignoring others. Examples of products as dissimilar as motorcycles and 'real ale' illustrate the folly of misjudging consumer taste. The collapse of Rolls-Royce at the beginning of the 70s showed how lack of financial awareness when developing new products can undermine the whole enterprise.

Having stressed the need for a balanced approach to design, the rest of this section will investigate the particular demands made by production departments. This seems appropriate in a book which is written for production and operations managers, but readers are urged not to forget all the other responsibilities of designers.

(a) Designer's Responsibility for Quality, Time and Cost of Production

Decisions made at the design stage of a new product can have long-term influences on the efficiency of the production department. By careful attention to the three areas stated in the sub-heading, the designer can ensure that his creations are successful from a manufacturing point of view.

As far as *quality* is concerned, the designer must aim to achieve the standards demanded by the specification, but at the same time not to exceed the capabilities of the production department. This may not be an easy task because the determinants of quality are frequently difficult to identify. For example, the specification may be explicit enough in the terms in which quality of the new product is described – for example, in terms of minimum acceptable working life, accuracy of performance and other aspects. The designer must decide how these are affected by features of the production process, as well as by his choice of materials, particular design solutions, etc. If he knows that a certain manufacturing operation can only achieve, say, very poor dimensional tolerances, he must decide whether such an operation can be used for the new product. If it cannot, he must devise an alternative solution.

In many companies, manufacturing quality standards are set down in written form in manuals or data sheets. These standards will take account of the equipment and skills available in the firm; they may also specify the grades and types of material that may be used for different applications. In such firms, the responsibility of the designer is to be familiar with these standards and to work within them. Where no published standards exist, the designer must discover them for himself – this can only be done by thoroughly understanding the production system, the skill level of the worl force and the nature of existing products. *Time and cost* of production are similar in that both need to be kept to a minimum and the design of any new product should reflect this. Further, these two aspects are usually closely interdependent – a cheap grade of material may require slow machining speeds and thus generate high labour costs; a simple design solution rather than a complex one may allow unskilled labour to be used rather than highly-paid skilled workers and may reduce production times as well.

Clearly the skill of the designer can have substantial impact on production times and costs. It is a skill which depends upon aptitude, training and experience certainly, but it depends also upon close co-operation between production managers and designers and upon a 'sense of value' within the firm as a whole.

In order to achieve the goal of minimum product costs, there are many possibilities to be explored and many 'trade-offs' to be evaluated. As an indication of the scope of the topic, some examples are given below of measures that should be considered at the design stage.

(i) *Labour costs* can be minimised by:
   (a) taking the skill out of each operation;
   (b) reducing the number of operations;
   (c) reducing the time of essential operations that cannot be eliminated;
   (d) eliminating the possibility of errors during manufacture.

(ii) *Material costs* can be minimised by:
   (a) using as few components as possible;
   (b) choosing component dimensions to make economic use of raw material;
   (c) using the cheapest materials consistent with quality standards;
   (d) specifying existing materials as far as possible.

(iii) *Equipment costs* can be minimised by:
   (a) specifying existing equipment rather than new equipment;
   (b) designing jigs, tools etc. to facilitate economic production;
   (c) selecting cheap rather than expensive processes.

In general, costs can be minimised by adopting policies of

standardisation. For example, the use of existing components rather than designing new ones is a form of standardisation. Not only can this save the designer's time, but also means that longer production runs will be possible and that larger material orders can be placed, both of which lead to economies compared with having short runs of several different components. Even if an existing component cannot be used in the new product, it may still be possible to choose an existing material rather than a new one so that purchasing economies and stockholding savings can be achieved.

An awareness of the benefits of standardisation may lead to a similar awareness of the value of *specialisation*. In large design departments it will be found advantageous if there is some specialisation of tasks – standardisation of components and materials will be encouraged if individual designers are able to develop expertise in particular areas. Another aspect of specialisation is where excellence in manufacturing skills is recognised and exploited by designers. Such excellence may be within the firm or outside; some highly successful companies have a policy of always specifying the most economical supplies of components, regardless of source. Designers should always recommend the use of bought-in parts from specialised suppliers if these really do represent the best value obtainable.

Standardisation and specialisation are both concerned with the *reduction of variety* in design and in manufacture, a third form of which is *simplification*. This is concerned with the avoidance of unnecessary complexity in either the design of products or the ways they are made. Most of the approaches for achieving minimum cost listed under the 'labour', 'material' and 'equipment' headings, are examples of simplification.

Minimum cost of production, like other aspects of design work, represents a goal for the designer. In fact, a perfect design can never be achieved – there is never enough time or knowledge available and some subsequent improvement is always possible. 'Good' design is that which consistently yields better-than-average results for the firm. Although the doctrines of standardisation, specialisation and simplification are by no means new or unfamiliar, they are a proven key to the achievement of design which is 'good' from a production viewpoint. Thus it is important that production managers and others, as well as designers, should appreciate the benefits that can result from a preoccupation with variety reduction in all its manifestations.

(b) Need for New Products to be Compatible with Existing Production

Designing to appropriate standards of quality and to minimum levels of cost and time are certainly major responsibilities of designers with respect to production. Where new production facilities are being created specifically for the new product, these may be the only responsibilities. But where existing production systems are to be used, there are other factors which must be considered before the design is completed to ensure that the new product will be *compatible*. This is a topic which is covered in few texts[10] yet, in the writer's experience, would seem to be the greatest cause of friction between production managers and designers.

Compatibility must be achieved with the production process and with existing products. It involves ensuring that design features are appropriate to existing methods and that they do not cause disruptions to occur. An extreme example of non-compatibility might be where a product was designed to be built using equipment not present in the factory. Another example could be where manufacture of the new product would cause overloading of a particular process.

The key to the problem lies in the designer's knowledge of the production set-up. Many designers have practical experience of production and fully understand the limitations and capabilities that they must work within. Unfortunately, many do not have this experience and, quite simply, do not appreciate the systems that they are supposed to be designing for and succeed only in antagonising their production colleagues. When this situation arises, the responsible production manager will adopt a constructive attitude and ensure that the design department is provided with a detailed picture of the true nature of his department. This information should cover:

(a) type of production system (e.g. batch, line, etc.);
(b) processes available (e.g. casting, welding, etc.);

(c) handling and storage facilities;
(d) nature of the workforce and skills available;
(e) list of preferred sub-contractors and their skills;
(f) breakdown of current products;
(g) utilisation of processes and machines;
(h) quality limits and inspection procedures;
(i) materials used and stockholding facilities.

Only with this basic knowledge can designers hope to achieve compatibility; the more complete the knowledge, the better the chances of a smooth start-up of production. It may be useful to have a 'check list of compatibility questions' so that the designer can satisfy himself he has attended to all contentious points. Three basic questions are important:

(i) *Is the new design compatible in terms of existing production technology?*
(a) Are existing *batch/flow line systems* satisfactory? If not, what degree of modification is required?
(b) Is the *proposed volume* of production compatible with existing volumes?
(c) Will the new design demand new *standards of quality*?
(d) Will changed demands on machines affect the *plant maintenance system*?

(ii) *Is the new design compatible in terms of labour requirements?*
(a) Are existing *skills* adequate? If not, is it feasible to demand different skills from those which already exist?
(b) What about the *pattern of working*? Does the new design involve a change to existing shift work arrangements?
(c) How might the new design affect the operation of *incentive and payments* schemes?

(iii) *Is the new design compatible in terms of 'control'?*
(a) Will existing *production control* methods be satisfactory?
(b) Can existing *costing procedures* be adopted?
(c) Will new methods of *checking quality* be required? Will the *frequency* of inspection be significantly different?

(d) Are existing *material control and handling* systems adequate?

Each production operation is unique and has its own special problems and opportunities, so designers must draw up their own checklist of 'compatibility parameters'. It would be misleading to attempt to present a generalised review of parameters. Statements like 'operation cycle times tend to be short in line systems and long in batch systems' are not helpful to designers – and in many cases, systems of production are neither 'line' nor 'batch', but a hybrid of the two.

The ideas expressed in the last few pages around the theme 'designing for production' will not appeal to all designers – or production specialists. In many, perhaps most, companies in the UK there is an assumption that production departments should adapt to whatever demands are made. 'It is the job of Design to dream up the ideas and of Production to make them work' sums up a common attitude. In fact, what frequently happens is that the ideas *do not* work and a great deal of wasted energy is expended. Both production managers and design managers are jealous of their own specialisms and see co-operation as a threat to their autonomy. This is an attitude that can be seen in other departments too, and is reflected in the highly segmented way in which many companies organise themselves. If managers were more concerned with 'success' rather than 'survival', they would be eager to reap the benefits of co-operation. The message for top management is that successful innovation must be seen to be a major objective and that it is the responsibility not only of designers, but of all functions in the organisation to achieve it.

4 Programmes of Re-design and Value Analysis

So far, only design work in relation to new products has been explored, but effort needs to be directed to existing products as well. Sooner or later, all firms operating in competitive markets risk finding that their products are less profitable than they used to be. This is because other manufacturers will have introduced alternative products which are cheaper or more attractive (or both).

Unfortunately, many companies think that design stops at the launch of a new product and are unprepared when sales eventually start to decline. Their response may be limited to an inadequate 'face-lift', or even worse, to resignation to the fate of having to abandon the particular market altogether. In many cases, such a response would be unnecessary if a 're-design policy' had been worked out and implemented.

(a) Product Re-design Programmes

To ensure long-term prosperity, all companies should adopt some means of critically reviewing their products or services. Rather than waiting for disaster to strike, the object of the review should be to identify at an early stage those products which are beginning to lose their attraction to customers. The mechanism of this review can vary a great deal – in some companies the marketing department may operate a continuous review of product performance; in other companies an occasional review might be thought adequate. Wherever responsibility lies, the following points should be observed:

(i) *Priority assessment* Very few companies manufacture only a single product, so most firms need to identify which products are most valuable to them. Points like annual sales value and contribution to overheads are clear indicators, but so are brand image and the extent to which a product fills a gap in the market.

(ii) *Basis of review* Ideally this should be on a continuous basis – information constantly updated, not only for the product under review but also for its competitors.

(iii) *'Trigger points'* Each firm must decide the point at which a re-design exercise should be initiated. Depending on the type of product, it may be on the basis of a single indicator such as falling market share or a combination of different factors. A very good case can be made in support of a policy of holding regular re-design exercises, as well as maintaining the 'watching brief' to detect failing competitiveness. The rate of progress in most branches of technology is sufficiently fast that few designs more than two or three years old cannot be improved, usually in ways that achieve savings in production costs. So most firms should think in terms of a two-edged approach:

(a) product reviews to give advanced warning of loss of competitive advantage and to initiate re-design exercises;
(b) routine re-design exercises to enable advantage to be taken of latest technology and thus to maintain profitability at the highest possible levels.

(iv) *Re-design exercise* Usually, the most obvious way to re-design a product will seem to be to hand it over to the design department, perhaps to the individual or team which did the original work. When it looks as though fairly drastic changes might be required this may be the only realistic course. However, there are serious drawbacks to this practice. For a start, the fact that the existing design is familiar to the design department – perhaps even viewed with some pride – might severely diminish the prospects of any really inspired changes. Also, even where the design department does have good working relationships with the rest of the company, it may be very difficult for it to evaluate the implications of change proposals.

To overcome these problems, some kind of collaborative re-design exercise is recommended. Unlike the process of designing a new product, where complex specifications have to be skilfully converted into design solutions, the problem in a re-design exercise is usually the less complex one of modifying existing solutions to achieve useful improvements. Thus, designers might be joined by representatives from other departments to tackle the project on a team basis. Where these representatives are truly involved in the exercise, rather than being regarded simply as 'advisors' to the design specialists, quite exciting results may be obtained. Value Analysis is a set of techniques based on such a multi-disciplinary team approach.

(b) Value Analysis

Value Analysis is so called because it focuses upon the 'values' offered by the product to customers. It aims to reduce the direct manufacturing cost of the product while preserving, or improving, these values – basically the technical, artistic, ergonomic and economic features described earlier in this chapter. In essence, Value Analysis operates by:

(a) identifying value features or functions of the product;
(b) examining alternative ways of achieving these;
(c) choosing the way that entails least cost.

It works by changing the design of the product and also, where appropriate, by changing the method of manufacture. It is an extremely thorough procedure; every component of the product is examined in turn, so the maximum possible cost saving can be achieved. At the same time, because it involves a team representing (typically) production, marketing and accounting as well as design, the needs of the customer and of all functions within the company are efficiently and comprehensively satisfied.

Value Analysis techniques have been used for more than 30 years and there are numerous references which may be consulted for details of methodologies and case histories.[4,11,12] Some experts describe procedures involving twelve or more steps, but for most applications a much simpler approach[13] is satisfactory.

(i) Familiarisation stage The first step must be to find out as accurately as possible the present costs and values associated with the product. Cost elements for each component will probably be available from the accounting representative on the team. As far as possible these elements should be broken down into labour costs and material costs, and should be recorded for reference during subsequent stages of the exercise. Value elements may be more difficult to identify and this is where the benefit of the team approach will become clear. The marketing representative should be able to give an informed opinion about the values which the customer seeks in the product and its competitors. But frequently this opinion is challenged, alternative assessments considered and a con-

sensus achieved. Again this result should be noted for reference at later stages.

Apart from the identification of costs and values, this stage is an opportunity for all team members to understand the product and how it works. To assist in this, certain information may be helpful – perhaps in the form of drawings, scale models, sample components etc.

(ii) Speculation stage This is the most crucial part of a Value Analysis exercise. Taking each component in turn, the team subjects it to critical examination. The first question is always 'Can we eliminate it?' Surprisingly often the answer is 'Yes'. It may be necessary to alter an adjacent part to ensure that the function is not lost, but usually there will still be an immediate cost saving. If the component *is* essential and cannot be eliminated, then the team must try to find other cost savings by making some change to it. Free-ranging 'brainstorming' techniques may be used by the team to produce ideas for change, although without an experienced team leader, inhibitions may prevent the realisation of full potential. In most exercises, the best results are probably obtained by using a 'structured' approach – a checklist of appropriate questions that will give the team a basis for generating ideas. For example: 'Can we use a standard part?' 'Can we use a cheaper material?' 'Can we use less material?' and so on.

(iii) Evaluation stage After each component has been analysed in turn, the team will find that there is a small number of changes which can be made without affecting the product as far as the customer is concerned, but which will bring cost benefits to the company. The effect of each change must be examined and the total effect of all changes in combination must be evaluated. Only when the team is certain that the product remains at least as good as it was originally, can it recommend that the changes should be implemented.

(iv) Implementation stage The team should complete its analysis by calculating the extent of the overall cost saving which has been identified. To do this, anticipated labour and material costs should be estimated and compared with the

sums noted at the beginning of the exercise. The team should also estimate the cost of making the changes – new equipment, redundant stocks of existing materials, etc. – and deduct this from the overall saving.

After the changes have been introduced, the team should follow up the results to confirm that its predictions have been realised. If they have not, then the reasons should be identified and appropriate action suggested.

The foregoing is intended only as a guide to the basic methodology of Value Analysis. Many refinements are possible which can be of great help when dealing with complex products.[14] The importance of the team approach in Value Analysis cannot be over-emphasised. Bringing together people from different parts of the company to participate in Value Analysis on a part time or occasional basis can produce benefits in addition to the effective re-design of a company's products.[13] Barriers between departments will be dismantled as problems are shared and understood. Participants will identify themselves more closely with the company and its products as a result of their greater understanding.

5 Conclusion

In many companies, senior production or operations managers have direct responsibility for design activities. It is essential therefore that they understand the problems that designers have to deal with. In particular, this chapter has stressed the importance of a close working relationship between design and the other functions in the company. Designers cannot do their jobs properly if they are considered to be specialists who must work in isolation from the rest of the company and the outside world. At all stages in the design of new products and during the re-design of existing products, the active participation of a wide range of company personnel may be highly desirable to ensure a 'balanced' approach to design.[15]

This chapter has sought to give an impression of the activities which designers undertake and also the nature of their responsibilities. All too often, there is a mis-match between design and other departments, particularly production, caused by a lack of knowledge and a lack of common objectives. This need not be the case if managers take the trouble to understand what is happening in their companies and to compare it with what *needs* to happen if successful innovation is to be achieved.

References

1 Mayall, W.H., *Principles in Design*, Design Council, London, 1979.
2 Buck, C.H., *Problems of Product Design and Development*, Pergamon 1963.
3 Leech, D.J., *Management of Engineering Design*, Wiley 1972.
4 Buck, C.H. and Butler, D.M., *Economic Product Design*, Collins 1970.
5 Blanco White, T.A., Jacob, R. and Davis, J.D., *Patents, Trade Marks, Copyright and Industrial Designs*, Sweet and Maxwell 1978.
6 Oakley, M.H., The importance of being useful, *The Guardian*, 20 December 1979.
7 *Applying for a Patent*, Patent Office, London, 1978.
8 Myrants, G., *The Protection of Industrial Designs*, McGraw-Hill 1977.
9 Miller, C.J. and Lovell, P.A., *Product Liability*, Butterworth 1977.
10 Harding, H.A., *Production Management* (3rd edn), Macdonald and Evans 1978.
11 Miles, L.D., *Techniques of Value Analysis and Engineering* (2nd edn), McGraw-Hill 1972.
12 Gage, W.L., *Value Analysis*, McGraw-Hill 1967.
13 Oakley, M.H., How to analyse value, *Management Today*, November 1979.
14 Raven, A.D., *Profit Improvement by Value Analysis, Value Engineering and Purchase Price Analysis*, Cassell 1971.
15 Topalian, A., *The Management of Design Projects*, Associated Business Press 1980.

5
The Thermimax Burner

J S BAYLISS

Marketing Executive,
Dunlop Ltd

1 Introduction*

Dunlop Engineering Group is one of five major groups which make up Dunlop Limited, a UK company with an annual turnover approaching £1500m. In the early 1970s, Engineering Group employed about 5000 people and consisted of four manufacturing divisions. Products included: vehicle wheels and suspension systems; aircraft tyres, wheels, brakes and accessories; equipment for building tyres. Also on the site was a New Products Division whose remit was to find, develop and bring to commercialisation new products which could be added to the Group's existing business.

This Division became involved with an interesting new material then being studied by BP Limited with a view to its use in *oil* burning systems. After some preliminary work by the Division, it was seen that a novel form of *gas* burner might be developed from the original concept. Accordingly, Dunlop recruited a combustion engineer and research started in earnest.

By 1975, development had advanced to the extent that gas

* To protect commercial confidentiality, some data in this case study has been disguised. The study was prepared in 1979.

burners had been sold in prototype quantities, the most notable sale being to a petro-chemical complex in the Middle East. The burner had been christened the 'Thermimax'.

Already, the burner offered real advantages to users, mainly on account of the remarkably good gas/air mixing achieved at the burner face. Some of the most important of these advantages were:

(i) Low noise level
(ii) High thermal efficiency
(iii) Controllable flame shape – easily tailored to suit different applications; for example from the long thin flame required for firing down tubes to the short fat flame ideal for oven and furnaces.
(iv) Controllable flame size – output could be turned down to low heat release without losing stability or efficiency.
(v) Ability to work reliably in very dusty atmospheres where other burners tend to 'clog-up'.
(vi) Extreme flame stability – tests showed the 'Thermimax' capable of burning in draughts that extinguished competitors' products.

From the manufacturing point of view, only 7 sizes covered a wide range of outputs, from 50,000 Btu/hr* for a domestic central heating boiler, to 10 million Btu/hr required in major industrial applications. Nevertheless, the design of the burner still resulted in a considerably more expensive product than the competition. This was mitigated by the fact that a burner system is usually sold as a 'package' consisting of burner head, wind box, air and gas controls, burner control system, fans etc.

2 Market Survey

In view of the promising nature of the development to date,

* The 'British thermal unit' is still widely used in many parts of the world. The metric S.I. (International System of Units) unit is the 'kilowatt', but this is rarely used in this context; Continental Europe uses the 'kilocalorie'.
1 kilowatt = 3412 Btu/hr; 1 kilocalorie/hr = 3.968 Btu/hr.

it was decided that a thorough market survey should be undertaken to determine how best to go commercial. A summary of the finding of this survey is as follows:

(a) Domestic Boiler Market

Below 50,000 Btu/hr, burners can be of very simple design and yet still be effective and efficient – a state of affairs which makes for a large number of competitors in what, in cash terms, is a small market. The volume of sales in the UK domestic market was estimated at £2½–3m p.a. Within Europe there was considerable manufacturing overcapacity and so imported burners were available at very low prices.

(b) Commercial Heating Market

This market segment includes heating systems in office blocks, hospitals, theatres, shops, schools and hotels. The requirement is normally for a central heating boiler system, sometimes with a large hot water facility as well. Outputs are in the range 150,000 up to 5 or 6 million Btu/hr, but there is a definite watershed in the market at 1 million Btu/hr.

Below this level, although not as bad as in the domestic market, there was overcapacity at the time of the survey and many satisfactory packaged burners were available at extremely competitive prices. Above 1 million Btu/hr there was considerably less competition, a result of the increased design complexity and the associated need to invest in development and to provide comprehensive advisory and servicing capability. Profit margins were much better than at the lower end of this market segment. There was a strong preference for gas fired equipment in the wake of the 1973 oil price rises, although it was considered that the UK market for 1 to 4½ million Btu/hr burners at £3/4 to £1m p.a. in 1975 was still smaller than oil burner sales. In view of the policy of British Gas to restrict new gas sales in this sector and the fact that customers would not normally exchange an oil boiler for a new gas one unless replacement was necessary anyway, then only a steady moderate growth rate was predicted.

Moreover, the new burner did not offer any significant

working advantages over existing packaged burners and without a price advantage would find market entry an uphill struggle. However, there would be a small number of users with special requirements within this sector, such as small process heating applications where the Thermimax's versatility would be admirably suited. But total potential sales were considered to be less than £50,000 p.a.

(c) The Industrial Tariff Market

Customers with an annual demand in excess of 100,000 therms* make up this market – that is, large commercial establishments and industrial users of process heating and space heating. The market can be subdivided into:

(i) Boilers Gas had become a major fuel only recently and the majority of installations were oil-fired. Typically, the Gas Corporation was supplying gas on interruptable contracts where the supply could be cut off at short notice to ensure continuity of supply to high tariff customers during periods of peak demand. Consequently, those already with oil-fired units were tending not to convert to gas-only systems, but instead were buying installations capable of running on either oil or gas, usually via twin nozzles or heads. This policy enabled advantage to be taken of fluctuations in relative fuel prices. However, sites which did not have existing oil storage facilities were disinclined to incur the costs of installation and so there continued to be a growth in demand for gas-only equipment, although it was considered unlikely to reach much more than a 10% share of the market. Demand in 1976 for all types of burners in the range of ½m to 3m+ Btu/hr was estimated at £6–7m, over half being dual-fired and less than 10% gas-only. Sales of gas-only boilers were expected to grow to a ceiling of £1m in 1977/78.

Although there was a definite demand in this sector for specially designed burners to suit particular boilers, there were some half dozen companies who were well-regarded and who, between them, were capable of more than satisfying the needs of the market. It would not be sensible to enter this market without an oil and a dual-fuel burner. On the gas-only side,

* 1 therm = 100,000 Btu.

the burner would have to be tailored to suit the needs of individual boiler manufacturers who, in the main, expressed contentment with existing suppliers.

(ii) Other Space Heaters Within this category are indirect and direct fired warm air heaters and overhead radiant heaters. The Thermimax burner was considered particularly suitable for the direct fired type. In this type of heater, the products of combustion are fired directly into the space to be heated. While highly efficient, these systems are safe only in locations where there is a plentiful and unavoidable supply of fresh air. Because of the high efficiencies involved, burner demand was predicted to increase from £80,000 p.a. to £300,000 p.a. over 5 years.

(iii) Process Heating Process Heating involves a heat release range from ½m to 100 million Btu/hr and includes appliances such as dryers, ovens, tanks, and furnaces. In general, the higher the heat release, the more common the use of oil, but in certain applications the cleanliness of gas is an overriding factor. The demand for gas-only burners was estimated at £¾–£1m p.a., and for oil and dual-fuel at £5–£6m p.a. The same half dozen suppliers operate in this sector as in the boiler sector, but there is a much greater demand for customer-designed equipment. It was felt that the product advantages of the Thermimax would be sufficient to enable a foothold to be established in the market. However, the diverse nature of the demand would mean that the costs of selling to and servicing this market would be higher than in the other segments already discussed.

(d) The Petro-Chemical Market

This market segment includes the supply of burners for:

(a) Reforming furnaces such as in ammonia, ethylene hydrogen and methanol plants;
(b) Fired heaters used to heat process fluids;
(c) Crude oil heaters in refineries.

Market characteristics were identified as:

(i) Size £3–£4m p.a.;

(ii) Upsurge in demand especially in the Middle East where there was a trend to process more fuel near to source;
(iii) Only 4 or 5 major competitors;
(iv) Relatively few customers (about 20) most of whom operated worldwide and had major offices in the UK;
(v) Technical capability was crucial and considerable development effort was involved in producing competitive products. The gas-fired Thermimax had already shown that it was not only suitable but in many ways technically superior. It was also price competitive.

Burners represent a very small part of the total cost of a petro-chemical complex, but if they prove unreliable, the whole complex can be brought to a halt. It would be a long haul to persuade operators to change to new untried equipment, whatever the technical advantages offered. Even so, a 10% market share appeared to be an achievable target with a gas-only burner, rising to 30%+ if an oil and dual-fuel burner could be developed.

3 New Product Decision

Presented with this report it was necessary to take a decision on what to do. The burner did not fit into the activities of any existing Division in the Engineering Group, and so a new undertaking would have to be formed if work was to continue. To be worthwhile to Dunlop, any new Division had to achieve rapidly a turnover of £1m p.a. rising, in the long run, to £10m p.a. Financial studies indicated that 15% profit on turnover at £1m was readily achievable for burner sales. The following different courses of action were defined and debated by senior management:

(i) Discontinue further activities – possibly seeking a purchaser for the rights to the burner in its existing form.
(ii) Continue development, aiming at one of the market segments. In this case, turnover from a gas-only burner would not meet the financial criteria dictated by company policy.

(iii) Continue development with a view to introducing an oil burner and a dual-fuel burner, and aim the burner(s) at a specific market segment.
(iv) As (iii) but in the meantime enter the market place with the existing burner.
(v) Obtain a licence from an overseas manufacturer of oil/dual-fuel burners, of comparable technical quality and suitable for the same market segment(s).
(vi) Acquire an existing burner company and add the Thermimax to its product range. (To consider this option properly it was necessary to look at the profitability in 1975 and predicted profitability of existing UK burner companies). Depending on the size of company chosen, either a cash or a share exchange would have to be considered as well as, in the case of a private company, its willingness to be acquired.
(vii) Acquire a company making products which use burners (and, possibly, whose product range would be made more competitive by adopting Thermimax).
(viii) Develop a range of products to be sold in association with the new gas burner. As in options (iii)/(iv) the timing would be crucial.
(ix) Obtain a licence for a range of associated products.

Clearly these options were not mutually exclusive and in the event a combination of options was adopted. First, a major policy decision was taken to form an umbrella Division, within which new small business units could be established and allowed to grow, sharing between them certain essential overheads, such as accounting, planning and personnel functions. This meant that ventures would be given more time to reach self-sufficiency than if they were to stand alone. Second, it was decided to go commercial immediately, get out into the market place and learn first-hand through operating experience more about the optional growth paths available. It was agreed that further development would be concentrated on refining the gas burner to meet specific UK market needs, rather than to try for an oil burner – considered to be at least a 2 year programme. Instead, an existing design of oil burner would be sought with a view to obtaining a licence for it. Third, the UK agency for a range of thermal heaters and rapid steam generators was obtained as a means of adding to the turnover.

4 Operating Experience

As expected, the first two years proved to be tough going – a new manufacturer breaking into an existing market. It soon became clear that results would be obtained more quickly by concentrating on process applications, rather than going for the petro-chemical market. Once the business was more firmly established, attention *was* again switched to the petro-chemical market with a certain amount of success; but this is still seen as a long-term growth sector at the time of writing.

On the process side, sales built up slowly as, not unnaturally, manufacturers of appliances such as air dryers and ovens could only adopt the new burner in new designs. Generally it was not economic to change designs simply to accommodate the Thermimax. Hence, most early sales were to end-users who for some reason were dissatisfied with their existing equipment or for whom a standard design was not suitable. This meant that each burner-based combustion system sold had to be specially modified to suit customer requirements and the Division found itself in a different type of business from the anticipated one of supplying original equipment manufacturers – something that could not be clearly foreseen until first-hand market experience had been gained.

A large potential demand was soon recognised for gas fired tank heating systems, used for direct heating of process fluids such as dyes, electroplating baths, rinsing baths, hot dipping and the like. The readily controllable flame shape possible with the Thermimax meant that a very cost-effective tank heating system could be quickly designed and marketed. The heater consisted of a tube immersed in the liquid and located at the bottom of the tank; a long thin flame was fired down the tube. Again, initial sales growth proved to be slow, but now, 3 years later, tank heaters form about half of the total turnover of the enterprise.

After the first year's operations it became clear that a suitable oil burner would not be easily found, although many possibilities had been assessed. Further, there had been little success with the agency already obtained so the whole range of alternatives had to be reassessed – but this time with first-hand market knowledge.

Again option (ix) (p. 75) was chosen as the main platform, but this time the agency for a range of industrial warm air units was negotiated. This was a logical step as it had been realised that the combustion requirements of an overhead radiant tube heater based on the Thermimax (with the burner firing down the inside of a small – 100 mm or so – diameter tube) were similar to those of the already proven tank heater. It was felt that a marketable unit could be developed within a few months which, together with the range of warm air units would provide an area of rapid expansion. This decision was based on the results of a further market survey which showed that there were only two effective competitors for each product type. With increased concern about energy costs and the need to use floor space economically, the advantages offered by these products in these respects were expected to ensure rapid market growth. Also, it was the type of end-user market where product performance could be proved easily in practice by demonstration and where individual customers could try a new product without disastrous consequences if it went wrong.

In fact, it was just over a year before the overhead radiant tube heater could be launched, but the predicted rapid growth has now been achieved. The Division quickly became known in the market place and its promise of reliable, high quality products and good delivery was tested and proved.

Now, three years later, the Division is established in its chosen markets and growing steadily. The time for considering the next growth step is approaching; in broad terms the alternatives set out in 1976 still remain valid. This time, with yet more direct market experience, the decisions will be made with increased expectations of success.

6
Facility Decisions

D J BENNETT

Lecturer in Operations Management,
The University of Aston

Introduction: Facility Location and Layout

Operations, whatever their nature, require the employment of physical facilities. In manufacturing these take the form of buildings (factories, warehouses, administrative offices etc.) together with plant and machinery (furnaces, presses, assembly lines etc.) for converting materials into finished products.

Service operations will also inevitably require facilities. Banks, airlines and hospitals all require buildings while 'plant and machinery' can take various forms (computers, aeroplanes, X-ray equipment etc.).

In all types of operation, however, there are common decisions to be made relating to the facilities that are employed. Decisions relating to the placement of such facilities can be viewed at a macro and a micro level. The macro problem involves deciding on the best location for the building or other operational bases, while the micro problem involves the disposition or layout of 'plant and machinery' within a particular location.

Any approach that is taken to determine the best location of a facility or layout of 'plant and machinery' must obviously seek to optimise some measure of operating performance. Usually the objective is to minimise the cost of the product or service incurred by virtue of a particular location, but in certain situations such a simple approach may not be appropriate. For example, the siting of a facility which took into account all the social and environmental factors may be totally different from the one which sought only to minimise operating costs as may be demonstrated by the controversy surrounding the location of new international airports at London and Tokyo.

Factors Determining Location

A thorough approach to facility location would carefully consider a wide number of factors, some of which will be tangible (to which costs may easily be assigned), while others will be intangible (where costs cannot so easily or directly be calculated). Some of the tangible factors which could be affected by the siting of a factory are cost of land, buildings, labour, transport, power etc., while the intangible factors include community attitudes, legal constraints, competition for skills, effect of weather etc.

Of course, the dynamic nature of an industrial economy often mitigates against finding anything other than short-term solutions to location and layout problems. This is amply illustrated by the changing fortunes of areas which once thrived as a result of the industrial revolution, but declined due to changes in fuel and transport costs. Basic iron and steel, pottery and textile manufacture are all examples of situations where location was determined originally by local sources of raw material and power. In the fullness of time, however, this pattern has changed dramatically. Better and cheaper communications, and transmission of electrical energy to virtually any part of the country has meant that such industries are no longer so dependent on such factors and very often some of the intangibles mentioned earlier have a greater part to play in determining the location of industries.

This current picture, therefore, is of a smaller number of manufacturers who, by virtue of the size or nature of their product, are still tied to a certain location, while a growing number of manufacturers (the motor industry in particular) have become 'footloose' and are free to choose between an extremely large number of possible locations.

Government Influence

In any industrialised country, two hundred years of unco-ordinated industrial development will undoubtedly lead to economic imbalance and, in recent years, successive UK governments have appreciated that certain regions of the country have rates of economic growth which give cause for concern.[1] The symptoms of this are well known: low and falling levels of employment, a low rate of increase of industrial and commercial premises, slow growth in personal incomes and generally below-average earnings. In many of the older industrial areas these economic symptoms are reflected in the dereliction and decay of the physical environment, thereby deterring the modern industry which is needed to revitalise these areas. Over the years, governments have sought to reverse this trend in two ways.

The first of these has been to *discourage* the expansion of industry in the more prosperous areas by not permitting development, while secondly, they have attempted to *encourage* firms to move to 'areas for expansion' by designating regions as assisted areas.[2]

Attractive incentives in the form of grants, tax allowances, training assistance etc., have been offered in an attempt to encourage firms to move to these areas. A further dimension was added by the emergence of 'new' towns, many of which are not in the areas designated for expansion, but which still attempt to attract industry by offering subsidised housing and low cost industrial and commercial units.

However, the passage of time has again necessitated a change in strategy, because inner city areas within the economically more viable regions have also suffered decay. More recently therefore, proposals have been made to strengthen inner area economies and a far more flexible policy has been adopted with respect to industrial development in large cities.[3]

What, therefore, is the significance of all this to the operations manager? One could cynically say that operations managers should not concern themselves with matters of location and should leave such decisions to 'experts'. But expert advice often only comes in the form of opinion or a statement of options. The final decision must still be made by management and in particular the operations manager, being accountable directly for the cost and effectiveness of the goods or service provided, must be aware of all the factors which might influence the operation. Thus, it is necessary to be able to achieve a fully balanced view which takes into account not only the immediate costs and benefits, but those which are likely to affect the long-term fortunes and even the survival of the organisation.

Evaluating Alternative Locations

The most common type of problem a manager is likely to face is the need to choose, from a number of alternative sites, that which best benefits the operation. Such a problem usually arises as a result of having already considered the intangible factors (including those just described) and having narrowed the problem down to a small number of possibilities which are easily feasible.

The decision is therefore taken based on a simple economic analysis where both fixed and variable costs are taken into account. Fixed costs (such as rent, insurance etc.) would be treated as annual payments, whereas the variable costs (such as materials, power etc.) would be dependent on volume of output or level of activity.

For a fixed annual volume the various annual costs can be summed and compared for alternative sites, see figure 6.1.

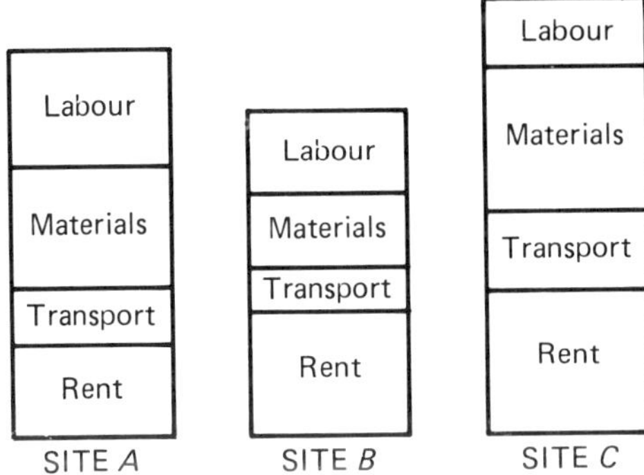

Figure 6.1 *Comparison of Annual Costs for Three Sites (Fixed Volume)*

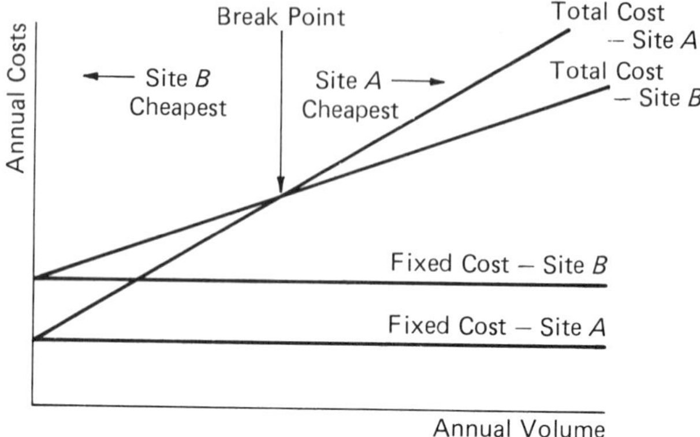

Figure 6.2 *Comparison of Annual Costs for Two Sites (Variable Volume)*

Where, however, the annual volume is variable or as yet uncertain, a graphical approach could be taken which highlights the 'break-points' and shows which is the best alternative at different output levels as in figure 6.2.

Location Models and 'Optimal' Solutions

The 'correct' solution to a plant location problem would be that location which is better than all other possibilities. This concept leads us to the idea of modelling the problem and obtaining an optimal result.

Such an idea is not new, for since the early 1900s theories have been developed aimed at achieving such a result by modelling the relevant variables either graphically or mathematically. The traditional approach is to assume a 'green field' situation where the facility can feasibly assume any one of an indefinite number of possible locations. The model is then 'organised' to 'settle' at that point which minimises some objective function (usually cost).

Such a theory is that of Weber (see Blowers[4]) which in its simplest form takes account of transport cost using the 'locational triangle' principle as shown in figure 6.3.

In this example 4 units of a finished good to be delivered to *C* are made up from 2 units of raw material supplied from *A* and 3 units supplied from *B*. An equilibrium point may be

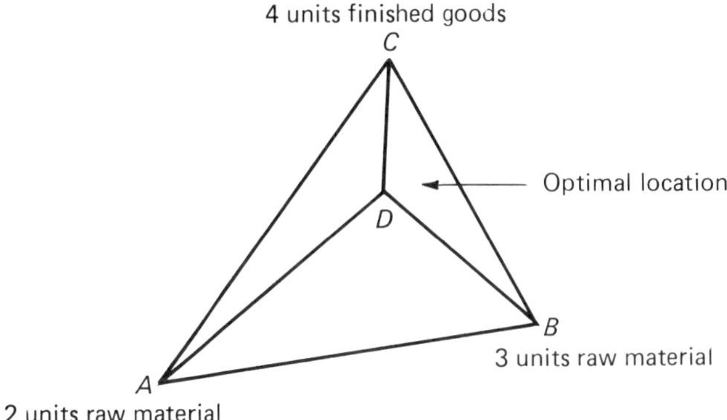

Figure 6.3 *Weber's Locational Triangle for Transport Costs*

found at *D* which minimises the total cost of transport. Further modifications may be made to the model to take account of additional costs (i.e. labour cost 'contours' may be added) and further assessments may be made in the light of the resultant total cost.

The Weber approach, however, still considers the company to be operating in isolation. Other theories developed by Hotelling and Losch, also described by Blowers, recognise the further dimensions of demand variation and competition. Still, these approaches only remotely approach a representation of the real situation which exists in industrial economies and, although they may provide a valuable means of describing and demonstrating the movement of industries, they are somewhat academic in value to the operations manager.

Perhaps of more immediate use are the recently developed techniques which have been generated by the 'operational research' school. These are generally more realistic in that they will not look for an optimal solution from within an infinite 'universe', rather they will start by taking a limited number of possibilities and seek to find the best by optimising some variable such as cost, distance travelled, capacity etc.

Linear and dynamic programming have both been used to solve the facility location problem and as an example of the approach which uses the transportation method (a special case of linear programming), consider the following problem.

A company making inexpensive modular furniture has two plants situated at York and Oxford. They sell through four 'direct-to-the-customer' discount warehouses which are located in Chester, Bristol, London and Norwich.

Forecasts have indicated that an increase in demand is expected which cannot be met by the two existing factories, so a third is to be built and the choice has been narrowed down to two possible locations, Northampton or Telford. Production costs at the plants would be the same but, because of the size of the product, transport costs between factory and warehouse are assumed to vary in proportion to distance and the quantity transported. Distribution costs (£ per module) for the existing plants are as shown in table 6.1.

Table 6.1 Distribution Costs (£ per module)

From:	*To:*				*Annual Capacity*
	Chester	Bristol	London	Norwich	
York	1.3	2.7	2.5	2.3	100,000
Oxford	1.7	0.9	0.8	1.9	80,000
Annual expected demand	90,000	50,000	100,000	60,000	

Distribution costs for the two plants under consideration, each of which would need an annual capacity of 12,000 units, would be as shown in table 6.2.

The transportation algorithm is described in detail in most textbooks of operational research techniques (see for example Sasieni, Yaspan and Friedman[5]). In essence the method seeks to determine the allocation of goods from factories to warehouses which minimises the transport costs incurred.

In our case two solutions would need to be found, one which

Table 6.2 Distribution Costs for Two Plants Under Consideration

From:	*To:*			
	Chester	Bristol	London	Norwich
Northampton	1.8	1.4	0.7	1.2
Telford	0.6	1.4	2.4	2.6

would assume choosing the Northampton site and one which would assume choosing the Telford site. In fact the two solutions would be:

To:

		Chester	Bristol	London	Norwich
	York	90,000	–	–	10,000
From:	Oxford	–	50,000	30,000	–
	Northampton	–	–	70,000	50,000

and

To:

		Chester	Bristol	London	Norwich
	York	20,000	–	20,000	60,000
From:	Oxford	–	–	80,000	–
	Telford	70,000	50,000	–	–

Multiplying quantities transported by the unit cost of distribution would give the following total distribution costs.

If Northampton site is chosen: £318,000
If Telford site is chosen: £390,000

If all other things are equal therefore, it would be preferable to build the new factory at Northampton.

As with most OR techniques, however, this method is based on a large number of assumptions such as for example:

(a) transport costs are assumed to increase in direct proportion to the number transported and to distance;
(b) demand expectations are fixed and not liable to variations;
(c) transport costs are, and always will be, the overriding factor determining location.

It may seem naive to make such assumptions, but at least the technique is of value in that it enables objective criteria to be employed in determining locations. However, in the final analysis, it must be recognised that such techniques still represent only one approach to the problem and their solutions may still be over-ridden in the light of other, perhaps intangible, criteria.

2 Facility Layout

Having described the macro or *location* problem, the supplementary situation is now that of deciding on the *layout* of facilities in the form of equipment, departments etc., within the total space available. This is the micro problem described earlier.

Once again, the objective is to obtain an 'optimal' solution based on maximising or minimising some performance measure. However, intangible factors make this a more difficult and complex problem than it may at first appear. An obvious example here is the need to maintain good working conditions, not only to satisfy the ever-increasing legislative measures, but also because research has indicated that conditions can have a direct effect on worker behaviour which in itself will influence the level of labour turnover, absenteeism and general industrial unrest.

The approach to layout planning would, therefore, take account of tangible and intangible factors as in the case with facility location. However, before any specific techniques are described it is necessary to recognise that there are certain basic layout arrangements.

The Basic Types of Layout

A set of facilities may be arranged in many different ways. However there are three fundamental types of layout that may be recognised in manufacturing situations. They have already been described briefly in Chapter 1 but will be elaborated on here:

(1) Fixed Position This is where the material or major component remains fixed while the equipment, labour, tools etc., are brought to this one place of work. Claimed advantages of this form of layout are:

(i) Handling of the product is reduced;
(ii) Workers can be given responsibility for the whole product and can be held accountable for quality;
(iii) Design changes are quickly adopted;
(iv) A high degree of flexibility is available.

(2) Functional (or Process) This is where equipment or processes of the same type are grouped together and products move between them usually in batches with the following claimed advantages:

(i) Higher machine utilisation is possible;
(ii) Wide product variety can be accommodated;
(iii) The work-in-progress generated can minimise the effect of machine breakdowns, shortages etc. and can accommodate scheduling changes.

(3) Product (or Line) This is where one product or component is continuously moved within one area or along a flowline, so that operations may be performed sequentially. The advantages are:

(i) Less handling and greater possibilities for mechanisation;
(ii) Shorter lead times and less work-in-progress reducing investment in materials;
(iii) Division of labour, leading to ease of training and wider application of semi-skilled workers;
(iv) Easier control.

Layout Planning

If cost minimisation is considered to be a reasonable objective in layout planning, then a purely quantitative approach would be adopted where, say, the total cost associated with moving materials was minimised. For example the objective function:

$$C = \sum_{i=1}^{n} \sum_{j=1}^{n} d_{ij} \; (e_{ij} \, C_{ij})$$

might be appropriate where a functional layout was being considered. Here, C is total cost of movement, d_{ij} is distance between departments i and j, e_{ij} is number of units or loads moving between departments i and j, C_{ij} is cost of moving a unit or load between departments i and j.

In the case of functional layout, attempts have been made to provide optimal solutions based on mathematical modelling (e.g. Wimmert[6]). However, experience has shown that large amounts of computation would be required and many assumptions would need to be made when formulating the model, so for these reasons such procedures are of limited value. As with many operations management problems therefore, it is probably better to employ 'heuristic' solutions, many of which have been taken to an advanced stage of development.

Two such possibilities are CRAFT (Computerised Relative Allocation of Facilities Technique)[7] and CORELAP (Computerised Relationship Layout Planning)[8] which have been devised in the USA and are in fairly wide use.

An extension to such a purely cost minimisation approach would be also to account for the intangible factors such as the safety, legal and environmental constraints.

A relationship chart, figure 6.4, represents a simple means of quickly highlighting the relative importance of departmental 'closeness'. This therefore provides the means of readily assessing such information while the planning procedure is on-going rather than it being necessary later to audit the layout.[9]

The design of product layouts (flowlines) is unique in that the objectives and constraints are different from those in functional layout situations. The cost of movement is less significant because the facilities are all adjacent. The objective is usually to achieve desired cycle times with the minimum of work stations and even 'balance' of workload at each station. Constraints relate to precedence (the order in which operations can be performed) and zoning (whether operations are permissible at certain stations). The problem of designing flowlines therefore goes hand in hand with the problem of operations scheduling. Further consideration of line design will therefore be left until Chapter 12 which relates to the planning and control of operations.

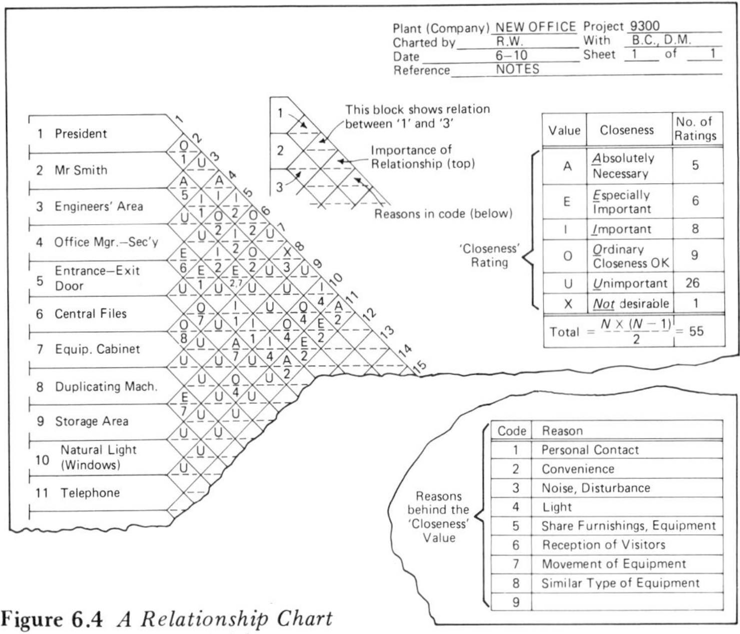

Figure 6.4 *A Relationship Chart*

Source: R. Muther[9]
Note: The relationship chart is extremely effective for planning all activities not tied together with a significant flow pattern. This chart was prepared for an office of consulting soil-test engineers. It indicates that Mr Smith must be near the Engineers' Area, the telephone to a lesser extent, still less to the office manager–secretary and central files, not at all near the duplicating machine or storage area. Reasons are filled in and recorded in lower half of the appropriate boxes. It is normally not realistic, in charting relationships, to include window or telephone availability. They are included here primarily to indicate the degree of detail to which the planner can go if need be.

3 Investment Decisions: Replacement and New Capacity

It has been assumed so far in this chapter that the organisation has decided on the number and type of facility to be used in its operations and need only solve the problems of location and layout.

Logically, however, before facilities are acquired, a process of selection and appraisal must take place in order that they can be fully justified.

Basically, facilities are acquired for one of two reasons: to replace existing capacity, or to provide additional capacity. The reasons for replacement could be:

(i) Existing plant has worn out;
(ii) A new process has been developed;
(iii) A superior facility is available.

While the reasons for adding capacity could be:

(iv) A new product or service is being offered;
(v) Existing capacity is insufficient to meet demand.

When considering new facilities, there are many physical and process factors to be taken into account in order that a short-list of appropriate alternatives may finally be evaluated. Assessment of such factors which include size, weight, speed, accuracy etc., would obviously represent an important aspect of the selection procedure, but since a discussion of these would be of a technical nature and specific to certain industries it is, therefore, outside the scope of this chapter.

Of greater interest to the operations manager are the economic considerations which would ensure that the investment is financially acceptable.

Operating Cost Considerations

Any economic appraisal of a new facility must take into account all the cost factors associated with its operation, as well as the capital costs incurred at the time of purchase and installation. Such on-going operating costs affected by a new investment may be:

(i) The cost of direct materials used (different processes may use different forms of material or may use them more efficiently);
(ii) The cost of labour required (differing amounts of labour may be needed or the degree of skill may vary);
(iii) The cost of overheads apportioned to the investment (there may be differences in setting time, the amount of maintenance required, the use of power etc.)

Where existing capacity is being replaced, it is usual to evaluate the costs associated with the new plant and compare them with those of the facility already in use.

However, where additional capacity is being justified, no such comparison can be made and the assessment must be on the basis of the 'income' resulting from the operation of the new facility.

Many companies would make use of a standard document when summarising the operating costs. Simplified examples of such documents are shown in figures 6.5 and 6.6.

In both of the cases illustrated, an annual sum is arrived at which represents the financial benefit derived from the investment. This benefit must now be compared with the capital cost of the replacement or new capacity in order to decide whether its purchase is justified.

There are many different criteria whereby such a decision can be made. Moreover, the use of a particular criterion may often lead to conflicting results so it is important to choose that criterion which best suits the organisation's corporate strategy. It should be remembered, therefore, that there is no *correct* technique for making investment decisions because the advantages vary according to the circumstances. The most

Operating Costs Affected				
Description			Costs per annum	
	Existing Facility	Proposed Facility	Existing £	Proposed £
Direct Materials Direct Labour Overheads – Setting – Maintenance – Power etc				
	TOTAL COST			
	SAVING PER ANNUM			

Figure 6.5 *Replacement Capacity – Cost Summary*

Operating Cost Affected	
Description	Costs per Annum Proposed
Direct Materials Direct Labour Overheads – Setting – Maintenance – Power etc.	
TOTAL COST	
INCOME	
RETURN PER ANNUM	

Figure 6.6 *Additional Capacity – Cost Summary*

common techniques currently in use in industry are based on either pay-back or rate of return criteria.

Pay-Back versus Rate of Return

The principle behind pay-back methods is that the period is estimated in which the expected financial benefits from an investment will add up to the capital expenditure incurred. In general, the shorter the period in which the capital outlay is expected to be recouped (i.e. the shorter the pay-back period), the more favourable will be the organisation's attitude towards the project.

This criterion recognises that early returns may be preferable to those accruing later and it may have some justification when later returns are particularly uncertain and where the risk is to be minimised.

However, no account is taken of the financial benefits accruing after the pay-back period and therefore the longer term advantages may be ignored. If an organisation wishes to maximise the long-term benefits of an investment, it therefore needs to take advantage of the benefits offered by the rate of return criteria.

There are several methods for calculating the rate of return. The most simple takes average income (or income for an early year) and simply relates this to the initial capital cost i.e. Rate of Return = Average Income/Initial Investment.

A more thorough method would be to reduce the average income to a 'real' figure by subtracting the depreciation (thus amortising the investment) and relating this to the average investment over the useful life of the investment, assuming the latter is known, i.e. Rate of Return = (Average Income − Depreciation)/Average Investment.

Rate of return criteria are useful in that they do try to take account of the benefits obtained throughout the life of the investment and thereby seek to be profit maximising, assuming profit maximisation is the objective. (Communist countries would probably rely on pay-back since their ideology would not usually support the concept of profit or return on capital.)

The rate of return methods described could be modified to take account of tax and more complex depreciation methods adopted, but they still suffer from the disadvantage of not paying sufficient regard to the *timing* of returns. This argument leads therefore to the concept of present value.

Present Value Criteria

The concept of present value is best illustrated by way of a simple example. If investment interest is paid at a rate of, say, 10% then £100 invested today will be worth £110 in one year's time, £121 in two years' time etc.

Mathematically, this process of compounding may be represented as:

$$S = (1 + i)^n P$$

where P is the principal sum invested; i is the annual rate of interest; n is the number of years invested; S is the total sum after n years.

We can therefore solve for P to determine the 'present value' of a sum S to be either received or paid n years hence:

$$P = \frac{S}{(1 + i)^n}$$

This process is called *discounting* and $\frac{1}{(1 + i)^n}$ may be regarded as the 'discount factor' that S must be multiplied by in order to find its present value.

Thus we have now demonstrated the principle of the time value of money which accepts that we can afford to pay an amount of money in the future by investing a smaller amount now or, conversely, we could receive an amount of money in the future by receiving a smaller amount now and investing it. Therefore, monies flowing into and out of an investment project (the cash flows) can be discounted to give their present value, hence the term 'discounted cash flow' (dcf).

The two dcf methods commonly used are the net present value (npv) and the yield method (sometimes called internal rate of return). The net present value is simply the sum of the present values of the net cash flows (positive or negative) for all years during the project's life. To calculate the present worth each net cash flow should be multiplied by the discount factor $\frac{1}{(1 + i)^n}$. In practice, tables would be used (see Appendix 6.1, p. 107) to calculate present values.

The relevant rate of interest would normally be the organisation's cost of finance, although the concept of 'opportunity cost' might be used in circumstances where the capital resources are limited.

If the npv is greater than zero, then the financial benefits are expected to be more valuable than the outlays on the project and to that extent the project is worthwhile. The yield of a project is the rate of interest which if used to discount the cash flow would make the net present value exactly zero. By the yield criterion, a project is worthwhile if its yield is greater than the organisation's required rate of return. Since all capital expenditure is included in the cash flow calculations and an interest charge is implicit in the discounting process, no separate provision for depreciation or charge on capital is necessary with present value methods. Alternative investments can easily be compared to see which has the highest npv or yield, even though they may be of unequal duration.

In order to demonstrate the relative differences between pay-back, rate of return and present value methods, consider the following example.

A company is considering the purchase of a new piece of plant and needs to choose between *A* and *B*. Plant *A* has a capital cost of £10,000 and after 10 years would have a salvage value of £2,000. Plant *B* has a capital cost of £12,000 and a salvage value after 10 years of £3,000. The running costs and expected income over the 10 year period are shown in table 6.3.

Table 6.3 Running Costs and Income for Investment Example

	Plant A			*Plant B*		
Year	*Running Cost*	*Income*	*Net Income*	*Running Cost*	*Income*	*Net Income*
1	1000	3000	2000	1000	3000	2000
2	1000	4000	3000	1000	3000	2000
3	1000	6000	5000	1000	5000	4000
4	1000	6000	5000	1000	5000	4000
5	2000	8000	6000	1000	8000	7000
6	2000	8000	6000	2000	11000	9000
7	2000	7000	5000	2000	11000	9000
8	3000	8000	5000	2000	10000	8000
9	3000	7000	4000	2000	10000	8000
10	3000	7000	4000	2000	9000	7000

Pay-back Period

Plant *A*

Capital Cost	= £10,000
Income Year 1	= £2,000
2	= £3,000
3	= £5,000
Total after 3 years	= £10,000

Plant *B*

Capital Cost	= £12,000
Income Year 1	= £2,000
2	= £2,000
3	= £4,000
4	= £4,000
Total after 4 years	= £12,000

Using the pay-back criterion, Plant *A* would be chosen since it has the shorter pay-back period.

Rate of Return

For Plant A, Average income $= \frac{£45,000}{10} = £4,500$ per annum

Assuming plant is depreciated to zero using a straight line formula,

Average depreciation $= \frac{£10,000}{10} = £1,000$ per annum

Average investment $= \frac{£10,000 + £2,000}{2} = £6,000$ per annum i.e.

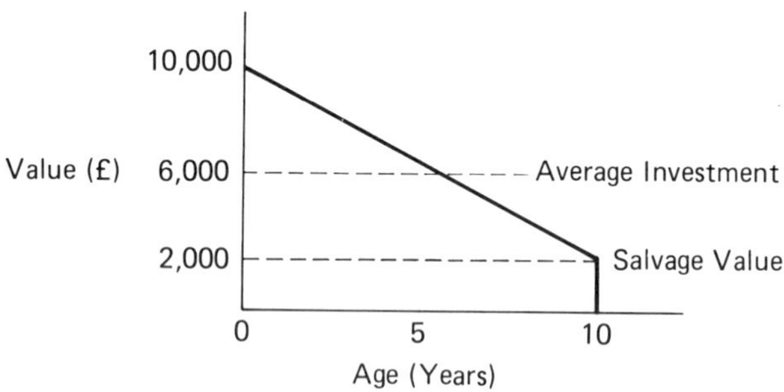

Rate of Return for Plant A $= \frac{£4,500 - £1,000}{£6,000} \times 100\%$

$= 58.3\%$

Similarly for Plant B:

Rate of Return $= \frac{£6,000 - £1,200}{£7,500} = 64\%$

Thus using a rate of return criterion Plant B would now be chosen since it has the highest rate of return.

Net Present Value

Assuming 15% interest rate the npv calculations are as shown in table 6.4.

Here, use of both items of plant results in a positive net present value, so either represents a profitable proposition.

Table 6.4 Calculation of Net Present Value for the two Alternative Investments

		Plant A		*Plant B*	
Year	*Discount Factor*	*Cash Flow*	*Present Value*	*Cash Flow*	*Present Value*
0	1.0000	–10000	–10000	–12000	–12000
1	0.8696	2000	1740	2000	1740
2	0.7561	3000	2270	2000	1510
3	0.6575	5000	3290	4000	2630
4	0.5718	5000	2860	4000	2290
5	0.4972	6000	2980	7000	3480
6	0.4323	6000	2590	9000	3890
7	0.3759	5000	1880	9000	3380
8	0.3269	5000	1630	8000	2620
9	0.2843	4000	1140	8000	2270
10	0.2472	6000	1480	10000	2470
		Net present value	+11860		+14280

However, out of preference, Plant *B* should be chosen since it has the highest npv figure.

4 Process Planning

A major activity of many manufacturing organisations concerns taking new or redesigned products and components through from the design stage to full-scale production. For manufacturers of complex assembled items, this might take several months or even years and any delays involved would not only impose heavy financial burdens, but could also provide competitors with a considerable marketing advantage. It is important, therefore, that strict control is exercised over these pre-production activities in order that unnecessary costs are avoided and to ensure that the time-span is not unnecessarily long.

The activities involved in taking new designs through to production are subject to the same conditions and constraints as any 'job' type of production operation. Many organisations will therefore find useful the planning and control techniques relevant to job production which will be described in Chapter 12.

At this stage, however, it is intended only to describe the major stages that form the framework for a pre-production plan.

In the case of a manufactured assembly these would be:

(a) Deciding on the logic for manufacture via assembly and flow charts;
(b) Taking the make or buy decisions;
(c) Selection of methods and processes;
(d) Designing workplaces.

These stages may be presented logically, via the diagram of the total 'process planning' system shown as figure 6.7.

Assembly and Flow Charts

The concept of designing for production has already been described in some detail in Chapter 4. However, even though a product has been designed for compatibility with existing production, a logic for manufacture will still be required which determines the product 'structure' or bill of materials.

Most complex products are built up via a number of sub-assemblies which are brought together throughout the various stages of manufacture. The precise nature of these sub-assemblies is, however, subject to variation and the way chosen will depend not only on the design itself but also on

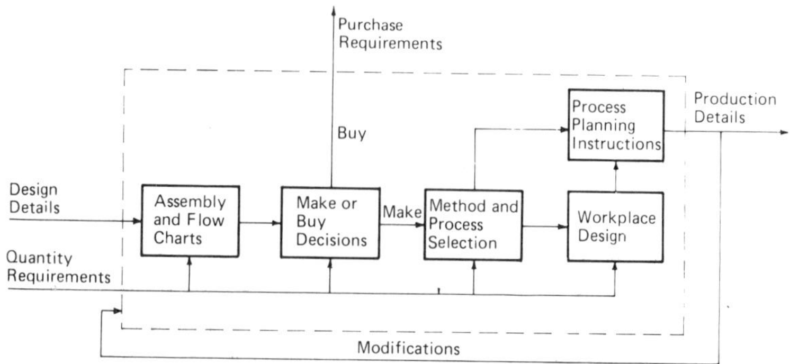

Figure 6.7 *The Process Planning System*

the quantities to be produced and company production policy.

Assembly charts are simply logic diagrams which describe the overall plan for the manufacture of assembled products and they are useful in that they can serve as a ready means to assess various alternative possibilities. The symbols used in such charts are usually those commonly used in method study to describe operations (O) and inspection (□).

Consider for example the manufacture of a simple domestic table lamp comprising a base, four rubber feet, stem, cable, bulb holder, shade and retaining ring. The logic for the manufacture of this device might be described via the assembly chart shown in figure 6.8.

Such an approach to a product's manufacture makes full use of sub-assemblies. This may be justified where large quantities are involved, particularly where the manufacturer is attempting to use the principle of 'division of labour' and specialisation of assembly skills. As an alternative approach, however, the logic shown in figure 6.9 may be equally valid.

This approach is based on the 'make-complete' concept of manufacture. It usually is a feature of small quantity production and is based on the 'job' concept described in Chapter 12. Even when larger quantities are being produced, however,

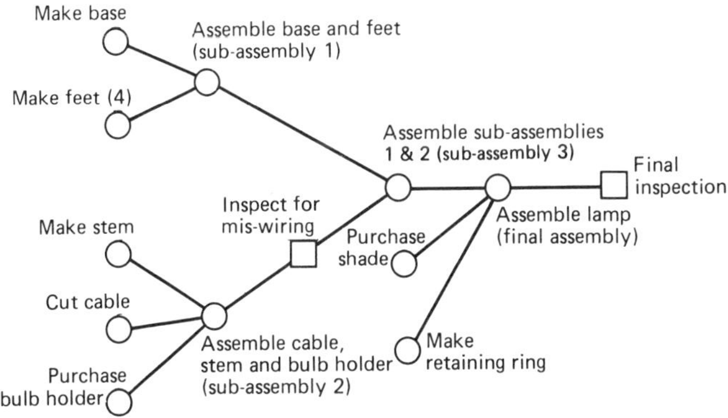

Figure 6.8 *Assembly Chart for Table Lamp using Several Sub-Assemblies*

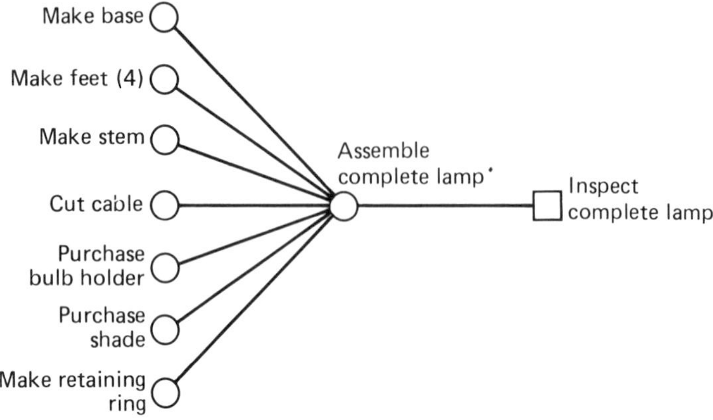

Figure 6.9 *Assembly Chart for Table Lamp using 'Make-Complete' Concept*

this method is sometimes used, since it is argued that assembly operators can identify with the complete product which leads to greater job enrichment.

The 'sub-assembly' and 'make-complete' concepts can even be illustrated in service situations. Consider for instance the systems used by airlines when passengers book and take a flight.

An 'assembly chart' which makes full use of 'sub-assemblies' could be as shown in figure 6.10.

This system would be used where large numbers of passengers are being 'processed' (i.e. charter flights etc.). Booking is done by a travel agent and seats are allocated at the departure gate just prior to boarding the aircraft. The 'division of labour' principle allows for efficient handling of large planeloads of passengers.

Alternatively, the 'make-complete' approach could be used, as illustrated in figure 6.11.

The 'make-complete' approach has obvious advantages for the passenger; only one 'transaction' has to take place. It is the sort of procedure therefore that might be adopted for prestige or first-class services. As with our manufacturing example, such an approach would usually be of more immediate value when dealing with small numbers of products

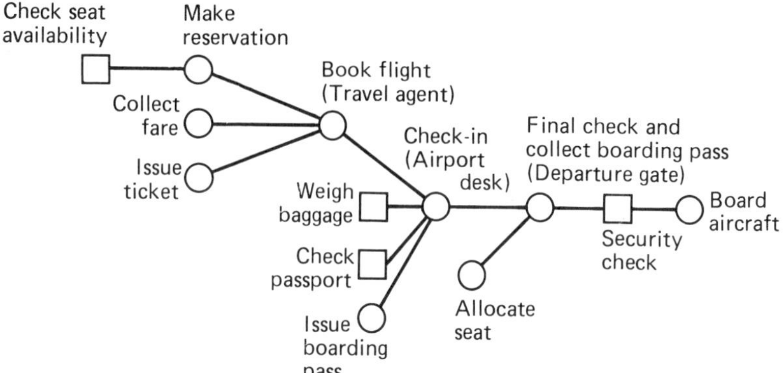

Figure 6.10 *Assembly Chart for Air Flight using Several 'Sub-Assemblies'*

(passengers) although, again, special circumstances might dictate otherwise.

The purpose of assembly charts is merely to illustrate the logic of manufacture and, because they show what part 'goes in to' another they are sometimes referred to as GOZINTO charts. If, however, movement and storage of materials or people (as in our passenger example) needs to be illustrated, an alternative could be the use of flow charts. Basically, the only difference between assembly and flow charts is the use, in the latter, of extra symbols to illustrate movement (⇨) and storage (▽).

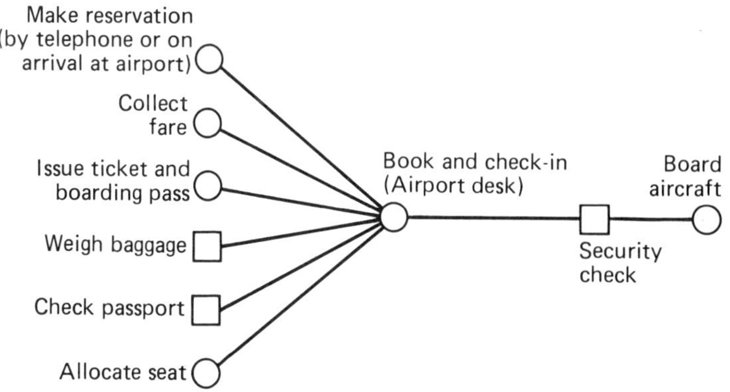

Figure 6.11 *Assembly Chart for Air Flight using 'Make-Complete' Concept*

Make or Buy Decisions

It would be extremely rare to encounter a situation of totally integrated manufacture i.e. where every single assembly or component part was supplied or made by the producer of the end product. There would obviously, in most circumstances, be a substantial number of common parts which would be bought from suppliers who, because they can specialise in the manufacture of such items, make it inappropriate for the non-specialists to attempt to make such items themselves.

This situation is obviously not unique to manufacturing. There are many examples in service industries where the specialist activities of another organisation may be called upon in order to keep down the final cost of the service to the customer. Many restaurants will buy ready prepared frozen vegetables, small airlines may have their fleet maintained by a company specialising in aircraft maintenance etc.

Sometimes the decision to buy parts is axiomatic. There are many obvious examples such as screws, rivets, nails etc. where it would be foolish to do anything but buy from another manufacturer.

However, the decision is not always so easy and a thorough evaluation of the relative costs would be necessary based on expected usage (in volume terms) of the item under consideration. Such an evaluation would consider the fixed and variable costs of manufacture by the user, together with the cost of buying in from an outside supplier. This is represented graphically in figure 6.12.

This illustrates the break-even point below which it is preferable to buy and above which it is preferable to manufacture. The graph is obviously only a simple representation of reality because it does not show the effect of quantity discounts for purchases nor the increases in fixed cost associated with higher volumes (because of the need to purchase additional capacity etc.). It does show however, that a quantity can be determined which can form the basis of the make or buy decision and which can be checked from time to time as the organisation's level of activity changes.

There are many occasions, however, when a decision is made to either manufacture and purchase when, on the basis described above, it may not necessarily be justified.

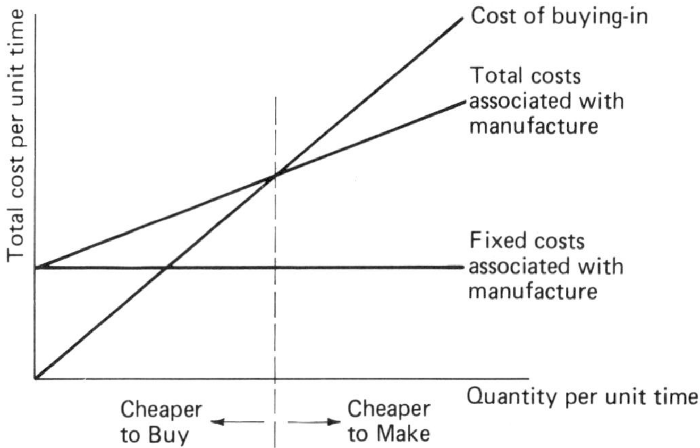

Figure 6.12 *Break-even Chart for Make/Buy Decision*

Some of the reasons why manufacturing companies choose to manufacture items rather than buy them include:

(a) closer control over quality;
(b) to ensure reliability of supply;
(c) to maintain trade secrets.

Conversely, companies choosing to purchase when it might in fact be cheaper to manufacture, might do so on the basis of:

(a) retention of goodwill with a supplier;
(b) reciprocal agreements (i.e. bartering);
(c) a desire to restrict the organisation's activities;
(d) provision of alternative sources of supplies;
(e) contractual obligation (e.g. in the case of Government work etc.).

Once the decision has been made to purchase rather than to make, we need proceed no further through the process planning system. Purchase requirements, specifications etc. are passed to a specialised buying function in order that orders and contracts might be placed with suppliers.

In the case where parts are to be made, the next stage is to decide on the details of manufacture.

Selection of Methods and Processes

There are basically three stages in the method and process selection procedure:

(i) Deciding which tasks are necessary;
(ii) Determining the order in which the tasks are to be done;
(iii) Determining on which work centre, machine or process the task is to be done.

In most industries, be they service or manufacturing, stages (i) and (ii) require a great deal of basic technical knowledge, being normally the job of an experienced member of the organisation's staff, and therefore outside the scope of this book.

The appropriate process can however be selected on the basis of an assessment of the relevant fixed and variable costs associated with using various alternatives.

For example, consider the case of a component which is equally capable of being produced on a manually operated, semi-automatic, or fully automatic machine. The fixed and variable costs associated with the three processes are shown in table 6.5.

The costs are shown in figure 6.13, from which it may be seen that the number produced determines the most appropriate process.

It is apparent that a fully automatic process can only be justified where volumes are sufficiently high for the lower incremental costs to offset the higher initial fixed costs.

Workplace Design and Process Planning Instructions

The importance of good workplace design as the concluding activity of process planning cannot be overstated. Many goods

Table 6.5 Costs for Three Alternative Processes

Process Type	*Fixed Cost – Tools, set up etc.*	*Variable Cost – Labour, power etc. per unit*
Manual	£5.00p	£0.15p
Semi-Automatic	£20.00p	£0.10p
Fully Automatic	£40.00p	£0.5p

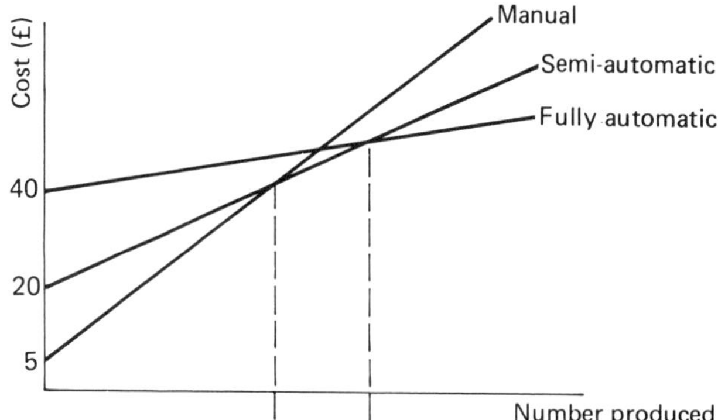

Figure 6.13 *Process Selection*

and services are produced with very little being done to ensure that tasks are being performed in the most effective manner.

In the case of manual tasks, such as assembly operations, the techniques of method study may be employed to ensure that unnecessary delays and redundant activities are avoided. Excessive movement can also be eliminated via the examination of work methods using flow charts, simultaneous motion charts etc. Additionally, the contributions of ergonomics will ensure that physiological and purely biological aspects of the job are also taken into account. Finally, it would be inappropriate for an operations manager in a modern industrial environment to ignore the psychological and sociological aspects of job design which consider the provision of job enrichment and job enlargement. Such an approach to workplace design would attempt to ensure that the intangible benefits associated with good quality, high morale, low labour turnover etc. are fully achieved, as well as the more traditional factors associated with a product's cost.

The procedure relating to process planning may now be summarised on a standard document (usually referred to as a process planning sheet) which forms basic input instruction to the production planning and control system. The process planning sheet will, together with drawings and specific details on machine set-up, comprise a complete set of production instructions and will include such things as raw material specification and sizes, operation sequence, set-up times and operation times.

In figure 6.7 (p. 98) the inclusion of modifications such as feedback within the process planning system highlights the dynamic nature of the procedures. Changes in design, manufacturing method, tools etc. will frequently occur and necessitate immediately updating the documentation. If the written instructions do no correspond with practice, an atmosphere of confusion and mistrust will soon arise which, in the long term, will contribute to a reduction in productive efficiency.

References and Further Reading

1 Hunt, Sir J., *The Intermediate Areas*, Report of a Committee under the Chairmanship of Sir J. Hunt, HMSO Cmnd 3998, 1969.
2 Department of Industry., *Regional Industrial Policy Changes*, January 1980.
3 *Policy for the Inner Cities*, HMSO Cmnd 6848, June 1977.
4 Blowers, A., *Economic Geography: Industrial Location Theory*, The Open University Press 1972.
5 Sasieni, M., Yaspan, A. & Friedman, L., *Operations Research: Methods and Problems*, Wiley 1959.
6 Wimmert, R.J., A mathematical method of equipment location, *Journal of Industrial Engineering*, Nov.–Dec. 1958.
7 Buffa, E.S., Armour, G.C. & Vollmann, T.E., Allocating facilities with CRAFT, *Harvard Business Review*, March–April 1964.
8 Lee, R.C. & Moore, J.M., CORELAP – COmputerised RElationship LAyout Planning, *Journal of Industrial Engineering*, 18, 195, 1967.
9 Muther, R., *Systematic Layout Planning*, CBI Publishing Inc. 1973.

Appendix 6.1 Discount Factors for use in Discounted Cash Flow Calculations

Present Value Factors – Interest Rates (1% to 14%)

Years	1%	2%	3%	4%	5%	6%	7%	8%	9%	10%	11%	12%	13%	14%
1	.9901	.9804	.9709	.9615	.9524	.9434	.9346	.9259	.9174	.9091	.9009	.8929	.8850	.8772
2	.9803	.9612	.9426	.9246	.9070	.8900	.8734	.8573	.8417	.8264	.8116	.7972	.7831	.7695
3	.9706	.9423	.9151	.8890	.8638	.8396	.8163	.7938	.7722	.7513	.7312	.7118	.6931	.6750
4	.9610	.9238	.8885	.8548	.8227	.7921	.7629	.7350	.7084	.6830	.6587	.6355	.6133	.5921
5	.9515	.9057	.8626	.8219	.7835	.7473	.7130	.6806	.6499	.6209	.5935	.5674	.5428	.5194
6	.9420	.8880	.8375	.7903	.7462	.7050	.6663	.6302	.5963	.5645	.5346	.5066	.4803	.4556
7	.9327	.8706	.8131	.7599	.7107	.6651	.6227	.5835	.5470	.5132	.4817	.4523	.4251	.3996
8	.9235	.8535	.7894	.7307	.6768	.6274	.5820	.5403	.5019	.4665	.4339	.4039	.3762	.3506
9	.9143	.8368	.7664	.7026	.6446	.5919	.5439	.5002	.4604	.4241	.3909	.3606	.3329	.3075
10	.9053	.8203	.7441	.6756	.6139	.5584	.5083	.4632	.4224	.3855	.3522	.3220	.2946	.2679
11	.8963	.8043	.7224	.6496	.5847	.5268	.4751	.4289	.3875	.3505	.3173	.2875	.2607	.2366
12	.8874	.7885	.7014	.6246	.5568	.4970	.4440	.3971	.3555	.3186	.2855	.2567	.2307	.2076
13	.8787	.7730	.6810	.6006	.5303	.4688	.4150	.3677	.3262	.2897	.2575	.2292	.2042	.1821
14	.8700	.7579	.6611	.5775	.5051	.4423	.3878	.3405	.2992	.2633	.2320	.2046	.1807	.1597
15	.8613	.7430	.6419	.5553	.4810	.4173	.3624	.3152	.2745	.2394	.2090	.1827	.1599	.1401
16	.8528	.7284	.6232	.5339	.4581	.3936	.3387	.2919	.2519	.2176	.1883	.1631	.1415	.1229
17	.8444	.7142	.6050	.5134	.4363	.3714	.3166	.2703	.2311	.1978	.1696	.1456	.1252	.1078
18	.8360	.7002	.5874	.4936	.4155	.3503	.2959	.2502	.2120	.1799	.1528	.1300	.1108	.0946
19	.8277	.6864	.5703	.4746	.3957	.3305	.2765	.2317	.1945	.1635	.1377	.1161	.0981	.0829
20	.8195	.6730	.5537	.4564	.3769	.3118	.2584	.2145	.1784	.1486	.1240	.1037	.0868	.0728

Present Value Factors – Interest Rates (15% to 50%)

Years	15%	16%	17%	18%	19%	20%	25%	30%	35%	40%	45%	50%
1	.8696	.8621	.8547	.8475	.8403	.8333	.8000	.7692	.7407	.7143	.6897	.6667
2	.7561	.7432	.7305	.7182	.7062	.6944	.6400	.5917	.5487	.5102	.4756	.4444
3	.6575	.6407	.6244	.6086	.5934	.5787	.5120	.4552	.4064	.3644	.3280	.2963
4	.5718	.5523	.5337	.5158	.4987	.4823	.4096	.3501	.3011	.2603	.2262	.1975
5	.4972	.4761	.4561	.4371	.4190	.4019	.3277	.2693	.2230	.1859	.1560	.1317
6	.4323	.4104	.3898	.3704	.3521	.3349	.2621	.2072	.1652	.1328	.1076	.0878
7	.3759	.3538	.3332	.3139	.2959	.2791	.2097	.1594	.1224	.0949	.0742	.0585
8	.3269	.3050	.2848	.2660	.2487	.2326	.1678	.1226	.0906	.0678	.0512	.0390
9	.2843	.2630	.2434	.2255	.2090	.1938	.1342	.0943	.0671	.0484	.0353	.0260
10	.2472	.2267	.2080	.1911	.1756	.1615	.1074	.0725	.0497	.0346	.0243	.0173
11	.2149	.1954	.1778	.1619	.1476	.1346	.0859	.0558	.0363	.0247	.0168	.0116
12	.1869	.1685	.1520	.1372	.1240	.1122	.0687	.0429	.0273	.0176	.0116	.0077
13	.1625	.1452	.1299	.1163	.1042	.0935	.0550	.0330	.0202	.0126	.0080	.0051
14	.1413	.1252	.1110	.0985	.0876	.0779	.0440	.0254	.0150	.0090	.0055	.0034
15	.1229	.1079	.0949	.0835	.0736	.0649	.0352	.0195	.0111	.0064	.0038	.0023
16	.1069	.0930	.0811	.0708	.0613	.0541	.0231	.0150	.0082	.0046	.0026	.0015
17	.0929	.0802	.0693	.0600	.0520	.0451	.0225	.0116	.0061	.0033	.0018	.0010
18	.0808	.0691	.0592	.0508	.0437	.0376	.0180	.0089	.0045	.0023	.0012	.0007
19	.0703	.0596	.0506	.0431	.0367	.0313	.0144	.0068	.0033	.0017	.0009	.0005
20	.0611	.0514	.0433	.0365	.0308	.0261	.0115	.0053	.0025	.0012	.0006	.0003

7
Facility Decisions Within Cadbury Schweppes Ltd

P SYMONDS

Industrial Engineering Manager,
Cadbury Schweppes Ltd

1 Introduction

All the types of decision outlined in the preceding chapter are taken in the real world operations of a company such as Cadbury Schweppes Ltd. However, it must be made quite clear that decisions taken at the micro level are far more frequent than those at the macro level. A company's location decisions for factories or depots are probably made at a rate of no more than one or two per year worldwide, whereas decisions concerning process equipment and plant layout may run into hundreds per year.

2 The Company

Cadbury Schweppes Ltd is the product of a merger in 1969 of two long established and well known companies. The Cadbury business is involved in the manufacture of confectionery and food products and has 33 wholly owned and 9 associate factory locations worldwide. The Schweppes business is soft drink manufacture, and it has 36 wholly owned factory sites and controls 261 franchise holders throughout the world.

In 1979 Group sales exceeded £1006 million, achieved from a worldwide turnover of more than 400,000 tonnes of confectionery and foods and 200 million dozen bottles of soft drink. The Group employs 47,000 people, 29,000 of whom are in the UK.

3 Examples of Factory Location Decisions

The past has always something to say to the future. Historically, Cadbury grew in an unplanned way. It exported its products on the back of a home trade, in the early years of this century, to what are now the Commonwealth countries. After the First World War tariff barriers were erected, and thus an extensive building programme in these countries was undertaken, chiefly in the 20s and 30s in Australia, New Zealand and South Africa. Today, these two major influences still exist for international facility location, i.e. a) a market potential, and b) tariff barriers. In 1972 Cadbury opened a new factory in Pennsylvania USA as a foothold in the massive North American market for its 'flagship' products. These had previously been exported in small quantities from the UK against increasingly severe tariff walls. In 1979 the Group acquired an American company, Peter Paul, in order to increase its market share, buy a distribution network, and extend a presence for its products alongside the traditional Peter Paul leaders.

Back in the UK, major factory sitings were made during the second half of the nineteenth century. The supply of raw materials seemed to be a major factor in these decisions, and thus transportation facilities of the time, the railways, the canals, and the Victorian ports were of consequence. This policy continued in the twentieth century with milk processing plants in rural Hereford, fruit processing plants in Cambridgeshire and on the east coast of Scotland, continuing into the 1960s with a potato conversion plant in North Yorkshire.

Increasingly however, Government influences have played a large part in factory siting. The location of a major cocoa conversion plant inside the Welsh border was taken with investment grants heavily in mind, as was the location of a biscuits and cakes factory in the Merseyside area.

In recent times, a major criterion, much in vogue with non-British companies, has been the industrial relations record of the area. The Group has never considered this criterion of primary importance, using its philosophy of managing situations with a pioneering form of industrial involvement between management and shopfloor.

In these days of ever increasing operating costs, facility rationalisation is equally as important as facility expansion. The maximum effective use of existing factory floor space is a high priority. One recent example of this was the movement of all Typhoo Tea production from its old building located in the heart of Birmingham to an existing modern factory location in the North West which had spare floor area. The decision involved many factors. Not only were savings made on total operating overheads, but also advantage was taken of the ability to establish more effective layouts with higher technology equipment.

Within the Group, distribution depot locations have been made on the basis of heavy Operational Research involvement. The development of distribution networks making maximum use of motorway geography follow the general theoretical analysis discussed in Chapter 6.

4 Examples of Plant Layout Decisions

On the micro scale, much of the choice of layout configuration is predetermined by the intrinsic engineering of the process. It must be remembered that the manufacture of confectionery, food and soft drink products is essentially a continuous process operation, where raw materials are fed in, modified and converted, and products finally wrapped and packed or bottled. The plant life of the modules which make up the layouts is usually considered to be in excess of 15–20 years. As such, some of the key questions to be asked when making layout decisions are – 'What is the expected brand life?' – 'What is the present level of technology and what is it likely to be in 5 years' time?' – 'How will the plant fit into existing buildings?'

In 1975 it was decided to re-equip the biscuit production facility in a factory. Since the time the original plant was installed in the mid 50s, baking technology had improved to the extent that modern ovens were physically more compact, more automatic and more efficient users of energy. In addition, biscuit handling and packaging machines had become more sophisticated and could now offer new concepts in packaging style.

The original plant had been laid out functionally, with one building housing baking and one housing wrapping and packaging. The connection between the two was through a complicated system of conveyors and manual movement. The new plant was laid out in straight lines, the compactness enabling all layouts to fit into one building. The advantages of the functional concept were kept however, because the layouts could be zoned horizontally across the lines into bakery, chocolate covering and packaging halls. The completed internal geography led to considerable operational economies both from the intrinsic engineering and from the layout design.

In the drinks industry, the technology for the rest of the 1980s has become available over the last few years. Recent investment has combined this with the development of the microprocessor. This combination has enabled the new standard bottling line to be three times as fast, using five times less employees, than the standard line of 5 years ago.

5 Investment Decisions

Investment decisions of all types are strictly controlled within Cadbury Schweppes. Divisional Boards have expenditure limits set, above which decisions are referred to the Group Main

Board. All applications for expenditure have to be prepared on a set of documents which are uniform worldwide and which promote and justify the particular case. The procedure is known as the ACE or Application for Capital Expenditure system.

The criteria on which these applications are judged vary from time to time, depending on such things as the prevailing interest rate, the availability of funds and the priority that the applicant's operating division has for the limited resources available. Nevertheless, all applications must exceed a predefined 'hurdle' rate of return, which is developed on a discounted cash flow basis and for which a standard computer package is available. There are normally 5 categories for Capital Expenditure which cover new products/capacity extension, cost reduction, essential replacement, health and hygiene, safety and legal requirements.

6 Make or Buy Decisions

The majority of Make or Buy decisions for the Group are self evident. Material input such as cocoa, sugar, fat, carbon dioxide, bottles etc. must all be bought in. However, there has been a history of making certain items when their supply or their quality has not been suitable. Cadbury built much of its machinery at one time. However, these days German, Swiss, Swedish and British companies are the major machinery suppliers.

Recently a decision was taken to cease production, in house, of a large proportion of the UK requirement of printed packaging material. The facilities have been sold and all such material is now bought in. An economic evaluation following the techniques described in Chapter 6 proved this to be the correct solution.

Interesting decisions can also be taken about the level of service a company needs to buy in – for example, computer services, secretarial services, office and factory cleaning services, security services and catering services to name but a few. Cadbury Schweppes has no firm policy on this point, but reacts to local situations and economies.

7 Work Place Design Decisions

In a process orientated industry, much of the ergonomic input is determined by the manufacturers of the bought-in equipment. However, the packaging of confectionery and food products still requires a good deal of manual intervention from its operators. To this end, most factories possess an Industrial Engineering service which, as part of its function, critically examines work place layouts to ensure maximum effective utilisation of its employees. Work place design is often developed in conjunction with the actual operators to ensure best operating practice and commitment to the design.

8 Conclusion

As with most leading companies, Cadbury Schweppes ensures that all facility decisions are made on the basis of thorough analytical investigation, using the techniques outlined in this book amongst many others, to establish effective production operations.

8
Direct Incentive Schemes

J McGREGOR

Lecturer in Operations Management, The University of Aston

1 Introduction

Incentive schemes may be divided into two, broad groups. the financial and the non-financial. These, in turn, may be subdivided even further, as shown below.

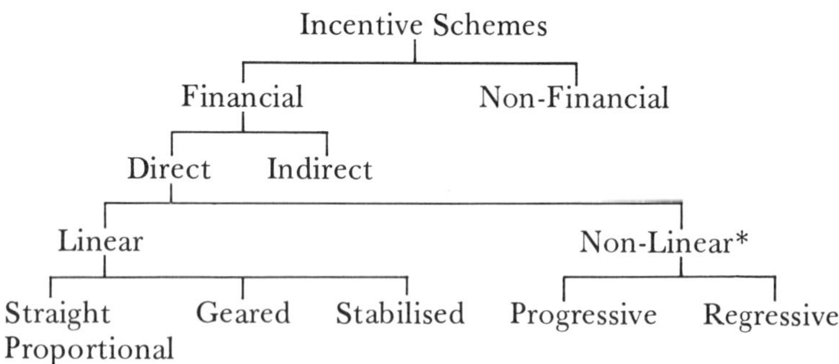

* Mathematicians term a line, which represents a functional relationship such as an equation, as a curve. A straight line is called a linear curve and represents a linear function. For simplicity, the term non-linear is used, in this chapter, to denote functions, which can be depicted by lines, which are not straight.

This chapter will examine direct, financial, incentive systems of the linear and non-linear types. Indirect bonus payment plans, such as profit sharing and non-financial methods of rewarding performance will not be reviewed.

The word 'financial' must be emphasised as, with some incentive schemes, privileges rather than money are earned. With a direct financial incentive or payment by results scheme, however, extra effort or output is rewarded by the payment of more money. Both extra cash and privileges can be combined in some plans, but the discussion here will be limited to the financial aspects only.

This examination of direct financial incentive payment systems will focus only on the basic, arithmetical aspects of such schemes. The motivational aspects will not be discussed. This is not to say that motivation is unimportant. It is, clearly, fundamental. But, what might be termed the pure 'mechanical' aspects are, also, extremely important and knowledge of this is a basic requirement of the intellectual tool-kit of the operations manager and of specialists such as the personnel manager, accountant or industrial engineer.

No attempt will be made to answer the riddle: 'Which is the best type of bonus system?'. The effects of what is often regarded as the first, known example of an incentive scheme – the offering of an apple to Adam by Eve – are still being debated. Perhaps the person best qualified to answer the riddle would be a theologian, or a proponent of the quantum theory with its concepts of multi-foliate reality. In other words, what is 'the best' is largely a matter of opinion, based on experience. In the absence of an adequate theory of behaviour, which enables one to predict, accurately, what the result of introducting a particular type of payment system will be, it is probably safer to point out that many organisations do use incentive schemes, and therefore, it is imperative to understand the structural linkages of such methods of remuneration. In consequence, in this discussion of direct, financial incentive schemes, the emphasis will be on the structural relationships between rating, performance, standard time, output, allowed time, payment and costs of linear and non-linear bonus systems, only. As far as possible, the terms used will conform to the definitions suggested in the *Glossary of Terms Used in Work Study and Organisation and Methods*[1].

2 Rating

When attempting to measure work, a work study practitioner assigns a numerical value to denote the rate of working of the person or persons being observed. It is assumed that most qualified workers, when working at a natural pace, are working at standard rating. The numerical value given to such a worker, by an observer using the British Standard rating scale, is 100. In theory, this rating scale extends from zero to infinity. Here, in the examples given, the range of ratings used will be limited to 50–150 (BS). The process of rating is central to the work study practitioner's approach to the measurement of work, and the measurement of work is the foundation on which bonus payment systems rest. Rating is not an exact science. It is based on experience and judgment. Ways of measuring and of trying to reduce the possible inaccuracy and the potential inconsistency of the rating process, have been developed. A much fuller treatment of this extremely important aspect is given in the ILO publication[2] and Whitmore.[3] It is sufficient to say, here, that if the rating is deemed to be incorrect, then the incentive scheme could be a failure.

3 Performance

Whereas rating recognises the rate of working over a short span of time, performance is based on the number of standard units of work completed in a longer period of time. If standard rating is consistently maintained over a working day, and not more than nor less than the appropriate relaxation and contingency allowances are taken, then a worker is deemed to have achieved standard performance.

4 Standard Time

A person's performance is calculated by comparing his or her output with standard output, which, in turn, is derived from the standard time for that output. Standard times are issued, usually, in the form: 'x standard minutes (or hours) per y units of output'. These standards are used for purposes of control and as one of the bases for standard costing systems. They are most useful for indicating deviations from standard and highlighting excess costs.

5 Output

This is best illustrated by an example:

(i) Assume: Standard Time = 10 minutes per unit of output
Working week = 40 Hours
There is no Lost Time

(ii) By calculation: Output per hour at Standard Performance = 6 units
∴ Output per 40 hours at Standard Performance = 240 units

(iii) Formula for calculating the output which can be expected at different levels of performance:

$$\text{Expected Output} = \frac{\begin{bmatrix}\text{Output at}\\ \text{Standard Performance}\end{bmatrix} \times \begin{bmatrix}\text{Observed}\\ \text{Rating level}\end{bmatrix}}{\text{Standard Rating}}$$

(iv) Using the British Standard Rating scale:

Observed Rating	*Formula*	*Expected Output per 40 Hours*
50	$\frac{240 \times 50}{100} =$	120
75	$\frac{240 \times 75}{100} =$	180
100	$\frac{240 \times 100}{100} =$	240

125	$\frac{240 \times 125}{100} =$	300
150	$\frac{240 \times 150}{100} =$	360

Clearly, by rearranging the terms of the formula, shown in (iii) above, and by substituting actual output for expected output, one can calculate a person's actual (observed) rating given the actual output.

The formula used to calculate expected output, described in (iii) above, should not be confused with the rather similar formula used to convert observed time to basic time:

$$\text{Basic Time} = \frac{\text{Observed time} \times \text{Observed rating}}{\text{Standard rating}}$$

The two formulae are, however, connected.

6 Allowed Time

Whereas standard time is the time which a person, working at standard rating (100 BS), would take to complete a task, allowed time is the time credited to that person for the calculation of incentive payment.

A clear distinction should be made between standard time, which is a form of bench-mark or target; actual time, which is the time actually taken to complete a specified task and which may or may not coincide with standard time; and allowed time, which is used for pay purposes.

For example, if the standard time is 10 minutes per unit of output and it has been agreed that employees, who work at standard performance, should be paid 20% bonus, then the standard time would be increased by 20% to give an allowed time of 12 minutes. The worker would be credited with 12 allowed minutes for every unit of output produced, even if it actually took him or her only, say, 8 minutes to complete each unit. The proportion, by which the standard time is increased to give the allowed time, is called the bonus factor.

7 Payment

The design of a payment by results scheme depends, among other things, on:

(i) The past history of incentive schemes in the organisation
(ii) Local wage rates
(iii) The financial state of the company
(iv) The power of the workforce
(v) The national economy
(vi) Legislation

In addition, all incentive schemes incorporate two factors, either implicitly or explicitly:

(i) Bonus factor
(ii) Gearing factor, sometimes referred to as the share factor

Frequently, these two factors are not made explicit in payment by results schemes. They are, however, always present, whether recognised or not.

(i) Bonus factor

As stated earlier, the bonus factor is the proportion by which standard time is increased to give allowed time. The formula is:

Allowed time = Standard time + (Standard Time × Bonus Factor)

Example:

Standard time = 60 minutes per unit of output
Bonus factor = 1/3
∴ Allowed time = 60 + (60 × 1/3)
= 80 minutes

The bonus factor also determines the point, on the performance level scale, at which incentive is first paid. Figure 8.1 illustrates the effects of changes in the value of the bonus factor (*B* in figure 8.1), for the straight proportional type of incentive scheme.

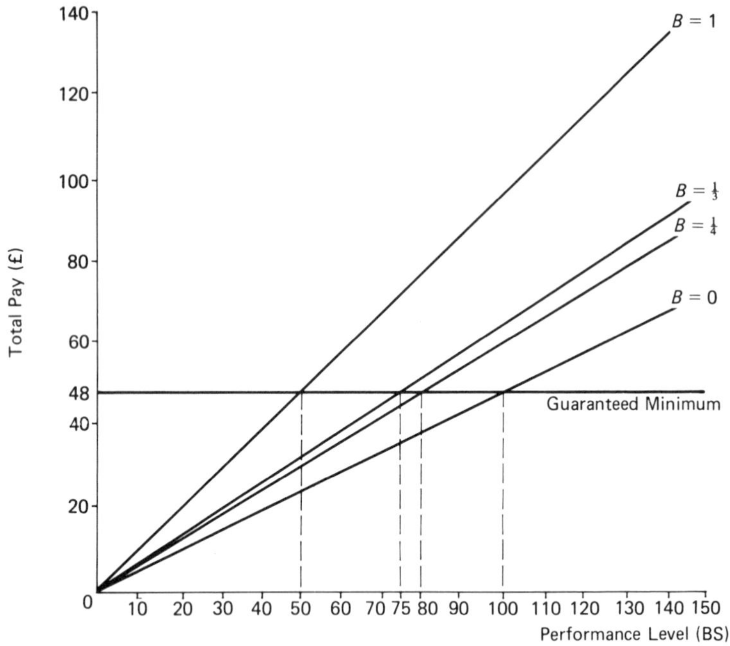

Figure 8.1 *Linear – Bonus Factors (B). (Straight proportional) K = 1*

The assumptions made in constructing figure 8.1 were:

(a) Bonus factor – various values
(b) Incentive pay is based on the hourly rate
(c) Hourly rate = £1.20
(d) A 40 hour week, with no lost time
(e) Guaranteed minimum = £48.00 for 40 hours
(f) Standard time = 60 minutes per unit of output

Notice that as the bonus factor (percentage) increases, so the point on the performance level scale, at which the operator starts to earn bonus, is decreased. This occurs, in fact, with all types of direct linear and non-linear, financial incentive schemes.

To calculate the point, on the performance level scale, at which the payment line crosses the guaranteed minimum payment line, the following formula can be used:

$$R = \frac{100}{1+B}$$

where R = performance level, and B = bonus factor.

This formula assumes that the worker should earn B amount of bonus at standard performance (100 BS). If the bonus percentage, represented by the factor B, is to be earned at some level of performance other than 100, then that other level of performance will be used in the dividend of the formula instead of 100.

For example, $R = 120/(1+B)$ would indicate that B amount of bonus would be earned at 120 performance level and R is the level above which bonus is earned.

It should not be assumed that the bonus factor must invariably be 33.33%, although this figure, inherited, it would seem, from Bedaux, has become something of a tradition amongst many operations managers. Bonus earnings level, at standard performance, can be any negotiable figure.

Neither should it be assumed that incentive earnings are always calculated from the basic, weekly salary. Bonus can be based on a separate incentive calculator rate, which might be greater than or less than the normal hourly rate. For simplicity, all the examples in this chapter assume that incentive earnings are calculated from the base rate.

Similarly, for the sake of simplicity, lost time has been ignored. The problem, of how and how much should be paid, during periods of lost time or non-productive or non-incentive working, can be of Byzantine complexity. It is, therefore, avoided here. It can, however, be a problem of great importance, as the case study, which follows this chapter, tries to show.

(ii) Gearing Factor

Whereas the bonus factor determines the percentage incentive earnings of a worker, the gearing factor determines whether that worker receives the whole of that bonus or not. For example, labelling the gearing factor as K and assuming the conditions outlined on p. 120 for figure 8.1, with a bonus factor value of 1/3rd, then someone working at a performance level of 100 BS should earn £16 bonus (£48 × $\frac{1}{3}$). If the value of the gearing share factor (K) is 1, then the full bonus earned will be paid. However, if the value of $K = \frac{1}{2}$ or 2, then £8.00 or £32.00 respectively will be paid, (see figure 8.2). Figure 8.3 has been drawn, based on the same assumptions of hours worked etc., to show the effect of having a different bonus factor value. It will be seen that changes in the value of K alter the gradient of the payment line from that of the 'basic', $K = 1$. Changes in the bonus factor alter the point, on the performance level scale, at which incentive is first paid.

The formula for calculating the incentive paid at standard performance is: Incentive Paid = Incentive Payment Rate × Bonus Factor × Share Factor.

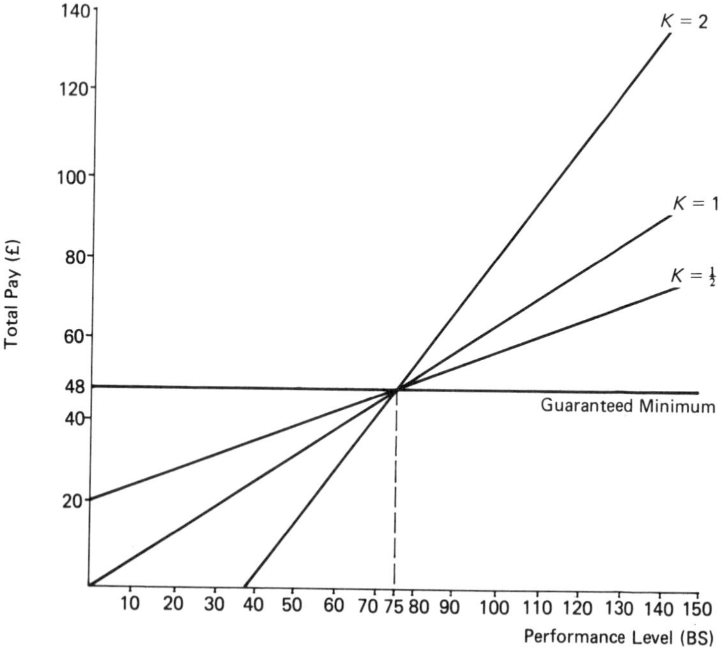

Figure 8.2 *Linear – Share Factors (K) for B* $= \frac{1}{3}$

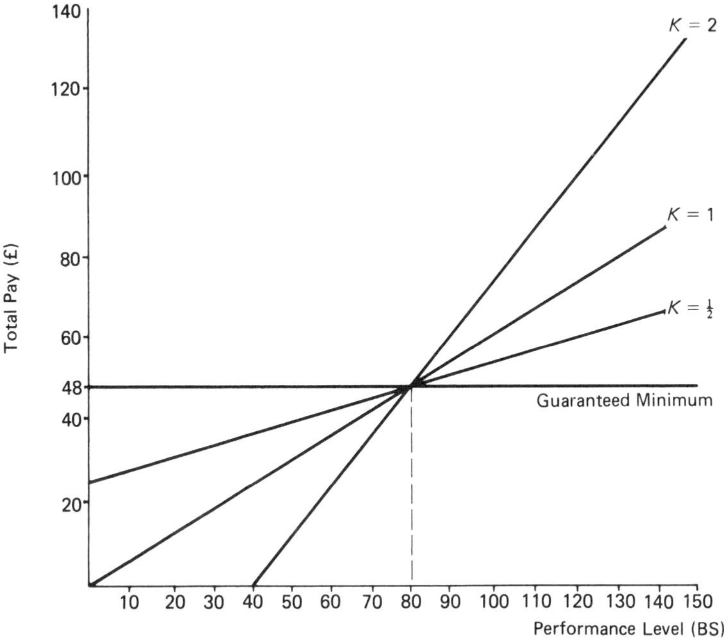

Figure 8.3 *Linear – Share Factors (K) for B = ¼*

Example:

Incentive Payment Rate	= £48.00 per 40 hours
Bonus Factor	= ¼
Share Factor	= 1½
Then Incentive Paid at 100 BS	= £48.00 × ¼ × 1½
	= £18.00

8 Direct Linear Schemes

There are three basic, direct linear financial incentive schemes.

They are:

(i) Straight Proportional, where the share factor is $K = 1$
(ii) Geared, where $K > 1$
(iii) Stabilised, where $K < 1$

(i) Straight Proportional Scheme

For a straight proportional type of payment by results scheme, basic pay and bonus may be calculated in the following ways:

(a) Time Saved Method With this method, which is sometimes called the premium bonus plan, basic pay and incentive pay are calculated separately.

First: Calculate the allowed time by the formula:
Allowed time = Number of units produced × Allowed time per unit of production

Second: Calculate the actual time taken to complete the units produced. (From attendance sheets or similar records, remembering that, actual time = attendance - lost time).

Third: Calculate the basic pay from the formula:
Basic pay = Actual time × Hourly rate

Fourth: Calculate the time saved, as follows:
Time saved = Allowed time – Actual Time

Fifth: Calculate the bonus pay:
Bonus pay = Time saved × Rate paid per unit of time saved × Share factor

Sixth: Total the basic and bonus pay

Example:

Assuming the conditions stated on p. 120 for figure 8.1, and a bonus factor of $\frac{1}{3}$ and a performance level of 110 (BS) – i.e. 44 units of output:

1. Allowed Time = 44 units × 80 allowed minutes
= 3520 allowed minutes

2. Actual time	= 40 Hours attendance – 0 lost time
	= 2400 minutes
3. Basic pay	= 40 Hours actual time × £1.20 per hour
	= £48.00
4. Time saved	= 3520 Allowed minutes – 2400 Actual minutes
	= 1120 minutes
5. Bonus pay	= 1120 minutes saved × 2p per minute*
	= £22.40
6. Total pay and incentive	= £48.00 + £22.40
	= £70.40

This result can be checked with tables 8.1 and 8.4 (pp. 127 and 135) and the graphs in figures 8.1 and 8.2.

(b) Allowed Time Method This method gives basic pay and incentive in one step. The formula is:

Total pay and incentive = Number of units produced × Allowed time per unit of output × Rate paid per unit of allowed time

Example:

Assuming the same conditions as given for the time saved method, above:

Total pay and incentive = 44 units × 80 allowed minutes × 2p per allowed minute*
= £70.40.

(c) Standard Time Method This method, like the allowed time calculation, gives basic pay and incentive pay in one step:

* The 2p per (allowed) minute was derived by dividing £1.20, the hourly rate, by 60 minutes.

$$\text{Total pay and incentive} = \text{Number of units produced} \times \text{Standard time per unit of production} \times \text{Rate paid per unit of standard time}$$

Example:

Assuming conditions as in the two previous examples:

Total pay and incentive = 44 units × 60 standard mins. × $[2+(\frac{1}{3}\times 2)]$ pence per standard minute
= £70.40

(*Note*: The rate paid for each standard minute is the monetary rate per allowed minute, increased by the bonus factor.)

(d) Price per Piece Method Strictly speaking this is not the same as the piecework price method of calculating pay, as, historically, piecework carried no guaranteed minimum wage. In fact, however, the mechanics of the calculation are, essentially, identical.

Again, this method enables basic pay plus incentive pay to be worked out in one step:

$$\text{Total pay and incentive} = \text{Number of units produced} \times \text{Price per piece}$$

Example:

With the same conditions as before:

Total pay and incentive = 44 units × £1.60 per unit
= £70.40

Note: The price per unit or piece can be determined in two ways:

First: Price per piece = Standard time per unit of production × Rate paid per unit of standard time

= 60 standard mins × [2+($\frac{1}{3}$×2)] pence per standard minute
= £1.60

Second: Price per piece = Allowed time per unit of production × Rate paid per unit of allowed time
= 80 Allowed mins. × 2p
= £1.60

It will be seen from table 8.1 and figure 8.2 that the characteristic of a straight proportional payment by results scheme is that increases in earnings are directly proportional to increases in performance level, once a certain minimum pay level has been reached. This is because the share factor $K = 1$. From table 8.1 and figure 8.2, a person working at 75 (BS) earns no bonus. If that person increases his or her performance by one third, a bonus of one third of £48.00 is paid (£16.00). If performance is raised by 100% to 150 (BS) then the incentive paid is 100% of £48.00.

Table 8.1 Linear Schemes – Incentive Pay ($B = \frac{1}{3}$)

Performance Level	*Incentive Pay*		
	$K = \frac{1}{2}$	$K = 1$	$K = 2$
	£	£	£
50	–	–	–
60	–	–	–
70	–	–	–
75	–	–	–
76	0.32	0.64	1.28
80	1.60	3.20	6.40
90	4.80	9.60	19.20
100	8.00	16.00	32.00
110	11.20	22.40	44.80
120	14.40	28.80	57.60
130	17.60	35.20	70.40
140	20.80	41.60	83.20
150	24.00	48.00	96.00

Notes: $K < 1$ – Stabilised scheme
$K = 1$ – Straight Proportional scheme
$K > 1$ – Geared scheme

(ii) Geared Scheme

With a geared financial incentive payment scheme, the rate at which bonus is earned increases at a rate greater than the rate of increase in output and performance level. This is because the share factor exceeds unity. The rate of change of the bonus element is constant. From table 8.1 and figure 8.2, it will be seen that someone who increases his output, and hence his performance level, by one third from 75 to 100 (BS) is paid a bonus of two-thirds of £48.00 (£32.00) when $B = \frac{1}{3}$ and $K = 2$.

This type of bonus payment method could be used where penalties, for late delivery of product, are punitive. The danger of run-away earnings, however, is clear, and particular care must be taken to set accurate time standards.

The time saved method of calculating bonus earnings can be used with linear geared schemes.

(iii) Stabilised Scheme

With stabilised payment by results plans, the rate at which incentive is earned decreases as the rate of output increases. The rate of change of the bonus element is constant, as in the straight proportional and geared schemes. With the stabilised plan, the share factor is less than one. Table 8.1 and figure 8.2 illustrate this.

This type of payment system is preferred by managers when they are not too certain of the accuracy of the time standards and they consider that there is a danger that earnings may escalate, uncontrollably.

The time saved method of calculating bonus can be used with stabilised schemes.

9 Non-linear Schemes

Non-linear schemes may be divided into two types:

(i) Progressive
(ii) Regressive.

Broadly speaking, the progressive type of non-linear payment by results method in which the rate of change of bonus earnings rises as the performance level increases, corresponds to a geared, linear type of incentive payment plan. The regressive, non-linear scheme in which the rate of change of incentive earnings falls as the performance level rises, corresponds to the stabilised, linear type of scheme.

One problem which arises, when devising non-linear bonus schemes, is that of constructing a formula to give the required earnings at different levels of performance. Two formulae are given below, but there are others. One empirical way of tackling this problem is to construct a formula, plot the results and see if the resultant curve gives the desired effect. If not, try another formula. Another, possibly simpler but, perhaps, less satisfying way, is to draw a curve of the requisite shape, and then construct a table of incentive earnings from it.

(i) Progressive Scheme

(a) A formula, which can be used as the basis of a progressive, non-linear, payment by results scheme is:

$$\begin{aligned}\text{Total Pay} = {} & \left[\text{Hours on Incentive} \times \text{Basic Hourly Rate}\right] \\ & + \text{Gearing Factor} \times \left[\frac{(\text{Performance level})^2}{\text{Constant}}\right. \\ & - \left\{\begin{matrix}\text{Guaranteed} \\ \text{Minimum for} \\ \text{possible hours}\end{matrix}\right\} \times (\text{Hours on Incentive}) \Big/ \left(\begin{matrix}\text{Possible} \\ \text{Hours on} \\ \text{Incentive}\end{matrix}\right)\end{aligned}$$

Instead of 'Performance level' it might be more convenient to use:

$$\frac{\text{Actual Output}}{\text{Standard Output}} \times 100 = \text{Performance level}$$

The 'constant' shown in the total pay formula will vary,

depending on the values of the share factor and the basic hourly rate.

Example:

Assume:

1. $B = \frac{1}{3}$
2. $K = 1$
3. All other conditions as on page 120.

The first step would be to derive the 'constant'. The formula for total pay, given above, is based on the equation:

$$Y = \frac{X^2}{a}$$

where $a =$ 'constant'. Because $B = \frac{1}{3}$, the formula must ensure no bonus at a 75 (BS) performance level, therefore, the equation would become:

$$Y = \frac{X^2}{a} - \text{Guaranteed Minimum}$$

What is the value of the constant a when the performance level $X = 75$, the incentive earnings $Y = 0$ and the guaranteed minimum is £48.00?

$$0 = \frac{75^2}{a} - 48$$

$$\therefore a = 117.2$$

Putting 117.2 into the formula for total pay, shown in 9(i)a) above, gives earnings of £48.00 at 75 (BS) and £85.3 at 100 (BS). If these amounts are considered to be unsuitable, then the value of the gearing ratio or the bonus factor can be changed and a fresh value for a calculated.

(b) Table 8.2 gives the incentive earnings, based on the formula for total pay given above, for the values of $K = \frac{1}{2}$ and 1 and a 'constant' of 117.2. Earnings for a straight proportional and linear geared scheme are shown, also, for comparison.

(c) Figure 8.4 shows total earnings graphically.

Table 8.2 Incentive Pay – Non-Linear – Progressive ($B = \frac{1}{3}$)

PERFORMANCE LEVEL	*INCENTIVE PAY*			
	Straight Proportional	*Linear Geared* $K = 3$	$K = \frac{1}{2}$	$K = 1$
	£	£	£	£
50	–	–	–	–
60	–	–	–	–
70	–	–	–	–
75	–	–	–	–
76	0.64	1.92	0.64	1.28
80	3.20	9.60	3.30	6.60
90	9.60	28.80	10.50	21.00
100	16.00	48.00	18.50	37.00
110	22.40	67.20	27.50	55.00
120	28.80	86.40	37.50	75.00
130	35.20	105.60	48.00	96.00
140	41.60	124.80	59.50	119.00
150	48.00	144.00	72.00	144.00

(ii) Regressive Scheme

(a) Regressive, non-linear payment plans, like stabilised, linear schemes, are favoured, usually, when operations managers are particularly uncertain of the time standards. One formula, which is easy to use, is:

$$\text{Total Pay} = \left[\text{Hours on Incentive} \times \text{Basic Hourly Rate}\right]$$

$$+ \left[\text{Gearing Factor} \times \frac{\text{Time Saved}}{\text{Allowed Time}} \times \text{Hours on Incentive} \times \text{Incentive Hourly Rate}\right]$$

Example:

Assume: 1. $B = \frac{1}{3}$
2. $K = 1$
3. All other conditions as on p. 120

Then, for a performance level of 100 (BS) total pay is:

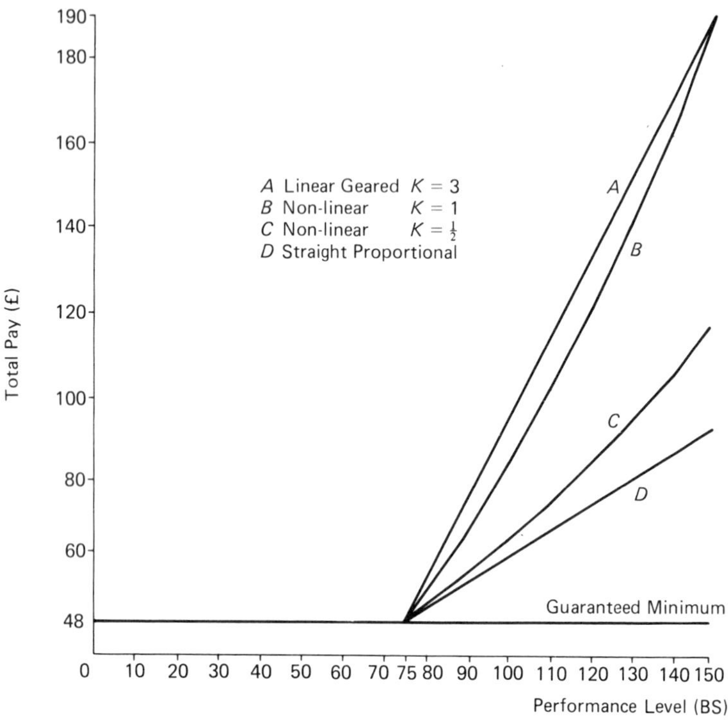

Figure 8.4 *Non-Linear-Progressive* $B = \frac{1}{3}$

$$(40 \times 1.20) + (1 \times \frac{800}{3200} \times 40 \times 1.20) = £60.00$$

(b) Table 8.3 gives the incentive earnings, based on the above formula, for values of $K = \frac{1}{2}$, 1 and 2. Earnings for a straight proportional plan, based on the same assumptions, are included for comparison.

(c) Figure 8.5 shows total earnings in graphical form. The effects, of changing the values of K and of B in non-linear schemes, are the same as for linear types of bonus payment schemes.

(d) The formula given in 9(ii)a) above is, sometimes, written as:

Table 8.3 Incentive Pay – Non-Linear – Regressive ($B = \frac{1}{3}$)

PERFORMANCE LEVEL	INCENTIVE PAY			
	Straight Proportional	Non-Linear $K = \frac{1}{2}$	$K = 1$	$K = 2$
	£	£	£	£
50	–	–	–	–
60	–	–	–	–
70	–	–	–	–
75	–	–	–	–
76	0.64	0.32	0.63	1.26
80	3.20	1.50	3.00	6.00
90	9.60	4.00	8.00	16.00
100	16.00	6.00	12.00	24.00
110	22.40	7.64	15.28	30.56
120	28.80	9.00	18.00	36.00
130	35.20	10.15	20.30	40.60
140	41.60	11.14	22.28	44.56
150	48.00	12.00	24.00	48.00

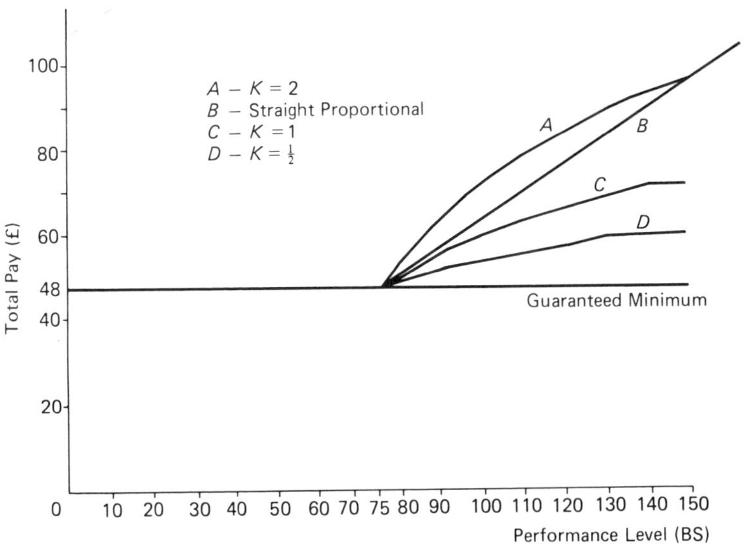

Figure 8.5 *Non-Linear – Regressive* $B = \frac{1}{3}$

$$\text{Total Pay} = \left[\text{Hours on Incentive} \times \text{Basic Hourly Rate}\right] + \text{Gearing Factor} \times \left[1 - \frac{100}{X_2\,(1+B)}\right] \times \text{Hours on Incentive} \times \text{Incentive Hourly Rate}$$

where B = bonus factor, and X_2 = actual performance level of the worker.

10 Costs

It is essential that managers or industrial engineers or whoever is concerned with the design, introduction and running of incentive schemes understand the behaviour of the costs associated with such schemes. Incentive schemes cost more (money), in an absolute sense, than flat rate payment systems. Incentive plans are relatively cheaper and can benefit a firm in two ways – always assuming that the scheme works successfully.

First, there should be an initial 'saving' due to the increase in productivity of the work force. For example, a firm, in which each of its workers is paid £40.00 a week and each worker produces 20 units a week, would have a labour cost of £2.00 per unit. If this firm, on introducing a straight proportional scheme ($B = \frac{1}{3}$), paying each of the workers £48.00 per week plus bonus, managed to raise individual output to 40 units a week, its labour cost would be £1.60 per unit, although the firm's wages bill would, in fact, have increased – assuming the usual guarantee of no redundancies as the result of the introduction of the new payment scheme.

Secondly, the firm benefits because the same amount of overhead costs can, now, be spread over a larger number of units, which have been produced, so the total cost of each unit is reduced.

A point that must be emphasised is that, not all bonus schemes lead to ever-reducing operator costs per unit as and if production increases. From table 8.4 and figure 8.6 it can be seen that, once the bonus starting point has been reached, operator costs remain the same when $K = 1$, irrespective of increases in production. The inclusion of overhead costs, however, would show reduced total cost per unit, as output

Table 8.4 Total Pay & Operator Cost per Unit of Production – Linear ($B = \frac{1}{3}$)

PERFORMANCE LEVEL	*OUTPUT*	*TOTAL PAY*			*OPERATOR COST PER UNIT OF PRODUCTION*			
		$K = \frac{1}{2}$	$K = 1$	$K = 2$	$K = \frac{1}{2}$	$K = 1$	$K = 2$	*Flat Rate*
		£	£	£	£	£	£	
50	20	48.00	48.00	48.00	2.40	2.40	2.40	2.40
60	24	48.00	48.00	48.00	2.00	2.00	2.00	2.00
70	28	48.00	48.00	48.00	1.71	1.70	1.70	1.71
75	30	48.00	48.00	48.00	1.61	1.61	1.61	1.61
76	30.4	48.32	48.64	49.28	1.59	1.60	1.62	1.58
80	32	49.60	51.20	54.40	1.55	1.60	1.70	1.50
90	36	52.80	57.60	67.20	1.47	1.60	1.87	1.33
100	40	56.00	64.00	80.00	1.40	1.60	2.00	1.20
110	44	59.20	70.40	92.80	1.35	1.60	2.11	1.09
120	48	62.40	76.80	105.60	1.30	1.60	2.20	1.00
130	52	65.60	83.20	118.40	1.26	1.60	2.28	0.92
140	56	68.80	89.60	131.20	1.23	1.60	2.34	0.86
150	60	72.00	96.00	144.00	1.20	1.60	2.40	0.80

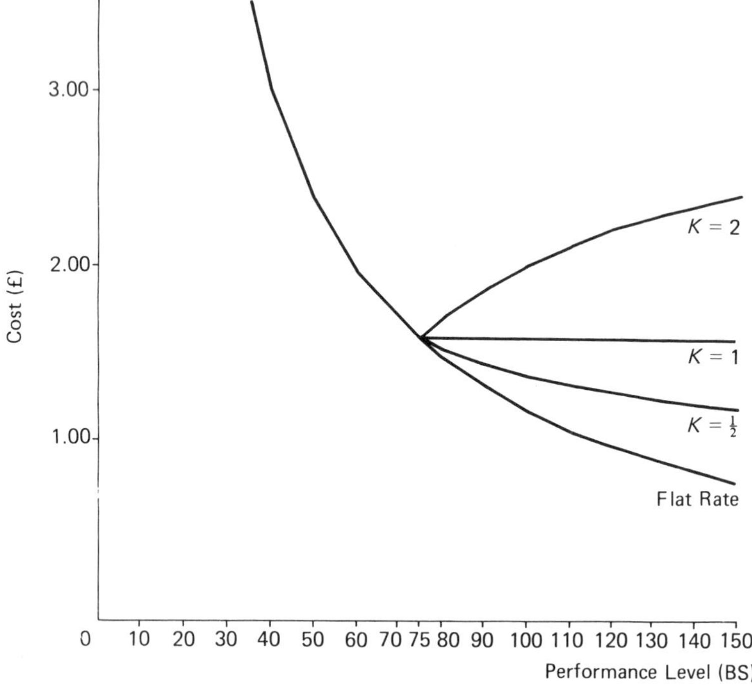

Figure 8.6 *Linear – Operator Cost per Unit of Production* $B = \frac{1}{3}$

increases. Table 8.5 illustrates this. Note that even where $K > 1$ and operator costs per unit increase with increased output, the total cost per unit diminishes. It is most important not to assume that costs always behave in this way and every case must be analysed very carefully before introducing any scheme.

Finally, notice from tables 8.4 and 8.5 what the relative costs might have been if the management had been able to achieve reasonable standards of performance without paying any incentive!

Tables 8.6 and 8.7 and figures 8.7 and 8.8 also show the operator cost per unit of production for typical progressive and regressive, non-linear type incentive systems. Figure 8.9 is included to show the pattern which cost curves can take, when an incentive scheme is based on a formula, very similar to the one described here, on page 129. It emphasises the

Table 8.5 Total Cost per Unit of Production – Linear ($B = \frac{1}{3}$)

TOTAL COST PER UNIT OF PRODUCTION					
Performance Level	*Output*	$K = \frac{1}{2}$	$K = 1$	$K = 2$	*Flat Rate*
		£	£	£	£
50	20	7.40	7.40	7.40	7.40
60	24	6.17	6.17	6.17	6.17
70	28	5.28	5.28	5.28	5.28
75	30	4.94	4.94	4.94	4.94
76	30.4	4.88	4.89	4.91	4.87
80	32	4.68	4.73	4.83	4.63
90	36	4.27	4.40	4.67	4.13
100	40	3.90	4.10	4.50	3.70
110	44	3.62	3.87	4.38	3.36
120	48	3.38	3.68	4.28	3.08
130	52	3.18	3.52	4.20	2.84
140	56	3.02	3.39	4.13	2.65
150	60	2.87	3.27	4.07	2.47

Note: In this table the simplifying assumption has been made that £100.00 of overhead costs could be 'attributed' to each worker.

point that the cost consequences of a payment by results system should be examined very carefully and certainly *before* the scheme is introduced.

11 Three Famous Incentive Schemes

The names Bedaux, Halsey and Rowan are, probably, among the best known of management 'pioneers', and surely the most often-quoted in discussions of bonus schemes. Figure 8.10 gives typical examples of their incentive plans.

(i) Bedaux Scheme

This was a direct, linear scheme, where the bonus factor was probably one third and the gearing factor three-quarters. In this scheme, the managers and supervisors were given the quarter share deducted from the operators' bonus earnings.

Table 8.6 Total Pay & Operator Cost per Unit of Production – Non-Linear -- Progressive ($B = \frac{1}{3}$)

Performance Level	Output	TOTAL PAY				OPERATOR COST PER UNIT OF PRODUCTION			
		Straight Proportional	Linear Geared $K = 3$	Non-Linear $K = \frac{1}{2}$	Non-Linear $K = 1$	Straight Proportional	Linear Geared $K = 3$	Non-Linear $K = \frac{1}{2}$	Non-Linear $K = 1$
		£	£	£	£	£	£	£	£
50	20	48.00	48.00	48.00	48.00	2.40	2.40	2.40	2.40
60	24	48.00	48.00	48.00	48.00	2.00	2.00	2.00	2.00
70	28	48.00	48.00	48.00	48.00	1.71	1.71	1.71	1.71
75	30	48.00	48.00	48.00	48.00	1.60	1.60	1.60	1.60
76	30.4	48.64	49.92	48.64	49.28	1.60	1.64	1.60	1.62
80	32	51.20	57.60	51.30	54.60	1.60	1.80	1.60	1.71
90	36	57.60	76.80	58.50	69.00	1.60	2.13	1.63	1.92
100	40	64.00	96.00	66.50	85.00	1.60	2.40	1.66	2.13
110	44	70.40	115.20	75.50	103.00	1.60	2.62	1.72	2.34
120	48	76.80	134.40	85.50	123.00	1.60	2.80	1.78	2.56
130	52	83.20	153.60	96.00	144.00	1.60	2.95	1.85	2.77
140	56	89.60	172.80	107.50	167.00	1.60	3.09	1.92	2.98
150	60	96.00	192.00	120.00	192.00	1.60	3.20	2.00	3.20

Table 8.7 Total Pay & Operator Cost per Unit of Production – Non-Linear – Regressive ($B = \frac{1}{3}$)

Performance Level	Output	TOTAL PAY				OPERATOR COST PER UNIT OF PRODUCTION			
		Straight Proportional	Non-Linear			Straight Proportional	Non-Linear		
			$K = \frac{1}{2}$	$K = 1$	$K = 2$		$K = \frac{1}{2}$	$K = 1$	$K = 2$
		£	£	£	£	£	£	£	£
50	20	48.00	48.00	48.00	48.00	2.40	2.40	2.40	2.40
60	24	48.00	48.00	48.00	48.00	2.00	2.00	2.00	2.00
70	28	48.00	48.00	48.00	48.00	1.71	1.71	1.71	1.71
75	30	48.00	48.00	48.00	48.00	1.60	1.60	1.60	1.60
76	30.4	48.64	48.32	48.63	49.26	1.60	1.59	1.59	1.63
80	32	51.20	49.50	51.00	54.00	1.60	1.55	1.59	1.69
90	36	57.60	52.00	56.00	64.00	1.60	1.44	1.56	1.78
100	40	64.00	54.00	60.00	72.00	1.60	1.35	1.50	1.80
110	44	70.40	55.64	63.28	78.56	1.60	1.26	1.44	1.79
120	48	76.80	57.00	66.00	84.00	1.60	1.19	1.38	1.75
130	52	83.20	58.15	68.30	88.60	1.60	1.12	1.31	1.70
140	56	89.60	59.14	70.28	92.56	1.60	1.06	1.26	1.65
150	60	96.00	60.00	72.00	96.00	1.60	1.00	1.20	1.60

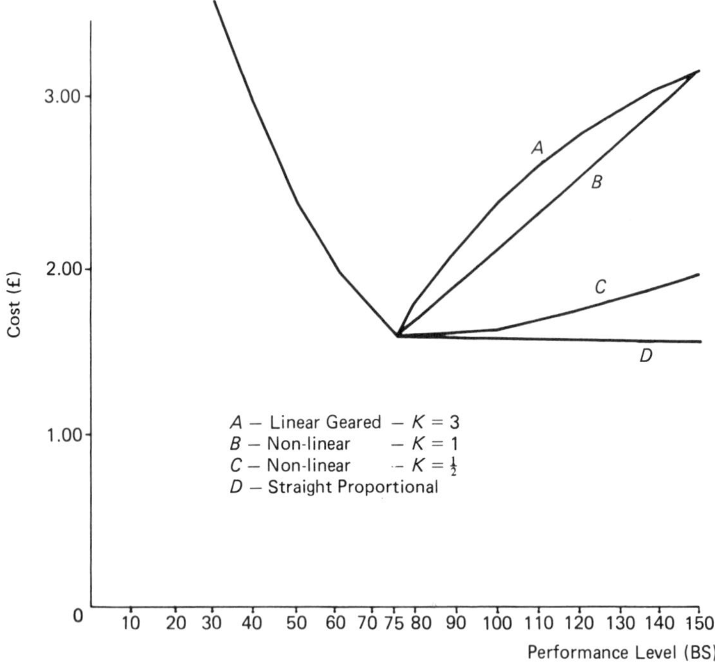

Figure 8.7 *Non-Linear – Progressive – Operator Cost per Unit of Production* $B = \frac{1}{3}$

(ii) Halsey Scheme

This was a direct linear scheme also. Halsey appears to have used different values for the bonus and gearing factors on different occasions. In the example in figure 8.10, the bonus factor was 0.7 and the gearing factor approximately 0.75.

(iii) Rowan Scheme

This was a regressive, non-linear scheme based on the formula:

$$\text{Premium Time} = \text{Time Taken} \times \frac{\text{Time Saved}}{\text{Time Allowed}}$$

The effective bonus and gearing factors, in this example, are 0.7 and 0.6, respectively.

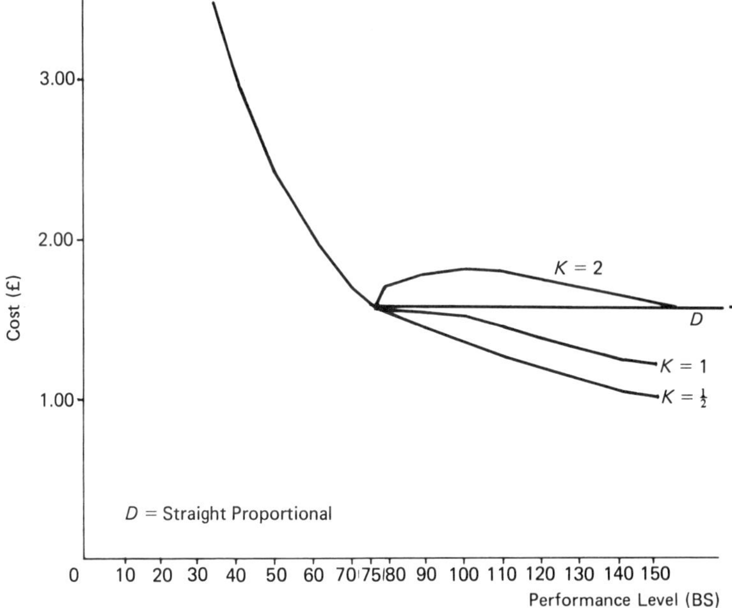

Figure 8.8 *Non-Linear – Regressive – Operator Cost per Unit of Production* $B = \frac{1}{3}$

12 Conclusion

As the schoolboy wrote: 'in the last paragraphs a writer must present his final confusions'. Considering the multiplicity of types of payment by results systems there is probably more than a germ of truth in the howler. A cursory glance at Lytle[4] is sufficient to suggest that there are as many different bonus plans as there are, or have been, management consultants or industrial engineers. This is hardly surprising, however, because not only should payment systems be tailored to suit individual organisations and their circumstances, but managers will, inevitably, try to repeat their successful experiences. Despite their apparent differences, however, these schemes are basically similar, and a knowledge of the factors, which have been des-

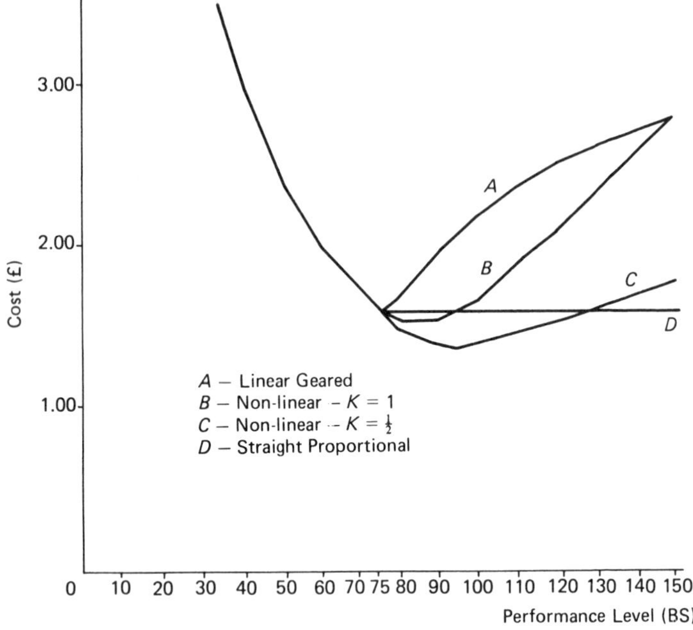

Figure 8.9 *Non-Linear – Progressive – Operator Cost per Unit of Production* $B = \frac{1}{3}$

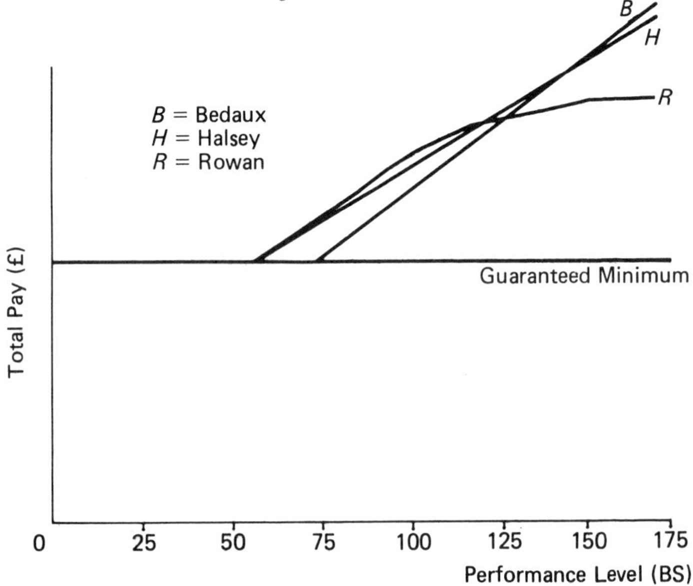

Figure 8.10 *Bedaux, Halsey & Rowan Schemes*

cribed in this chapter, should enable a manager to understand how these direct linear and non-linear schemes work.

It is also important that managers remember that incentive plans are introduced in order to reduce the total cost of a product or service. This may and probably will mean that operator earnings are increased. Were it not for the relationship between overhead costs and volume of output, the lowest earnings curve would be the best plan, from a managerial viewpoint. When comparing incentive payment methods, the best one from an *economic* position is the one which results in the lowest total cost per unit curve. Where a bonus scheme might lead to increased scrapped work, however, the potential savings from any increased output must be compared with the possible higher costs of rejected work, and, in such cases a flat rate of pay may be preferable. Alternatively, an incentive scheme based on quality or rejected output or on both quality and output might be feasible. In either case, the basic principles enumerated previously would still apply. They would also be applicable if the schemes were for individuals or for groups.

Whether financial incentives are successful motivators or not is still arguable. What does seem clear is that, to be successful, such schemes must be acceptable. It is interesting to note, also, that there does not seem to have been any marked abandonment of bonus payment methods in industrialised societies. Until this occurs it is important that managers be fluent in the simple, arithmetical interconnections between those variables of a pay plan which are thought to be quantifiable. The infinitely more complex variables governing human behaviour, which usually manages to bend or subvert the 'quantifiable' factors, are another matter altogether. But then why employ managers if behaviour were completely predictable?

Lytle, in his classic work,[4] summed up the matter neatly:

> By no means consider an incentive plan as a cure-all! It is not even a primary remedy for industrial ills, but a phase of control effective only after such primary measures as: correct processing, improved lay-out, job standardisation and evaluation have been thoroughly carried out. It is like oats for a horse; oats cannot change the breed, but can maintain the spirit. The simile is fortunate because in both cases overdoses as well as underdoses are disastrous.

Disaster will be much less probable if operations managers are versed in, at the very least, the basic, structural, quantitative aspects of direct financial incentive schemes, which have been discussed here.

References and Further Reading

Terminology

1 *Glossary of Terms Used in Work Study and Organisation and Methods*, British Standards Institution, BS 3138, 1979.

Work Measurement

2 *Introduction to Work Study*, International Labour Office, Geneva, 3rd (revised) edn, 1978.
3 Whitmore, D.A., *Work Measurement*, Heinemann 1975.

Incentive Schemes

4 Lytle, C.W., *Wage Incentive Methods*, Ronald Press 1942.
5 *Payments by Results*, International Labour Office, Geneva, 1951.
6 Avery, M., *Time Study, Incentives & Budgetary Control*, Business Publications 1964.
7 O'Connor, T.F., *Profitable Productivity*, Emmott 1966.
8 *Payment by Results Systems*, HMSO Report No. 65, 1969.
9 Baggott, J., *Cost and Management Accounting*, W.H. Allen 1973.
10 Gould, C.T., *Incentives*, Institute of Work Study Practitioners, 1974.
11 Lloyd, P.A., *Incentive Payment Schemes*, British Institute of Management 1976.
12 Husband, T.M., *Work Analysis and Pay Structure*, McGraw-Hill 1976.
13 Beacham, R.H.S., *Pay Systems*, Heinemann 1979.

9
Productivity Measurement at Felton & Co Ltd

H WILLIAMS

Management Consultant, Imperial Group Ltd
and
J McGREGOR

Lecturer in Operations Management,
The University of Aston

1 Introduction

The aim of this case is to try to demonstrate the connections between performance level, output, pay and costs and to show the use which managers can make of these important elements of information when attempting to solve problems of productivity.

No attempt has been made to illustrate other important aspects of managing such as, for example, the raising of capital, or the health and safety of employees.

This case is based on a real company, but names have been changed and figures greatly simplified.

2 Felton & Co Ltd

H. Gantt and Partners, management consultants, have been

retained by Amalgan (Holdings) Ltd, to advise on ways of increasing productivity in one of its subsidiaries, Felton & Co Ltd.

Mr Barth, of H. Gantt and Partners, was given this task. He learned that Felton & Co Ltd, manufacturers of electrical components, had been established in 1911 and acquired by Amalgan (Holdings) Ltd in 1978. Felton & Co Ltd occupied a large, modern factory on an industrial estate, in a large town in the Midlands. At present, the company employed eighty-five staff and five hundred and twenty semi-skilled operators.

Mr Barth attempted to ensure that everyone at Felton & Co Ltd knew who he was and understood what he was trying to do. To this end he tried to meet and to talk to as many people as possible, and to learn the management and union structures and agreements. The Managing Director suggested that Mr Barth should investigate the payment system as 'the incentive element appears to be lacking'.

3 Present Incentive Scheme & its Implications

The consultant discovered that the incentive scheme for the employers in the production departments was based on time-study standards, set by a work-study engineer, who had left the firm six months previously and who had not been replaced. Records of production, earnings and lost time were patchy or non-existent, so Barth decided to check the time standards, analyse earnings and obtain an estimate of the amount of lost time in the production departments. To this end, he did some short time-studies, arranged for an analysis of earnings to be made and did a rated activity sampling study to get an overall view of the level of productivity. He also requested a forecast of sales for the next twelve months and information on the extent of any back-log of unfulfilled orders.

The results of the rated activity sampling study were:

Total number of observations (n)	=	350	=	100%
Number of occasions 'waiting for work' (p_1)	=	105	=	30%

Number of occasions 'waiting – no reason' (p_2)	=	70	=	20%
Number of occasions working (q)	=	175	=	50%
Average Rating	=	105 (BS)		
Required level of confidence	=	95%		
Required limits of accuracy	=	±5%		

Using the formula:*

$$\sigma = \sqrt{\frac{p \times q}{n}}$$

$$1.96\,\sigma = 5$$

$$\therefore \quad \sigma = 2.55$$

$$\therefore \text{ For } p_1: \quad 2.55 = \sqrt{\frac{30 \times 70}{n}}$$

$$\therefore n = 323$$

$$\therefore \text{ For } p_2: \quad 2.55 = \sqrt{\frac{20 \times 80}{n}}$$

$$\therefore n = 246$$

Barth was interested to see that, when working, the operators were working slightly above standard performance (100 (BS)), but that waiting time seemed extremely high. He was somewhat puzzled by the 'waiting – no reason'.

Further investigation showed the following:

(i) The standard times, which had been issued, originally, by the recently departed work-study engineer, agreed very closely with the results from Barth's own time studies.

(ii) The original standard times had been increased, by a factor of $\frac{70}{60}$, by the management, instead of awarding an increase in pay.

(iii) Waiting time was paid at the performance level achieved whilst on incentive. It paid the operators, therefore, to book 'off incentive', as quickly as possible. They achieveu

* See *Introduction to Work Study*, 3rd (revised) edn, ILO, 1978, p. 197.

their desired level of earnings by working slightly above standard performance, when working, and then booking 'off incentive' and recording 'waiting time'. Barth discovered that no analysis of waiting time was made by management.

(iv) An allowance of 10% had been included in the standard times to cover relaxation (fatigue).

(v) The payment by results scheme was based on a guaranteed minimum of £20.00 for 40 hours attendance, with an incentive element of £60.00 for 100 (BS) performance level, giving a total of £80.00 for 40 hours at standard performance. Management had insisted on this large bonus proportion in order to 'encourage output'.

From the payment tables used by the wages office, Barth noted that £80.00 was paid at 100 (BS) performance level and £20.00 at 25 (BS). Using the formula:

$$R = \frac{100}{1+B}$$

(See page 121, Chapter 8)

Barth calculated that the Bonus Factor was $B = 3$ and, that, as the ratio of earnings to performance level (20/25 = 80/100) was directly proportional, the scheme was, in fact, a straight proportional one and an operator would expect to earn £2.00 per hour at standard performance.

Barth decided to compare operator costs per standard hour under various circumstances:

(i) Original Standards

In 40 hours 1 operator produces 40 Standard Hours of work at 100 (BS).

Total Pay at 100 (BS) for 40 hours = £80.00
∴ Operator Cost per Standard Hour = £2.00

(ii) Present Standard – Assuming No Lost Time

In 40 hours 1 operator produces

$$\frac{40 \times 60}{70} = 34.29 \text{ Standard Hours of work at 100 (BS).}$$

Total Pay at 100 (BS) for 40 hours = £80.00
∴ Operator Cost per Standard Hour = £2.33

(iii) Present Standards – Assuming 50% Lost Time & Standard Performance

Operator attends for 40 hours, but works productively for 20 hours. In 20 productive hours 1 operator produces $\frac{20 \times 60}{70} = 17.15$ Standard Hours at 100 (BS).

Total Pay:	Incentive (productive) time	= 20 hours × £2.00
		= £40.00
	Non-productive time	= 20 hours × £2.00
		= £40.00
	∴ Total pay	= £80.00

∴ Operator Cost per Standard Hour $= \frac{£80.00}{17.15}$

= £4.67

(iv) Present Standard – Assuming 50% Lost Time and 105 (BS) Performance Level

Operator attends for 40 hours, but works productively for 20 hours. In 20 productive hours 1 operator produces $\frac{17.15 \times 105}{100} = 18.00$ Standard Hours at 105 (BS).

Total Pay $= \frac{£80 \times 105}{100}$ = £84 at 105 (BS)

∴ Operator Cost per Standard Hour $= \frac{£84}{18} =$ £4.67

Barth then calculated the potential output of the factory under various conditions:

(i) Original Standards – No Lost Time – 100 (BS) Performance

Annual capacity: 520 operators × 40 Hours × 50 weeks
= 1,040,000 Standard Hours

(ii) Original Standards – 10% Lost Time – 100 (BS) Performance

Annual capacity: 520 × (40–4) × 50
= 936,000 Standard Hours

(iv) Present Standards – 10% Lost Time – 100 (BS) Performance

Annual capacity: $520 \times (40–4) \times \frac{60}{70} \times 50$

$= 802{,}286$ Standard Hours

(v) Present Standards – 50% Lost Time – 105 (BS) Performance

Annual capacity: $520 \times (40 \times 20) \times \frac{60}{70} \times \frac{105}{100} \times 50$

$= 468{,}000$ Standard Hours

4 Projected Work-load

Barth now received the sales forecast and back-log of orders, which he had requested. He calculated the total standard hours required to produce each product and then converted sales forecast and back-log of orders to standard hours, in order to calculate the future demands on the factory.

Backlog of Orders

Product Type	*Quantity*	*Original Standard Hours per Product*	*Total Standard Hours*	
			Original	*Present*
A	200	300	60,000	70,000
B	300	200	60,000	70,000
C	3,400	30	102,000	119,000
			222,000	259,000

Sales Forecast – Next 12 Months

Product Type	*Quantity*	*Original Standard Hours per Product*	*Total Standard Hours*	
			Original	*Present*
A	350	300	105,000	122,500
B	250	200	50,000	58,333
C	7,500	30	225,000	262,500
			380,000	443,333

At this juncture Barth learned, from the Managing Director of Felton & Co Ltd, that the Chairman of the parent company had written to say that Feltons must show a profit within the next eighteen months or be closed down.

Barth showed the Managing Director the results of his analysis. An output of 936,000 standard hours of work should be the target, he thought. At the present level of output, of 468,000 standard hours, it was hardly surprising, therefore, that the company was finding it difficult to make an adequate profit, in the face of keen pricing competition. Moreover, if output could be increased to 800,000 or 900,000 standard hours, then the factory would work its way through the back-log and forecast of orders within some eight to eleven months.

5 Recommendations

Barth advised that the following steps be taken:

(i) All recruitment of operators be stopped immediately. Special cases to be reviewed by the Managing Director.
(ii) A system for recording the amount and reasons for lost time be instituted immediately.
(iii) A control system, showing operator and departmental costs and efficiencies be developed and installed, as quickly as possible.
(iv) A new pay scheme should be devised, as quickly as possible.
(v) The Union representatives should be informed of the financial situation and of the company's intention to negotiate a new payment system to improve output.
(vi) An immediate marketing campaign be instituted. If possible, products *A* & *B* should be promoted, in particular, as their work content was high. (Relative profitability must be considered, also).
(vii) New products should be developed.
(viii) Investigate the possibility of finding alternative employment, for Feltons' employees, within Amalgan's other companies.

From the Personnel Department, Barth obtained information about the composition and skills possessed by the workforce.

He learned that:

(i) Labour turnover was 15% p.a.
(ii) Part-time workers: 26 (full-time equivalents).
(iii) Due to retire within the next twelve months: 14.

Using this information, Barth calculated that the workforce would be approximately 400 people in a year's time, and it would require roughly 400 X (40–4) X 50 = 720,000 standard hours of work to keep the factory running.

Reflecting on the problems of introducing a new payment by results system, Barth felt that the two most important changes must be:

(i) To change the present system of paying for lost time to one which discouraged booking of non-productive time.
(ii) To issue 'correct' standard times. In his experience, issuing standard times, which had been inflated to give extra money, invariably led to decreases in productivity.

Barth thought that the precarious financial situation of the company would give the management some leverage to negotiate a different system of paying for non-productive time.

6 Proposed Scheme

To overcome the lost time booking problem, Barth proposed that lost time should be paid at a fraction of average earnings. To begin, management could suggest a figure of, say, 0.6 and 'retreat' to 0.9 if necessary. The property of this system was that total earnings would decrease, each week, if lost time was booked. Operators would, therefore, Barth felt, put pressure on managers to avoid non-productive time and so increase departmental efficiency. Barth gave the following example:

Week 1

30 Hours Productive Time X £2.00	=	£60.00
10 Hours Non-Productive Time X £2.00 X 0.7	=	£14.00

Total Pay		=	£74.00
Average earnings	$= \frac{£74.00}{40}$	=	£1.85 per hour

Week 2

30 Hours Productive Time X £2.00	=	£60.00
10 Hours Non-Productive Time X £1.85 X 0.7	=	£12.95
Total Pay	=	£72.95
Average earnings either: $\frac{£72.95}{40}$	=	£1.82 per hour
or: $\frac{£74.00 + £72.95}{80}$	=	£1.84 per hour

As to the question of issuing 'correct' standard times, Barth considered that the company could afford to offer some increase in pay, which would compensate operators for the loss of the time, which had been added on to the original time standards. Working back from figures supplied by the company's accountant, Barth calculated that actual operator cost per standard hour should not exceed £3.00, if the company was to make a reasonable profit. To give himself some margin, remembering that it could take some time for the managers to reduce the amount of lost time, within their control, to 10% or less, Barth thought that the standard operator cost per standard hour should not exceed £2.50. This meant that, with a straight proportional type of scheme which Barth favoured, the company could afford to pay 40 X £2.50 = £100.00 at standard performance. Barth thought this too high and suggested an initial offer of £84.00 at standard performance. He pointed out that, inflating standards by the factor $\frac{70}{60}$ was tantamount to paying operators some 14% extra money. Management should not be surprised, therefore, if, in the negotiations, a demand for £80.00 (the present expected total earnings) plus some £14.00 was tabled, making the expected total earnings at standard performance £94.00 per week.

Barth proposed one further change to the existing incentive scheme. He suggested that the incentive element should be reduced considerably by raising the guaranteed minimum payment to £60.00 for 40 hours. He recognised that there was a risk that a person might not trouble to achieve a performance level, which would earn this figure, but considered that risk to be minimal. It was, he thought, an inducement to accept the new payment scheme. It was up to managers to see that members of their department achieved standard performance.

Summarising his proposals, Barth suggested that the new payment by results scheme, for the production workers, should:

(i) Be a straight proportional type system.
(ii) Have a guaranteed minimum wage of £60.00 for 40 hours attendance.
(iii) Pay £84.00 for 40 hours at standard performance. This meant:
  (a) Bonus factor of 0.4
  (b) Bonus would be earned above 72 (BS) performance level.
  (This to be the initial bargaining position.)
(iv) Pay non-productive time at a fraction (to be determined by negotiation) of average earnings.
(v) Payment to be made for good quality work only.

His final recommendation was that, whatever the mix of bonus factor and guaranteed minimum pay negotiated:

(i) The standard operator cost per standard hour should not exceed £2.50.
(ii) Payment should be based on 'true', non-inflated time standards.

7 Conclusion

In the event, the management and the union representatives agreed to a guaranteed minimum wage of £66.00 per 40 hour week, a total basic and bonus pay of £88.00 at standard performance, lost time to be paid at 0.7 of average earnings, and 'correct' standard times to be used. Furthermore, it was agreed that a value-added incentive scheme, which would be in addition to the new payment by results scheme, would be considered in the near future, 'should the firm attain a financially more stable position' – which it did!

10
Costing for Operations and Production Management

J B COATES

*Senior Lecturer in Accounting,
The University of Aston*

1 Introduction

Correctly defined and relevant cost information is of fundamental importance to the efficient functioning of operations and production management. This is a fact not uniformly perceived across firms as a whole for reasons frequently attributable to both members of the operations management team and their company accountants. This chapter aims to establish the validity of the assertion, outlining the basic objectives and elements of a costing system, the nature and limitations of the information it produces and illustrating with examples, the need to ensure that cost information is defined in such a way as to be relevant when special decisions have to be made.

'Costing' as a term should be taken to mean much more than a routine calculation of costs of products or factory or office sections. All too often it appears in practice to be little more then just such a routine and even this may be carried out in a manner which leaves little real meaning to be attached to the resultant figures. In other circumstances, 'costing' may conjure up a vision of a repressive control system, with managers seeing little more to it than an attempt to put a strait-jacket on their spending.

Technically, the term costing is too narrow as a description of the modern industrial accounting approach. It is preferable to consider costing[1] as an activity within the scope of the services provided by the management accounting function. Routine calculations of the costs of products and departments is then seen as an input to the latter service, which incorporates it along with other information into data on which general management can base decisions with respect to planning and control of the business.

What has to be made clear is that costing in this sense (it is still commonplace to hear the function of management accounting referred to for simplicity as 'costing'), when carried out in a positive manner, is not being done for its own sake, but for a wide variety of purposes. Control is certainly amongst these, but planning can scarcely be carried out properly without proposals being translated into financial terms. The variety of applications where cost data could be required to assist in decision-making also raises problems: cost data produced in a particular form by the accounting system is unlikely to be valid for all applications and further, the system cannot be expected to produce information for all possible decision situations. This point emphasises the need for users of cost information to fully appreciate the nature and limitations of the data they receive and to be clear themselves on the cost requirements – the so-called 'relevant' costs – of particular problems; company accountants cannot be expected to prepare information as a matter of routine, for all cases. A reasonable dialogue and understanding between accountants and users of accounting information is very necessary, but often lacking in practice.

2 Costing and Operations Management

In terms of the activities within a company with which these two functions are principally concerned, there is a substantial identity of interest. Indeed, costing/management accounting information is probably relevant to all aspects of operations management. Without attempting an exhaustive listing, some of the obvious areas are:

product planning
capacity planning
production planning and control
inventory planning and control
process planning

Each of these activities will be executed at least in part, if not wholly, with reference to costs. They are not, of course, mutually exclusive areas.

(a) Product Planning

By this is meant planning the range of products (and services) a company is to produce. Cost of production is an element (not the sole one) in pricing considerations and in determining the profit per unit earned by each item. What is not always appreciated is that 'profit per unit' is not the only yardstick on which to base judgments, the more significant one being profitability: the power of the product to *earn* profits. Cost measurements for profitability analysis are often not the same as those applied to defining profit.

(b) Capacity Planning

At first sight this would seem a problem principally concerned with forecast production levels, machine hours, man hours, floor space and so on, i.e. largely physical measurements. These inputs are of course essential, but they must be translated into appropriate cost information related to incidence and timing, item by item, so that matters such as financing, tax and ultimately profitability can be examined. The operations management team, besides being responsible for much of the physical data preparation, may well be required to provide at least preliminary costings and hence should understand the format in which the data will be required. This particular subject is taken up in detail in Chapter 6.

(c) Production Planning and Control; Inventory Planning and Control

These two aspects of operations management are clearly related, especially from a cost point of view. At an elementary level, one must consider the economics of production run lengths against levels of stock holdings of each type of stock: raw material, work in progress and finished goods. If reference is to be made to economic order/batch quantities, these will require special cost items such as stock holding costs.

(d) Process Planning

Production of a given item may be achieved through a variety of manufacturing processes within a given production unit: the costs may well vary substantially between these. Again at a simple level, a choice may exist between using conventional or single or multi-spindle lathes for turning a metal component: before drawing up a standard process routeing, the cost implications of selecting a particular route (which in the example given, would be substantially different) must clearly be examined.

(e) Other Areas

The multiplicity of operations management problems is generally matched, as indicated, by the need for costs to be analysed. Other areas for example could be in the determination of the level of maintenance cover to be provided: an input to the decision will be the cost of downtime, including the knock-on effects of a particular machine or group of machines being idle. Maintenance also figures centrally in life-cycle costing assessments[2] which again will come within the scope of operations management. An aspect of activity closely related to the above is the cost of queues, where these develop in relation to the levels of service provided, for example, at stores' counters. The overall assessment of production against non-productive time and causes of lost time of vital importance to the calculation of costs and how actual costs incurred are monitored and controlled.

Altogether, costing and operations management can be seen

to be complementary to each other in virtually all aspects of significance in industry. Ignorance of this by either side is certain to lead to poorer results for the company as a whole than would otherwise be the case. However, attention will now be concentrated on discussing the nature of accounting information and its applications to operations management problems.

3 Computation of Product and Departmental Costs

The vital point to be accepted here is that there are numerous methods which may be employed to arrive at product and department costs. The choice of which method to employ depends in part on the purposes for which the information is required and in part on the actual manufacturing processes and their supporting services. In either case though, there is still considerable scope for variation in the actual computation methods adopted, since they ultimately rest on the judgment of the company accountants: there are no set rules other than to say that a sensible, common sense approach to the problem is the best way to tackle it.

In general, certainly for special decisions, this means the user of the cost information should ensure a thorough knowledge of how and for what other purposes the information he is using was developed.

(a) The Mechanics of Computation

The basic mechanics apply in any costing situation. Here it will be assumed the sole objective is to derive the costs per unit of output and the costs of running defined sections of the firm: the product and department costs. The former naturally provide a yardstick (but not necessarily a determinant) for pricing decisions and the latter the basis for responsibility accounting, with managers given cost budgets for running their sections and comparative actual cost information on achievement relative to budget.

The routine of developing this cost information starts with

the classification of each cost incurred into one of three categories:

material
labour
expense

The firm is divided into a set of cost centres[1] (basically the 'departments' above) and costs will be analysed and accumulated against each centre. Some costs will arise directly and solely as a result of the activities carried on by a centre, said to be 'allocated' to it; others arise as the result of using facilities and services common to a number of other cost centres, a share of these costs being divided amongst, 'apportioned', to all centres receiving the service.

In the process of costing, the allocations are the direct costs of running the centre and may include operator wages, supervision salaries, depreciation costs of plant, insurances etc., all provided they are identifiable as arising solely within the centre. Other, indirect, costs are apportioned, for example the factory rent and rates bill, heating and lighting charges, higher level supervision and so on. Some basis must be found for making an equitable charge of these items to each centre, an obvious example being the use of the square foot floor area to divide out rent and rates; however, there is frequently a choice of the charging out method, with the resultant cost totals varying according to method adopted, i.e. not as a function of the activity of the centre.

It should also be noted that the designation of cost centres is not a fixed matter: they may be defined as narrowly as ultimate planning/control/ analytical requirements demand and as the benefits appear to exceed the costs of further and further breakdown of the information. Typically cost centres are formed within sections of the manufacturing plant e.g. machining areas, assembly areas, paint shop, perhaps even individual items of high cost plant; various section plant/ administrative service activities; sales and distribution units.

Once the initial allocations and apportionments have taken place across all cost centres, the primary basis for responsibility accounting has been obtained.

For total department costs and product costing, the process of apportionment has to be taken a stage further. Costs can be regarded as value-added to products (which may start out as raw materials, semi-finished parts or orders for a service) as each item is routed through the production unit. This means the costs attributed intially to centres not directly involved in the production process must be reapportioned to the latter areas and another formula applied to link the final production costs to the product. For example, maintenance may be one such service department whose costs could be charged to user departments on the basis of the number of man hours maintenance service they have received. Figure 10.1 illustrates the situation.

Since many service departments provide services to each other, an iterative process may be used to 'clear' their centre accounts and achieve a full reapportionment of cost to production centres.[3] Cost may then be added to products completing production operations in each centre, applying a number of possible bases:

- percentage on direct labour cost
- percentage on direct material cost
- percentage on direct prime cost (direct labour plus direct materials)
- rate per man hour
- rate per machine hour

Unfortunately, some firms choose to use the so-called 'blanket' or 'uniform' rate for all these costs lumped together, the basis for product costing usually being:

$$\frac{\text{Total Indirect Cost to be Recovered}}{\text{Total Direct Labour Cost Incurred}} \times 100$$

i.e. there is no attempt to produce separate rates for individual cost centres. Except for very simple situations, this is usually an unsound costing practice where some products may be penalised and others subsidised in relation to the facilities they use. This also means that control and other cost analyses are likely to be difficult to carry out.

The terms 'direct' and 'indirect' cost are also applied to product costing, but in a different manner from their use for department/cost centre costing. The direct costs are again the

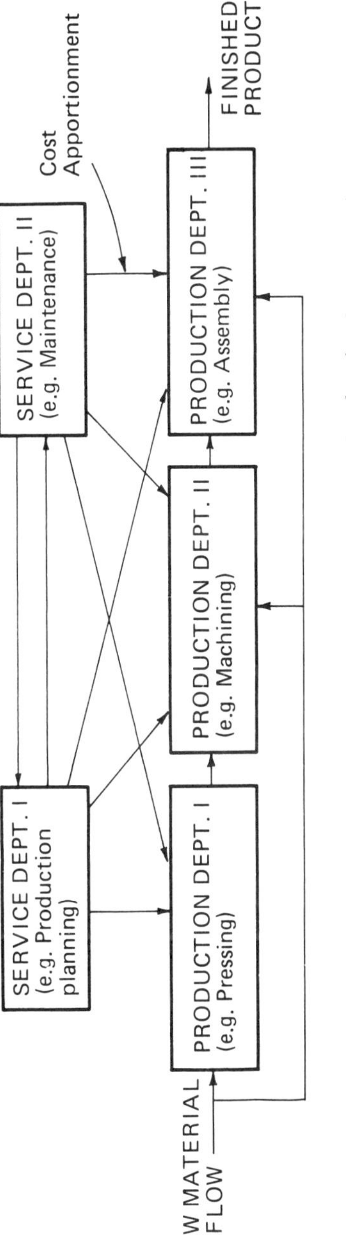

Figure 10.1 *Re-appointment of Service Department Costs to Production Department*

identifiable costs, in practice generally meaning only direct material and direct labour[1] which are identified as measurably involved in the manufacture of the product i.e. the actual materials used and the labour employed on transforming it. Most other costs are indirect in one form or another, for example the depreciation cost of a general purpose lathe will probably be spread over a range of parts which are machined on it. These indirect costs are synonymous with the more popularly used term 'overhead' cost; other terms are 'oncost' and 'burden'.

The structure of the product cost can be outlined as:

Cost Element	
Direct Costs: (Material Labour Expense)	Determined by design, work measurement allowances etc.
Indirect Factory Costs	Added to the direct costs by application of an appropriate recovery rate, for example, machine/process time required
Indirect Administration Selling and Distribution Costs	Added to total factory costs as a percentage of factory value-added, or possibly directly to a product if special identification can be made e.g. a special advertising campaign.

The same structure with modifications, is applicable to organisations whose 'product' is a service. In general, the process of costing can be seen to be very flexible. In any given case, how it is carried out will depend on company management's decision with the advice of its accountants. Enough has been described here to show why it is necessary for users to appreciate fully how the routine has been performed.[4,5]

(b) Controllable and Non-Controllable Costs

The distinction between controllable and non-controllable costs is made largely for responsibility accounting purposes.

Controllable costs are those considered to be within the individual manager's sphere of responsibility of control. Once again however, sharp distinctions cannot be drawn. For example, whilst the level of material costs incurred may clearly be affected by the efficiency of material utilisation realised by production processes under a given manager's control, at the same time his 'control' over items such as floor space, depreciation costs and so on may not appear to exist, since they are determined outside his section. However, the efficiency of the section's operation obviously affects the ease with which such costs are absorbed. All costs are controllable at some level over some period of time: clear objectives in the definition of 'controllable' *versus* 'non-controllable' are again needed.

4 Fixed and Variable Costs

A further classification of cost frequently referred to both in textbooks and in practice is the division of expenses between fixed and variable. The division is based on taking a relatively short-term view of the costs which are expected to be incurred, say in the next budget period, i.e. looking no more than 12–18 months ahead. Over a limited time span such as this, it will be found that certain expenses can be expected to remain relatively constant (fixed) regardless of the level of activity in a given department or in the business as a whole, an example being the charge for depreciation of existing buildings and plant and equipment. Some costs may be established as fixed by the process of budgeting itself, for example, how much is to be allowed for expenditure on education and training, research and development, advertising, publicity and so on. These budgeted fixed expenses though are of a different character from the kind exemplified by depreciation charges and this distinction should be borne in mind.

Variable costs are those which vary with the level of activity of a department. Truly variable costs are relatively few in number and probably the most significant is direct material. Direct labour, though often given in examples as a variable cost is really only so (and then only partially) when employees are paid on a piecework basis. Then it is only piecework payment which is the variable cost.

There is an intermediate category of semi-variable expenses, i.e. part fixed, part variable, but the items comprised here are also relatively few in number. Diagrams illustrating the respective cost functions of each of the categories are shown in figure 10.2.

The term 'activity' is used as the basic independent variable because it is a general term, which can be taken to refer to the 'output' of individual departments as well as 'output' in the more general sense of final products and services.

Diagrams like those of figure 10.2 and the general concept of fixed and variable costs are easy to draw and described and should be easy to grasp. However, this obscures the actual practical difficulties of the analysis: it is time-consuming to do; data may not be readily available; it is most unlikely that even the 'fixed' costs will be rigidly fixed and there may be a substantial scatter of actual data readings around the straight lines of the variable costs. The linearity of the cost function is often an untested assumption, especially when cost behaviour studies have not been carried out.

The breakdown of costs into fixed and variable is regarded as an essential step in deriving information for short-term planning and control and special decisions. Shortcomings in the means employed to arrive at this distinction may lead to subsequent problems, a point of caution which can only be emphasised here as a warning against adoption of too naive an approach in subsequently using the information.

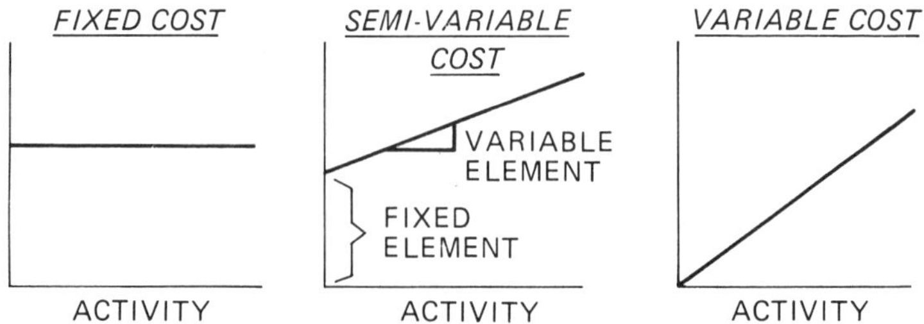

Figure 10.2 *Short-Run Classifications of Cost Variability with Level of Activity*

These then, are the fundamental classifications of cost; they are drawn on in a number of ways to produce cost analyses, but before looking at some example applications, certain cost concepts should be noted:

(a) *Full (or absorption) costs* are where all costs incurred by a company are processed through into product and department costs; specifically this includes both fixed and variable costs.
(b) *Marginal (or variable) costs,* where only variable costs are included in the analysis.
(c) *Direct costs*, where all costs whether fixed or variable, which are directly associated with a particular operation, for example, the direct operating costs of a machining centre, are included (note that direct costs in an American company may refer to marginal costs as defined in the UK).

This analysis may apply to the whole of the management accounting routine; thus we may have the accounting system referred to as 'an absorption costing' or a 'marginal costing' system. Once again, due to the very different nature of the information produced in each case, it is necessary to be completely clear about the basis employed before attempting to use that information.

In addition, the terms 'job' and/or 'process' costing[1] may be met with. These refer to the cost collection routine defined according to the nature of the industry in which a firm is operating. Job costing is conventionally found in industries where each job accepted by the firm is basically of a one-off nature in, for example, the production of large electrical generators. Each job is identified by a job order number and costs are booked directly to that number. At the other extreme, in continuous process manufacture such as is found in chemicals, petroleum refining and so on, there is no means of and no point in attempting to separate out individual orders – the product is homogeneous and is not produced in discrete batches. Here, as the name suggests, the cost accounting system is centred on the process. The mechanics of operation of the two differ, but this is not a matter of significance here, between the extremes of the pure one-off and continuous process. There are several variants of each basic type for example, to deal with batch manufacture.

Let us turn now to consider the application of costing information.

5 Standard Costing and Budgetary Control: often referred to today as Variance Accounting*

As with most cost analyses of significance, the exercise is a forward-looking one. Information on past costs is of little relevance except:

(a) as a guide to expected future costs and as a means to assist in their estimation;
(b) in order to compare actual outturns against previously estimated future costs.

Standard costing and budgetary control in a nutshell means estimating the costs and benefits of carrying out a future production programme and then keeping control of this plan through continuous comparison of actual against planned results. Should everything go according to plan, then in principle there is no need for subsequent management intervention.

If, as is more likely to be the case, the comparisons show deviations from the plan, then these are highlighted in the form of variance statements, which direct management attention to where the differences are arising, how large they are and why they are appearing. Management can concentrate attention on those areas where difficulties (or potential difficulties, where trend analysis is used) are most serious.

The system normally operates within the time period of a company's financial year and within the framework of a forecast of the sales of the goods and services it supplies. The budgets referred to included both revenue and cost budgets; to avoid the artificial impression of discrete time periods created by working to a financial year, many companies now operate 'rolling' budgets which keep the future under con-

* Author's note: readers should recognise the different use of the word 'variance' by accountants and statisticians, the latter interpreting the word as the standard deviation squared.

tinuous review: for example, as one month of a 12 month programme is completed, a further month is added at the end, so that a 12 month period is constantly being examined.

The sales budget is obtained from forecast sales quantities (see Chapter 23) and expected prices. So far as the activity of the organisation is concerned, management has to ensure that a forecast presented to it is realistic, acceptable and within the capacity of company resources to complete. Once agreed this way, it becomes the focus around which all other budgets and standards are developed, and is often referred to as the Master Budget of Sales. It may well be the case of course, that a realistic sales forecast cannot be achieved within a company's current level of resources, when the practical operating capacity level will become the focus for the budgeting process; the practical capacity could also be constrained for many reasons: shortages of skilled labour; material supplies; machining capacity, being amongst obvious examples.

Whatever the limiting factors – market size, machine time etc., budgets are drawn up to be consistent with them. They may be classified for many purposes: by the nature of the expense involved e.g. the labour and materials budgets; by function e.g. production, administration; by department or budget centre. Planning and control aspects are present in all cases, but it is the budget centre budgets which are more important here, because direct managerial responsibility is exercised most widely at this level.

Individual managers participate in the budget process (or should do), providing estimates of resource requirements and costs for their centres to meet planned activity levels, agreeing proposed changes for services from outside departments, perhaps having to agree to modifications to their own initial estimates. The extent of involvement naturally varies with the position in the managerial hierarchy and the extent of responsibility for operations. Foremen for example, will typically be held accountable for labour and material utilisation, plant utilisation and the level of direct services such as maintenance required; their main responsibility lies with the physical consumption of these resources and not the prices which have to be paid for them, though as an example of the kind of controversy that can arise, responsibility for higher than expected prices being paid for material could be attributed to a foreman when poor utilisation has led a buyer to have to purchase further quantities in smaller batches at less advantageous prices.

Budgets then, are created for defined 'budget centre' areas of activity, but where does the basic information come from for them?

(a) Standard Cost

Any cost figure is composed of two elements: quantity and price per unit. Where it is sensible to measure each one individually, a standard may be set relating to a standard quantity usage and a standard price to be paid. These standards should be based on agreed future levels of usage and price. To take the examples of direct material and labour:

	Standard	*Measured/Determined by*
Direct Material	Usage	Methods Engineer
	Price	Buyer
Direct Labour	Efficiency	Work Study/Measurement
	Rate	Personnel/Company Management

Thus if the level of activity agreed calls for 100,000 units of output and the agreed standards for material are 0.5 kg per unit of output at a price of £1.0 per kg, the budget for material is obviously £50,000. Other items which can be broken down and measured in a similar manner will produce budgets in a similar way.

A standard then is a unit concept: unit of resource required per unit and price per unit of resource. For many items however, the unit standard will be obtained from a total budget figure which cannot be broken down into its component elements, for example depreciation of plant, equipment and buildings.

An amount representing the depreciation of these assets will be included in absorption costing: to obtain a standard cost per unit of product, the calculation will be:

$$\frac{\text{Total Depreciation (£)}}{\text{Total Budgeted Activity (Standard Hours)}}$$

The standard hour concept introduced here is a measurement

of work content rather than time, though the initial basis is frequently:

1 Standard hour = 1 Clock hour

i.e. the amount of work represented by one standard hour is determined as the quantity of output, net of allowances, achievable in one hour's time at an agreed pace of working. It is the common denominator for measuring output in the usual situation where a company produces a number of heterogeneous products, e.g. chairs, tables, cupboards, where common production facilities may be used. To plan capacity requirements and assess plant utilisation, production programmes in this case must be calculated in terms of the number of standard hours required to complete each operation: the capacity requirements to manufacture a chair then become comparable with those for manufacturing a table.

A standard product (full) cost is then obtained as follows:

Cost Element	*Measured as :*	*Standard cost per unit (£)*
Standard Direct Material	Number of kilograms per unit × standard price per kg	'*a*'
Standard Direct Labour	Number of standard hours to complete product × standard direct labour cost rate per hour	'*b*'
Standard Indirect Cost:		
(i) Variable	As for direct labour or on a total budget	'*c*'
(ii) Fixed	Total budget ÷ budgeted level of activity	'*d*'
TOTAL		$a+b+c+d$

(b) Cost Control

Having established a planned level of activity (the master budget of sales) and costed it out on the basis of standards, attention is subsequently directed toward maintaining the plan in the light of actual results. Correction to deviations from plan are carried out on an *ad hoc* basis, though continuous uni-directional changes may ultimately force a revision of either the whole or some element of the original plan. It is a management by exception approach – if the plan were to be achieved perfectly, there would be no need for management intervention.

(c) Cost/Budget Variances

Deviations are indicated by the variances, simple arithmetic differences: expected cost (revenue) minus standard/budget cost (revenue).

An example variance calculation is as follows:

Assume 10,000 components have been manufactured, with a standard direct material allowance of 1 kg per component and a standard price of £1/kg. Material drawn from stores was 10,500 kilogrammes and the actual price paid for the material was £1.05/kg.

If the standards had been followed, we *should* have only required 10,000 kgs from store and the total price paid for the batch *should* have been £10,000. Thus the differences from expected cost are:

Total variance	£11,550 (actually paid) minus £10,000 (expected cost) = £1550.
Price Variance	10,500 (£1.10 – £1.00) = £1050 (unfavourable)
Quantity Variance	£1.00 (10,500 – 10,000) = £500 (unfavourable)

The manner of calculation of the individual variances applies to all cases where it is possible to break down the cost between a quantity and a price element. It will also be observed there is an implicit assumption that total cost of the item in question (direct material here) is proportionately *variable* with the quantity used. Unfortunately, the terms applied to the variances differ: 'usage', 'efficiency' and 'productivity' are terms used to describe quantity variances; 'price' and 'rate' to the price variances.

The main variances may be further sub-divided, for example,

material usage could be refined to obtain that part of the difference due to variations in the *mix* of materials (e.g. in an alloy) and the *yield* from a process (e.g. a certain loss is usually allowed for in a metal casting process).

A further important category is the *volume* variance. This arises in respect of fixed costs and actual level compared to the planned level of activity. Assume that the total fixed cost is correctly estimated at £100,000 and that plant activity was forecast at 100,000 standards hours' output based on the master sales budget. The recovery rate for fixed expenses for purposes of standard cost calculations is obviously £1.0/std. hr. Assume the actual number of standard hours produced to have been 90,000, then the recovery of fixed costs in production will have been only £90,000 – an under-recovery of £10,000.

By comparison with truly variable costs, an under-recovery of fixed costs resulting from a fall in planned output represents a definite loss; conversely, when output is higher than planned. The volume variance can also be subdivided into several components: of principal interest are capacity variances arising from differences in planned against actual capacity utilisation and efficiency/productivity variances, due to producing a greater/smaller quantity than standard performance during actual operation time.

For control purposes it will generally be necessary for analysis of variances to take place as close to the event in time which caused them as possible. With modern data processing methods this is not such a problem as formerly: the further away in time that the analysis takes place, the less likely is it that causal events will be properly recalled and effective action taken. It is frequently possible to reduce the delay period for comparisons to be made by working on the physical variances alone, e.g. labour time and material usage, without waiting for a fully costed statement to appear.

Deciding which variances are worth investigating also poses a problem. Since some variance from expected cost will probably be the order of the day for a large number of items, it will be necessary to select the most significant of these to analyse: to attempt to appraise them all would be too time-consuming and expensive. No totally satisfactory guide can be given, but one yardstick which may assist is to consider the ratio:

$$\frac{\text{Standard Cost Variance}}{\text{Original Standard Cost}}$$

This provides a scaling factor, though it must still be seen in relation to the absolute size of the variance and original standard cost.

(d) Reconciliation of Planned with Actual Results

The master budget for a commercial organisation will clearly centre round a realistic and acceptable target profit figure, probably related to the value of capital required to support it. Variances from standard and the budgets derived from the master plan will ultimately lead to a difference of actual against forecast profit. When end-period accounts are drawn up – annual, quarterly etc. – a reconciliation of budgeted against actual profit will be made. An outline of this is as follows:

		£
	Budgeted Sales	a
Add or *Subtract*:	Sales Variances	
	Mix Volume	b
	Actual Sales	$a \pm b$
Less:	Standard Cost of Actual Sales	c
	Standard Profit in Actual Sales	$d = a \pm b - c$
Add or *Subtract*:	Cost Variances	
	Material Labour Indirect Expense	e
	Actual Profit	$d \pm e$

Figure 10.3 illustrates how the standard cost variances pyramid down from the variance on the expected operating profit.

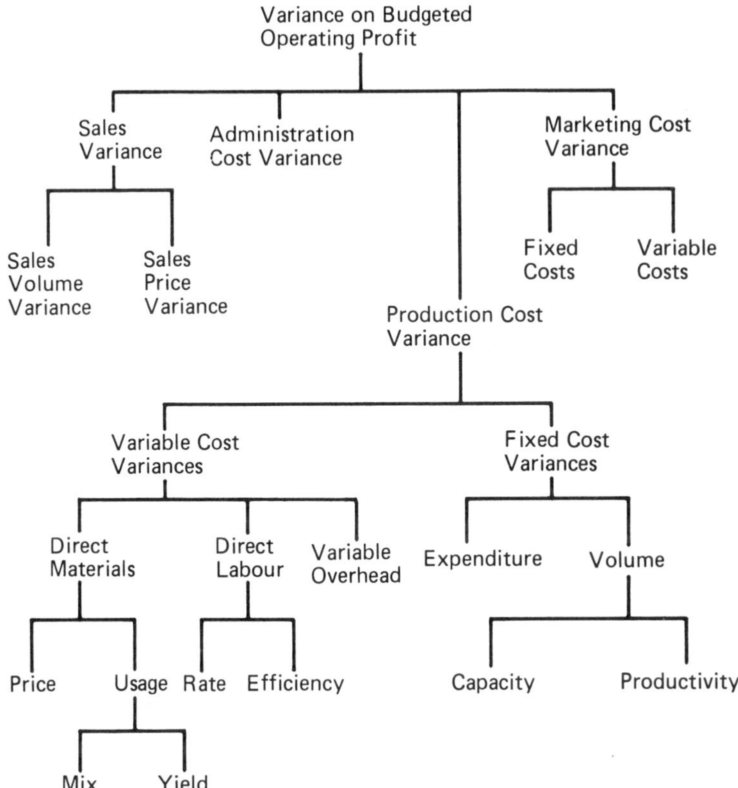

Figure 10.3 *Diagram Illustrating the Link between the Overall Variance on Budgeted Profit and the Individual Contributory Elements (each can be further subdivided to provide greater detail.)*

6 Costs for Planning and Special Decision-Making

It should be realised that even the most comprehensive costing/standard costing system is unlikely to be able to supply all the information for making all planning and other special decisions. For example, it would be most unlikely to be able to find a figure for 'cost of lost sales' say, due to a machine breakdown. This information generally has to be put together as a special exercise. Even where decision information can be readily obtained from the system, the user has to ensure that the data really is relevant to the solution of the problem on hand. Information for planning and decision-making may well cut across lines of traditional cost classification. The user guide is to think in terms of the information 'relevant' to the problem and to be wary of simply accepting figures which are described in a way which seems to fit what is required, for example to use a figure for product profit per unit when what is really required is product profitability.

There are many areas of analysis where this approach to obtaining data has to be used. Some common ones are:

Product profitability
Make or buy
Manufacturing method
Stock-holding policy
Product pricing
Transfer pricing
Cost of labour turnover
Cost of machine down-time

Note that these problems refer to the short-run period and do not include any capital expenditure element.

(a) Product Profitability

The agreed master budget plan described in Section 5, results in a certain standard profit forecast. This is aggregated from the forecast sales of the individual product/service lines supplied, less the estimated costs of those sales. The question now is how to determine the mix and quantity of these individual lines which gives an acceptable profit performance.

The key here is to distinguish profit per unit from profitability. The latter defines a product's profit earning capacity. Conventionally, *profit per unit* is found as:

price per unit *less* absorption cost per unit.

It is the absorption cost which is the non-relevant figure here. The required cost is basically the marginal (or variable) product cost. Providing a company has made an analysis of cost behaviour patterns and made an appropriate classification of costs into fixed and variable elements, it should not be difficult to obtain the marginal products costs; even if the underlying accounting principle is absorption costing, a company using a standard costing system usually will have variable cost information built into the flexible budget.

Profitability is measured by a product's *contribution margin.* This is the difference:

price per unit *minus* variable cost per unit.

Essentially, by concentrating on those product lines which return the highest contribution in relation to the resources they require, the company will ultimately maximise its net profit figure. The reasoning simply is that provided fixed costs have been correctly defined for the short-run period in question, then their total cost is not going to change, hence the only relevant costs to consider are those which will change as a result of a decision of the kind to produce more of product *X* and less of product *Y*, i.e. the variable/marginal costs. The greater the total contribution that can be earned, the more effectively is fixed cost covered and the greater the resulting net profit figure. However, productive resources are not unlimited and therefore contribution earned must be related to the quantity of resources required to generate a product's contribution figure: the ultimate guide is contribution per unit of resource consumed. A simple numerical example illustrates this:

Given the following 4 products, which should be produced on the basis of the following information, given that only 9000 production hours are available?

	PRODUCTS			
	A	*B*	*C*	*D*
Sales Demand (units)	5000	4000	3000	6000
Contribution per unit (£)	5	6	6	2
Production Time (hours per unit)	2	3	2	1
Contribution per production hour (£)	2.5	2	3	2

As *C* offers the highest contribution per product hour, the total sales demand for C of 3000 should be produced which takes 6000 hours. This leaves only 3000 hours for product A which is next best in order of priority at £2.50 per product hour, resulting in a 3000/2 = 1500 unit production run.

Solution: Make 3000 units C = £18,000
Make 1500 units A = £7,500
Total Contribution = £25,500

No other solution produces a higher total contribution or therefore, a higher final net profit figure. If it is not acceptable that only C & A should be produced and in this particular combination, then the cost of departure from the plan will be immediately apparent.

Production time is the only resource constraint in the example; more realistically there could be many present such as market size, materials, labour skills etc. Where there are a number of constraints operating simultaneously on a large number of product lines, then a more formal mathematical[6,7] method has to be adopted to obtain an answer.

(b) *Make or Buy*

Assume a short-run situation where capacity on a machine or group of machines is insufficient to meet demand; the manufacturer has to purchase supplies from outside suppliers to meet the full production programme. Again, another four products are assumed to be involved, with the following relevant production and cost data:

	A	*B*	*C*	*D*
Production				
Units per machine hour	0.25	0.4	0.5	1.00
Costs per unit				
Marginal cost (p)	20	30	18	13
Fixed Cost (p)	8	14	6	4
Total Cost (p)	28	44	24	17

Outside Supplier				
Price (p)	30	42	25	15

Apparently the internal cost of manufacture inside is higher in some cases than buying from the outside supplier, but it would be wrong to assume these are necessarily the best candidates for outside purchase. The objective of this exercise is to obtain the extra supplies for the least cost: the marginal cost of internal manufacture is lower in all cases than the outside price, but the total fixed cost will not change, whether manufacture takes place inside or outside the company; in any event, since a full capacity situation is being considered, it is fully absorbed. So fixed costs are not relevant to the problem and neither therefore are the total costs. The relevant comparison is the marginal cost of internal manufacture against the outside supplier price and in relation to the machine capacity (productive time) released by subcontracting a unit of one of the products. Thus a unit of Product *D* purchased outside saves one machine hour for an extra cost of 2p; Product *A* saves 4 machine hours for an extra cost of 10p, i.e. 2.5p per machine hour. The least cost order priority sequence for outside purchase on this basis will be found to be DACB. This cost based approach to planning sub-contract work at least affords a logical approach to the problem.

(c) Other Decision Problems

Space does not allow for further detailed examples; all that can be said is that marginal/variable cost analysis often presents a starting point for the process of determining relevant costs. As the extent of a problem increases, it may be necessary to consider the so-called 'incremental' costs, i.e. ones which arise when changes contemplated reach a certain level. For example, if output is increased beyond a certain point, it may become necessary to employ another chargehand or foreman, more direct service labour and so on.

(d) Production Planning and Control and Costing

A brief section now indicates the inter-relationship of an activity such as production planning with cost and financial effects. Production planners will often participate in the establishment of the agreed budget production programme. Therefore, they have the month by month task of detailed planning and monitoring results.

The original budget will have assumed a certain level of capacity utilisation and probably an estimate of the frequency that machines will require re-setting, in order that the production unit is properly serviced by machine setters. Matters frequently go wrong, for example, when unexpected machine breakdowns or interruptions to material supplies occur, or an attempt is made to give priority to a new order just obtained. All these factors interrupt the pattern of the original plans and efforts to restore the latter can often make things financially more serious, for example, if, in order to keep customers going after a shortfall in production has occurred, machines are changed over to different products and re-set more frequently than originally envisaged, production runs will tend to be shorter and batch costs inevitably higher. The situation then develops a vicious spiral of its own because the more frequent changeovers lose more production time and so it becomes increasingly more difficult to meet customer orders.

In addition, failure to meet plans then may affect the cash flow of the business, again to an ever-increasing extent; penalties may be incurred; administrative costs rise; problems with export documentation and its cost will also often appear. These are just a few examples of possible consequences.

Financial difficulties often result in demands to reduce stock levels. Once again, however, without a proper cost analysis, the supposed cure by saving on costs of stockholding may produce a situation much worse, by the impact on factory operation raising the level of operating costs.

7 Conclusion

In reality, no aspect of business activity can avoid having a cost consequence. The latter may be very complex in its individual elements and their inter-relationships, but every effort should be made to understand them and how they function; to do otherwise means a great deal of guesswork in management.

References and Further Reading

1 *Terminology of Management and Financial Accountancy*, Institute of Cost and Management Accountants 1974.
2 *Life-Cycle Costing in the Management of Assets :A Practical Guide*, Department of Industry 1977.
3 Churchill, N., Linear algebra and cost allocations: some examples, *Accounting Review*, October 1964.
4 Sizer, J., *An Insight into Management Accounting*, Pelican 1979.
5 Horngren, C.T., *Cost Accounting: A Managerial Emphasis*, Prentice-Hall 1979.
6 Lucey, T., *Quantitative Techniques*, DP Publications 1979.
7 Taffler, R., *Using Operational Research*, Prentice-Hall 1979.

11
Ely's Drop Forge Ltd

J B COATES

Senior Lecturer in Accounting,
The University of Aston

1 Introduction

Ely's Drop Forge is a typical black country forge, of medium size, employing 75 direct operators and 40 indirect/staff employees. It is heavily associated with motor industry production and its fortunes naturally reflect those of the motor industry in general. The management of the company has tended to view accounting as a distinctly non-productive expense in the past and consequently maintains only the simplest (and incomplete) costing routines; final accounts are produced according to the requirements of the Companies Acts.

However, on the engineering side, management prides itself on having a programme of modernisation and technical advance in production equipment and has an efficient (again in the equipment availability sense) die-sinking capacity within the firm. Altogether, its technical expertise, both with respect to the equipment it owns and its operators, maintenance, production and design engineering staff and production management, is of good standard. Quality of goods produced is also high.

Currently the firm is anticipating that it will experience over the next two years one of the most serious trade recessions for some time which will affect in varying degrees all the markets it supplies. Management therefore decided to carry out a study of the company's efficiency in production from a financial point of view, to see what economies could be made either from cutting out certain activities and expenditures or instituting better controls where possible. In addition, it was decided to study proposed orders more closely from now on to see how profitable they really were. (In the past, orders were accepted at a price which 'seemed' reasonable, without any detailed calculation of profit and little understanding of what was meant by the term 'profitable'; furthermore, it had been policy to meet customer requirements at all times.)

The company has recently taken on a new accountant with considerable interest in costing and management accounting aspects. He believes that substantially improved management accounting information would be of great value to management decision-making in the current situation and also that with modern data collection and processing equipment the expense of introducing the systems basic to providing this information would not be excessive.

The company's production area consists of:

(a) Raw material store
(b) Forge furnace
(c) Hammer and forging presses
(d) Clipping presses
(e) Bending, straightening and coining presses
(f) Cutting off equipment
(g) Heat treatment
(h) Testing
(i) Finished goods store and despatch area
(j) Die tool store

Fixtures and small tools principally for the tool room are purchased directly from outside when required or made internally.

A production incentive scheme is part of the direct labour payment system, so reasonable records exist related to production output rates. Stores' issues of raw material against production orders have been well recorded, so that material utilisation rates can be established with reasonable accuracy.

Production is concentrated on the following product groups:

crankshafts
con-rods
steering arms
suspension links

but wide variations exist within the main groups, for example, as between parts for cars and commercial vehicles.

Initial Cost Analysis

A preliminary investigation of costs based on actual costs incurred over the past twelve months provides the following information:

Raw material: Steel bar
sizes: 75 mm–250 mm
costs vary according to size

Direct Operator Rates (Basic):
£2.00/hour
(operators are paid a bonus on top of basic wages in relation to agreed output rates on batches of goods produced, which on average bring operator rates to £3/hour)

Production Overhead: (with an estimated breakdown between fixed and variable cost elements).

	Variable £	Fixed £	Total £
Direct Labour (including holiday pay, NHI etc)	–	30,000	30,000
Production management and services staff such as planners, designers etc.		60,000	
Depreciation of Plant	–	100,000	100,000
Maintenance	5,000	15,000	20,000
Power, light, heat	40,000	20,000	60,000
Consumable stores	2,000	1,000	3,000
Shop floor clerical wages	–	8,000	8,000
	47,000	234,000	281,000

Tool Room:

	Variable	Fixed	Total
Operator Wages & holiday pay, NHI etc		25,000	25,000
Depreciation of Plant		50,000	50,000
Power, light, heat	2,000	1,000	3,000
Consumable Stores	500	100	600
	2,500	76,100	78,600

Planning of work for the tool-room is the responsibility of the senior tool-room operator, working in conjunction with the production manager and design engineer.

Administration, Selling and Distribution:

	Variable £	Fixed £	Total £
Administration	–	80,000	50,000
Selling & Distribution	10,000	60,000	60,000
	10,000	140,000	150,000

Administration expenses are largely salaries; distribution expenses inlcude a bonus element based on value of orders obtained paid to sales engineers (who also act as salesmen) as well as vehicle depreciation and other running costs.

Production management aim to achieve 55% production plant utilisation in general. The remainder of the time goes on set-up, maintenance and operator allowances. A year ago substantial overtime was being worked, including some week-end working. This has now been stopped with the agreement of the workforce due to the relatively low level of orders and the likelihood of further weakening of the market. It means that there are no serious capacity restrictions on output, but management wishes to be able to identify more clearly the break-even point of the plant overall.

Three orders recently obtained are presented here for analysis; cost estimates and customer proposed prices are given.

	Orders		
	A	*B*	*C*
Total quantity (units)			
per annum	50,000	10,000	2,000
per 4-week period (units)	4,000	800	
weekly (units)			40
Set-up time (Hours)	3	5	7
Total Production Operation Times per Batch (Hours)	40	20	10
Costs per Batch (£) (Summarised totals)			
Direct Material	250	60	20
Direct Labour	120	60	30
Set-up	18	30	42
Total Overhead Additions:			
Fixed	260	130	90
Variable	24	12	10
Tool & Die	40	20	15
	702	312	207
Price Customer willing to pay (per batch, inclusive of set-up & tool-charge)	£720	£280	£175

In view of the anticipated down-turn in activity, management wishes to know what arguments there are in favour of accepting any of these orders.

2 Terms of Reference

The first task of the new company accountant was to consider the following questions:

(a) How should the structure of the company be analysed from a costing point of view, i.e. how should it be broken down into sections (cost centres) for purposes of collection and analysis of cost data? What costing methods should be adopted?

(b) How should cost estimates for orders be provided such that realistic pricing could be done and comparisons of actual costs made against the original estimates?

(c) On the basis of the data provided could a general break-even point for the plant be established?

(d) Give specific examples as to how *A, B* & *C* could be analysed to show whether or not they should be accepted, and if not, at what prices could they be accepted?

(e) What additional cost analysis would be required beyond those suggested?

3 Suggested Proposals from the Company Accountant

(Not to be taken as exhaustive or necessarily of 'best practice' for the industry chosen as the context of the case study).

(a) Structure

The first proposal is to divide the company into various sections so that costs can be analysed more clearly in relation to the functions performed. This will provide a basis both for planning ahead and control of expenditure.

Activities could be separated out as follows:

Production Units:

Forge furnace
Hammers
Forging presses
Clipping presses
Bending, straightening and coining presses
Cut-off equipment
Heat treatment
Testing
Materials handling
Production management & supervision

Tool-room
Stores
Production Service Departments (planning, design etc)
Administration
Selling & Distribution

Costing/estimating should aim to derive material and direct labour cost and usage rates as accurately as possible, together with set-up and tool costs, for individual orders. Indirect (overhead) expenses should then be recovered in a realistic manner: some companies for example might only have a single recovery rate for the whole of the production unit. For Ely's it is suggested that although the final market is broadly defined as the 'motor industry', the range of products obviously implies a range in production equipment which should be distinguished for costing purposes.

Tonnage of output is a traditional measure in the drop forging industry; direct labour costs are also widely used as a means of overhead recovery. However, it is proposed that consideration should be given to establishing the following overhead recovery rates for the various cost centres:

(i) based on tonnage for materials handling, heat treatment;
(ii) machine hour rates for main sections in both the production department and tool room as well as operating hours for the forge furnace,
(iii) direct labour hour rates for benching operations;
(iv) set-up times to be estimated as accurately as possible;
(v) allocations and apportionments for general overhead expenses such as rates, insurances, supervision, management and administration to be made on equitable bases and included in the hourly rates;
(vi) selling and distribution expenses to be recovered in general on the value-added element of factory costs.

The above implies that unit costs and ultimately estimated costs for orders will be based on the absorption costing principle. However, with the basic split given between variable and fixed cost elements, it will be indicated later how the marginal costing principle can be adopted to provide the product profitability requested by management.

(b) Cost Estimation

Where orders for particular products are for large quantities over long periods, work measurement techniques are currently used to establish standard production methods and rates. Estimation is scarcely a problem in these cases and estimates provided for re-negotiation of contracts should be relatively easy to up-date.

Problems for cost estimation tend to arise on small batch enquiries, where these are received at irregular intervals and include many non-standard items. The company needs to be able to respond as rapidly and realistically to these enquiries as it does for the 'main' items; the dangers of not doing so are on the one hand lost opportunities or on the other the possible acceptance of unprofitable work. The means to respond rapidly and realistically are often not available or rest on the experience of a single person who has worked with the company for a long time.

A basic guide for this small order work is to keep good records of what has actually been done on past orders. 'Near-neighbour' comparisons – i.e. matching new enquiries with similar orders received and executed in the past – can provide very useful information. Organisation of data collection and a referencing system have to be given considerable care and attention, and include not only the production data, but die and tool information as well.

An outline cost estimation sheet is shown overpage to illustrate what could be done.

A similar document allowing comparison of actuals with estimates should be used to summarise the out-turn on each job.

A further subdivision on these documents would break the cost figures down into their cost estimate sheet.

(c) Estimation of the Break-even Position as Expressed in Terms of Capacity Utilisation

It is sometimes difficult to define this unit of measurement for the plant as a whole, but it can be expressed in terms of potential operating hours (given the number of shifts to be worked) derived from production plant operating hours or direct labour hours.

Total costs and revenues can then be related to capacity utilisation, distinguishing the fixed and variable cost elements in the total costs. The break-even point can also be found algebraically in terms of cost or quantity, but this requires specification of a budgeted contribution margin, perhaps used as a target for all orders to aim for.

COST ESTIMATE No.

Material specification . . . . Customer. . . . .
Description . . . .
Production Method . . . . Part Number . . . . . .

Production Cost Estimate	£ p	*Die & Tool Cost Estimate**	£ p
1. Material Quantities (gross, net) @ £/ton		1. Die Materials and tools	
2. Material Handling @ £/ton		2. Die & Tool Costs:	
3. Forge Furnacing @ £/hour		(a) machinery (various operations) @ £/hour	
4. Set-up Hours @ £/hour		(b) Bench-work @ £/hour	
5. Forging Hours @ £/hour		3. Total Cost	
6. Heat Treatment £/ton			
7. Brinell		Die & Tool Cost per Forging: $= \frac{\text{(3) Total Cost}}{\text{Number of Forgings per Impression}}$	
8. Inspect and Test £/hour			
9. Dies & Tools £/forging			
10. Carriage			
11. Total Estimated Cost			
12. Profit Margin			
13. Selling Price			

*N.B. Distinguish new dies, resinks and repairs

From the company data already available, together with sales revenue, direct material and direct labour, the company can be shown to have the following total revenue and cost position:

			£
Total Revenue:			1,100,000
Total Cost:	Variable	Fixed	
	£	£	
Direct Material	300,000		
Direct Labour	100,000	200,000	
Production Overhead	47,000	234,000	
Tool Room	2,500	76,100	
Administration, Selling & Distribution	10,000	140,000	
Total	359,500	650,100	1,009,600
Net Profit (before tax etc.)			90,400

This information relates to a practical capacity of 3500 operating hours per week over a 50 week period and actual utilisation of 2000 hours per week. Cost and revenue functions are assumed to have a linear relationship with operating hours.

The break-even chart (figure 11.1) illustrates how tight the current position is – a decline of about 11% from the present operating level brings the company to the break-even point. If it can be assumed that costs are under control, then given the company's normal capacity utilisation it can be seen that sales margins have probably already been severely squeezed with little profit in the operation, even when it is well up with anticipated utilisation figures. (Higher product prices would increase the slope of the Total Revenue line.)

The overall contribution earned was £740,500, the difference between Total Revenue and Total Variable Costs. A target contribution rate could therefore be expressed as:

£0.74 per production hour,

to maintain existing rates. Contribution is also the measure of

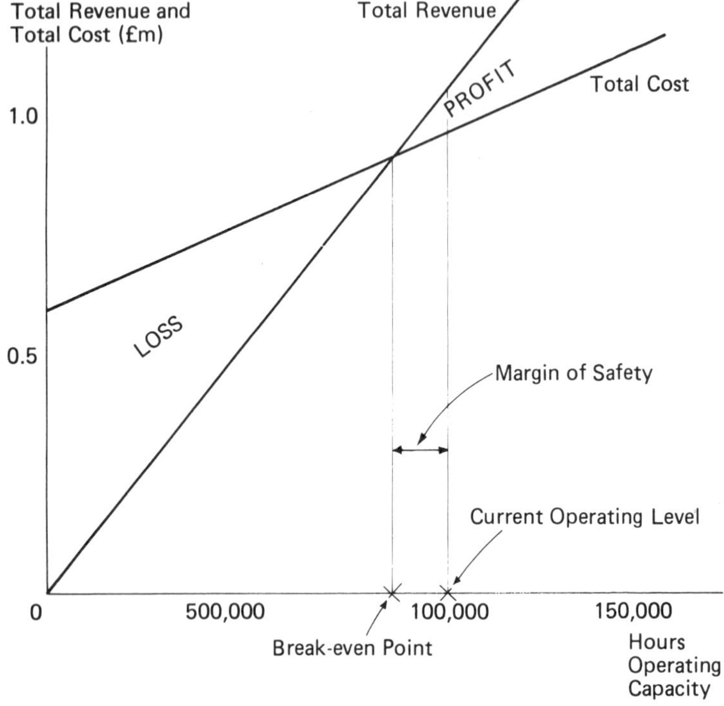

Figure 11.1 *Break-even Analysis for Ely's Drop Forge Ltd*

product profitability. Calculating the financial (sales) break-even point algebraically gives us:

$$\frac{\text{Total Fixed Costs (£)}}{\text{Total Contribution (£)}} \times 100 = \frac{650{,}100}{740{,}500} \times \text{£}00 = 87.8\%$$

of the current actual production hours.

(d) Examples of the Cost Implications of Specific Orders

Order A Gives a positive contribution and a net profit, provided the call-off rate does not become too frequent, and is well within the hoped-for plant utilisation range. Compare estimated contribution with target contribution (similarly for *B* & *C*).

Order B Net profit is negative; however, there is a positive contribution to the fixed costs of the business and hence the order would be worth considering in terms of a declining market, certainly so unless it is strongly felt that to accept the order would weaken the company's bargaining position against the customer in question both now and in the future. Taken at face value on the full cost basis it would receive less chance of being accepted.

Order C It is more questionable for this order to be accepted. Although there is a positive contribution, the terms attached to delivery would mean a low plant utilisation rate if set-ups followed the call off rate, certainly if it were matched by similar requirements in other orders. Even though the extra set-up costs may be covered in the estimated price per batch, the capacity loss may not be compensated for and if work has to be accepted at prices which do not produce a profit, this one deals a double disadvantage by demanding above average plant time, (but is it comparable with similar orders on the type of plant required?).

4 Conclusion

Clearly for future planning, an estimated sales volume should be projected, together with appropriate selling price and cost of production estimates. From the broad projection of activity level, up-dated cost rates and prices, an overall contribution target can be established, broken down by different classes of business. This serves as a yardstick for acceptability of orders in terms of the plan.

If feasible, the plan should be developed for a range of projected levels of activity and price/cost combinations. This would permit upper and lower limits to be studied and the final plan to be determined in the light of assessed variations.

12
Operations Planning and Control

D J BENNETT

Senior Lecturer in Operations Management, The University of Aston

1 Introduction – Control of Operations Systems

In any manufacturing or service industry, good planning and control is an essential part of the efficient day to day running of the various productive activities.

It is the intention in this chapter therefore to describe the concept of control and to present the various approaches and techniques that may be used in order to make most effective use of the resources available.

A great deal is said about industries becoming more 'productive' via investment in new machinery and equipment. However, surveys have shown that in many organisations, the most significant reason for low productivity is under-utilisation of existing resources due to poor planning and control, material shortages, inefficient labour allocation etc.

Before describing individual problem areas and their solutions however, it is important to discuss briefly the concept of control in the operations management context and to describe the basic elements of an operations system.

Any operations system is a process which seeks to transform inputs (capital, materials, labour etc) into outputs (goods and

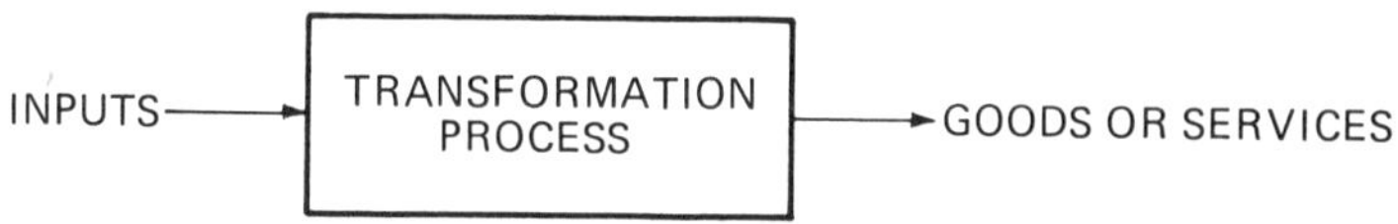

Figure 12.1 *An Open-Loop Operations System*

services). This process can therefore be represented in a simple diagrammatic form (figure 12.1).

The system illustrated is termed the 'open-loop' type. As it stands, however, such a system suffers from a lack of control in that the output quantity, quality, time, mix etc. may fail to meet the organisational objectives. A closed-loop system on the other hand measures some feature of the output and feeds this back to a comparator which regulates the process on the basis of any deviations from the set objectives (figure 12.2.)

To a production manager, the most important features of a manufactured product which must be controlled are quality and production information. Thus the main areas of interest are quality control and production control.

Quality control will be dealt with in Chapter 21, so we shall concentrate here on the planning and control of production activities while, at the same time, considering how these can relate to a service environment.

2 Optimising the Product Mix

A major, but in practice often ignored, aspect of production planning relates to finding the best mix of products or services.

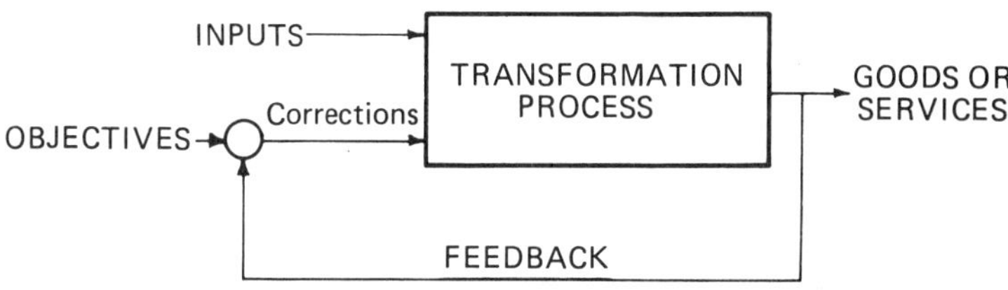

Figure 12.2 *A Closed-Loop Operations System*

The term 'best' in this context is obviously bound by the overall objectives of the organisation. However, the main objective of most operations is either profit maximisation or cost minimisation (exceptions to this may be charities, armed services etc. which may be set-up for humane or strategic reasons). Therefore, the optimum will be that mix of products or services which seeks to satisfy an overall profit or cost objective.

In considering profit maximisation as an objective, it is self evident that maximum profit is not obtained solely by maximising output since certain products and services may be inherently more profitable than others. In theory, therefore, the organisation might only concentrate on those which provide the greatest individual profit. However, this is not usually realistic, due to the constraints which exist in terms of material and labour availability, capacity of facilities, market requirements and so on.

The real nature of the problem is so complex that the immediate reaction is to tackle it merely by intuition. It may be appropriate, however, to reduce the real situation to a model which only contains those factors and dimensions that are strongly related to the organisational objectives.

Assume for instance that several products or services (n) are being considered. If X_j is the number of each produced and C_j is the profit per unit, then the total profit would be:

$$P = \sum_{j=1}^{n} C_j X_j = C_1 X_1 + C_2 X_2 \ldots C_n X_n$$

This would then be subject to a number of constraints. For instance, if only b units of material were available for use and each product used a_j units then:

$$\sum_{j=1}^{n} a_j X_j = a_1 X_1 + a_2 X_2 \ldots a_n X_n \leqslant b$$

and so on for the other resources.

This approach obviously assumes a linear relationship between quantity and profit, material usage etc. Hence the term 'linear programming' which is used to describe this type of model.

Complex computer programmes using the 'Simplex' algorithm are available which can solve problems comprising a large number of variables (different products or services). However, the general approach may be demonstrated by a two variable problem which it is possible to solve graphically.

Example

A manufacturer is engaged in the manufacture of two types of glue, 'Holdtite' and 'Fastbond'. The profit from Holdtite is £300 per tonne and from Fastbond it is £450 per tonne.

Both glues require processing through the same three plants: *A*, *B* and *C*, having weekly capacities of 24, 44 and 60 hours respectively. Plant capacity is the only constraint on output.

Processing times per tonne in the three plants are as follows:

	Plant *A*	Plant *B*	Plant *C*
'Holdtite'	4 hours	4 hours	12 hours
'Fastbond'	4 hours	10 hours	6 hours

Evaluate the weekly quantities of each glue which should be produced in order to maximise profit.

If the weekly quantitites of Holdtite and Fastbond are X_1 and X_2 respectively, then the total profit P obtained would be:

$$P = 300\,X_1 + 450\,X_2$$

The constraints are the three plant capacities, i.e.:

For Plant *A*	$4X_1 + 4X_2 \leqslant 24$
For Plant *B*	$4X_1 + 10X_2 \leqslant 44$
For Plant *C*	$12X_1 + 6X_2 \leqslant 60$

Negative quantities cannot be made, so for completeness:

$$X_1 \geqslant 0 \quad \text{and} \quad X_2 \geqslant 0$$

Plotting the constraints using X_1 and X_2 as axes will give a *feasible area* in which any solution must lie (figure 12.3).

An arbitrary profit line is now drawn. Assuming a profit of, say, £900 then:

$$900 = 300\,X_1 + 450\,X_2$$

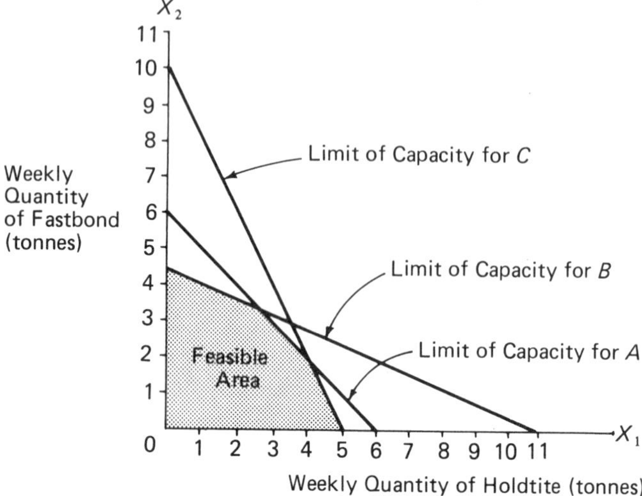

Figure 12.3 *Feasible Area for Product Mix Problem*

This profit line is shown plotted in figure 12.4. The maximum profit line is a line parallel to the arbitrary profit line which just touches the bound of the feasible area. The values of X_1 and X_2 at this extreme point are the quantities of Holdtite and Fastbond which produce the largest weekly profit. In this case it is 2.7 tonnes and 3.4 tonnes respectively. Yielding a profit of (2.7 X 300) + (3.4 X 450) = £2340.

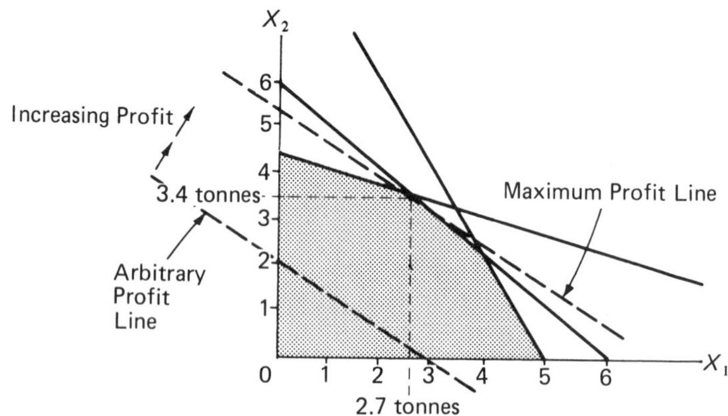

Figure 12.4 *Maximising Profit for Product Mix Problem*

This same graphical technique cannot obviously be applied to a problem with more than two variables, so the approach used is to analyse the resultant multi-dimensional model to identify that 'corner' or 'edge' which will yield maximum profit. The Simplex method (see Sasieni, Yaspan & Friedman)[1] is an iterative procedure which does this by investigating each apex in a logical fashion until a solution is found on which no improvement can be made.

The practical deficiencies of the linear programming approach must be recognised by operations managers; in particular the linear relationships and relatively small numbers of contributory variables are obvious fallacies. However, the general approach is beneficial in that it does provide an indication of the relative importance that should be attached to each of the organisation's product lines.

The effect of increasing a resource can easily be investigated by altering the constraint that it imposes and thereby computing the subsequent change in profit.

3 Capacity and Load Evaluation

No operations system has limitless capacity; indeed, capacity limitations and their effect on product mix have just been discussed with respect to overall profit maximisation.

For individual departments and work centres, a knowledge of the availability of capacity together with load requirements is also necessary for:

determining the amount of sub-contracting required;
planning overtime requirements;
assessing the need for possible manpower reductions;
planning movement of labour between work centres and departments;
deciding on additional equipment capacity etc.

Loads on departments and work centres may be determined by either:

(i) Aggregating demand data derived from forecast input to a stock ordering system (see Chapters 14 & 16) or

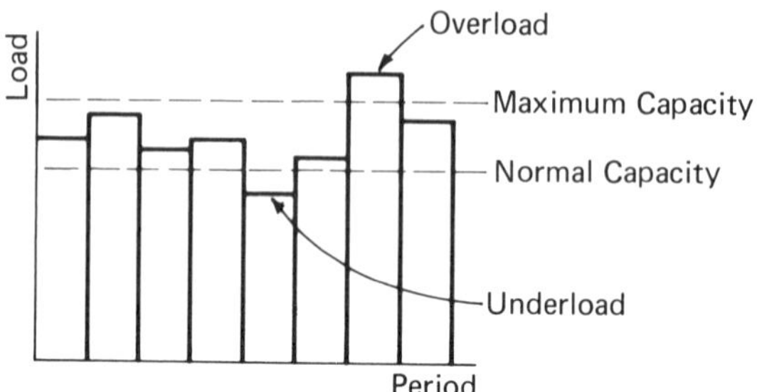

Figure 12.5 *Work Centre Load Chart*

(ii) Subtracting lead-time allowances from due-date of firm orders and aggregating production requirements at each start date (see Chapter 18).

Load requirements can then be compared with available normal and maximum capacity (see figure 12.5).

Additional uses of the capacity plan are for:

(a) meeting due dates
(b) controlling work-in-progress levels
(c) reducing lead times
(d) regulating queue length
(e) reducing bottlenecks
(f) minimising idle time

Capacity and load planning on individual work centres is obviously monotonous and time-consuming if done manually. The increasing use of computers in operations planning and control has therefore made the technique a more feasible proposition for all types of organisation.

4 Monitoring and Progress of Operations

The most commonly used method of monitoring and controlling operations is by the use of some form of bar chart or 'Gantt' chart where load is shown against a time scale. Completion of jobs or activities at any point in time is also shown on the chart providing some visual indication of progress to the planner (figure 12.6). The basic Gantt chart, as perceived by Henry

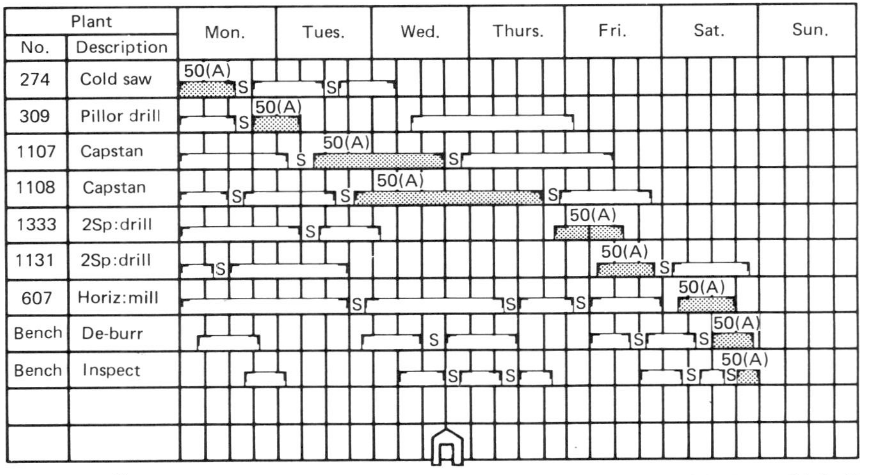

Source: Burbidge,[2] reproduced with kind permission of the author and MacDonald & Evans Ltd

Symbol	Description
	Start task.
	Finish task.
S	Setting-up.
50	Thick black line shows 25 out of 50 complete.

Symbol	Description
S	Time gained against plan. Next task shown above line, at correct starting time.
	Time lost against plan. Next task shown at correct starting time. Lost time written off.
50	Number of items shown at left.
(X)	Identification symbol central in brackets.

Symbols used on Gantt Charts

Figure 12.6 *The Gantt Chart for Monitoring and Progressing Operations*

Gantt in 1917 using the basis of time as a planning medium, is a simple manual device and may merely comprise a piece of graph paper or one of the many proprietary wall charts which are available.

Alternatively, the chart may be built into a computer programme, as is the case with some of the production control packages.

The use of a Gantt chart to derive a job schedule on a series of facilities is also illustrated in Chapter 20 under scheduling and process monitoring. Its usefulness is as a vehicle with which to plan the sequence of a series of operations and to evaluate the throughput time (or 'makespan').

The sequence is monitored by recording against each facility the extent to which each operation has been completed. At any point in time the performance of a facility may readily be observed by comparing the planned completion with the actual achievement.

5 Production Control

Production Control has been defined as the function of management which plans, directs and controls the material supply and processing activities of an enterprise, so that specified products are produced by specified methods to meet an approved sales programme, these activities being carried out in such a manner that the labour, plant and capital available are used to the best advantage.[2]

Although this definition obviously relates to manufacturing, the main features are equally relevant in a service context and in particular, emphasise the importance which must be attached to resource utilisation as well as 'customer service'. Any organisation not only has to satisfy a client population, but must also survive in a climate of high interest rates, material and labour shortages, cash flow difficulties, cash limits etc.

Much is said and written about production control *systems* and their design and operation. There are, however, as many systems as there are firms, each one being unique and purpose-built for a particular situation.

In practice, however, production control may be broken down into a number of common elements which may be found throughout all manufacturing and service operations.

Firstly, as a broad categorisation, distinction may be drawn between *planning* on the one hand and *control* on the other.

Planning may be done throughout the various levels within the organisation with broad plans being drawn up at the highest level, probably in product terms rather than in any detail. At the lower levels, the broad plans will need to be reduced to a far greater degree of detail specifying actual number of components, tool and material requirements etc.

Burbidge gives the name *programming* to the top level activity where delivery plans for products are determined to meet the sales programme. The middle level activity is termed *ordering* and relates to the placing of orders for materials and parts on purchasing and processing departments. The bottom level activity is *despatching* where plant, labour, materials, tools, etc. are brought together in order that parts and assemblies are completed according to due-date requirements.

The basic elements of control are *progressing* and *inventory control*. Progressing, adopting the principles of control described earlier, comprises the measurement of actual achievement, together with the feed back of results, so that 'variances' may be derived by comparison with the relevant plans. It should be noted that progressing may be applied at all planning levels and that for effective organisational control, every production plan should be regularly subject to such a routine.

Scientific approaches to inventory control will be described in some detail in Chapter 16 so we shall here merely restrict discussion to the function of stocks within the context of production control.

Inventory control is often thought of as being a separate function from production control. It is, however, a central activity which embraces both 'direct' raw materials and purchases, work-in-progress and finished goods, together with 'indirect' consumable materials. Since all of these stock areas are inextricably linked to production, then policies for their control must be determined by the organisation's overall production or operations policy. In particular, it must be recognised that all stocks cost money and that they represent a certain amount of capital tied up in operational activities, being in many cases as great as 40% of total assets employed. It is important therefore that inventory control is approached with more than simple off-the-cuff judgment and that *systems* are designed which provide effective monitoring and regulation of stock movements.

Although we have implied that no universal system exists which will embrace all operations in every organisation, it is however possible to categorise the planning problems, and their associated solution techniques, according to the particular broad type of production being employed.

To recap on what has already been described in the introductory chapter, we can classify production as:

(i) the *job* type, in which all orders are different, having their own designs, tools, planning etc.;
(ii) the *batch* type, in which repeated batches of an item are produced usually for stock and subsequent consumption;
(iii) the *flow* type, where production is continuous and more-or-less in line with the demand.

Recognising the fact that the approach to production planning will be determined by the type of production or operations system, the relevant techniques associated with job, batch and flow situations will be described and discussed.

6 Job Production Planning

With improved customer choice and the ever-increasing demand for variety, the job type of operations system is again becoming prevalent. Proper planning and control of job production is of the utmost importance, since it often involves a high level of investment and, if not adequately managed, may lead to costly and ineffective use of resources.

For many years the Gantt chart has been the primary mechanism for coping with the planning of job production. Here, each *phase* of the project is represented as a 'bar' drawn against a time scale. In this respect it differs slightly from the chart described previously which showed the load against a number of facilities.

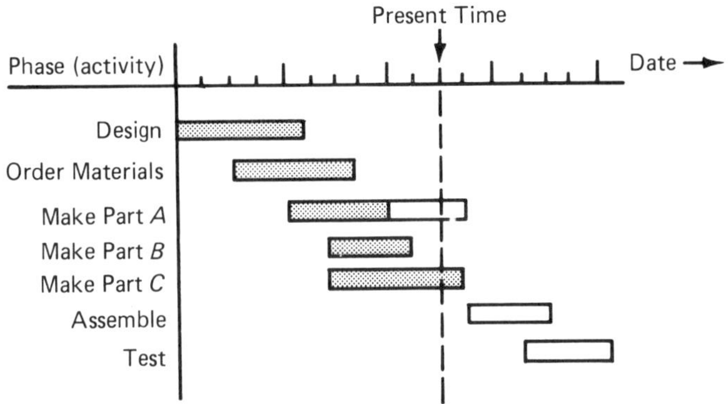

Figure 12.7 *Gantt Chart for Planning and Controlling a Project*

As before however, as each phase is completed, then this may be shown on the chart and progress may be compared with the plan at any time throughout the duration of the project (see figure 12.7).

The Gantt chart approach however has many weaknesses which make it less attractive for planning the more complex type of project common in modern industries, such as constructing a motorway, building a ship, introducing a new motor car etc. In these cases, factors such as dependency of one activity on another, identification of 'critical' activities, manpower and resource allocation become important considerations and a better method of planning and control is desirable.

A more appropriate method of planning the complex project was found in the area of *network analysis* and, from the late 1950s, a host of very similar planning techniques, based on activity networks, have been developed, for example:

PERT – Programme Evaluation and Review Technique
CPM – Critical Path Method
PRISM – Programme Reliability Information System for Management
PEP – Programme Evaluation Procedure
IMPACT – Integrated Management Planning and Control Technique
SCAN – Scheduling and Control by Automated Network Systems

The differences between the techniques arise primarily as a result of the particular job for which the technique was originally developed. However, because of their similarity they do not warrant separate treatment and so a general description of network models and their analysis will follow.

Networks may be of the *activity on node* type or of the *activity on arrow* type. We shall confine ourselves, however, to the more common activity on arrow networks, such diagrams consisting of two basic elements – *activities* and *events*.

Consider the example of a small project. Table 12.1 shows all the activities, their duration, and their predecessors.

Table 12.1 Project Precedence and Activity Duration

Activity	*Immediate Predecessors*	*Duration (Days)*
A	–	2
B	–	3
C	*A*	4
D	*A*	5
E	*C*	6
F	*D*	3
G	*D* & *B*	4
H	*E*	7
I	*F*	2
J	*F* & *G*	3

The activities when drawn as a network will appear as figure 12.8.

Note the use of dummy activities – – → to complete precedence requirements. Their duration is naturally 0.

The Earliest Event Time (EET), Latest Event Time (LET) and Event Slack (S) may now be calculated for each event in the project. This will be shown on the network above each event node as follows:

S

EET	LET

Earliest Event Times (EET) for each 'head' event are found by *passing forward* through the network progressively, *adding* the activity duration to the EET for each 'tail' event. Where

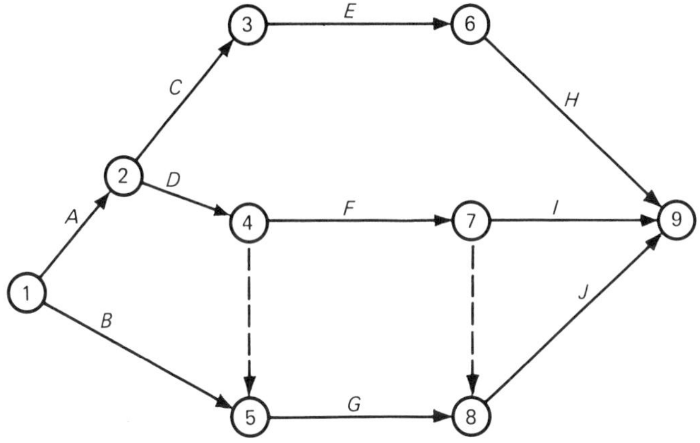

Figure 12.8 *Network of Activities in Table 12.1*

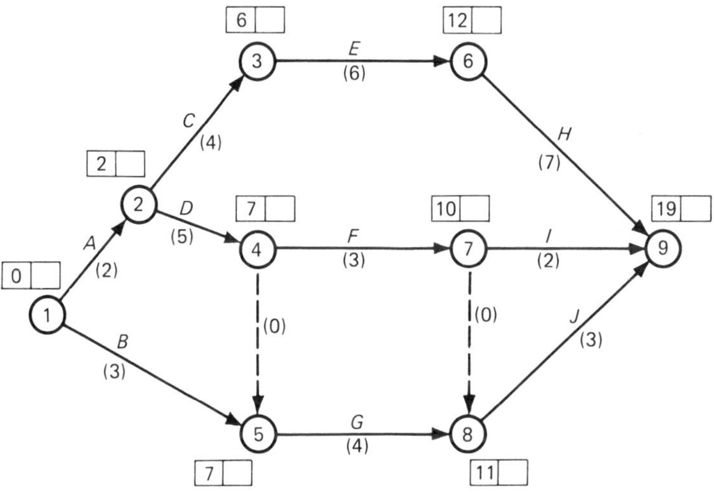

Figure 12.9 *Calculation of Earliest Event Times*

there is more than one route to an event, the highest calculated value is used (see figure 12.9).

The EET for the first event (the start) is assumed to be 0.

Latest Event Times (LET) are found for each tail event by *passing backwards* through the network progressively *subtracting* the activity duration from the LET for each head event. Where there is more than one route to an event, the lowest

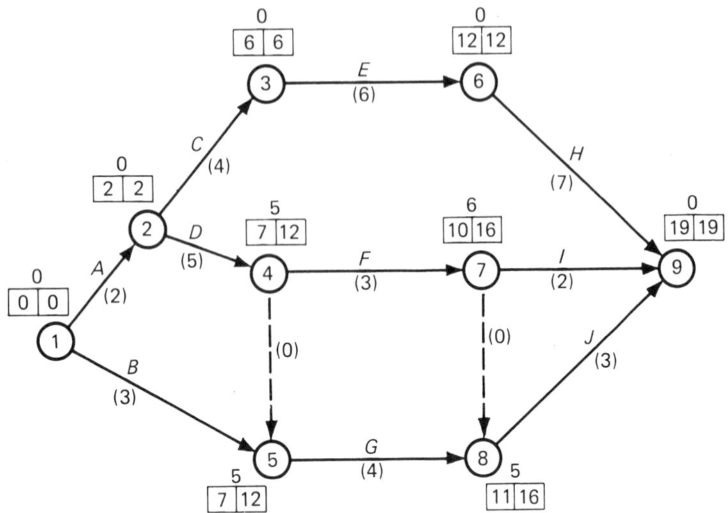

Figure 12.10 *Calculation of Latest Event Times*

calculated value is used. The LET for the last event (the finish) is the same as its EET (see figure 12.10).

For each activity, the Earliest Start Time (ES) is given by the EET of the tail event, while the Latest Finish Time (LF) is given by the LET of the head event. The total FLOAT associated with each activity is given by:

TOTAL FLOAT = (LF – ES) – activity duration
i.e. for activity *D*

	Activity *D* Duration 5	Total Float = 5
Time (Day)	2	7	12

Free float is the amount of float associated with an activity if the subsequent activity commences at its earliest start time.

Thus, FREE FLOAT = TOTAL FLOAT – HEAD EVENT SLACK

i.e. for activity *B*

	Activity *B* Duration 3	Free Float = 4	Head Event Slack = 5
Time (Day)	0	3	7	12

Independent float is the amount of float associated with an activity if the subsequent activity commences at its earliest start time *and* the preceding activity is completed at its latest finish time.

Thus, INDEPENDENT FLOAT = FREE FLOAT − TAIL EVENT SLACK

i.e. for activity *I*

Head Event Slack = 0

Tail Event Slack = 6	Activity *I* Duration 2	Ind Float = 1

Time (Day) 10 16 18 19

Table 12.2 shows the various Floats calculated for the example.

Table 12.2 Network Analysis Float Calculations

Activity	*Duration (Days)*	*ES*	*LF*	*Head Event Slack*	*Tail Event Slack*	*Activity Floats Total*	*Free*	*Independent*
A	2	0	2	0	0	0	0	0
B	3	0	12	5	0	9	4	4
C	4	2	6	0	0	0	0	0
D	5	2	12	5	0	5	0	0
E	6	6	12	0	0	0	0	0
F	3	7	16	6	5	6	0	−5 (say 0)
G	4	7	16	5	5	5	0	−5 (say 0)
H	7	12	19	0	0	0	0	0
I	2	10	19	0	6	7	7	1
J	3	11	19	0	5	5	5	0

Each of the float values shows the amount of flexibility that exists within the network. In particular, activities *A, C, E* and *H* all have zero total float. This chain of activities has no flexibility and if any of them are delayed the whole project completion time will be increased. These critical activities

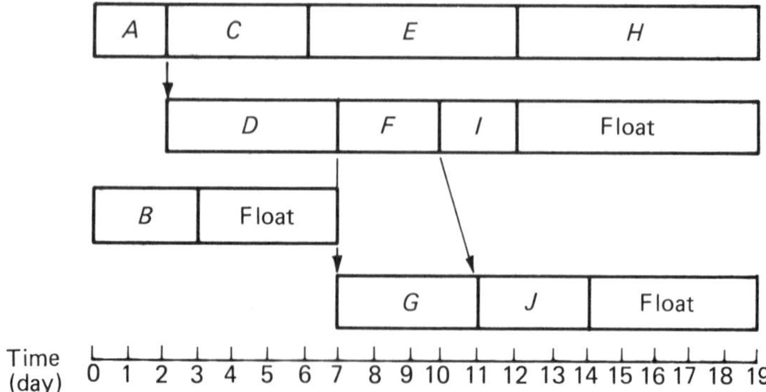

Figure 12.11 *The Sequenced Gantt Chart*

therefore represent the *critical path* through the project network and are those activities which require the greatest attention in order that delays do not occur.

The chains of activities and free float may be presented visually on a *Sequenced Gantt Chart* which has the additional advantage of showing the user the degree of flexibility associated with each of the project activities (see figure 12.11).

The usefulness of the sequenced Gantt chart is in resource smoothing i.e. manipulation of activities in order to regulate the amount of any resource (e.g. labour, equipment etc.) which is required.

For example assume the labour requirement for each activity is as shown in table 12.3.

Table 12.3 Labour Requirements for Each Activity

Activity	*Labour Required*
A	2
B	3
C	3
D	4
E	5
F	4
G	5
H	6
I	4
J	4

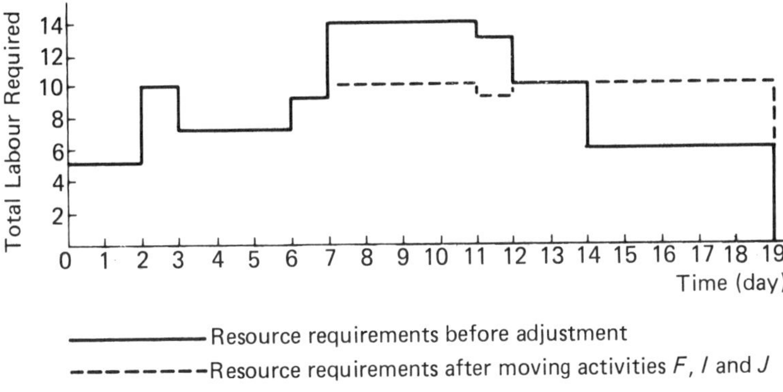

Figure 12.12 *Resource Requirements*

As the activities stand at present, the maximum labour requirement would be fourteen (for days 7 to 11). This can be reduced to ten by moving *F* and *I* to 11–16 and *J* to 16–19 as shown in figure 12.12.

7 Batch Production Planning

In intermittent batch production, each individual batch requires processing through a number of operations on a series of facilities. Here, the basic question to be answered is – in what order should jobs be assigned to facilities, bearing in mind that in different situations it may be necessary to achieve different objectives.

It is important to distinguish between two basic classes of problem which involve firstly *sequencing* and secondly *despatching*.

The term sequencing usually relates to a situation where all jobs to be processed are known and available and processing is done on a series of facilities (see figure 12.13).

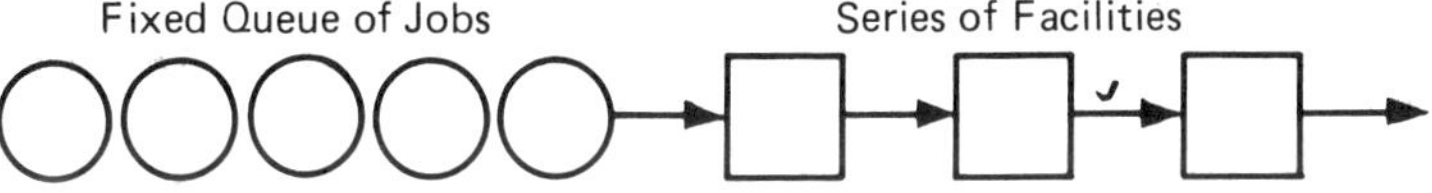

Figure 12.13 *Diagrammatic Representation of Sequencing Problem*

Figure 12.14 *Diagrammatic Representation of Despatching Problem*

The objective in the case of the sequencing problem is usually to minimise the total throughput time. No mathematical solution to the general problem has been found to date, although the simple problem comprising a number of jobs processed through two facilities may be solved using Johnson's algorithm[3] described in Chapter 20, p. 364. In certain cases the algorithm may be extended to a three machine sequence, but beyond this no exact solution procedures exist.

Optimal sequences can be derived using branch and bound techniques,[4] but they are probably too complex and unwieldy to be of any really practical value. More promising results may be obtained from the use of 'heuristics' which give good, but not necessarily optimal, solutions.

The despatching problem is where a queue of jobs is processed by a single facility and, moreover, further jobs may join the queue as time proceeds (see figure 12.14).

Despatching is far more representative of the practical industrial situation, because jobs usually queue and are ordered at each facility rather than remaining in the same sequence throughout. Whereas the sequencing problem is only a very simple concept, despatching can operate in a far more complex environment having, for instance:

transport between various operations;
many unique routeings through facilities;
variety of due dates etc.

The objective in sequencing was simply to minimise the total throughput time, but despatching may operate within different (and often conflicting) objectives, for example:

(i) Minimisation of facility idle time.
(i.e. in an attempt to gain the best use of capacity)
(ii) Minimisation of number of late jobs.
(i.e. in an attempt to provide good customer service)
(iii) Minimisation of average throughput time.
(i.e. in order to reduce the amount of work-in-progress)

The nature of the despatching problem does not lend itself to rigorous mathematical solutions and the most common approach is to use priority rules.

Priority rules may be classified into two types: static and dynamic, (also see page 331). Static rules are those in which the value of the priority function does not change with time. Such rules as 'earliest due date first' and 'shortest processing time first' may be classified as static, and could even be applied to sequencing problems since, without arrivals into the queue, sequencing is a static situation. Dynamic rules on the other hand give a priority value which changes with time.

e.g. priority value = (due date − time now) − remaining processing time

or, priority value = (due date − time now) − (remaining processing time + time for last operation).

With both these rules the priority value depends on 'time now' and will therefore need to be continually modified. In practice, however, priority values will be calculated on a daily or weekly basis but, nevertheless, dynamic rules will be more costly to operate than static ones.

The effectiveness of a chosen priority can only be assessed by putting the rule into practice and judging with regard to the three criteria described earlier. This, however, could be time-consuming and also expensive if a poor rule were chosen. An alternative is therefore simulation, which is quicker but usually simplifies the situation by making numerous assumptions, for example:

the operation times (including set-up) for all jobs are known and are independent of processing order;
operations once started must be completed;
no facility may process more than one job at a time;
transport between facilities is neglected;
operations must be carried out in a predetermined order;
machines and labour are available in known quantities;
the 'splitting' of batches is not permitted.

Most computer aided despatching systems make use of priority rules, but are in a position to use more complex formulae than the manual systems. Moreover, many packages involve the use of a factor or factors which may be varied by the user and tested until the desired results are obtained.

8 Flow Production Planning

In flow line production, whether it be the manufacture of a component on a transfer line, the production of liquids and gases in process plant, or the assembly of a complex finished product, facilities are laid out in such a way that all the necessary operations (or tasks) are performed *sequentially* as the product passes from one facility (or work station) to another. The production planning problems of flow production are therefore rather unique in that the operation sequence and capacity loading of each facility is pre-determined by the design or layout of the plant and the 'share' of the total work content that each work station is allocated. Usually, once a line has been set up, it determines the way in which a product is manufactured for perhaps several years and, hence, anything other than a minor change in sequence or loading involves a rearrangement of the entire line at prohibitive cost.

Lines may be of two types. The assembly type produces a single finished product by bringing together materials and components at a series of work stations. Alternatively, a series of operations may be performed on a single object as with a machine transfer line or in some types of service operation. The assembly line is perhaps the most common type of flow line (see figure 12.15).

The second type of line is the analytical type where a number of finished outputs are produced from a single raw material. An obvious example is oil refining where crude is refined and blended into petrol, paraffin, heating oil etc. (see

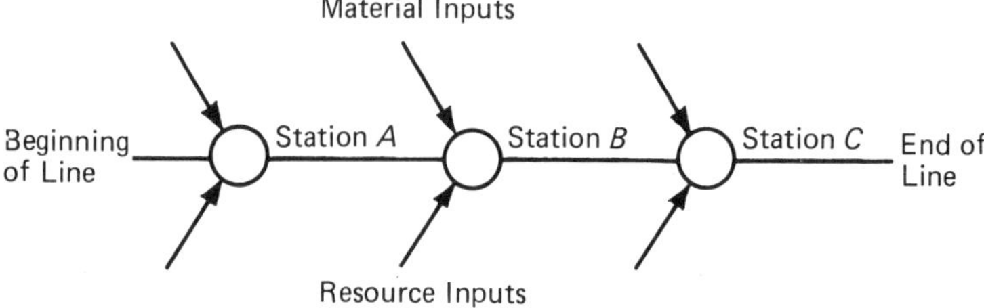

Figure 12.15 *The Assembly Function*

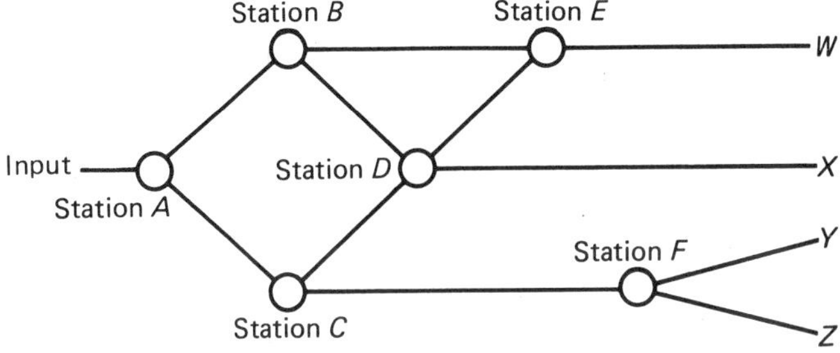

Figure 12.16 *The Analytical Function*

figure 12.16). Although less common than the assembly type, the analytical function is probably older and the use of lines in the meat packing industry can be traced back to the nineteenth century. In fact it is sometimes claimed that this provided the inspiration for Henry Ford's Model 'T' production line.

Whatever the type of line being considered, the basic decisions which need to be made are as follows:

(i) Deciding on output rate or cycle time;
(ii) Determination of required number of stations;
(iii) Allocation of tasks to each station;
(iv) Deciding on whether any station duplication or multiple manning is needed.

The objective of good flow line design is to provide high resource efficiency and good balance of load between the work stations.

There are, however, constraints on the problem of flow line design which may affect the final solution, the two most significant being:

(i) Precedence Constraints – which are restrictions on the order in which tasks can be done, i.e. certain tasks will have *predecessors* which must be carried out before subsequent tasks can be performed;
(ii) Zoning Constraints – which are restrictions on where certain tasks or combinations of tasks may, or may not, take place.

To understand the problems associated with flow line design consider the following example.

Example

Table 12.4 shows the precedence constraints and times for a number of tasks which comprise the assembly operations of a simple product. The total work content for the assembly is 59 minutes.

Table 12.4 Precedence for a Product Assembly

Task	*Immediate Predecessors*	*Time (Minutes)*
1	–	6
2	1	15
3	1	8
4	2	7
5	2, 3	6
6	4	4
7	4, 5	8
8	6, 7	5

Diagrams for flow line task precedence are usually drawn using activity-on-node notation. The precedence network for the example will therefore appear as in figure 12.17.

If the assembly is to be produced continuously on a flow line, the tasks must be divided between a number of work stations. This could be done arbitrarily as shown in figure 12.18.

Here the cycle time, which determines the output from the

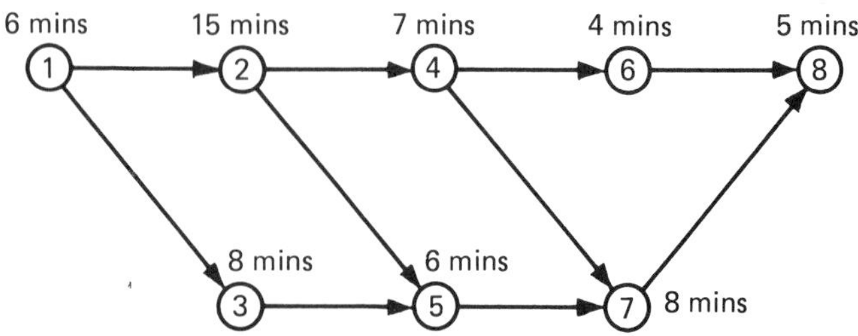

Figure 12.17 *Precedence Network for Product Assembly*

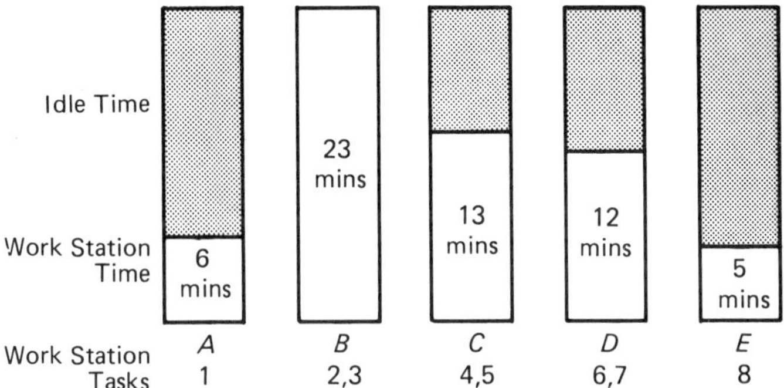

Figure 12.18 *Arbitrary Work Station Loading*

line, is 23 minutes, which with five work stations gives a total available work station time per assembly of 5 X 23 = 115 minutes. Line efficiency is therefore (59/115) X 100% = 51%.

The line efficiency is obviously very low and, moreover, the balance of the line is very uneven, one work station only being allocated 5 minutes of assembly time.

Clearly, a better solution would be preferred, having more even balance and, perhaps, a shorter cycle time. A simple problem such as the one shown could probably be manipulated to give an improvement by eye, but a typical complex set of tasks (a motor car may have over a thousand final assembly operations) would obviously need a more rigorous approach.

Whilst 'exact' solutions based on mathematical treatments such as linear programming have been developed by, for example, Bowman,[5] they are really only of academic value since their procedure is so complex that realistic problems would require vast computations which would be an impractical proposition even with the assistance of a computer.

A number of heuristic methods have therefore been developed which are of more practical value to production planners.

Perhaps the most widely quoted of these is that developed by Kilbridge and Wester,[6] the procedure for which has been modified somewhat by Starr[7] to further simplify its operating procedure.

The approach used is to assign a number to each task describing how many predecessors it has. The first operations assigned to stations are those with the lowest predecessor numbers but, where there is a choice, the operation with the longest time that can be used is chosen. Hence shorter operations are saved until later for ease of manipulation. Consideration must obviously be given to precedence and zoning constraints when tasks are assigned to stations.

The example may be solved using this heuristic by first setting up a working table of the number of predecessors for each operation e.g. table 12.5.

Table 12.5 Working Table Showing Number of Task Predecessors

Task	*Number of Predecessors*	*Time (Minutes)*
1	0	6
2	1	15
3	1	8
4	2	7
5	3	6
6	3	4
7	5	8
8	7	5

If we wish to design a line to produce assemblies at a rate of 28 per day, then a cycle time is required of:

$$\frac{60\ \text{(mins/hour)} \times 8\ \text{(hours/day)}}{28\ \text{(items/day)}}$$

$$= 17\ \text{minutes (approx.)}$$

Table 12.6 Resultant Task Allocation

Work Station	*Task*	*Time*	*Cumulative Time*
A	1	6	6
	3	8	14
B	2	15	15
C	4	7	7
	5	6	13
	6	4	17
D	7	8	8
	8	5	13

Since the work content is 59 minutes, the number of stations required is 59/17 = 3.5; i.e. at least 4.

The procedure described gives the solution shown in table 12.6.

The task network has therefore been divided as shown in figure 12.19.

Work station loading is as shown in figure 12.20.

A cycle time of 17 minutes has therefore been achieved using four work stations giving a total available work station time of 4 X 17 = 68 minutes. Line efficiency is therefore 59/68 X 100% = 87%.

This is obviously a preferable solution to that given previously, since line efficiency is much higher and balance is much improved, the lowest work station time being 13 minutes.

The heuristic just described represents one of the more elementary procedures for laying out flow lines and, as such, lends itself readily to manual use. There are, however, many other heuristics involving varying degrees of complexity which, in some cases, require use of a computer to be applied effectively.

The Ranked Positional Weight heuristic (RPW) developed by Helgeson and Birnie[8] is a well-proven method which, although involving slightly more computation than that developed by Kilbridge and Wester,[6] provides good solutions more quickly than many alternative methods while still capable of being manipulated manually.

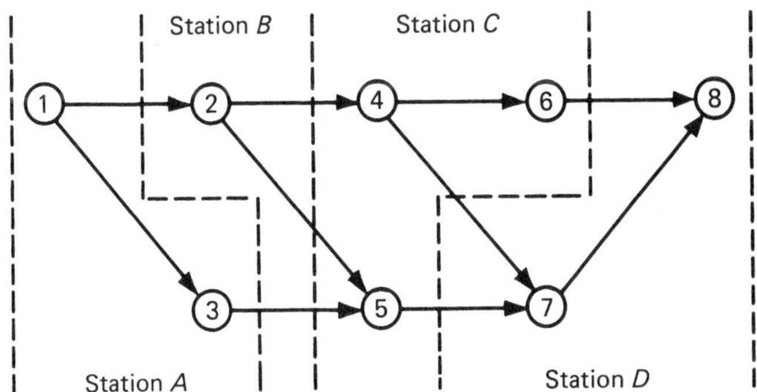

Figure 12.19 *Network for Product Assembly Showing Task Allocation*

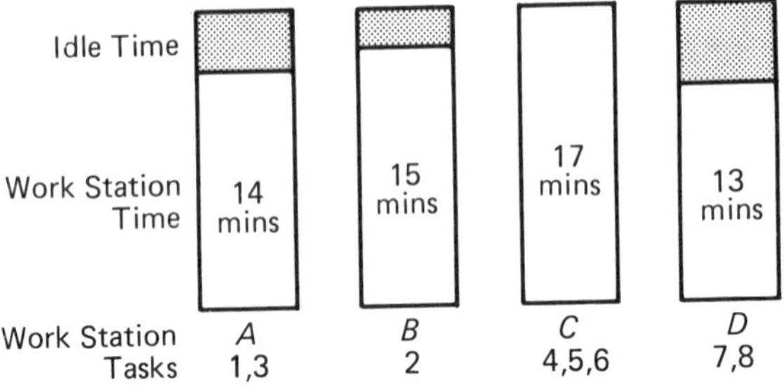

Figure 12.20 *Work Station Loading*

The technique is illustrated by the following example. Consider the sequence of tasks shown on the following diagram, figure 12.21.

Each task is assigned a *positional weight* which is the sum of that task's time and the times of all *subsequent* tasks.

i.e. for element 7 the positional weight
$= \text{time for } 7 + \text{time for } 9 + \text{time for } 11$
$= 3 + 5 + 4$
$= 12$

Positional weights for the eleven tasks are therefore given in the following working table (table 12.7).

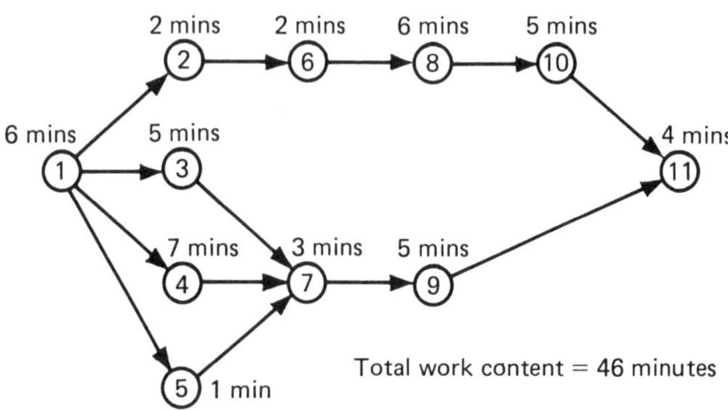

Figure 12.21 *Precedence Network*

Table 12.7 Working Table Showing Positional Weight for Tasks

Task	*Positional Weight*	*Rank*	*Time (mins)*
1	46	1	6
2	19	3	2
3	17	4	5
4	19	2	7
5	13	7	1
6	17	5	2
7	12	8	3
8	15	6	6
9	9	9	5
10	9	10	5
11	4	11	4

Tasks are now allocated to work stations in order of *descending* positional weights (a ranking of 1 to 11 has been given in the above table) in a similar manner to the previous example, again with consideration of precedence and time constraints.

i.e. If a cycle time of 16 minutes is required:
number of work stations necessary

$$= \frac{46}{16}$$

$$= 2.9$$

i.e. at least 3

Table 12.8 Resultant Task Allocation using Positional Weights

Work Station	*Task*	*Time*	*Cumulative Time*
A	1	6	6
	4	7	13
	2	2	15
	5	1	16
B	3	5	5
	6	2	7
	8	6	13
	7	3	16
C	9	5	5
	10	5	10
	11	4	14

Assigning tasks to work stations by descending order of positional weights gives the following solution (table 12.8).

Heuristic techniques for planning flow production obviously vary in their complexity. Those which are designed to be used manually necessarily need to be relatively simple. However, the systematic approach adopted by such solution procedures obviously means that more complex algorithms can be developed which may still be manipulated by computer.

Of the many computer based heuristics that have been developed to solve the flow line balancing problem, perhaps the best known is COMSOAL (computer method of sequencing operations for assembly lines) which was developed by Arcus.[9]

Its iterative procedure lends itself to massive and complex problems which would be too unwieldy to tackle manually. For example the Chrysler Corporation used COMSOAL to solve a one thousand operation, 203 station problem resulting in a line efficiency of 98.52% (i.e. 1.48% idle time). The computation used 2 minutes of computer time.

9 Conclusion

This example of the use of computers in flow line planning clearly illustrates the improvements in performance that are achievable in the area of operations planning and control. Indeed, computers have been applied to the solution of all the problems described in this chapter and this is bound to become an increasing trend as the cost and availability of computing brings it within the reach of every small manufacturing and service operation.

References and Further Reading

1 Sasieni, M., Yaspan, A. and Friedman, L., *Operations Research : Methods and Problems*, Wiley 1959.
2 Burbidge, J.L., *Principles of Production Control*, 4th edn, Macdonald & Evans 1978.
3 Johnson, S.M., Optimal two- and three-stage production schedules

with set-up time included, *Naval Research Logistics Quarterly*, March 1954.
4 Ignall, E. and Schrage, L., Application of the branch and bound technique to some flow shop scheduling problems, *Operations Research*, May–June 1965.
5 Bowman, E.H., Assembly-line balancing by linear programming, *Operations Research*, May–June 1960.
6 Kilbridge, M. and Wester, L., A heuristic method of assembly line balancing, *Journal of Industrial Engineering*, Vol. 12, No. 4, 1961.
7 Starr, M.K., *Systems Management of Operations*, Prentice-Hall 1971.
8 Helgeson, W.B. and Birnie, D.P., Assembly line balancing using the ranked positional weight technique, *Journal of Industrial Engineering*, Nov–Dec 1961.
9 Arcus, A.L., COMSOAL: a computer method for sequencing operations for assembly lines, in E.S. Buffa (ed.), *Readings in Production and Operations Management*, Wiley 1966.

13
Scheduling Production in a Jobbing Fabrication Shop

T BERNARD TATE

*Beta Systems**

1 Introduction

Fabrication is a term applied to the manufacture of assemblies by techniques such as bolting and welding, mainly structures for subsequent erection. The bulk of the workload in the shop concerned in this study consisted of assembly, the manual bringing together of two or more steel parts, and the subsequent welding or bolting, in which the tool is brought to the job rather than the job to a machine. However, this work is preceded by several preparation operations such as sawing and burning (flame-cutting) in which usually it is the material that is moved as in a conventional machining operation. For both preparation and finishing, as for the first mentioned operations, together with painting and dressing (grinding), the man hours available were the only constraint on capacity in practice, not the availability of machines.

This shop was one of three 'Works' that constituted one of

* Editor's note: This chapter details the author's experience as a practising consultant.

four 'Branches' of a company that manufactures and erects steel structures for factories and multi-storey buildings. My original task as consultant was to help the Company assess whether or not a network based package might be suitable for scheduling production in the Works. PERT packages were already being studied as means of improving overall planning, by co-ordinating the arrival of materials and drawings prior to the fabrication, assembly, transportation and construction of the various 'Phases' into which each job was usually broken down. However, it soon became apparent that the real objectives of production management could not be met just by implementing on the shop floor either multi-project PERT or any of the current network-based scheduling packages.

2 Prevailing Method of Scheduling

Before a contract for such construction work is awarded, it is usual for a customer to request price and delivery quotations from a number of would-be suppliers. These estimates are made on the basis of general information on the design and tonnage of steel involved. Estimates of the standard hours required for each of about 10 operations are then converted into financial terms. Detailed drawings are prepared by the supplier as part of the contract, when awarded, and so the estimates are not as accurate as they would be if the drawings were made available to him by the customer at the time of the quotation.

When a contract is finally awarded, the contract estimator may take account of any variations in the final specification and re-estimate the standard hours where necessary. The project engineer then breaks down the contract into 'phases', (a 1000 ton job into about 5 phases), each with a planned start date, and a finish date or due date for delivery to the construction site, which enables the customer to phase the arrival of the other construction site requirements. The start date depends on when detailed drawings can be prepared and agreed with the customer, and on the arrival of materials, usually from British Steel, as well as on a conceptual 'backward schedule' from the due date. When the phases have been defined, the Planning Department break down the estimated hours by phase, approximately. When the detailed drawings become available at the Works a phase is then broken down into batches, for which times are estimated by 'applicators' at the Works. These times are used later in group incentive bonus calculations. However, payments are related to an aggregation of performance, and the detail at batch level is required for control purposes. It should be noted that the difference between the sales estimate and applicated hours varies, some types of work being easier to estimate than others in the absence of detailed drawings. It should also be noted that it is sometimes convenient for the works to lump together batches from different phases, just as in the manufacture of parts for different assemblies, but such lumping together across phase boundaries is rare and discouraged.

The prevailing method of production planning was for Branch Central Planning to spread the tonnage in each phase from earliest start to due date, week by week. The hours required in total each week, for all current phases, were calculated by multiplying the average rate per ton for each particular contract or phase, aggregating them, and then comparing this total with the total man hours available. Any severe overloads and underloads were identified, and an attempt made in conjunction with the Works to reallocate the distribution of hours on specific phases so as to achieve a more feasible total load. Two kinds of schedule, a four-month one in weeks and a 12-month one in months, were updated once a month and posted to the Works, who each week reported tons produced by contract, and recorded it on the plan by hatching out completed tons.

Each month the Works would examine what jobs were in fact in progress or available to start, and would calculate the anticipated overloads and underloads on key operations for up to 4 months ahead. Frequently this would cause them to change their projections of completion at the fortnightly planning meetings, at which progress against plan was reviewed.

A general appraisal of this system follows.

3 Appraisal of Prevailing System

The central scheduling system was not designed to anticipate loads and overloads by operation, and the sheets prepared at the Works often showed overloads of some resources and underloads of others of up to 80%, within any given month. This situation is likely to arise when the proportions of the work content of jobs accounted for by each operation differ markedly between successive jobs. The effect on projected finish dates was not as severe as it would be in a machining shop for three main reasons:

(i) A resource group such as welding can be spread over a variable number of jobs as opposed to each job needing to be completed before the same operation on the next one can be started.
(ii) The actual hours per week allocated to a particular job is not a predetermined quantity – operations may be conducted quite slowly, a few hours per week, or more quickly by allocating more men to them, up to some practical limit where the men get in each other's way.
(iii) A resource group may be augmented by men from other resource groups, given notice, and again within limits.

Nevertheless some clearly identifiable costs do arise owing to overloads and underloads not being anticipated sufficiently early.

(i) 3% to 4% of time was lost as 'idle time', costing at the time about £5 per hour.
(ii) Subcontracting costs were incurred that could have been avoided with better planning.
(iii) Buffers of stock were maintained at erection sites to reduce the effects of late deliveries.
(iv) Nevertheless, many deliveries were late.
(v) Men were paid their own rates for doing jobs at which they were less skilful.
(vi) Work in progress was high.
(vii) Inter-company transfers of raw material and finished product were expensive.

(viii) Considerable overtime was scheduled to cope with specific overloads.

Some quantification of this problem was attempted for the period September–November 1975. The figures arrived at and given below, were subjective estimates of orders of magnitude rather than extracts from accounting documents.

Symptom	*Quantification*
Average 'idle time'	1000 hours/week
'Avoidable' subcontracting	1000 tons p.a.
Stocks relating to this works at subcontractors	1000 tons
Average jobs late	1/week (50%)
Average lateness of late jobs	2 weeks
Time on non-prime operations	100 hours/week
Average work in progress	1000 tons (£300,000)
Intercompany transfers	10000 ton miles p.a.
Overtime	200 hours/week

Management evaluated these costs in annual terms as follows:

Idle Time	£ 50,000 p.a.
Avoidable subcontracting	£ 10,000 p.a.
Subcontractor stocks	£ 60,000 p.a.
Lateness	£100,000 p.a.
Non-prime work	£ 5,000 p.a.
Work in progress	£ 60,000 p.a.
Intercompany transfers	£ 2,000 p.a.
Overtime	£ 20,000 p.a.
Total	£307,000 p.a.

Not all of these effects were due to the fact that phases were not scheduled down to an operation level. Sometimes drawings or materials are late, which can cause both unexpected underloads before they arrive and unforeseen overloads when they do arrive. Also, the standard times, although accurate to about 5% on average, are for particular operations wrong by more than this, and the work in progress always exceeds that predicted from a schedule based on the 'expected values' of operation durations whose values differ from these expected values. Some scrap occurs, machines break down, and the requirements of the customers change.

However, one criticism could be levelled at the scheduling system, and this was that re-scheduling was not carried out sufficiently often. During the course of a month, about 25% of jobs are affected by at least a week as a consequence of changes of the kinds referred to in the preceding paragraph, and so a monthly schedule fails to reflect the effects of a serious number of such changes which is an issue separate from not being able to anticipate these changes.

What contribution might better scheduling make to these costs, bearing in mind the 'uncontrollable' variables such as changing customer requirements and late materials? Management made the following guesses at the probable effect on each of the eight costs of an 'ideal' scheduling system:

	%	Value (£ p.a.)
Idle time	20	10,000
Avoidable subcontracting	20	2,000
Subcontractor stocks	20	12,000
Lateness	20	20,000
Non-prime work	20	1,000
Work in progress	20	12,000
Inter company transfers	20	400
Overtime	20	4,000
		£61,400 p.a.

This appraisal was undertaken informally at the beginning of the research, and the above represents a more precise version arrived at several months later. However, the totals were of the same order of magnitude. This appraisal was of course for the Works picked out for initial implementation, whose turnover, at £2,500,000 p.a. was the smallest of the three.

The prevailing system was a manual one, occupying four men, full time at Branch Headquarters, of which about 7 man weeks a month were involved in producing the two kinds of chart and keeping them up to date. Each Works had a Works

Planner who prepared the overload and underload predictions and relayed apposite information back to Headquarters. About two man days a week could be said to have been involved with the information used by Headquarters planning system.

4 Client Set and its Objectives

The leading decision-makers in the Branch had the titles Production Manager and Operations Manager. Their responsibility and authority was much wider than these titles suggest and covered most of the activities in the company. Their main objectives with regard to scheduling were to fill capacity, cut costs and meet delivery dates. The Branch staff who performed the manual scheduling appeared to share these objectives and not to feel threatened by the possible advent of a computer.

The staff at the Works selected were not greatly affected by the monthly schedule currently being produced and saw their problems as caused by late drawings and materials rather than badly set launch dates and due dates. They shared the objectives of increasing the workload, cutting costs and meeting due dates. They had a tendency to be conservative about their mode of operation, and would resist any extension of the authority of the project engineers, but proposals to change the method of producing the overall plan were not seen as threatening, and the possibility of planning by activity was welcomed. The project engineers had the most direct interest in meeting the due dates of the individual jobs, with some potential conflicts of interest between their own jobs and those of other project engineers, and the factories. The men on the shop floor had the usual long-term financial and security objectives. They also liked to 'hold back' some of the documentation on completed work as a method of exercising control over their earnings, and to avoid the detection of exceptionally 'good' jobs, which resulted in a slight lag after the work was completed before the paperwork could reflect this.

The Company had very little experience with computers,

despite being fairly large (turnover exceeded £100 million p.a.), but a small Company Head Office Staff had been set up to promote the use of computers, and generally assist in the planning and development of computing throughout the four Branches with their sixteen Works (at that time). Because of the lack of computer expertise in the Branches they were slightly inclined to favour packages such as WASP,* with which one of the senior advisers at Head Office had had some previous experience. The Branch Operations Manager had, however, on a previous occasion, decided that WASP as then developed would not meet the bill. One of the Head Office senior advisers asked me to give an independent opinion on the suitability of WASP for this particular application. It should be stressed, however, that all the Head Office computer advisers were much keener to encourage the Branches to begin to use computers than to insist, at this stage, that the best possible use should be made of them, and that no-one could make a move until a microscopic examination had established that no improvement could be envisaged on whatever course of action had been proposed.

Perhaps before listing some of the alternatives, the potential value of better delivery should be mentioned. Established reliability is as important in obtaining new business as the specific delivery promised in a particular quotation. In addition, penalty clauses for lateness were built into the contracts for certain jobs.

What options did the company have?

Alternative Courses of Action

(i) Maintain current manual systems.
(ii) Increase manpower commitment to the Branch Headquarters activities, and issue an overall schedule every week or fortnight.
(iii) Increase manpower commitment at Branch Headquarters and schedule by operation (ten at the selected works).
(iv) Combine (i) and (ii).
(v) Buy WASP implement, and run on a bureau.

* WASP – A machine shop scheduling package developed at the Atomic Energy Research Establishment Harwell (Gower).[1]

(vi) Buy WASP and run on a Head Office computer.
(vii) Buy WASP and install a company computer.
(viii) Buy some other package.
(ix) Rent a package.
(x) Develop a 'home-made' computer system.

In order to understand these possibilities, a little more must be said about the means of evaluating a system in terms of the objectives discussed.

5 Choosing a Measure of Effectiveness

To summarise these interests and objectives crudely is not difficult, because everyone was interested in cutting costs and improving delivery, but without too great a capital expenditure. In principle, guesses could be made at the values of each of these three variables for the existing situation and each of the nine alternatives. However, the analysis proved somewhat simpler than this, and also sounder, because of a hypothesised relationship between the operating costs and delivery performance and the overloads and underloads.

It seems clear that each of the eight symptoms noted in Appraisal of the Prevailing System would be reduced if the overloads and underloads could be avoided without breaking delivery promises, which indeed, at an aggregate level, was the objective of the manual system. It was hypothesised that the 'ideal' system would have an effect equivalent to an 80% reduction of the overloads for the same average load. The problem then becomes: 'What is the best way of reducing the overloads and underloads?' The overloads and underloads thus become intervening variables in a conceptual objective function whose structure can be ignored, providing the capital and systems costs of the preferred solution are not greater than those of the other possibilities.

In preparing a detailed schedule, management have two choices for each operation on a job, the start time, and the resources to be allocated each week. They can allocate these resources so as to reduce the greatest overload, minimise the sum of the overloads, minimise the sum of the overloads expressed as percentages, minimise a sum weighted by how far ahead they are, or the weighted, squared percentage overloads, or some other related objective function. The values taken by the variables are constrained by the need to keep jobs moving through the Works, by it being impossible to begin some operations until others are partially completed, by the fact that resources are not unlimited, although they are flexible, and by the desirability of meeting due dates.

The measures to be considered, whose values are to be predicted, become: capital cost, system cost, and effect on overloads and underloads.

Rough Appraisal of Alternatives

(i) No capital cost, incremental running cost, or effect on the overloads or underloads. For May and July 1976 the monthly overloads for five key areas were:

	May 1976		July 1976	
Saw and Drill	–490	–34%	–214	–25%
Plating	– 42	– 1%	–392	–15%
Welding	–394	–12%	30	2%
Painting	–162	–19%	–498	–77%
Other Trades	910	+17%	+565	+20%
	+188		–509	

(ii) (iii) and (iv) Once the need to manipulate the schedules at an operational level of detail had been grasped in order to have a significant impact on the overloads, with regard to both start dates and overlaps, management's original opinion that computer assistance was required was put beyond any shadow of doubt.

(v), (vi), (vii), (viii) and (ix) None of the usual packages is designed to maximise any objective function, and none at all is directed to minimising overloads. Whilst finite scheduling packages produce feasible schedules, they do not make good choices about scheduling because they do not evaluate any alternatives. But in any event, because of the flexibility of capacity, what was wanted in the first instance was an 'optimal' infinite capacity schedule that would flex the resources allocated to each operation on each job, thus affecting their durations. The maker of one package suggested that writing a 'front-end' for his package, that would do this as a preliminary exercise, might cost about £15,000. Without such a capability, one package would have cost £5,000, plus £5,000 p.a. to run (half of which estimate is for increased manpower) and would have cut overloads by an estimated 20%, worth say 2/8 of £61,400, the estimated savings for a 80% reduction, i.e. about £15,000 p.a.

(x) Since the problem had not been formulated mathematically, never mind solved, an attempt to do so involved some risks, both of a technical and a commercial nature. The technical risk was that it could not be solved, and the commercial risk was that the solution of the paper scheduling problem would not prove valuable in practice. However, the Branch elected to undertake both these risks.

A proposal was formulated to:

(a) Provide a means of calculating and printing a load and overload table, and a schedule of operations for each job prepared by scheduling forward to infinite capacity, with manually input resources per week and minimum duration before overlap, for each operation.

(b) Provide an automatic algorithm, either heuristic or exact, for systematically reducing the overloads resulting from the forward schedule to infinite capacity by altering the resources per week (which were to be regarded as constant throughout the duration of the operation), and the overlaps, but respecting due dates.

(c) If time permitted, provide an algorithm for producing a finite capacity schedule that did not permit overloads, but attempted to minimise lateness, relaxing the constraint that weekly resource consumption, although not constant, must be the same each week.

The proposed system was to be written in BASIC, the simplest programming language, with an interactive interface via a teletype terminal with a remote computer.

The evaluation was assessed as follows: Capital Cost £3,500, Incremental System Costs £2,400 p.a. Estimated effect on overloads 40%, worth say £30,000 p.a.

Since this proposal dominated the 'package' solution on all three criteria, it was accepted, despite the technical and commercial risks involved.

6 Outline of Solution

The initial computer package was written to a specification agreed with management, although various details were altered by mutual consent during this process. It operated on three files of data, one for jobs, one for resources, and one containing some variable parameters such as the current date and number of jobs. Six programmes were involved: one to create the job file, one to update it, one to create the resource file, and one to update it, one to schedule, and one to print the results.

The development of the system was somewhat by trial and error, as the Company found they wanted to add further facilities, or improved means of operating the system were devised. For example, it was not found possible to develop the finite capacity optimisation within the budget, but this was later commissioned by the company. Subsequently, the original budgeted development cost of £3,500 swelled to £7,500, as more features were added. The scheduling algorithms are not detailed for commercial reasons, as previous agreed with the company, but they were neither complex nor optimal, and so their exact nature is perhaps unimportant.

Although infinite 'optimisation' to infinite capacity was available by March 1976, nine months after commencement, serious efforts to match the print-outs with the shop floor were only made in August and September, following the commission of this effort in a later phase of the study.

It should perhaps be noted that whilst the complexity of the problem is greater in some ways than average, a number of frequently occurring features did not have to be catered for:

Assemblies
'Dis-Assemblies'
Different routes for different parts
Preferred and secondary choice routes for individual parts
A 'standard' file for repeat items

The system was soon extended to one of the other two Works, an operation which took only two hours computer time, and then later to the third Works.

The current operational procedure is to update the files each fortnight. The print-outs are then discussed with the management of the Works and various actions taken such as:

Increase the planned level of a resource in certain weeks;
Postpone the due dates of certain phases, and notify the customer;
Increase the 'maximum' resources per week allocated to jobs that would otherwise be late;
Change the overlaps set for selected operations.

The changes are incorporated in the following run.

7 Appraisal of System

It is satisfying that the company liked the system, and wanted both to increase its features and extend its scope of operation.

But the prime test is whether it is saving any money.

The following measurements were taken at the first Works at the beginning of the months of October and November 1976.

	November 1976		*October 1976*	
	Average Overload (hours)	*%*	*Average Overload (hours)*	*%*
(i) Saw and Drill	–608	–40	–406	–30
(ii) Plating	–140	– 4	+293	+ 8
(iii) Welding	– 70	– 4	–170	– 8
(iv) Painting	–500	–62	–600	–75
(v) Other Trades	–402	– 7	+118	3
	–1710		–765	

It will be noted that the situation still seems extreme, and that the underloads seem to have increased. Nevertheless, comparing the two most comparably overloaded months, the two extreme percentages are less in October than in July. The mean absolute percentage overload is 25% rather than 28%, and if the absolute values of the mean percentages are subtracted from these, one has a 4% 'adjusted deviation' in October instead of a 5% one (i.e. a 20% drop), as forecast for the 'front-ended package'. In terms of hours, which is what the programmes tried to level at that time, the mean absolute 'deviation' fell from 340 hours to 317, a 7% drop, but this is an understatement in view of the greater overall underload in October. The mean 'adjusted' overload fell from 238 hours to 164, a 31% drop.

Results from such a small sample could not be regarded as having statistical significance, but it is reasonable to enquire whether any of the measures, the costs associated with scheduling, had improved. The most important factor here is that overtime had been stopped, so the results were achieved with much less opportunity for flexibility, but with an executive management action that ensured a gain.

The estimated measures for October were as follows, with a corresponding evaluation when cast over the whole year:

	Value in October	*Value on Previous Basis*	*% Savings*	*Value £000's p.a.*
(i) Idle time	500 hours	1000	50	25,000
(ii) Avoidable subcontracting	83 tons	83 (per month)	0	0
(iii) Subcontractor stocks	1000 tons	1000 tons	0	0
(iv) Jobs late	3 (38%)	4 (per month)	44	44,000
(v) Average lateness	1½ weeks	2 weeks		
(vi) Non-prime work	300 hours	400 (per month)	25	1,000
(vii) Work in progress	1000 tons	1000	0	0
(viii) Inter company transfers	833 ton miles	833 (per week)	0	0
(ix) Overtime	0 hours	400 (per month)	100	20,000
			Total	£90,000

Naturally it was too early to expect an improvement in factors (ii), (iii) or (viii) and perhaps one should not have expected much impact on (vii) (work in progress). Nevertheless, on the basis of this sample, about whose selection little choice existed, the estimated savings were in excess of those originally forecast. The running costs were about as forecast, i.e. £120 per month for this factory, and although the capital cost was twice as high, most of the improvements had yet to be implemented. The effects must be attributed to the efforts of management to act on the information made available, rather than the clever scheduling, but only because the new system enabled confidence to be developed in the picture and predictions it gave. The banning of overtime led to the men doing more productive work in a day, which helped mop up the 'idle' time. Incidentally, this led to an initial inaccuracy in the programmes: the capacity in 'standard hours per week' had increased, without an increase in the number of men, which is food for thought in a more general cost reduction context. Here it led to the introduction of a systematic re-appraisal and monitoring of capacity, which has been retained.

Even putting the company share of the development cost as high as £5,000, the benefits were still high for a scheduling study, with a benefit to cost ratio of 5 to 1 instead of 1 to 1 for the small works alone, and benefits amounting to 3.6% as opposed to 1% of turnover. The man weeks in system design and implementation amounted to about 50, including company input, i.e. about 20 per direct employee taking the one factory by itself, or 0.4 taking all three works. This was quite a long time in view of the complexity factor (Complexity 1) of only about 25, because the man weeks should have been predicted as 0.2 × 125 + 0.3 × 25, i.e. 32.5.

The difference in development time may be due to the development of the algorithms, but the difference in performance is more likely to be due to other factors, one important one being the feasibility study.

8 Conclusion

Implementation at the two remaining Works took place in the following year, but the same pressure as at the earlier, smaller Works had not been applied by the end of April 1977, and longer gaps had developed in the scheduling system as a whole between receipt of information and its incorporation into a schedule and subsequent discussion at a planning meeting.

It was planned to rectify these deficiencies during the summer months of 1977, following which a similar evaluation was to have been made. Although the formal evaluation did not take place, due partly to management changes, increases in load have been handled with planned, marginal increases in overtime and staffing, and no worsening of delivery performance. Consequently it may be claimed that the feasibility study shaped the systems design in a direction which has turned out to be advantageous to the company on the basis of the post project appraisal, and that it is unlikely that this particular direction would have been followed had the feasibility study not been undertaken, with a resulting disadvantage to the company.

References

1 Gower, D.N., *Production Control by Computer – the WASP System*, Atomic Energy Research Establishment, Report No. 6259, 1970.

14
Forecasting

C D LEWIS

Professor of Operations Management,
The University of Aston

1 Introduction

Forecasting is a necessary prerequisite for many of the methods and procedures used in Operations Management. Without some reasonable estimate of the future requirements, it is obviously impossible to plan for the future.

The different types of forecasting methods can best be categorised by reference to the time period on which they are based. For instance, at a retail outlet a company may be using as its information base the demand per *week*, at the wholesaler level a company may be concerned with the demand per *month* and overall company performance might be based on the sales per *year*. In each of these cases the time period concerned is different, as might well be the forecasting method employed.

Table 14.1 categorises the various forecasting methods by time period from an hour up to a decade. However, at the manufacturing level with which Operations Management is primarily concerned, the predominant forecasting method used is short-term forecasting since the time period is usually of the order of one calendar month.

Some of the areas in which forecasts are used are:

Table 14.1 Forecasting Methods Categorised by Time Period

Forecasting Method	*Time Period*	*Example*	*Techniques Used*
Immediate-term	hour, day	electrical power forecasting	various; linked to time of day, weather forecast and even TV programmes
Short-term	week, month	demand and sales forecasting	exponential smoothing methods, moving averages
Medium-term	quarter, year	economic and market forecasting	simple and multiple regression techniques, econometric models
Long-term	year, decade	technological forecasting	'think tanks', DELPHI techniques etc.

Inventory control which is concerned with the planning and provision of inventories to act as a buffer between supply and demand. The methods and techniques used to achieve this are fully detailed in Chapter 16. Before any stock control policy can be implemented, it is obviously necessary to have a reasonable estimate of the likely demand for the material, product or service being considered during the inevitable period of delay in obtaining further supplies.

Production planning and scheduling which is concerned with, amongst other things, the drawing up of future plans for the loading of the various production or service facilities. Again, this can only be successfully achieved if a reasonable estimate of the demand for those facilities is available early enough for the plans to be implemented.

Manpower planning which is concerned with the planning of future requirements for labour rather than material or production facilities. Although this is often regarded as a medium-to long-term area of planning, concerned with the length of training periods, labour turnover rates etc., in shift working situations in particular, it can become very much a short-term problem for which accurate forecasts are required.

Financial planning which is concerned particularly with the task of ensuring that a company has sufficient liquidity to continue in business. Many companies have been forced into liquidation not because they have not been producing a profitable product or service, but because they failed to see in advance that at a particular time in the future their financial commitments could not be met from their trading revenue. Very often, on investigation, this may be found to be a very short-term situation, but if some form of bridging facility is not available, the company may be forced into liquidation even though, in theory, future prosperity can be predicted. The use of forecasting techniques to predict cash flows both in and out of a company are being used increasingly to give advance warning of likely cash crises, which can then be avoided either by stimulating income or reducing cash outflow.

2 Short-term Forecasting: Basic Concept

In some situations, production of the manufacturing organisation's final product may be exactly specified in advance, and demand at lower levels of production is totally *dependent* on demand at the higher level (e.g. one car requires exactly five wheel assemblies). In such situations, demand at the material and component level can be discovered by exploding the known sales programme into the material and component parts, then aggregating totals of each part. Techniques such as material requirements planning (MRP), which produces a time schedule of requirements to meet the desired schedule of the finished product, do work successfully and are gaining increasing acceptance. This has been particularly true over the last few years with the increased storage and processing power of computers, a necessary development for the widespread introduction of MRP procedures in view of the large numbers of items involved. A detailed description of MRP procedures is given in Chapter 18.

Where demand at the various levels of production is not interdependent, a valuable approach is to study past values of demand at the appropriate level of production, whether that be raw material, work in progress or finished goods. Such a study may reveal systematic trends within the demand data. If it can be assumed that past demand patterns will be continued into the future, then the extrapolation of those trends can be used to predict future demand. The identification of such trends and the development of predictive models based on them is termed forecasting, and as has been explained earlier, where monthly data is generally involved, the forecasting techniques are usually referred to as 'short-term'. This chapter will therefore concentrate on short-term forecasting with particular emphasis on exponential smoothing methods. A recent survey by the American Production and Inventory Control Society indicated that the percentage of that Society's membership using exponential smoothing methods in the formulation of sales and demand forecasts had risen from 9% in 1961, through 19% in 1966 to 30% in 1973. At the same time, a decline in the use of subjective forecasting methods such as 'sales manager's estimates' and 'executive opinion' was noticed.

In a so-called stationary situation, successive values of the item to be forecast exhibit a random variation about a reasonably steady average. Superimposed on this stationary element one might also find a linear growth element. To expect demand to increase by a fixed amount per month would, of course, be extremely naive; therefore in general, as well as there being random variation in the stationary element, there could also be random variation in the growth element. Over and above the stationary element with superimposed random growth, there might also be a seasonal element, i.e. for particular months of the year a higher or lower value compared with the average monthly value could be expected. It is evident that the situation could be yet further complicated by having random variations in the seasonal factors, and in practice other changes not associated with either the linear or seasonal trend can make the real life situation even more complicated.

This discussion indicates how complicated situations could be *composed* but, in forecasting, the problem is that data already exist. What one wishes to establish is which underlying models might best explain those particular data. Hence, the process of forecasting is essentially one of *decomposing* existing data values into certain model types (possibly with linear or seasonal characteristics) whose parameters can be estimated.

The remainder of this chapter will examine in order of increasing complexity the forecasting techniques used in stationary, growth and seasonal situations. Throughout, it will be assumed that *demand* for the product or services being supplied is the item forecast, simply because demand forecasting is one of the major applications of short-term forecasting, and also because this approach provides a link between this chapter and the chapter on inventory control. However, although demand is in this instance the item being forecast, obviously in other situations the item being forecast could be sales, manpower requirements, cash revenue or whatever.

Since few forecasts will always remain 'in control', simply because the general assumption that what has happened in the past will be continued into the future becomes invalid because of sudden changes or discontinuities in the data being considered, the monitoring of forecasts to effect the detection of such changes is also examined in some detail.

Finally, specifically for demand forecasting situations, the method of selecting the appropriate forecasting method is considered.

3 Forecasting Average Demand in a Stationary Situation

The Moving Average

If demand remains fairly steady over a reasonably long period of time, an obvious approach to estimating average demand is to take an arithmetic average of the last n periods of demand data; this traditionally is called a moving average. If d_t denotes the observed value of demand in period t, then the moving average in period t is defined as

$$m_t = \frac{1}{n}(d_t + d_{t-1} + d_{t-2} \ldots d_{t-n+1})$$

This value of m_t is used as a forecast of demand in period $t + 1$.

Such a moving average, although simple in concept, has several major disadvantages when used for forecasting purposes. These disadvantages are:

(i) When starting a moving average, at least n items of demand data are required.

(ii) The most recent $n - 1$ values of demand must always be stored for further forecasts to be made, as any average based on less than about a dozen values tends to be too sensitive for forecasting purposes. When forecasts based on twelve or more data periods are made for many items (as is generally the case in manufacturing organisations) the amount of accumulated data storage becomes prohibitive.

(iii) The sensitivity of a moving average is inversely proportional to the number of data values included in the average. It is relatively simple to increase the sensitivity by reducing the number of periods incorporated and thus discarding demand data. However, in order to decrease the sensitivity, the number of periods must be increased and very seldom will the demand data be available for the additional necessary past time periods.

(iv) With an orthodox moving average, all data included within the average are equally weighted by $1/n$. In most forecasting situations, with some specific exceptions, demand data can be assumed to become less relevant as they grow older. For forecasting purposes, therefore, one generally requires an average which gives greater weight to more recent observations.

4 Exponential Smoothing Methods

The exponentially weighted average

Most of the disadvantages of the moving average can be overcome by using weights which decrease with time. Because, for a mathematically true average, the sum of weights must be unity, what is ideally required is an infinite series of weights with decreasing values which converge at infinity to produce a total sum of one. Such a series is the exponential series with successive weights.

$$\alpha + \alpha\,(1-\alpha) + \alpha\,(1-\alpha)^2 + \alpha\,(1-\alpha)^3, \ldots$$

which sum one at infinity if α lies between zero and one. Choosing a value of 0.2, the first seven values of such a series would be

0.200, 0.160, 0.128, 0.102, 0.082, 0.066, 0.052

which sum to 0.79. It is apparent that if sufficient values are taken, the sum will approach a value of one.

Incorporating the exponential series as the weighting series yields an exponentially weighted average (u_t) defined by

$$u_t = \alpha d_t + \alpha\,(1-\alpha)\,d_{t-1} + \alpha\,(1-\alpha)^2\,d_{t-2} + \alpha(1-\alpha)^3\,d_{t-3}, \ldots$$

or

$$u_t = \alpha d_t + (1-\alpha)\,[\,\alpha d_{t-1} + \alpha\,(1-\alpha)\,d_{t-2} + \alpha\,(1-\alpha)^2\,d_{t-3}, \ldots$$

Since the term in square brackets is precisely u_{t-1}, the exponentially weighted average can be rewritten very simply as

$$u_t = \alpha d_t + (1-\alpha)\,u_{t-1}$$

As before, u_t is used as a forecast for period $t + 1$. A numerical illustration is given in the first five rows of table 14.2.

It is apparent that the exponentially weighted average

Table 14.2 Fully Expanded Forecasting Schedule with $\alpha = 0.2$ (* = estimate)

		Jan.	Feb.	Mar.
1. This month's demand	d_t	60	70	55
2. Last month's forecast for this month	u_{t-1}	70.00*	68.0	68.4
3. α x this month's demand	αd_t	12	14	11
4. (1 − α) x last month's forecast for this month	$(1-\alpha)u_{t-1}$	56.0	54.4	54.7
5. This month's forecast for next month	$u_t = \alpha d_t + (1-\alpha)u_{t-1}$	68.0	68.4	65.7
6. This month's forecasting error	$e_t = d_t - u_{t-1}$	-10.0	2.0	-13.4
7. α x absolute value of this month's forecasting error	$\alpha \mid e_t \mid$	2.0	0.40	2.68
8. (1 − α) x last month's mean absolute deviation	$(1-\alpha)\text{MAD}_{t-1}$	10.00*	9.60	8.0
9. This month's mean absolute deviation	$\text{MAD}_t = \alpha \mid e_t \mid + (1-\alpha)\text{MAD}_{t-1}$	12.00	10.00	10.68
10. This month's estimate of standard deviation	$\sigma_t = 1.25\ \text{MAD}_t$	15.0	12.5	13.4
11. α x this month's forecasting error	αe_t	-2.0	0.4	-2.68
12. (1 − α) x last month's smoothed error	$(1-\alpha)\bar{e}_{t-1}$	1.00*	-0.80	-0.32
13. This month's smoothed error	$\bar{e}_t = \alpha e_t + (1-\alpha)\bar{e}_{t-1}$	-1.00	-0.40	-3.00
14. Trigg's tracking signal	$T_t = \bar{e}_t/\text{MAD}_t$	-0.08	-0.04	-0.28

April	May	June	July	Aug.	Sept.	Oct.	Nov.	Dec.	Jan.
80	90	65	70	75	60	80	90	100	95
65.7	68.6	72.9	71.3	71.0	71.8	69.4	71.6	75.2	80.2
16	18	13	14	15	12	16	18	20	19
52.6	54.9	58.3	57.0	56.8	57.4	56.6	57.2	60.2	64.2
68.6	72.9	71.3	71.0	71.8	69.4	71.6	75.2	80.2	83.2
14.3	21.4	-7.9	-1.3	4.0	-11.8	10.6	18.4	24.8	14.8
2.85	4.28	1.57	0.25	0.79	2.36	2.11	3.69	4.95	2.96
8.54	9.11	10.71	9.82	8.05	7.07	7.54	7.72	9.12	11.25
11.39	13.39	12.28	10.07	8.84	9.43	9.65	11.41	14.07	14.21
14.1	16.7	15.3	12.6	11.0	11.8	12.1	14.3	17.6	17.7
2.85	4.28	-1.57	-0.25	-0.79	-2.36	2.11	3.69	4.95	2.96
-2.40	0.36	3.71	1.71	1.16	1.56	-0.64	1.17	3.88	7.06
0.45	4.64	2.14	1.46	1.95	-0.80	1.47	4.86	8.83	10.02
0.03	0.34	0.17	0.14	0.22	-0.08	0.15	0.42	0.62	0.70

overcomes the problem of storing data (since all previous data are neatly compacted into a single figure represented by u_{t-1}) and also overcomes the problem of starting up with no previous data (since, once an initial guess for u_{t-1} is made, when fresh data, d_t, arrive, the next forecast can be directly evaluated). The sensitivity of the forecast can be changed at any time, simply by changing the value of α which is known as the exponential smoothing constant. This is typically chosen from a range of values between 0.05 and 0.3; the values of 0.1 and 0.2 are the most used.

In stationary demand situations, because no growth or seasonality is assumed, the forecast for any month in the future is the same as for one month ahead. It is accepted, of course, that the further ahead that forecast is made, the wider will be the possible range of demand values that could be expected to fall either side of that average value.

An alternative method of calculating the exponentially weighted average is to re-organise the original equation into the form

$$u_t = u_{t-1} + \alpha (d_t - u_{t-1})$$

In this form the forecast can be evaluated graphically by saying that the new forecast u_t will be equal to the old forecast u_{t-1} plus one-fifth (with $\alpha = 0.2$) of the gap between the old forecast and the current demand value. This procedure is shown for a set of random demand values in figure 14.1. The gap $(d_t - u_{t-1})$ is in fact the current value of the forecasting error which is denoted as e_t. The previous equation can therefore be rewritten

$$u_t = u_{t-1} + \alpha e_t$$

The forecasting error is calculated in the sixth row of table 14.2.

Whilst in practice the majority of mathematically based short-term forecasts are evaluated by computer, for those situations where a manual evaluation makes more economic sense, the nomogram shown as figure 14.2 can be used. Because the nomogram method is so simple to use, it can readily be used by personnel with absolutely no mathematical background. Typical applications have been with forecasting of demand for oils and lubricants by an order clerk in a

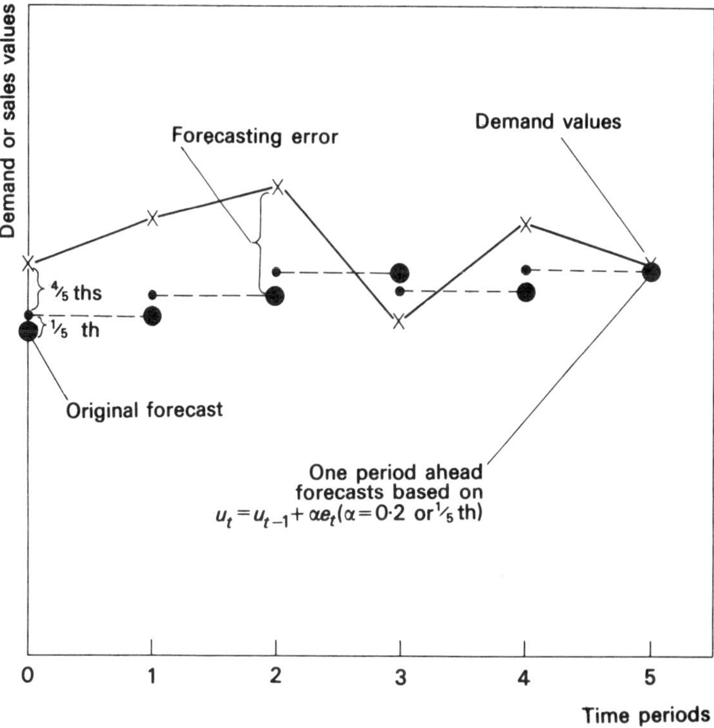

Figure 14.1 *Graphical Construction of Forecasts based on an Exponentially Weighted Average*

machine shop and the prediction of bedlinen requirements by ward sisters in a large hospital.

5 Calculation of the Standard Deviation of Demand

The Mean Absolute Deviation

Examination of figure 14.3 reveals that, although the average demand has remained at approximately 100 units over the whole year, after June a distinct change in the pattern of demand has occurred. It is apparent that it is the spread of demand values about the average which has changed significantly, rather than the average level of demand itself. Such a change would not be detected as a change in the forecast and

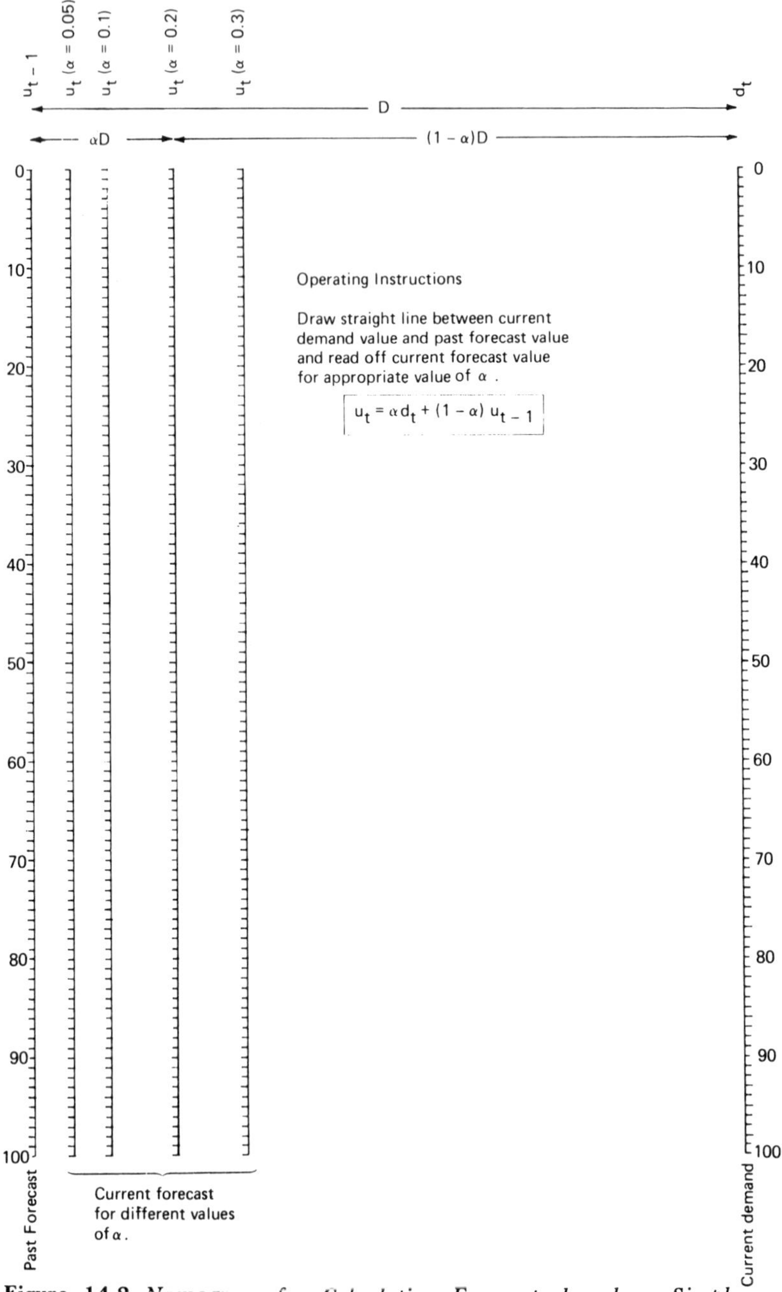

Figure 14.2 *Nomogram for Calculating Forecasts based on Simple Exponentially Weighted Averages*

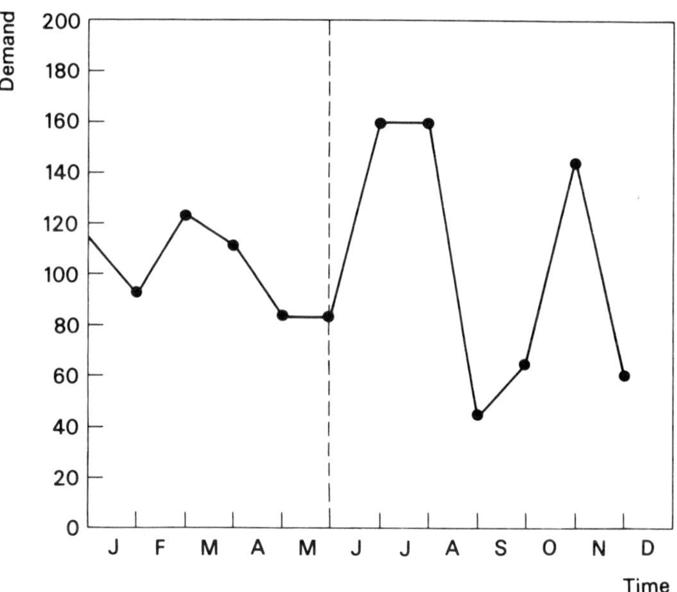

Figure 14.3 *Change in the Spread of Demand about a Steady Average Value*

could, therefore, only be detected by a separate measure of 'spread'.

The statistic most used in short-term forecasting to measure spread is known as the mean absolute deviation (MAD). As its name indicates, the mean absolute deviation is simply the mean or average of the absolute values of errors or deviations from the long-term average level of demand. With the present forecasting model, the mean absolute deviation can be calculated as the exponentially weighted average of the absolute value of forecasting errors, where $|e_t|$ denotes the absolute value of e_t. (See rows 7–9 of table 14.2.) A measure of variability of demand which is particularly useful is the standard deviation σ. It may be shown that, for all practical purposes, the estimated standard deviation for period t is given by $\sigma_t = 1.25\ \mathrm{MAD}_t$. (See row 10 of table 14.2.)

The standard deviation defines the degree of variation about the forecast that one can usually expect. For instance, in table 14.2 the forecast of 80.2 (row 2) produced in January as a prediction of what is expected in the following February is accompanied by a standard deviation value 17.7 (row 10). For most practical purposes it can be assumed that the actual demand in February will fall within an envelope of ± two standard deviations either side of the forecasts which in this case is 80.2 ± 2 × 17.7 which defines an envelope from 44.8 to 115.6. An examination of all the figures in table 14.2 reveals that this relationship, known as the 95% confidence limits, is never violated.

It cannot be stressed too highly that any forecast without some form of confidence limits can be most misleading. A forecast of 1000 with 95% confidence limits of 900 to 1100 (meaning that on 95% of occasions the actual demand value should fall within those limits) is totally different from the same forecast with limits between zero and 2000. In the second case (where the standard deviation is obviously 500) the forecast is so imprecise that all that can be inferred is that there might be some demand next month!

6 Non-stationary Demand Situation

Where the average demand value does not remain relatively constant over a period of time, the assumption of a stationary demand process can no longer be substantiated and forecasts based on the simple exponentially weighted average are no longer appropriate.

The variation of an average with time is known as a trend and such trends in a demand situation can vary in character and type.

(a) Character of Demand Trends

(i) Linear trends

A linear trend is one in which the average demand value increases or decreases linearly with time. A product with a linearly increasing trend could be typified by a new product with ever increasing sales or by a product in an expanding market retaining its percentage of that market.

A product with a linearly decreasing trend could be typified by a product rapidly becoming obsolete.

(ii) Seasonal trends
A seasonal trend is one in which the average demand value varies in some cyclical fashion in sympathy with some imposed time cycle. In the demand situation with which manufacturing organisations are concerned, this time cycle is invariably a yearly one in which the average demand in some months is up, compared with the overall yearly average, and in some months is down. Fashion goods such as clothes and shoes are naturally subject to such seasonal trends, but a large section of this country's engineering industry is similarly affected by the sales of cars which decline with the approach of winter and increase in the spring.

(iii) Combined linear and seasonal trends
As the name indicates, this type of trend is a direct combination of the two already mentioned. A good example of this was to have been seen in the sixties and early seventies in the bookings for airline seats over the past decade. The increasing use of air transport over the years provides the linear element of the trend and the seasonal pattern of travel within each year (as influenced by peak demands during Christmas, Easter and summer holidays) provides the seasonal element based on an annual time cycle.

(b) Types of Demand Trends

(i) Additive trends
As well as having certain characteristics, demands trends can also be distinguished by their type. An additive type of trend is one in which an approximately regular amount is added to or subtracted from each consecutive demand value, as influenced by the character of the trend. For instance, with a linear additive trend, an average increase in demand of ten units for each consecutive month might be expected.

(ii) Ratio or multiplicative trends
A demand trend of a ratio type is subject to a percentage increase or decrease, as influenced by the character of the trend. Thus, the demand for an item with an increasing linear

ratio trend might be expected to increase at say two per cent per month.

(iii) Combined additive and ratio trends
This type of trend, which is of course a direct combination of the two already mentioned, tends to be rather complicated from the point of view of mathematical analysis, and is usually dealt with, other than by sophisticated computer programmes, as either just an additive trend or just a ratio trend.

When describing any demand trend it is necessary to describe both its type and character. The more usual trends for which relatively simple forecasting models have been developed are:

(c) Examples of the More Common Trends found in Practice

(i) Linear additive trend
A project subject to such a trend would have an average demand value increasing (or decreasing) by an approximately fixed quantity with each time period. Figure 14.4 shows such a demand situation which is distinguished from a linear ratio trend case (figure 14.5) by the fact that although the average demand value is increasing, the spread or variation of individual demand values about that average remains virtually constant.

(ii) Linear ratio trend
A product subject to a linear ratio would either increase (or decrease) its average demand value by an approximately fixed percentage with each successive time period. (Figure 14.5

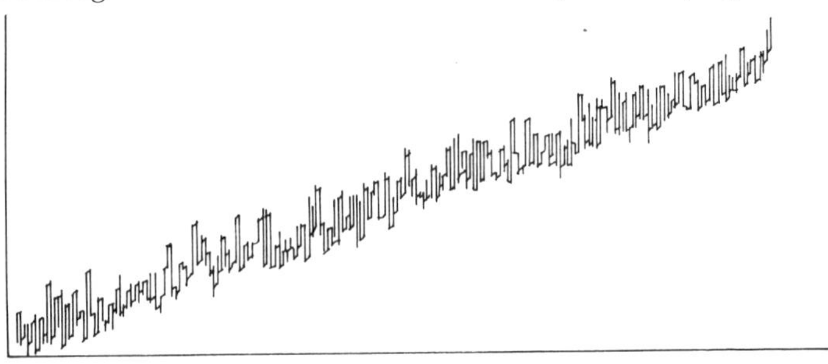

Figure 14.4 *Demand Pattern Subject to a Linear Additive Trend* (i)

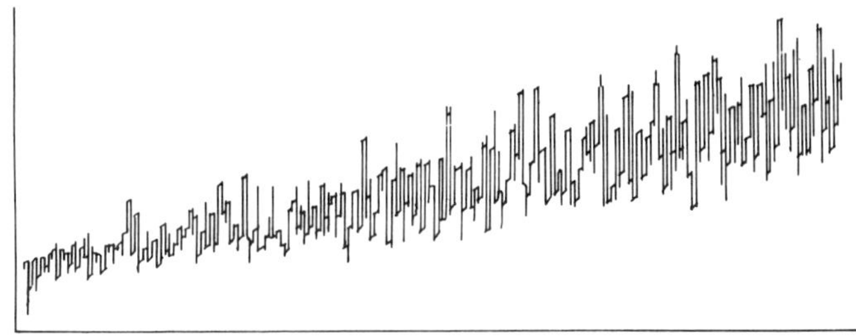

Figure 14.5 *Demand Pattern Subject to a Linear Ratio Trend* (ii)

illustrates such a demand situation from which it can be seen that not only does the average value increase with time, but so also does the spread or variation of individual demand values about that average.)

(iii) Combined linear and seasonal additive trend

This type of trend also covers the situation of the pure seasonal additive trend with no linear element. Generally, however, models dealing with seasonal trends tend also to accept the possible influence of some linear element. This is because if a linear element is present in the data, its effect can upset completely the analysis made by a pure seasonal model. A linear and seasonal additive trend demand situation over a four year period is shown in figure 14.6. Note the two annual demand peaks being repeated year by year.

Having discussed the different trend types and characters

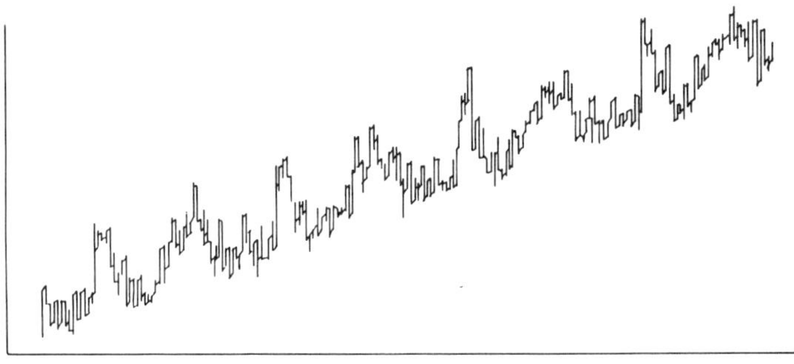

Figure 14.6 *Demand Pattern Subject to both a Linear and a Seasonal Additive Trend*

that are more likely to occur in an industrial demand situation, the mathematical forecasting models developed specifically for some such trends will now be detailed.

7 Linear Additive Trend Forecasting Models

When dealing with a linear additive trend model, it is assumed that the underlying process generating d_t has an average which changes linearly with time, thus

$$d_t = \mu + \lambda t + \epsilon$$

where μ is the process average; λ is the process growth rate; and ϵ is a process error with zero mean (noise).

Several forecasting models have been proposed to meet this demand situation.

(a) Holt's Method

The method proposed by Holt is based on estimating λ, the factor which measures the degree of linear growth (or decline) with time. This growth factor is estimated by b_t which is calculated as the exponentially weighted average value of the difference between the current exponentially weighted average value of demand u_t and the immediate past value u_{t-1}; this difference $(u_t - u_{t-1})$ represents for the current period the growth rate of u_t. A feature of the method is that the value of the immediate past growth factor b_{t-1} is included to update the current value of the exponentially weighted average demand value as this always lags behind the actual demand in linear situations.

The equations describing Holt's model are, in the order in which they are used,

$$u_t = Ad_t + (1 - A)(u_{t-1} + b_{t-1})$$

and $$b_t = B\,(u_t - u_{t-1}) + (1 - B)b_{t-1}$$

where A and B are arbitrarily chosen exponential weighting factors with values between zero and one.

To estimate the expected demand in the future with any

type of trend model, it is necessary to make specific reference to the period for which the forecast is being considered. Throughout it will be assumed that such forecasts are calculated for the period 'T' time periods ahead, that is at time $(t+T)$.

In Holt's model, having estimated the growth (or decline) factor b_t a forecast of what demand can be expected in the future, i.e. f_{t+T}, is equated as the estimate of the demand average at the current time (u_t) plus the expected increase due to the growth factor b_t and the number of time periods that this is assumed to operate for, namely for T periods. Hence,

$$f_{t+T} = u_t + b_t T$$

(b) Brown's Double Smoothing Method

This method of Brown's (1959) accepts that after initial transients have died down, a simple exponentially weighted average will always lag a true linear trend in demand by an amount given by

$$\text{LAG} = \frac{1-\alpha}{\alpha}\lambda$$

where λ is the slope of the process trend.

Brown has also shown that a double exponentially weighted average $\bar{u}_t$ defined as

$$\bar{u}_t = \alpha u_t + (1-\alpha)\,\bar{u}_{t-1}$$

will, after transients have died down, also lag the primary smoothed average u_t by the same amount as u_t lags d_t. Under steady state conditions the actual and estimated lags can be equated so that

$$u_t - \bar{u}_t = \frac{1-\alpha}{\alpha}b_t$$

where λ is now replaced by its estimate b_t and hence

$$b_t = \frac{\alpha}{1-\alpha}(u_t - \bar{u}_t)$$

Thus the forecast for d_t at any time T is given by

$$f_{t+T} = f_t + b_t T$$

or

$$f_{t+T} = 2u_t - \bar{u}_t + \frac{\alpha}{1-\alpha}(u_t - \bar{u}_t)T$$

8 Seasonal Models

Holt–Winters De-seasonaling Method

The Holt–Winters method maintains that not to take into account a linear trend in demand patterns subjected to seasonal fluctuations necessarily means that any linear trend effect will automatically be incorporated in the de-seasonaling factors which will then become unduly biased. Holt–Winters, therefore, incorporate a linear trend factor in the exponentially smoothed average (used to estimate the demand's process average) before estimating the de-seasonaling factors. Hence;

$$u_t = A\frac{d_t}{F_{t-L}} + (1-A)(u_{t-1} + b_{t-1})$$

where F_{t-L} is the smoothed de-seasonaling factor calculated at the corresponding period of the last seasonal cycle (L being the number of periods in the seasonal cycle), and the current de-seasonaling factor calculated now but not used for a further L periods ahead, is evaluated as:

$$F_t = C\frac{d_t}{u_t} + (1-C)F_{t-L}$$

and the estimate of the linear trend factor is then calculated as usual by:

$$b_t = B(u_t - u_{t-1}) + (1-B)b_{t-1}$$

and the forecast for period $t+T$ is given by:

$$f_{t+T} = (u_t + b_t T)F_{t-L+T}$$

where F_{t-L+T} is the last calculated de-seasonaling factor corresponding to the period $t - L + T$ and A, B and C all lie between zero and one. Due to the relative complexity of growth and seasonal models compared with simple exponential smoothing, they are usually implemented on a computer, although examples of organisations who have implemented seasonal models by manual calculations are not unknown.

9 Monitoring Forecasting System

The Trigg or Smoothed Error Method

Once any routine system for making forecasts has been set up, it is necessary to have some form of monitoring method to indicate when demand becomes so different from the level expected that the forecasting system breaks down. All forecasts are delayed in their response to sudden changes, and the resultant lags brought about by such delays naturally produce larger than usual forecasting errors.

Once a monitoring method has indicated a lack of control in forecasting, questions can be asked as to what is responsible for this sudden change, whether the change is likely to be sustained or not, and if not, when is it likely to end. Such information obviously cannot be derived from the forecasting system itself; it is in this type of situation that the market intelligence of the company's salesforce may give useful clues.

The monitoring method proposed in 1964 by Trigg is based on the definition of a tracking signal whose value indicates, with specified degrees of statistical confidence, the failure of a forecasting system because of a change in the demand pattern.

Defining the smoothed error, $\bar{e}_t$, in period t as the exponentially weighted average of forecasting errors in previous periods:

$$\bar{e}_t = \alpha e_t + (1 - \alpha)\, \bar{e}_{t-1}$$

Trigg's tracking signal for period t (denoted T_t) is defined as the ratio of the exponentially smoothed error to the mean absolute deviation:

$$T_t = \frac{\bar{e}_t}{\text{MAD}_t}$$

This tracking signal ranges between +1 and −1; the higher its absolute value, the more likely it is that the forecasting model is out of control because of a sudden jump in demand. Table 14.3 gives statistical confidence levels for various values of the tracking signal, on the assumption that the value of the smoothing constant α is 0.2. Thus, if the calculated value of Trigg's tracking signal becomes larger than 0.74, this would indicate with 95% confidence that the forecasting system was out of control.

Now refer back to rows 11–14 of table 14.2 which present calculations of smoothed errors and tracking signals for the twelve month period. The low absolute value of the tracking signal in March, April and May (0.28, 0.03, 0.34) does not suggest that the jump in demand from 55 in March to 80 in April and to 90 in May (row 1) represents a fundamental change in demand. However, because the tracking signal rises to 0.70 in the final period, this confirms with about 94% confidence that the four successive high values of demand of 80, 90, 100 and 95 from October onwards do represent a genuine or significant change in underlying conditions of demand.

When starting the calculations for the tracking signal it is essential to provide reasonable estimates for the immediate past values of the mean absolute deviation (MAD_{t-1}) and, to a lesser extent, the smoothed error ($\bar{e}_{t-1}$). Without such initialisation the first tracking signal will be either +1 or −1, indicating to all eagerly awaiting the first computer print-out that everything is totally out of control! A reasonable working assumption for initialising these variables is to set MAD_{t-1} equal to one tenth of the initial forecast estimate u_{t-1} and $\bar{e}_{t-1}$ equal to one fiftieth.

Table 14.3 Tracking Signal Confidence Levels ($\alpha = 0.2$)

Level of Confidence (i.e. Cumulative Probability)	*Absolute Value of Trigg's Tracking Signal T_t*
80%	0.54
90%	0.66
95%	0.74
98%	0.81
100%	1.00

A fairly obvious method of using the tracking signal for many products would be simply to highlight those items whose tracking signal exceeded a value of say 0.70. This rather naive approach is unfortunately embodied in much of the computer software in this area. It may highlight as out of control a wildly varying number of items each time an analysis is made. This is not usually very helpful for the investigating team which is trying to find the reasons why certain forecasts have gone out of control and which is attempting to get the forecasts back in control. (The reasons might be a competitor's strike temporarily reducing market competition and thus creating a sudden surge in sales, or alternatively a sales promotion having the same effect.) What such a team requires is a system which highlights a fixed number of items.

10 Adaptive Forecasting

(a) The Adaptive Response Rate Forecasting Method

Adaptive forecasting is a term used for forecasting methods which adapt themselves to the nature of the demand information with which they are dealing. The basic requirement of any such adaptive forecasting method is that as the demand data become relatively more changeable, so the forecast itself responds and becomes more sensitive. Conversely, as the demand becomes relatively more stable, so the forecast becomes less sensitive in order to filter out extraneous 'noise'. In technical terms, this requires that the value of the exponential weighting constant should decrease as demand becomes more stable. Trigg's proposal (in 1964) for a tracking signal to be used for monitoring purposes in forecasting situations was followed by a proposal, in 1967 in conjunction with Leach, which advocated the use of this same tracking signal in an adaptive response rate forecasting method. In essence, the Trigg and Leach method of adaptive response rate forecasting can be described as follows.

Having defined what is required of the exponential smoothing constant for adaptive forecasting, it is obvious that the modulus or absolute value of Trigg's original tracking signal fits all the requirements. It increases in value when demand data become more changeable; it decreases in value as demand becomes more stable and by definition it lies within the extreme limits of zero and one.

Hence, in the stationary demand situation, the forecast for any period in the future using the Trigg and Leach adaptive response rate forecasting model is given by:

$$f_{t+T} = \tilde{u}_t = |T_t|\, d_t + (1 - |T_t|)\, \tilde{u}_{t-1}$$

where again;

$$\bar{e}_t = \alpha e_t + (1 - \alpha)\, \bar{e}_{t-1}$$

$$\text{MAD}_t = \alpha\, |e_t| + (1 - \alpha)\, \text{MAD}_{t-1}$$

and

$$T_t = \bar{e}_t / \text{MAD}_t$$

Using this method, when forecasts tend to go out of control due to sudden changes in the demand average, the value of $|T_t|$ is automatically increased and therefore gives more weight to recent data and the forecast 'homes' rapidly into the new average level. Once the system has settled at the new level, the value of $|T_t|$ is automatically reduced again to prevent the forecasts responding to continual small demand fluctuations (noise). This adaptive response to sudden changes compared with simple exponentially weighted averages as shown in figure 14.7 can also be adapted to linear and seasonal trend models. It is particularly useful when initialising a forecasting system where assumptions made can be greatly in error.

One slight disadvantage of this method, ironically, is that as forecasts are greatly improved, forecasting errors are reduced which in turn alters the values calculated for the tracking signal. In fact, this error reduction invalidates the use of the tracking signal for monitoring purposes when forecasts are of the adaptive response rate type. If both the improved forecasts derived from adaptive response rate forecasting and also monitoring facilities are required, this author has suggested that a non-adaptive forecast must be generated simply to generate a value of Trigg's tracking signal for monitoring purposes.

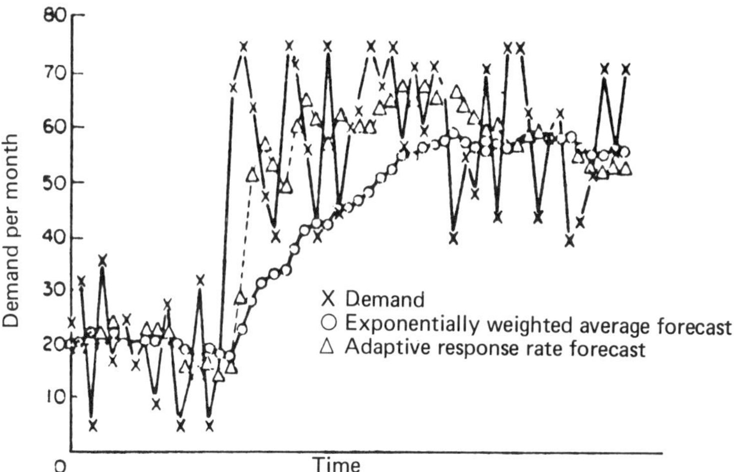

Figure 14.7 *Improved Response of Adaptive Response Rate Forecast to Step Change in Demand*

(b) Delayed Adaptive Response Rate Forecasting Method

Shone has suggested a slight modification of Trigg and Leach's formula which, it is claimed, reduces the response of the adaptive response rate to spurious period impulses, whilst maintaining the forecast's improved response to other types of demand changes. Shone's modification of Trigg and Leach's method is simply to use the one-period delayed value of the tracking signal T_{t-1} rather than the current value T_t.

Then the adaptive rate response rate forecast is given for the stationary demand situation by:

$$f_{t+T} = \widetilde{u}_t = |T_{t-1}|\, d_t + (1 - |T_{t-1}|)\, \widetilde{u}_{t-1}$$

and the characteristic of this type of adaptive response rate forecast compared with that of the original Trigg and Leach proposal is indicated in figure 14.8.

11 Grouping Methods: Pareto or ABC Analysis

The forecasting methods so far described can be invaluable where it is important to obtain regular and up-to-date forecasts of demand, but it would be foolish to spend time and energy

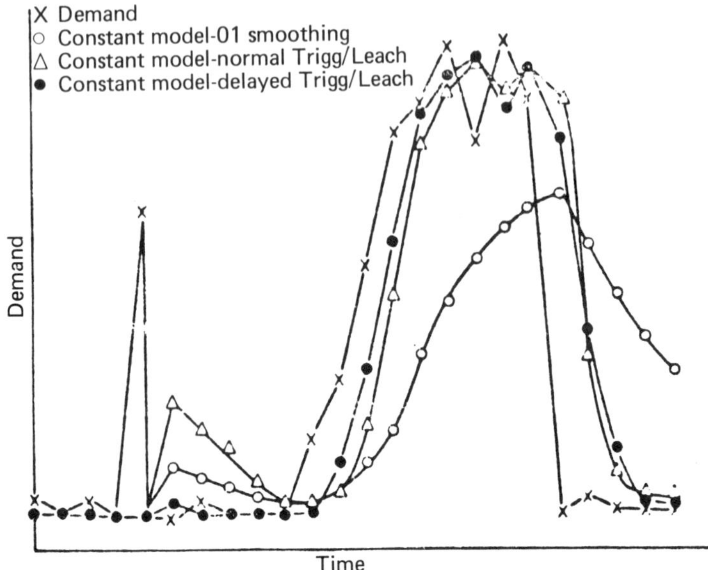

Figure 14.8 *Improved Response of Delayed Adaptive Response Rate Method*

applying them to unimportant or very slow-moving products. It is, therefore, worthwhile classifying a firm's products into several different groups and examining what kind of forecasting system (if any) is most appropriate for the products of each group.

In most industrial organisations a few items represent a large proportion of annual usage value turnover, profit, invested capital or some other indicator of 'importance'. In fact, the distribution of items follows a Pareto distribution, as illustrated in figure 14.9.

The particular shape of a company's Pareto curve can vary in detail depending on the type of organisation being studied, but as a general rule it can be said that approximately:

the first 10% of the stocked items represent 60% of the usage value: these items are termed 'A' items;

the next 30% of the stocked items represent 30% of the usage value: these are termed 'B' items;

the remaining 60% of stocked items represent only 10% of the usage value: these are termed 'C' items.

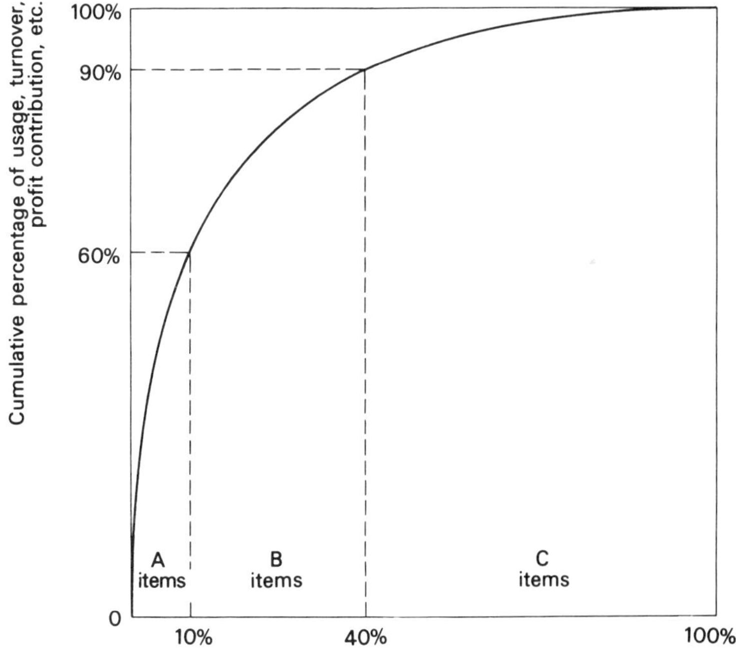

Figure 14.9 *Pareto Distribution for Stocked Items*

The division of an organisation's stockholding into three such groups is known as Pareto or ABC analysis. We now discuss the most appropriate forecasting method for each group.

12 Choice of Forecasting Methods

(a) Category A Items

These are expensive or much used items, usually excluding engineering spares for which separate treatment is more appropriate.

With this category of item it will generally be advisable to monitor forecasts so as to identify rapidly changes in the demand pattern. Instigating a monitoring scheme for 'A' items is also reasonably practical because relatively few items are involved. The use of a monitoring scheme will generally preclude the use of adaptive forecasting methods of the Trigg/Leach adaptive response rate type and thus a non-adaptive forecasting system will normally be adopted. The specific choice between non-adaptive methods will generally be centred around the fact that the more comprehensive the forecast, the more accurate the results, but the higher the cost of implementation.

(b) Category B Items

These are medium cost or moderately used items. As category 'B' items are marginally less costly and less important than 'A' items, a rapid response of the forecast to sudden changes in the demand pattern is marginally more important than a sure identification of that change using a monitoring method. Thus an adaptive forecasting method of the Trigg/Leach adaptive response rate type would generally be most suitable. Also with this type of item there is less chance that short-term mathematical forecasts will be 'modified' in the light of sales and market intelligence and, hence, obtaining more responsive forecasts will be well worthwhile. With 'A' items, such is their importance that a certain degree of manual intervention will always take place with the mathematically forecast figures and this feature would nullify the particular advantages of an adaptive type of forecasting method.

(c) Category C Items

These are low cost items or 'small runners'. Because this category represents a large number of stocked items of low usage value, it is usually inadvisable to operate a formalised forecasting scheme, simply because of the high implementation costs involved. Such items are often controlled by a two-bin inventory system (explained in Chapter 16) and, because of their cheapness, relative overstocking can frequently be permitted in order to insulate against any significant variations in demand. Because many 'C' items are standard, and hence rapidly available from several suppliers, it may not be necessary even to take this precaution. It is, therefore, not usual to have a formalised system of forecasting for 'C' items. Rough annual assessment of demand is usually sufficient.

13 Conclusion

This chapter has covered the more important forecasting and associated techniques in the short-term forecasting area. While some may appear somewhat complicated, unfortunately as patterns of data become more complicated, so do the methods by which they must be analysed. However, the reader can take comfort from the fact that in computer terms the models suggested in this chapter are readily calculated and indeed all commercial computer installations have forecasting software (programmes) available.

References and Further Reading

1 Brown, R.G., *Statistical Forecasting for Inventory Control*, McGraw-Hill 1959.
2 Brown, R.G., *Smoothing, Forecasting and Prediction of Discrete Time Series*, Prentice-Hall 1962.
3 Holt, C.C., *Forecasting Seasonals by Exponentially Weighted Moving Averages*, Office of Naval Research, Memo No. 52, 1957.
4 ICI, *Short-term Forecasting*. ICI Monograph No. 2, Oliver & Boyd 1964.
5 ICI, *Cumulative Sum Techniques*, ICI Monograph No. 3, Oliver & Boyd 1964.
6 Lewis, C.D., *Demand Analysis and Inventory Control*, Saxon House 1975.
7 Trigg, D.W., Monitoring a forecasting system, *Operational Research Quarterly*, Vol. 15, 1964.
8 Trigg, D.W. and Leach, A.C., Exponential smoothing with adaptive response rate, *Operational Research Quarterly*, Vol. 18, 1967.
9 Winter, P.R., Forecasting sales by exponentially weighted moving averages, *Management Science*, Vol. 6, 1960.

15

Selecting a Forecasting Method for Inventory Control in a Maintenance Environment*

K A TURNER
and
J G WESTON

London Transport Executive

1 Introduction

Increasing amounts of research are being done into the problems of controlling inventories in manufacturing industries, and also to an extent into after sales spare parts operations. However, nothing like so much work has been done to discover the problems of ensuring material is available for large scale maintenance operations, where major capital equipment and rolling stock need to be serviced.

This case-study outlines investigations to improve the methods used to control the spare parts required to maintain London Transport's bus fleet, and in particular the selection of an appropriate forecasting method.

* Reproduced from *Proceedings of 14th European Technical Conference on Production and Inventory Control* by kind permission of the authors and the British Production and Inventory Control Society.

2 Outline of Maintenance Operation

London Transport runs about 5,500 buses of 8 different types from 67 bus garages. Day to day maintenance is carried out at garages, while mechanical and electrical units are over-hauled and repaired at Chiswick Works, and body work re-furbished at Aldenham.

When Mechanical and Electrical units fail they are removed from buses at garages and returned to Chiswick for repair, while buses are sent to Aldenham for overhaul once every 6 years.

To facilitate the overhaul of mechanical units while keeping buses in service, a float of extra units is held, part of the float being held at garages, and part at Chiswick Works as 'Work in Progress'.

To give an indication of the level of activity at Chiswick Works, output of engines in 1979 is likely to be in the region of 2,500, gearboxes 3,000 and starter motors 5,000. Most other significant units are overhauled. The exact number depends on their failure rate.

Spare parts are held in two main storehouses – at Chiswick which contains 40,000 parts valued at £6.5m and at Aldenham which stocks 30,000 parts valued at £2.4m.

These two storehouses issue day to day requirements of consumable parts such as fan belts, brake liners and bus lamps direct to garages, and also provide the two overhaul works with material to enable them to carry out more thorough repairs and overhauls. The average daily requisition throughput is 900 at Chiswick and 500 at Aldenham.

Inventory control is based on an ICL 1900 batch based system, with a slave 2904 on-line computer used to capture issue and receipt data and stock balance information via Visual Display Units.

Re-order decisions are based on a re-order point system, the re-order and expediting levels derived from computer forecasts, worked out by an exponentially smoothed moving average, which is updated monthly from current consumption. A variable buffer stock is used to take account of differences in demand during lead time.

A further system is available where it is considered that automatic forecasts would be unreliable. Here fixed levels are input by Stock Controllers, based on manually calculated estimates provided by the engineers.

Re-order quantities are largely based on the standard EOQ principle.

A detailed investigation was started in early 1978 to evaluate the overall performance of the system and to identify areas of weakness. The main areas examined were:

accuracy of computer forecasts and engineers' estimates;
buffer stocks and service levels;
methods of measuring service levels.

This case study examines the analysis of the accuracy of computer forecasts and engineers' estimates.

3 Forecasting Methods

(a) Accuracy of Forecasts and Estimates

Exponential smoothing has been used for forecasting future demand for an item. The smoothing factor is reduced (from 0.33 to 0.1 over a year) as more information is obtained. There are three features of the method as employed by LT which have led to biases of the forecast:

reliance on an initial engineer's estimate for the first 6 months;
ignoring exceptional demands;
pre-averaging of demands.

This section discusses these and the suggested changes proposed in our study.

(b) Engineers' Estimates

In the original design of the stock control system engineers' estimates could continue to be used for expensive and critical items. This approach was also applied to forecasting. The need to input a manually calculated estimate to start an item on the forecast system has meant that the accuracy of the estimate is a very important influence on the size of inventory. Nearly one third of all items which were nominally on the forecast system were in fact in the initial 6 months gestation period.

The accuracy of estimates had been measured by comparing the last estimate provided with consumption in the previous year. The results showed that:

(a) the estimates were generally very inaccurate and on average overestimated by around 30–40%;
(b) the overestimate was generally higher for the slower moving items;
(c) as could be expected, there was a direct relationship between the estimate bias and inventory performance with weekly cover rising and nil stocks falling as the bias increases.

The influence of the engineers' estimates is both large and adverse. It was decided to limit its effect by removing the 6 months gestation period for the estimate and allow the exponential smoothing system to update the estimate immediately.

(c) Ignoring Exceptional Demands

If the demand in a month lay outside a range of two standard deviations from the expected value, a Stock Position Report (SPR) was produced, but no use made of the demand in forecasting. Since high demands are more common than low, this procedure underestimated usage. (The SPR produced also uselessly overloaded the stock control clerks.) The effect of the feature was investigated with the alternative forecasting system (see below) and a decision made to widen limits to four standard deviations so that fewer exception reports are produced. In addition, forecasts are now updated even if the demand is outside the control limits.

(d) Pre-averaging of Demands

Demand in a month was pre-averaged before being used in a

forecast; that is divided by the interval in months since the last non-zero demand. (Months with zero demand are ignored in this updating process). This is a reasonable procedure to adopt if the size of demand is related to the length of the interval, but when, more often, the size of demand is independent of the interval, demand is overestimated. Three alternative methods were therefore investigated and compared with this system.

(a) *'Plain' forecasting*
This is exponential smoothing without pre-averaging. It updates the forecast with a monthly demand irrespective of whether or not it is zero. In common with the other methods, it updates the forecast using a smoothing factor set initially high but to reduce to a long-term level of 0.1.

(b) *'Adaptive' forecasting*
In this modification to the plain system, the smoothing factor is itself calculated based upon the departure of demand from forecast. (The Trigg & Leach method).[1] In principle this should make the forecast far more responsive to changes which occur in demand level.

(c) *'Separate' forecasting* of demand and interval
This is a refinement to take account especially of slow moving items. However, it is generalised to be applicable to all types of item. Separate forecasts are made of non-zero demand and of the interval between months in which demand occurs. For example, if the demand pattern is

200 0 200 0 200 etc.

then demand is 200 and the interval is 2 months. The forecast used would be the demand divided by the interval – in this case = 100. In principle the method should remove sources of bias and permit a greater range of items to be considered.[2]

4 Evaluation of Forecasting Methods

The four forecasting methods were compared using a computer simulation model which generates demands according to defined parameters and calculates the forecasts.

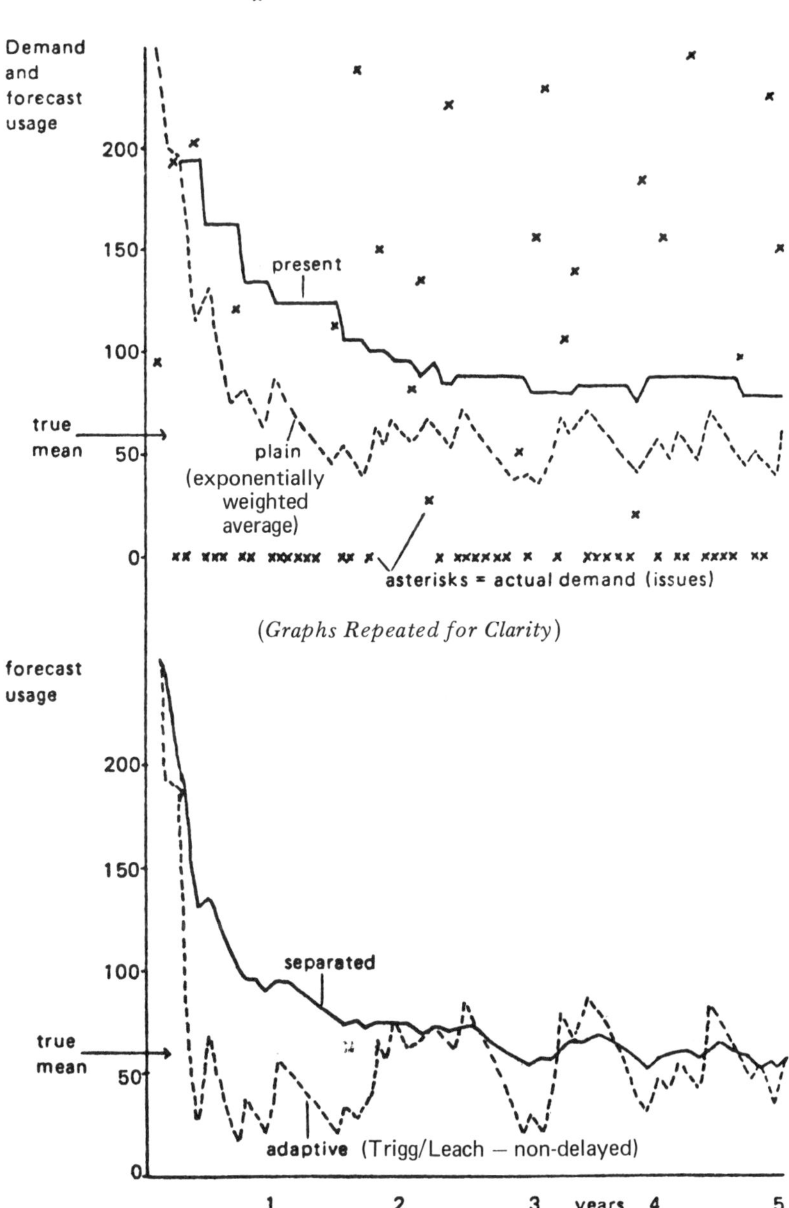

Figure 15.1 *Illustration of the Responses of the Four Forecasting Methods Investigated*

An example of output from the model is shown in figure 15.1. This shows the behaviour of forecasts over a 5 year period assuming an initially high estimate. The demand averages around 60 units, but fluctuates, so that about 8 months in a year have zero demand. The graphs show the over-estimation of the current pre-average system and demonstrate the erratic behaviour of adaptive forecasting.

The forecast methods were modelled in different situations and their performance summarised on a number of criteria in table 15.1.

The bias of the forecast is calculated for the last two years of the simulation and is derived from the average forecast compared with the average actual demand. It has been necessary to define the average forecast used here as the maximum of the forecast in the months a non-zero demand occurs, and the forecast in the month after. This is because the ordering of new stock can be initiated either as the demand occurs, or

Table 15.1 Summary of Performance of the Four Forecasting Methods Investigated

Criteria of Performance Method	*Present (pre-average)*	*Plain*	*Adaptive*	*Separated*
Bias of forecast	+ 25%	+ 17%	+ 40%	+ 13%
Stability	Medium	Medium	Bad	Good
Response to				
(a) high initial forecast	Bad	Good	Excellent	Medium
(b) increasing demand	Poor	Good	Good	Poor
(c) decreasing demand	Bad	Good	Good	Poor
Intelligibility of method	Medium	Good	Poor	Poor
Ease of Implementation	Excellent	Good	Poor	Poor
Generality to items	Poor	Medium	Medium	Good

when the forecast is updated.

Stability of a forecast is desirable where the underlying average demand is not changing. The responsiveness of the forecast was examined to an initial high estimate (such as shown in figure 15.1), demand increasing at 10% per annum or decreasing at 10% per annum. Pre-averaging is especially bad in response to decreasing demand, as the effect of the cut-off is reduced and the forecast is only updated after the demand occurs.

5 Results

It is clear from table 15.1 that the Adaptive method is a poor one for this type of item. It is far too unstable because it over reacts to the erratic demand pattern. It also is very highly biased because of this over reaction to non-zero demand.

In some ways the 'Separate' system is attractive – it has low bias, good stability and can be used for many slow moving items. However, it is unresponsive to changes in demand and would pose implementation problems. On balance, although better than pre-averaging, it offered insufficient real advantage over the simpler plain method.

The Plain system is better than pre-averaging on all performance categories and posed little difficulty in implementation. Because the bias depends upon the type of item, this aspect has been examined further. For infrequently used items, pre-averaging gives a substantially higher bias than the plain method, while for regularly used items it underestimates. Thus the pre-averaging method was leading to better service performance for low usage items than for frequently used items. This was clearly an undesirable feature.

As a result of this analysis, a change to the plain forecasting system was implemented in August 1979. At the time of writing it is too early to comment on the effect of the change in practice.

References

1 Trigg, D.W. and Leach, A.G., Exponential smoothing with an adaptive response rate, *Operational Research Quarterly*, Vol. 18, No. 2, 1964.
2 Crosston, J.D., Forecasting and stock control for intermittent demand, *Operational Research Quarterly*, Vol. 23, No. 3, 1972.

16
Inventory Control

C D LEWIS

Professor of Operations Management,
The University of Aston

1 Introduction

Inventory control is the science-based art of ensuring that just enough inventory (or stock) is held by an organisation to meet economically both its internal and external demand commitments. There can be disadvantages in holding either too much or too little inventory; inventory control is primarily concerned with obtaining the correct balance or compromise between these two extremes.

In 1979, the total UK investment in stock was valued at about £50,035m.* The different types of stock, and the purposes for which they are held, are as follows:

(a) *Raw material stocks* (represents about 35% of UK total) By holding stocks of raw material, an organisation decouples its primary production sections or processes (e.g. machine shops and press shops) from its raw material manufacturers or stockists. This allows primary production to be initiated in a shorter period of time than the raw material supplier's delivery time.

(b) *Work-in-progress or stocks-in-process* (about 38%) The holding of both raw material stocks and stocks of finished

* Source: *Monthly Digest of Statistics* (1979)

goods is generally a planned activity, whereas in-process stocks are likely to exist in any manufacturing organisation whether or not they are planned for. The de-coupling function provided by this category of inventory is to buffer the demand of a later stage in the production process (e.g. sub-assemblies and final assemblies) from the supply of an earlier stage (e.g. machine shops and press shops); this facility is essential for any production process. Without such de-coupling, all manufacturing stages would need to be perfectly synchronised – a practical impossibility.

(c) *Finished goods* (about 27%) The stocking of finished goods provides a buffer between the customer demand and the manufacturer's supply. In many cases, because the sizes of orders required by customers are much less than those supplied by the manufacturer, a wholesaler or stockist acts as intermediary.

We shall begin by describing the two basic inventory control policies, then discuss the costs and usage patterns which determine the design of an appropriate control system.

2 Inventory Policies

An organisation's stockholding policy is implemented by a series of rules which determine how and when certain decisions concerning the holding of stocks should be made. This series of rules is known as an inventory policy.

There are two basic types of inventory policies. Those in which decisions concerning replenishment are based on the level of inventory held are known as re-order level policies and those in which such decisions are made on a regular time basis are known as re-order cycle or periodic review policies.

(a) *Re-order level policy* An order for replenishment is placed when the stock on hand equals or falls below a fixed value M known as the re-order level. Stock on hand includes the stock actually held in stores plus any outstanding replenishment orders less demand orders which have already been committed

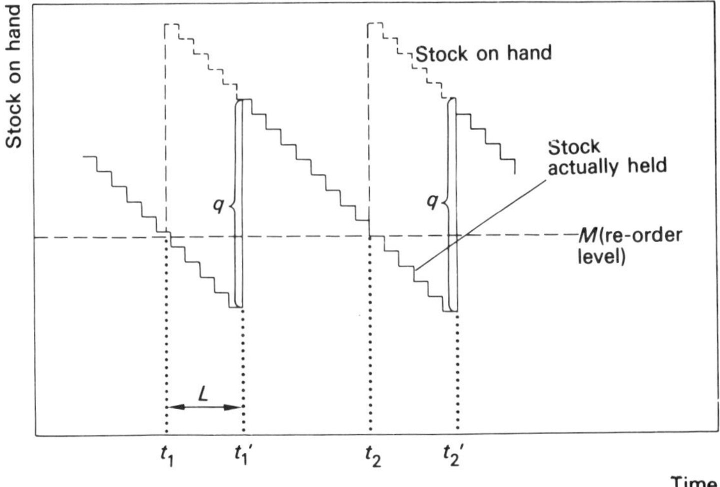

Figure 16.1 *The Re-Order Level Policy*

to the production programme. In this policy, therefore, the amount of inventory held must be reviewed continuously.

When a replenishment order is placed within a re-order level policy, it is generally for a fixed quantity. A typical example of inventory balances for a re-order level policy is shown in figure 16.1. The solid line in this diagram represents the inventory actually held, the broken line is the stock on hand (actual stock plus outstanding replenishments less committed stock). When the re-order level M is broken at time t_1, a replenishment order of size q is placed, but there is a delay before the order actually arrives; this delay is known as the lead time (L). At time t_1, the stock on hand immediately rises by q (since the moment the order is placed it is technically outstanding), but the actual stock continues to be depleted by successive demand withdrawals until the lead time expires and the replenishment order is received at time t_1'. The process is repeated as soon as stock on hand again falls to re-order level M at time t_2.

The excess of the re-order level over the expected demand during the lead time is called the safety stock or buffer stock (B). If the buffer stock is exhausted, then back-ordering may be permitted, whereby demand orders are accepted even when no actual stock remains, thus in effect allowing negative stock to build up.

The most common practical implementation of the re-order level policy is known as the two-bin system. Two bins of the stocked item are kept and a replenishment order is placed when the first bin becomes empty. Further stock is then withdrawn from the second bin until the replenishment order is received to refill the second bin, the remainder being placed in the first bin. The amount of stock held in the second bin, therefore, represents the size of the re-order level. In practice, of course, it is not always necessary to have two separate bins to operate this system; for instance a single bin with a dividing layer or partition serves exactly the same purpose. Some retailers operate by placing a 're-order now' card at an appropriate place in the stock of each item on the counter. However, this single- or two-bin adaptation of the re-order level method cannot be used for items that deteriorate or for items which have a limited shelf-life controlled with a first-in, first-out policy.

The single- or two-bin system operates most successfully with physically small items such as nuts, bolts, washers, etc., where committed demand orders are not generally allowed and usually only one outstanding replenishment exists at any time. The system obviously becomes impracticable when large items such as castings and sub-assemblies are involved, where space occupied does not necessarily represent number stored. To be really cheap and effective as a means of controlling stocks, the two-bin system is operated without any formal stock recording, and even auditors are now taking sample estimates of overall stock levels as evidence for audit assessment.

(b) *The re-order cycle or periodic review policy* The stock on hand is reviewed at fixed periods of time (R), and a replenishment order placed at every review. However, unlike the policy previously described, the size of a replenishment order is variable. This variable replenishment quantity is calculated as that amount of stock which, if there were no lead time, would bring the stock on hand up to some fixed maximum stock level, S. Thus, the size of the replenishment order is equal to S less the stock on hand, and can be different at

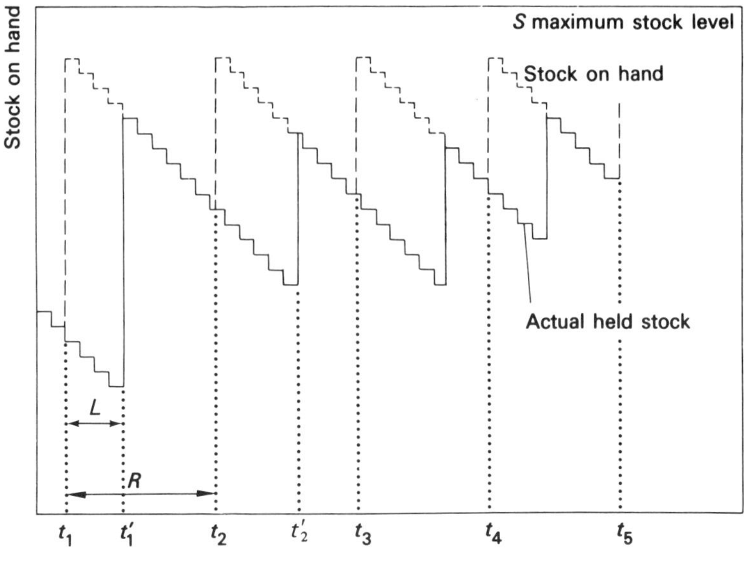

Figure 16.2 *The Re-Order Cycle Policy*

every review. This replenishment policy ensures that when the level of stock on hand is high at review, a smaller sized replenishment order is placed than when it is low. This can be quite clearly seen in figure 16.2 which shows a typical stock situation when operating a re-order cycle policy. Orders are placed at time t_1, t_2, t_3, which are a fixed time R apart; the first order arrives at time t_1'. In the example shown the lead times also vary.

The essential differences between the two inventory policies is that the re-order level policy is one of continuous review, and the operating system must allow replenishment orders to be placed at any time, rather than to be planned in advance as with the re-order cycle policy. One of the principle advantages of planned replenishment is that a single order can be raised to cover many replenishments being placed with a common supplier, thus considerably reducing the cost per replenishment. This advantage is offset by the fact that cyclical policies in general require higher average levels of stock in order to offer similar levels of service (one possible definition of the level of service being the probability of meeting demand 'off the shelf'.)

A domestic comparison can be drawn between the situations of working and non-working wives. The non-working wife, who has the opportunity to shop on any day and knows that her family consumes a maximum of ½ lb of butter per day, might operate a re-order level policy with a re-order level of ½ lb. Her stock holding costs based on an average ½ lb of butter (with ½ lb replenishments) would be very low, but against this she would incur high replenishment costs plus the lost opportunity cost of not working. By contrast, in this same situation, a working wife with the opportunity of shopping only on Saturdays would be forced to operate a cyclical policy such that on each Saturday she would replenish up to 7 X ½ = 3½ lbs of butter to ensure supplies to the following Saturday. Her storage cost would be relatively high (based on an average stock holding of 1¾ lbs of butter), but her replenishment costs very low (based on a single replenishment per week).

3 Inventory Operating Costs

There are three principal costs involved in operating an inventory system, namely the cost of ordering stock (C_0), the cost of holding stock (C_h) generally given as a percentage (i) of the stock's value (C_m), and the cost of running out of stock (C_s). We shall discuss these in turn.

(a) Ordering Costs (C_0)

(i) All purchase department costs (which usually include a healthy proportion of an organisation's telephone bill) could be included as part of the ordering cost if replenishment orders are obtained from outside. Such costs are usually apportioned across all stock items ordered through the department, so that the cost of ordering is generally assumed to be the same for all items irrespective of their value. Where replenishment orders are obtained within the organisation, the cost of ordering should include the cost of implementing the work's order and also any set-up cost that might be involved.

(ii) For purchased-out items, the cost of receiving goods (which should include any transport costs) might be included in the ordering costs. Again, these are usually allocated on an apportionment basis.

(iii) Those quality control costs incurred as a result of checking received replenishment orders might be included in the cost of ordering, but rarely are, as these costs are absorbed as general overheads.

(iv) Where replenishment orders for purchased-out items are overdue, or where internally manufactured items are behind schedule, the cost of 'chasing' or 'expediting' such overdue orders should be included in the cost of ordering.

At current UK prices in 1980 a manufacturer's order cost of much less than £15 is unrealistic, which highlights the advantages of multiple replenishment orders. High order costs also explain why manufacturing organisations stipulate minimum quantities below which they are not prepared to trade and why cheaper prices are quoted for cash transactions which can bypass much of the invoicing procedures and their associated costs.

(b) Holding or Storage Costs (iC_m)

C_m is the works prime cost of the stocked item (materials + labour + overheads or, perhaps more simply, materials + value-added, but not including profit). Holding cost is expressed as a percentage, i, of prime cost, where i is normally of the order of 25% p.a. and is made up as follows:

(i) the opportunity cost of capital invested in stock. This is usually taken to be the existing rate of interest encountered in obtaining capital from the company's normal sources or the rate of return the company estimates it could obtain by investing capital elsewhere, and has traditionally been of the order of 10%–15% (but see following note).

(ii) all costs directly associated with storing goods, i.e. storemen's wages, rates, heating and lighting, store's transport, racking and palletisation, protective clothing, weighing equipment, etc. (2%–6%).

(iii) deterioration costs, including the costs incurred in preventing deterioration (1%–4%).

(iv) obsolescence costs, including possible re-work or scrapping (4%–7%).

(v) fire and general insurance (1½%).

The above figures give a range for i between 17½% and 34½%, the median of 26% represents ½p in the £ per week.

Note: Until recently the effect of inflation on the prices of goods has not been regarded as an important enough feature to be included in the holding interest rate. However, with price inflation rates now at levels of 12% p.a. or so, it is very debatable whether this ignoring of the effects of inflation should continue. In principle, the expected rate of increase in stock prices should be deducted from the cost of holding stock, thereby promoting a tendency to build up stocks by 'buying now rather than later'. However, such a policy requires a further cash investment and such 'spare' cash is not generally available in times of inflation, especially since interest rates will tend to increase to reflect inflation.

(c) Stockout or Runout Costs (C_s)

These costs are most difficult to assess and to incorporate in mathematical inventory models, since they depend upon such imponderables as loss of customer goodwill, reduction in future orders, change in market share, etc. For this reason, stockout costs are frequently not computed in practice, and are generally only incorporated in the more sophisticated mathematical inventory models which are beyond the scope of this book. Instead, attention is focused on the level of service provided, without trying directly to evaluate that service. Of course, the cost of providing any service level indirectly implies a valuation of that service.

4 Demand: the Link with Forecasting

The design of any stock control system requires estimated values of the following three parameters:

D, the average demand per unit time;
σ, the standard deviation of demand per unit time; and
L, the lead time.

(If the lead time is variable, one needs also to estimate the mean and standard deviation of the lead time; we shall ignore such complications in this chapter.) The values of D and σ may be obtained from a forecasting model as discussed in Chapter 14. It would appear sensible to suppose that these values should be updated every time an analysis of the demand situation produced a new forecast. With computerised inventory control systems this is indeed the general practice but, where a manual system of stock recording is in operation using stock record or bin cards, such substitutions are not easily effected, particularly over a large number of items. It must be accepted that the manual system itself limits the degree of control that can be exercised over stocks, and in such situations it might be expedient to update control parameters in line with forecasts at annual intervals and whenever a significant change in demand occurs (see Chapter 14, Section 9).

5 Service Levels

The efficiency of any stock control policy is indicated by the level of service it offers to potential or existing customers in terms of providing stock 'off the shelf' or 'ex-stock'. Opinions as to which definition of service is best have varied widely, but the two most commonly used definitions are 'the probability of not running out of stock per occasion', and the 'proportion of annual demand met ex-stock'.

The probability of not running out of stock per occasion, as a measure of the effectiveness of a stock control system, has the advantage of being calculated fairly easily, but suffers from the disadvantage that it can also be misinterpreted very easily. A 95% probability of not running out of stock per occasion strictly interpreted means that, on average, for every 100 replenishment orders placed by the stockholder for his own replenishment, on 95 occasions customer demand will be met ex-stock before the replenishment order is received. On five occasions per 100, therefore, stockouts do occur before the replenishment order is received.

From the customer's point of view, the probability of not running out of stock per occasion does not indicate how frequently the holder of stock will be out of stock (unless the stockholder's frequency of replenishment is known, which is most unlikely, except where the stock is raw material or work in progress, and the 'customer' is in fact another department of the same firm). Moreover, it does not indicate how badly or how long the supplier will be out of stock when a stockout does occur and it certainly does not indicate what proportion of the customer's demand will be met ex-stock. From an even more practical point of view, it also does not cover the situation of part-deliveries, where a customer would be more than satisfied to receive a part-delivery on time and the remainder of the order at a later date.

Because the probability of not running out of stock per occasion is easy to calculate, it has been used up to now more than any other definition of service in spite of its many disadvantages, and is the method used by virtually all computer packages. Because (in this author's opinion) the probability of not running out of stock per occasion is more an indication of good housekeeping on the part of the supplier or vendor than a meaningful measure of service to the customer, this measure of service will be termed the vendor service level.

From the customer's point of view a more useful measure of the service offered by a stock control system is the proportion of demand met ex-stock per annum. Such a measure permits the customer to allow for an expected amount short over a year and to protect himself against it, either by arranging to absorb such a shortfall or by holding a limited amount of stock of his own. As this measure is more useful to the customer, it will be referred to here as the customer service level. Because the proportion of annual demand met ex-stock (the customer service level) can now, with advances in statistical theory, be calculated relatively easily, and indeed linked with the probability of not running out of stock per occasion (the vendor service level), it is increasingly being adopted as the measure of service offered by an inventory system, particularly in the USA.

6 Evaluation of Stock Control Parameters: Traditional Approach

(a) Re-order Level Policy

The traditional method of evaluating stock control parameters is to determine, quite separately, the replenishment order size (q) and the re-order level (M). The former is calculated as that size which minimises the total cost of ordering and storing. The latter is obtained by management specifying an appropriate vendor service level (i.e. probability of not running out of stock per occasion). It is obviously more sensible to take into account interactions between q and M, but because of its relative simplicity, the traditional method of separate evaluation will be considered initially.

(i) Economic order quantity The replenishment quantity is most usually evaluated on a criterion of minimising total annual inventory operating costs, comprising inventory storage costs plus replenishment ordering costs.

Annual inventory storage costs are given by the storage cost per item (iC_m) multiplied by the buffer stock (B) plus half the order quantity ($q/2$). Annual storage costs thus total:

$$\left\{B + \frac{q}{2}\right\} iC_m$$

Note that they increase with order size q.

The annual cost of ordering is the cost of placing a single replenishment order (C_0) multiplied by the number of replenishments (or cycles) per annum (A/q), where A is the annual demand. Annual order costs thus total $C_0 A/q$. Note that they decrease with order size q.

Combining these two costs, the total cost C of ordering q units each time is:

$$C(q) = \left\{ B + \frac{q}{2} \right\} iC_m + C_0 \frac{A}{q}$$

Setting the derivative with respect to q equal to zero to obtain a minimum yields:

$$\frac{dC}{dq} = \frac{iC_m}{2} - \frac{AC_0}{q^2} = 0$$

hence an optimal value

$$q^* = \sqrt{\frac{2AC_0}{iC_m}}$$

This is the so-called economic order quantity (EOQ) which minimises the cost of operating the present simple inventory system. A diagrammatic representation is provided in figure 16.3. Note that, at the optimum quantity, annual storage costs equal annual ordering costs.

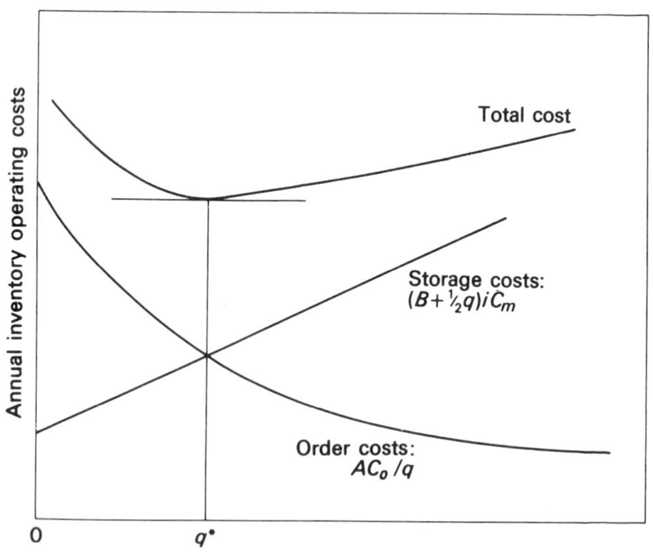

Figure 16.3 *Evaluation of the Traditional Economic Order Quantity*

To illustrate this, suppose demand (D) averages 100 per week, totally 5000 (A) in a 50-week year. Suppose the order cost C_0 is £10, the value of the product C_m is £1 per item and annual holding costs are 25% of this value. The economic order is given by:

$$q^* = \sqrt{\frac{2 \times 5000 \times £10}{0.25 \times £1}} = 632 \text{ items}$$

The above derivation of the economic order quantity assumed that replenishment occurred instantaneously rather than over a period of time. Although this assumption is usually valid for most 'purchased-out' items and for some items manufactured internally, it may be necessary to consider what the minimum cost quantity should be in situations where replenishment does occur over a period of time. The relevant replenishment quantity in this situation is the economic batch quantity (EBQ) which, using a similar approach to that for developing the economic order quantity, is given by

$$q_b^* = \sqrt{\frac{2AC_0}{iC_m\ (1 - D/p)}} = q^* \sqrt{\frac{1}{(1 - D/p)}}$$

where p denotes production rate (measured in the same units as demand D). To continue the previous example, if $D = 100$ per week and $p = 300$ per week, then $(1 - D/p) = 2/3$, hence

$$q_b^* = q^* \sqrt{\frac{3}{2}} = 1.225 \times 632 = 774 \text{ items}$$

In many manufacturing situations it is more sensible to express the economic batch quantity in terms of number of weeks of production q_b^*/p. Such values of weeks of production are always rounded to the nearest whole week or to the nearest production planning time unit. In the example, the economic batch quantity involves ordering 774/330 = 2.58 or 3 weeks' production each time.

The concept of the economic order (or batch) quantity was originally developed as long ago as the 1920s, and the simple square-root formulae shown here have become the parents of a whole family of formulae of ever-increasing complexity. Such formulae have been developed to take into account either (a) that some of the assumptions made in the original model may not be valid in many practical situations, or (b) that the criterion of minimum cost may not necessarily be the most relevant. Thus, it has been objected that the basic model takes no account of stockout costs or price breaks (quantity discounts), that cost of replenishment may not be independent of order size and that deviations from the optimum order quantity are not important because the total cost curve is relatively flat. Alternative criteria which have been proposed in certain circumstances include maximum profit per batch, maximum rate of return and minimum cost subject to restrictions on capital, storage space or set-up costs.

However, from all these theoretical considerations, one common factor which appears to be generally agreed is that although the values of individual economic order quantities may not always be relevant, *the ratio of the value of the economic order quantity for one stocked item to that of another is always relevant*. This concept can be shown to be valid by several different approaches and is also a very useful one as it relates the size of order quantities between items rather than in isolation. This feature of relative size means that if EOQ's for two different items come out at 300 units and 100 units, what is of most importance is that replenishment orders for the first item should be three times larger than for the second.

(ii) Re-order level The re-order level (M) is set equal to the expected (or average) demand during the lead time plus the buffer stock (B). The latter is an allowance for occasions when demand exceeds the average level. It is conveniently expressed as a specified number (k) of standard deviations of lead time demand. Assume that demand is normally distributed with a mean of D per week (or per month, etc.) and a standard deviation of σ per week. Assume also that demand in any week is essentially independent of demand in any other week. Then average demand over L weeks' lead time is DL and standard deviation of lead time demand is $\sigma \sqrt{L}$. The re-order level is given by

$$M = DL + k\sigma\sqrt{L}$$

The parameter k is called a standard normal deviate and

controls directly the vendor service level offered. From standard normal distribution tables (see table 16.1) we can extract information of particular reference to the inventory problem which shows the following relationship between k and stockout probability per occasion.

To illustrate this, let demand average $D = 100$ per week, with a standard deviation of $\sigma = 30$ per week, and let lead time be $L = 4$ weeks. Suppose a vendor service level of 97.7%

Table 16.1 Vendor Service Levels, Stockout Probability and Partial Expectation – Normal Distribution

Standard deviate, k	*Vendor Service level (%) P*	*Probability of stockout*	*Partial expectation, E (k)*
0.60	72.6	27.4	0.169
0.70	75.8	24.2	0.143
0.80	78.8	21.2	0.120
0.90	81.6	18.4	0.100
1.00	84.1	15.9	0.083
1.05	85.3	14.7	0.076
1.10	86.4	13.6	0.069
1.15	87.5	12.5	0.062
1.20	88.5	11.5	0.056
1.25	89.4	10.6	0.051
1.30	90.0	10.0	0.046
1.35	91.2	8.8	0.041
1.40	91.9	8.1	0.037
1.45	92.7	7.3	0.033
1.50	93.3	6.7	0.029
1.55	94.0	6.0	0.026
1.60	94.5	5.5	0.023
1.65	95.1	4.9	0.021
1.70	95.5	4.5	0.018
1.75	96.0	4.0	0.016
1.80	96.4	3.6	0.014
1.85	96.8	3.2	0.013
1.90	97.1	2.9	0.011
1.95	97.4	2.6	0.010
2.00	97.7	2.3	0.008
2.25	98.8	1.2	0.004
2.50	99.4	0.6	0.002
2.75	99.7	0.3	0.001
3.00	99.9	0.1	0.000

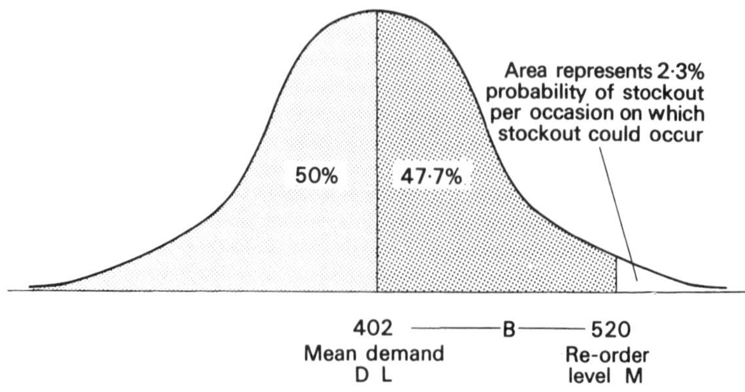

Figure 16.4 *Probability Distribution of Normal Demand during the Lead Time for 97.7% Vendor Service Level*

is required, hence $k = 2$. Then re-order level is

$$M = (100 \times 4) + (2 \times 30\sqrt{4}) = 520 \text{ units}$$

Of this amount, 400 units are active stock required to meet average demand during the lead time, and 120 units represent buffer stock (B) to meet above-average demand. The situation is illustrated in figure 16.4.

In many companies, re-order levels are expressed in terms of weeks (or months, etc.) of average demand rather than in units of stock. Thus a re-order level may be expressed as 'four weeks' supply' rather than as 400 units. To do this, simply divide the re-order level by the rate of demand, hence

$$\text{re-order level (in time units)} = \frac{M}{D} = L + \frac{k\sigma\sqrt{L}}{D}$$

In the present example, a re-order level of 520 units represents 520/100 = 5.2 weeks' supply. Too often, however, when this type of definition is used, the practice is to make the re-order level simply equal to the average lead time demand. Such a rule of thumb does not take into account more than average demand and, hence, results in a very low level of vendor service (theoretically only 50%).

It is quite straightforward to relate probability of stockout to expected number of stockouts per year. If A denotes annual demand and q the replenishment order quantity, then there will, on average, be A/q replenishment cycles per year. If P denotes the probability of *not* running out of stock, then the expected number of stockouts per year is $(1 - P)A/q$. For the numerical example just given, where the economic order quantity is $q = 632$ and annual demand is $A = 5000$, there would be 5000/632 or approximately 8 replenishments per year. If the *vendor* service level is 97.7%, then the average frequency of stockout would be:

$$(1 - 0.977)\frac{5000}{632} = 0.182 \text{ times per year}$$

or approximately once every 5½ years.

(b) Re-order Cycle Policy

Because the re-order cycle policy is a time based inventory system, the value of the vendor service level achieved when operating this policy has more relevance than when considering the re-order level policy. This is because with the review time being fixed, the *frequency* of stockouts can be directly related to the probability of a stockout. For instance, it follows that if a re-order cycle policy has a review period of one month and a service level of 91.6 per cent (i.e. 11/12) then the frequency of stockouts per year will, on average, be one.

For the re-order cycle policy there are two parameters whose values must be chosen, namely S, the maximum fixed inventory level from which all replenishment orders are calculated and R, the policy's review period.

(i) Economic review period It is possible for cyclical policies to find the so called 'economic review period' (ERP), if one is prepared again to consider that the minimisation of the annual cost of acquiring and holding stock is a reasonably valid criterion for operating an inventory system.

Using a similar approach as for the evaluation of the EOQ, it can be shown that m, the economic number of reviews p.a., is given by:

$$m = \sqrt{\frac{AiC_m}{2C_0}}$$

For the product considered earlier (see page 291 for details) the economic number of replenishments per annum, m, would be given by:

$$m = \sqrt{\frac{5000 \times 0.25 \times £1}{2 \times £10}} = 7.9 \text{ orders p.a.}$$

and hence the economic review period for a 50-week year becomes:

$$\text{ERP} = 50 \div 7.9 = 6 \text{ weeks}$$

(ii) Maximum stock level The maximum stock level (S) can be evaluated on the same basis as the re-order level (M) in the re-order level policy. Examination of figure 16.2 indicates that, since the replenishment decision taken at time t_1 has more influence on the possibility of a stockout at time t_2' rather than at time t_1', the period of risk in the re-order cycle policy is $(R + L)$ rather than (L), as was the case in the re-order level policy.

On this basis, the maximum stock level can be evaluated as:

$$S = D(R + L) + k\sigma\sqrt{(R + L)}$$

For the situation under consideration with $R = 6$, we obtain:

$$S = (100 \times 10) + (2 \times 30\sqrt{10}) = 1190 \text{ units}$$

7 Evaluation of Stock Control Parameters: Modern Approach

The vendor service level on which re-order level evaluation is based is the probability of not running out of stock per occasion i.e. subsequent to a replenishment order being placed. This concept of the service level offered by an inventory policy, although statistically convenient, is without doubt the most misinterpreted measure in stock control theory. It does *not* for instance mean:

(a) The proportion of time an item is available ex-stock; or
(b) The proportion of demand met ex-stock; or
(c) The proportion of the total number of items held in stock available ex-stock at any point in time.

As a measure of service it gives *no* indication of the:

(a) frequency of stockouts; or
(b) duration of stockouts; or
(c) the severity of stockouts in terms of number of units back-ordered.

Moreover, since the number of occasions on which stockouts can occur depends totally on the size of the replenishment order used, it is rather non-sensical to evaluate the re-order level without any regard to the size of that replenishment order. For instance, given a probability of not running out of stock per occasion of, say, 10/12 (i.e. a service level of 83%), if replenishment orders were placed monthly two stockouts should occur per year whereas if the replenishment order size were doubled and therefore only placed once every two months only one stockout should occur per year, in spite of the fact that the service level remains the same in both cases!

Why then, the reader might ask, given that the probability of not running out of stock per occasion gives rise to so many problems, was it ever chosen as a measure of the service offered by an inventory policy? The reason, quite simply, is that twenty years ago it was the most convenient measure that statistics could offer. However, since that time, not surprisingly, advances have been made in statistics and it is a relatively modest advance and its incorporation in stock control theory will be discussed in this section.

(a) Re-order Level Policy

Reconsidering the situation considered in Sections 6, but allowing the vendor service level (or probability of not running out of stock per occasion) to slump from 97.7% to 84.1%

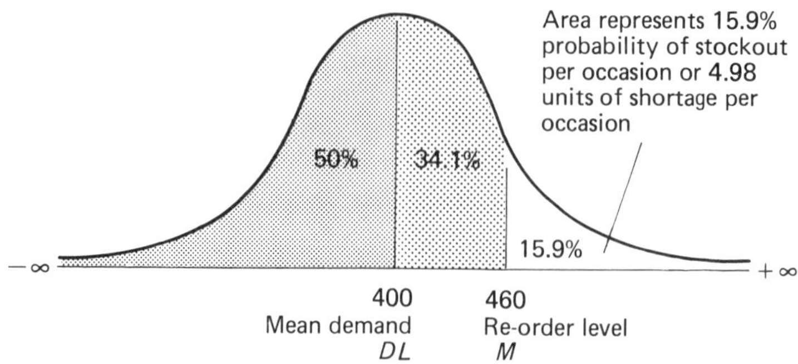

Figure 16.5 *Probability Distribution of Normal Demand during the Lead Time for 84.1% Vendor Service Level but 99.2% Customer Service Level*

(k = 1 from table 16.1), it is apparent that the required re-order level would be:

$$M = (100 \times 4) + (1 \times 30\sqrt{4}) = 460 \text{ units}$$

Illustrating this situation in figure 16.5, it can be seen that the area to the right of the re-order level of 460 units represents 15.9% of the total area under the normal curve. Now, if area (the first integral of the probability density function) represents probability, it can also be shown that the second integral represents the average number of units of demand occurring after stockout occurs, i.e. the number of units of shortage, which would be back ordered if that were permitted.

Referring to table 16.1, for a vendor service level of 84.1% the value of this second integral (known as the Partial Expectation $-E(k)$) is 0.083 which would make the potential number of units of shortage per occasion equal to:

$$0.083 \times 30\sqrt{4} = 4.98 \text{ units}$$

Since such occasions occur (when the annual demand A is 5000 and replenishment orders are based on the EOQ of 632) 5000 ÷ 632, i.e. eight times a year, it is apparent that the total number of units of shortage per year is given by:

$$8 \times 4.98 = 39.84 \text{ units}$$

These units of shortage represent only 0.79% of the total annual demand of 5000 units, indicating that 99.2% of annual demand is met ex-stock, or a 99.2% *customer* service level.

Thus a situation exists where a disastrously low vendor service level offered of 84.1% produces a most satisfactory observed customer service level of 99.2%, when due consideration is taken of the frequency of possible stockout occasions as controlled by the replenishment quantity. Further discussion on the advantages of joint evaluation of re-order levels and replenishment quantities is beyond the scope of this book, but can be simply implemented by a relatively simple formula from which P', the customer service level (defined as the proportion of annual demand met ex-stock), is given by

$$P' = 1 - \frac{E(k)\sigma\sqrt{L}}{q}$$

This simple equation not only links the customer service level P' with the vendor service level (defined as the probability of not running out of stock) as controlled by the standard Normal deviate k; but also relates the replenishment quantity q with the re-order level M, which is itself dependent on k. Readers will recall that the feature of not relating these two principle parameters of the re-order level policy was one of the main criticisms levelled at the traditional approach of establishing their values.

Examining this feature in detail, via the equation for P' it follows that if:

(a) q is increased
(b) for P' to remain the same for a given value of $\sigma\sqrt{L}$
(c) the partial expectation $E(k)$ must be increased resulting in
(d) the standard Normal deviate k being reduced, thus reducing the re-order level and vendor service level.

In descriptive terms this means that if the replenishment quantity were to be increased, resulting in higher stocks but fewer occasions per annum on which stockouts could occur, then automatically the re-order level would be lowered compensatingly to reduce such proposed increased stocks and also increase the probability of running out of stock. This latter feature would be acceptable, as the number of occasions on which stockouts could occur would also have been reduced.

The possible combinations of defined requirements and

resulting parameter evaluations that can be related using this concept are shown in table 16.2.

Table 16.2 Relating Customer and Vendor Service Levels and Re-order Level and Replenishment Quantity Values

Defining the	*and knowing the values of*	*one can evaluate*
Customer service level P' and the replenishment quantity q		The vendor service level as defined by the standard normal deviate k and the re-order level $M = DL + k\,\sigma\sqrt{L}$
Replenishment quantity q and the vendor service level (this automatically defines the re-order level M)	The standard deviation of demand per unit time σ, the lead time duration L and the average demand per unit time D	The customer service level P'
Customer service level P' and the vendor service level (this automatically defines the re-order level M)		The replenishment quantity q

(b) Re-order Cycle Policy

To evaluate stock control parameters for the re-order cycle policy such that the review period R and the maximum stock level S are evaluated jointly and the concept of the customer service level is introduced, we follow a similar line of discussion as for the ROL policy. Since there are $50/R$ occasions per annum when stockout could occur, and the average shortage per occasion would be $E(k)\sqrt{R + L}$ units, it follows that:

$$\frac{50}{R} E(k)\sqrt{R + L} = (1 - P')A$$

from which the customer service level P' is given by:

$$P' = 1 - \frac{50}{AR} E(k)\sqrt{R + L}$$

To prove the point that the customer service level always exceeds the vendor service level, considering a drop of VSL from 97.7% to 84.1% ($k = 1$, $E(k) = 0.083$) by a reduction in the maximum stock levels from 1190 to 1095 units, it follows that the customer service level in this new situation would be given by:

$$P' = 1 - \frac{50 \times 0.083 \times 30\sqrt{10}}{5000 \times 6} = 98.7\%$$

8 Evaluation of Stock Control Parameters: Conclusion

It is apparent that the introduction of the statistic known as the partial expectation has improved considerably the 'state of art' in evaluating stock control parameters. Rather than replacing the old concept, the new approach adds to it, thus allowing the additional new information and enhanced control to co-exist with traditional systems. The fundamental advantages of the modern approach are:

(a) That the two control parameters associated either with the re-order level policy or the re-order cycle policy are evaluated jointly rather than separately.
(b) That an additional measure of the effectiveness of stock control policies is produced which is much more meaningful to customers; this being the 'proportion of annual demand met ex-stock per annum' and appropriately termed the customer service level.

Table 16.3 summarises all the calculations concerned with the evaluation of parameters of both policies for a product whose:

average demand $D = 100$ per week
standard deviation of demand $\sigma = 30$ per week
annual demand for a fifty-week year $A = 5000$ p.a.
replenishment lead time $L = 4$ weeks
value of prime cost $C_m = £1$
holding interest rate $i = 25\%$ p.a.
associated ordering cost $C_o = £10$

Table 16.3 Summary of Stock Control Policy Information

POLICY	VSL = 97.7% $k = 2$ $E(k) = 0.008$	VSL = 84.1% $k = 1$ $E(k) = 0.083$
Re-order level	EOQ = 632 units ROL = 520 units CSL = 99.92%*	EOQ = 632 units ROL = 460 units CSL = 99.2%
Re-order cycle	ERP = 6 weeks S = 1190 units CSL = 99.87%*	ERP = 6 weeks S = 1095 units CSL = 98.7%

Note: *Readers might like to verify these values for themselves.

9 Categorisation of Stocked Items

When deciding which type of inventory policy to use for the different types of items held in stock by an organisation, a necessary first step is to group items using some measure or criterion of importance. Having grouped stocked items on a basis of relative importance, it is then possible to use the properties of the method of grouping itself to arrive at an overall comprehensive stocking policy. The situation is exactly analogous to that of forecasting and, in fact, the same approach may be used as described in the concluding section of Chapter 14 (see p. 267).

To recapitulate, ABC or Pareto analysis uses the well-known relationship that in virtually all inventory situations a large proportion of an organisation's investment, usually annual turnover or profit contribution, is associated with relatively few items. This general relationship was shown in figure 14.9 of Chapter 14. Although for different organisations the relationship can vary somewhat, it is still generally true that a few items are of great importance and a large proportion of items are, relatively speaking, unimportant.

Category A Items

These are the most important 20% of the items, representing 80% of, say, turnover. It is usual with valuable items such as these (typically three times the average individual value) to try to obtain a high degree of control of stocks. There is a tendency therefore to use inventory control policies of the periodic review type for this category of item. Such policies ensure that the stock position is reviewed regularly irrespective of demand, whereas in a re-order level type of policy it is the demand situation which determines when reviews take place. In the latter type of policy, if demand is particularly low for a period of time, the frequency at which reviews of the stock situation take place drops significantly compared with the average, and this can be a prime cause of dead stocks being created as items gradually become obsolete.

The pure re-order cycle policy ensures that replenishments are placed regularly at each and every review although the size of the individual replenishment order varies. Such a method of replenishment might fit in well with contract buying.

Category B Items

These are the next 15% of the items representing 15% of turnover. For these medium-cost items a re-order level policy is generally most suitable. Where replenishments for several items are obtained from a single source, however, again it may be practical to operate a regular review type of inventory policy to enable several orders to be placed simultaneously, thus reducing ordering and transport costs.

Category C Items

These are the large majority of items representing relatively little value. The re-order level of two-bin (or single-bin) policy is usually most appropriate for C items. This method offers a reasonable degree of control with a minimum of record-keeping. If space allows, a degree of overstocking can generally be allowed, simply because of the cheapness of the items involved, in order to reduce the probability of stockouts. Readers are reminded that the two-bin type of policy is not suitable for items that deteriorate as it is essentially a last-in first-out (LIFO) policy rather than a first-in first-out (FIFO) policy. For C items it is not usual to update stock control parameters in line with forecasts, as forecasts will not generally be made for this type of item – annual updating is, therefore, more usual. Often, in fact, this policy is operated with no paper records at all and auditors accept limited sampling as a method of assessing value for audit purposes.

10 Conclusion

This chapter has described the fundamental models and features of inventory control theory and in particular the theory behind most of the computer inventory control packages commercially available today. Because mathematical theorists find the field of inventory control a fruitful area within which they can devise increasingly more complex mathematical models of decreasingly practical usefulness, the literature in this field abounds. The following references, however, provide a comprehensive coverage to that which is important.

References and Further Reading

1 Brown, R.G., *Decision Rules for Inventory Management*, Holt, Rinehart and Winston 1967.
2 Buchan, J. and Koenigsberg, E., *Scientific Inventory Management*, Prentice-Hall 1963.
3 ICI, *Problems of Stocks and Storage*, ICI Monograph No. 4, Oliver & Boyd 1967.
4 Lewis, C.D., *Scientific Inventory Control*, Butterworths 1970.
5 Thomas, A., *Stock Control in Manufacturing Industries*, Gower Press 1968.

17
Inventory Control Systems for Retail Distribution*

R J READ

Retail Group R & D Manager,
W H Smith Ltd

1 Introduction

Within W.H. Smith & Son Limited, the Retail Group is headed by a Managing Director and three Directors responsible for the line operations of Buying, Distribution and Retail Shop Administration. The group has its own management executive comprising the four Directors and certain Senior Managers and they form the most senior decision-making body within the Retail Group.

The Buying Division is responsible for initial buying, product development and promotional plans.

The Retail Division selects sites and builds new or resited shops and controls the staffs and administers them. There are some 319 W.H. Smith Shops and 89 bookstalls divided into 21 Retail areas. The shops are located throughout England, Wales and Scotland.

The Distribution Division has large warehouses at Swindon and Dunstable which between them stock some 31,000 lines to meet approximately 60% of the volume demand. The

* Reproduced by kind permission of the author and the British Production and Inventory Control Society. This material was first prepared in 1979.

balance of 40% is supplied directly by the manufacturer. The departments within the Distribution Division are Staff Services, Operations and Inventory.

The Operations Manager controls the efficient running of the warehouses, transport and engineering and negotiates the cost of contracted distribution.

The Inventory Department is responsible for Retail Group inventory. Its task is to provide the right amount of stock (in financial and volume terms) to meet the needs of the Group. It must do this at pre-determined service levels (i.e. the ratio of orders fulfilled to orders placed) at acceptable cost.

Each line manager has a small development department which is responsible for providing industrial engineering, operational research and materials handling systems as appropriate. Their work includes stockroom design at branches, stock control systems both at Swindon and in branches and economic modelling.

The Distributing Director is also responsible for the development of business systems throughout the Retail Group and I as Retail Group R & D Manager report to him.

2 Inventory Control

The Buying Division is responsible for choosing lines, fixing margins and making the initial purchases of items. The Inventory Department at Swindon is then responsible for stocking and replenishing these lines at the central warehouses. With the exception of about 200 lines, the branch manager or his departmental managers are free to order stock from a catalogue which is tailored to their size and turnover. Naturally, the branch manager makes use of stock control systems devised by the Inventory Department and works to stock budgets also determined by them.

Let us look now in a little more detail at how the Inventory Department manages the stock held in the central warehouses. As we have already seen, goods are supplied to branches by one of two channels:

1. Directly by the manufacturer or
2. From the central warehouses at Swindon and Dunstable

The choice of channel is usually the one which produces the best margin for the company and this decision ultimately rests with the Distribution Director. He has at his disposal a mathematical model which calculates the marginal costs of going direct from manufacturer to branch or from manufacturer to warehouse to branch and he uses this to help him with his decision-making. I say 'help' here because, as with any model, we cannot programme in all the constraints.

The channel supply having been determined, further economies may be achieved in examining:

Pack size
Pallet stacking patterns
Delivery methods

Once the buyer has placed the initial order, the setting of the first and subsequent review levels and all future purchasing is done by the Inventory Department which seeks to minimise the costs of distribution while maintaining stocks at economic levels to produce the service levels required.

The Inventory Manager who is ultimately responsible for stock levels in the group has the task of directly controlling the stock and service levels from the warehouse to the branch and sets the target levels and systems for all branch stock. He also has a considerable influence on the buying decisions made by Buying Division.

3 The Purchasing Cycle

Once a year, members of the Retail Group devote considerable time and effort to producing a corporate strategy and sales and profit plan, taking into account as many factors as possible. These include:

Market share
Market growth

Price and Volume Analyses
Development of product range
Additional selling space
Re-allocation of space per product range
The extent to which additional sales may be generated by advertising and sales promotion.

The corporate strategy is converted from a sales and profit plan into a purchasing estimate of what is required to meet stockholding budgets set throughout the distribution pipeline.

The first stage of determining the provisioning estimate is to calculate the sales requirements, and the ideal supporting stock. Predictions of the stock holding levels of the year end are deducted from the provisioning estimate to establish the purchasing requirements.

Having established how much stock is needed, we have to schedule its delivery to the warehouses and determine the rate at which it should be ordered, delivered to warehouse and to branch. Stock budgets are therefore provided to branch management enabling them to interpret the rate of supply for each merchandise range. The branch stock level budgets are expressed in number of weeks' forward sales and are compiled taking account of the following factors:

1. The effect of operating stock control systems taking into account order review periods.
2. Manufacturers lead times and pack size limitations.
3. The value of display stock required.
4. Whichever is the greater of 1. or 2. above, plus additional values of stock delivered in anticipation of the selling peaks at Christmas and other times throughout the year. This avoids undue pressures on the central warehouse or on manufacturers' transport.

Warehouse stock levels depend on the characteristics of the merchandise. For example, Own Brand products produced in this country are usually readily available, whereas imported products have long and unpredictable lead times.

Ideally, the current month's deliveries to warehouse become the next month's deliveries to branches, though of course this rapid turn-round of stock is not always achieved.

A prediction of the demands for cash is made at the same time, based on the predetermined flow of merchandise through the least cost channel of supply.

Naturally, we aim to reduce the cost of holding inventory as much as possible, by trying to make the number of weeks' stock held less than or equal to the number of weeks' credit. There are some types of merchandise with which we do very well, for example, newspapers and magazines where the turn-round is measurable in hours rather than weeks. On the other hand, some of our slower selling lines such as the less familiar book titles are held for much longer periods, but this is essential for maintaining a service to our customers.

Naturally, the credit period which we enjoy with our suppliers – the time taken between receipt of their invoice and our payment of it – also has to take into account any settlement discounts.

Branch managers receive a regular statement of sales, stocks and the number of weeks' forward supply that these represent. Decisions to alter the rate of stock intake are taken by comparing actual performance to budgets. The aim in using this stock control system is to reduce branch stock to a minimum consistent with reasonable service levels and to hold any stock which is required to meet unpredictable supplies from the manufacturer at the centre rather than at the branch. This management control system is backed up by line by line branch stock control systems for all types of merchandise.

We can play tunes on the way in which we store stock and pay for it, in that we smooth the peaks and troughs of the distribution workload without incurring a financial disadvantage. For example, we will often arrange with manufacturers to receive in stock early if they have too little warehouse space. In return, we defer payment to them. This helps both the manufacturer and ourselves.

Stock budgets are applied to total stocks of a range of merchandise or to stocks in a single branch. The detailed processes involved in translating these plans into actions on a day-to-day or item-by-item basis are carried out by replenishment purchasing staff and these comprise the main activity of the Inventory Department.

4 Replenishment Purchasing

We have already seen that the channel of supply is one of the first distribution decisions to be made. The initial order is placed by the buyer and the responsibility is then passed to the replenishment purchasing manager. He has to find out how the line is likely to behave in conjunction with the buyer. He determines the lead time of supply, the review level at which the line will be considered for replenishment, the pack size, the pallet quantities and order multiples and any expected change in normal demand rates (to take account of promotions, or supplier closedowns etc.).

A computer print-out shows the state of the line at intervals which are either regular, or where the line falls below the review level, or where the line goes out of stock. The replenishment purchasing manager receives these latter two reports every day, plus a summary of the range for which he is concerned with showing the behaviour of all lines every 5, 10 or 20 days depending on the stability of the line.

As orders are created, so they are sent to suppliers with precise delivery instructions on them. They are entered onto the computer file so that at regular intervals a statement of the due deliveries can be given to goods-inwards staff to estimate forward workload. In addition, progress chasing has to take place on key lines and poor performing suppliers and short-term forecasts of cash requirements prepared for the Accounts Department.

The life blood of the replenishing purchasing section is of course the information which it obtains from the computer. Let us look in very broad outline at the computer system in use at W.H. Smith at the moment.

The core of the system is the central suite of programmes which updates the master file and produces picking lists for the warehouse.

History reports are produced at the same time for use in stock control, stock valuation, and in planning future requirements.

The output of the central processing system is also fed into retail branch accounts as all branches are charged for goods they receive from the warehouse at retail price.

The central system is fed with input from the branch stock control systems, which we will look at in more detail below, and by centrally determined allocations of central stock to branches. In addition, we should also mention that back-orders are kept if no stock is available at the centre. Stock is then supplied when this becomes available. In addition, the computer system is used to manage the volumes to be handled through the warehouse and by the transport system. This is done by holding or releasing back-orders as appropriate.

The central processing system has to be updated for goods received and any amendments which need to be made to the master file, such as price changes to a transaction processing system which is on line to a holding file. Soon we will be able to access the main file directly and amend it as necessary.

What we have seen so far is a very simplified description of the way central stock control is carried out at two levels – the control level and the day-to-day. Of course, like any progressive company, we are always looking at ways of improving our methods and currently we are examining the whole of our inventory procedures with this in mind. We are hoping to build in some form of automatic stock replenishment for our slower selling lines although we expect that we will still need to keep a closer (human) eye on our top selling lines and those which are subject to variations in supply and demand. We are also looking at information systems which should give us much more detailed information of sales and stock levels for the branches which should enable us to further reduce our stock levels and increase our service levels.

5 Branch Stock Control Systems

Let us take a look now at the way the branch manager controls his stock and the ordering of stock in his branch. I think if you were to come into our organisation and look at the different types of merchandise and outlets that we have, you would quickly realise that there is no one stock control system which will cope with all of these. In fact, we have quite a large number of separate systems. For example, the retail shops have one batch of systems whilst the airport stalls have another and the Bowes & Bowes chain of speciality bookshops have a quite separate one.

For simplicity, let us look at the ordinary retail branches with which I am sure readers are familiar. These branches sell a wide range of goods including stationery, books, periodicals, records, confectionery, and tobacco. We organise our stock control procedures on *A, B, C* lines – that is the *A* lines are the top 1%, accounting for 30% of the volume, the *C* lines are 85% lines, accounting for 20% of the volume and *B* lie somewhere inbetween. The figures are not precise.

Our *A* lines – the top 1% – are partly controlled by a Top Sellers system. This looks after about 80 lines. Branches report the stock level of each of these lines at weekly intervals and from this we calculate rates of sale. This, combined with an estimate of how long it takes to get goods from the warehouse to the branches and previous history of the way lines behave, allows us to calculate an order at the centre. This is then fed into the central computer system, which generates picking lists for the warehouse. The system has been highly successful in keeping down stock levels to very acceptable figures whilst maintaining service levels to the branches in the region of 94%.

Our Top Sellers system is one of two central branch stock control systems – the other is our Central Allocation system for high value goods. Here we need a separate system, because these are delivered to the branch by Securicor and require special handling and accounting and it is essential that for such expensive items we maintain stock levels at the lowest possible levels. Stock levels are therefore counted on a fortnightly cycle and in this case the branches work out their sales and their next order which is advised to the centre who will vary it according to the stock available and their special knowledge of any changes in range which may take place.

Our books are mainly *C* items in stock control terms, that is they are 85% of the lines which account for 20% of the volume. For example, we hold 31,000 lines at Swindon, of which 25,000 are books. For our really slow selling books, we use a system called SABRE which stands for Sales Activated Book Re-Ordering.

This is, in effect, a primitive Point of Sale system. A stock card is inserted in each book and removed when the sale is made by the assistant and the book re-ordered provided its sales have achieved certain target levels.

Our stationery and toys and games lines are controlled by a system known as the BSOB – Branch Stock Order Book system. This is a re-order level system. The sales assistant counts the stock every three weeks and provided this is in excess of the re-order level, no order is made. If the stock count is below this figure, a standard order quantity is ordered – the standard order quantity being determined centrally from computer history files. The system is simple to operate and relies on computer produced stock books which are themselves a spin-off from our master stock files. The system is also geared to take account of the size of the shop and the amount of its display stock and its turnover of any particular type of merchandise. We have up to six different catalogues depending on the size of the shop.

It has been our experience over the last five years of installing branch stock control systems that these are one of the more difficult things to do well. We find that we need really effective teams of people to train our shop assistants and branch management in the way that these systems should be operated. Bear in mind that with over 300 shops it is very difficult to police a stock control system, particularly as we have quite a number of these. However, we have been able to demonstrate quite convincingly that the BSOB system for general merchandise as we call it – mostly stationery lines – has been effective at the branch in maintaining service levels and reducing stock levels. At this point the reader might ask exactly what results do W.H. Smith achieve. Of course, stock and service levels for a central warehouse to the branch vary according to the nature of the merchandise. They also vary quite dramatically throughout the year, but our selling pattern and, therefore, our stock levels, are heavily influenced by the Christmas selling peak.

One very real problem is that we know a good deal less about the service levels between the branch and the customer. What we do know however is that our centrally controlled branch stock systems seem to give a very much higher service level than the ones which are operated by the branch. That is, there are many fewer stockouts. We are therefore looking at systems which will allow us to control stock centrally. However, you will realise that with 300 plus branches and perhaps 60,000 product lines in total, only half of which are supplied internally, this is no easy matter.

6 Comparison with Other Retail Companies

Let us now compare W.H. Smith with other High Street retailers. The reader will probably know that British Home Stores, Marks & Spencers and Mothercare are characterised by a relatively small number of product lines, tight margins, high sales per square foot and a high degree of central control. At the other end of the scale, W.H. Smith, Boots and Halfords, all have a very large number of lines, lower sales per square foot, lower stock turns and much less central control. It is also true to say that British Home Stores, Marks & Spencers and Mothercare tend to have very many high fashion items, particularly in clothes, and these require (as in the case of our central allocation system) a high degree of central control.

British Home Stores, Marks & Spencers and Mothercare all have very tightly controlled central stock systems, in some cases based on the Kimbal tag system or on simple stock counts. For those unfamiliar with the Kimbal tag, this is a small punched card which is attached to the item by the manufacturer. At the Point of Sale the tag is detached, later to be punch read at the central computer. This system can be remarkably effective in determining sales rates of individual lines. Obviously, the fewer lines the better when operating such a system.

We in W.H. Smith, our colleagues in Boots and in Halfords, are all looking at the new point of sale data capture systems. For the system to work, each item has to have a bar code on it. This bar code can be scanned by a light wand and the unique number of the product (and the fact that it has been sold) transferred to the central computer via cassette storage, floppy disc storage, or bubble memory. The sales data can then be integrated with other data about receipts and distribution from warehouse and transfers between the stores to arrive at an accurate figure for sales of each item. This information can then be built up into a picture for the whole group of merchandise within a branch and within all branches.

There are great potential benefits to be reaped particularly in reducing stock levels, increasing sales, reducing what we euphemistically call 'shrinkage' – that is theft – and for the first time it makes possible a high degree of central control in W.H. Smith's kind of business. Of course, these systems are expensive – their costs run to many millions of pounds – but we would expect to see prices come tumbling down over the next few years and at the same time the facilities and storage offered by the manufacturers of the point of sale terminals greatly increased.

The problem however is not so much a technical one of design of systems but in making sure that we know how to use the information and that we have the kind of organisation which is geared to this very sophisticated type of information system. We are currently looking at the whole problem of defining key information requirements for the Retail Group and of course Point of Sale is one of the things we are looking at very closely. We are already running experiments in our Portsmouth branch which look very encouraging, but each step along the way has to be seen to pay for itself.

We see one of the major hurdles being that of getting the manufacturers to put bar codes on their products. This is not a very costly exercise for them, but it is for us. You can imagine that labelling every product – which we already do for pricing purposes – with a bar code in addition would be expensive in terms of labelling equipment and time. We are, therefore, making strenuous efforts to persuade the manufacturers of records, books, periodicals and stationery to put European Article Number bar codes on their products. From their point of view they will have access to a great deal of marketing information which could prove extremely useful. We for our part will have to bear a large proportion of the costs of point of sale, though we expect that this will be greatly outweighed by the benefits. It may well take us four to five years to get the necessary 90% of our items coded. However, next year should see the first bar codes appearing on books and perhaps even records.

Of course, we recognise that these systems will all have an effect on our staff and indeed on our customers, but the effects are likely to be beneficial to both these groups. The sales assistants will be spared the task of stock counting at frequent intervals – though they will still have to count stock for reconciliation purposes every so often – and the customer will have an itemised bill which will say in clear English what he has bought – for example, a pencil or a ruler and its price. This of course is only possible because the POS tills will have what is called Computer Price Lookup – the wanding of the EAN number causes the till software and hardware to look up the price and item description and then instantly flashes this to a display in front of the cashier and customer.

7 Conclusion

I think you can see that these are exciting times for retailers. Perhaps the most recent revolution in retailing was the move towards self service with its considerable benefits in terms of cost reduction which have been passed on to the consumer. Point of Sale could have just as far-reaching benefits. The most obvious conclusions to come out of this short discussion are that we in retailing, like you in other areas of industry, must have good, tight information and control systems operating at the right levels of detail.

At the same time our systems must be capable of being understood and operated by the people under our control and we must be able to take advantage of the micro processor revolution which is just around the corner, if not already with us.

18
Material Requirements Planning

P G BURCHER

Lecturer in Operations Management,
The University of Aston

1 Introduction

In contrast to the classical inventory control approach to the planning and control of materials, as described in Chapter 16, the technique, known as material requirements planning (MRP), looks at a future requirement for the finished product in terms of a master production schedule and uses this and other information to generate the requirements for all the sub-assemblies, components and raw materials which go to make up the finished product.

This technique has, in essence, been used under different names for many years, particularly for the purchase of special materials in the jobbing industries, that is, the time-phasing of material ordering. However, the advent of low cost computing has brought the term material requirements planning to the fore in the planning and control of the manufacture of multi-component assemblies. In fact, MRP forms the central module of the majority of commercially available production control software packages.

As has been mentioned, MRP is concerned with the manufacture of multi-component assemblies and relies on the fact that the demands for all sub-assemblies, components and raw

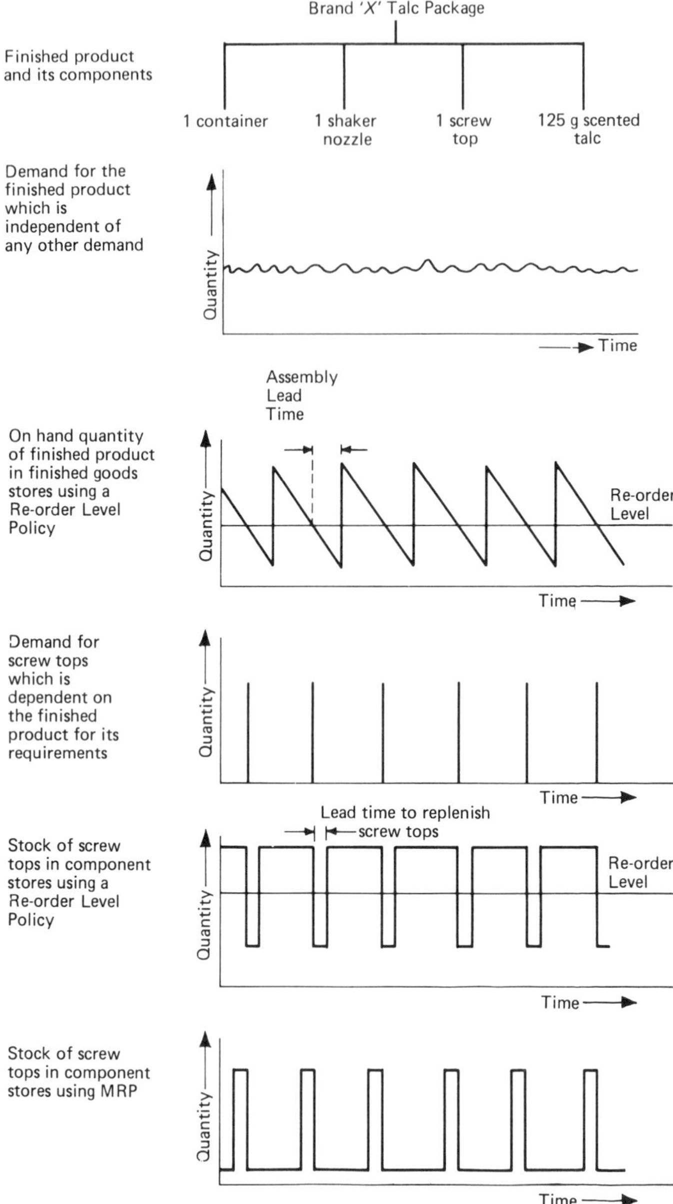

Figure 18.1 *A Comparison of the Behaviour of Component Stocks using a Re-order Level Policy and MRP*

materials are dependent upon the demand for the finished product itself. They are said to have 'dependent demands'.

There are also some items which have 'independent demands', that is, the demand for them does not depend on the demand for any other item. Notably, the finished product itself usually has an independent demand in that it depends solely on the customer purchasing the product. Components and sub-assemblies may also have independent demands in the form of spare parts sales requirements.

It is interesting to note that in a recent survey,[1] 92% of engineering companies produced assembled products, that is to say, they had to deal with a proportion of dependent demand items.

Independent demand items may be satisfactorily controlled using the classical inventory control approach, for example, the re-order level policy. However, for dependent demand items, MRP offers considerable advantages in ensuring that all the parts for the assembly of the product are available at the right time. It also reduces overall stockholding costs whilst improving the service that the stock is providing.

To illustrate this point a simple example is shown in figure 18.1.

This example shows that a saving in stock holding costs is one of the objectives of an MRP system.

In order to carry out its calculations, the MRP package requires three types of information to be supplied, namely:

(i) The *master production schedule* for the finished products;
(ii) The *bill of material* which contains details of which raw materials, components and sub-assemblies go to make up the finished products; and
(iii) Information concerning the *status of all materials* held in inventory.

Having performed its calculations, the package then produces reports, the majority of which are concerned with what and when to manufacture or order.

This system is shown in general outline in figure 18.2.

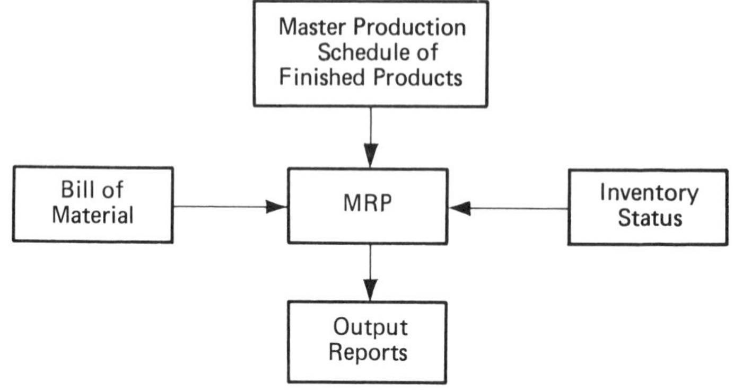

Figure 18.2 *General MRP System Outline*

2 Elements of the MRP System

The total MRP System (figure 18.2) consists of several elements: the inputs, the package itself which carries out the calculations and the output reports. Each element may vary in its exact description, depending on the company and product in any particular case, but it is important to understand the purpose of the element and the various choices which are available.

3 The Master Production Schedule

The master production schedule is a management commitment to produce certain volumes of finished products in particular time periods in the future and should not be confused with the term 'sales forecast'.

A master schedule is created for each finished product using known customer orders, sales forecasts and a knowledge of the manufacturing capacity. It is likely that the schedule will contain a major proportion of firm customer orders in the most immediate time periods and mostly forecasts in the later periods of the planning horizon (see figure 18.3).

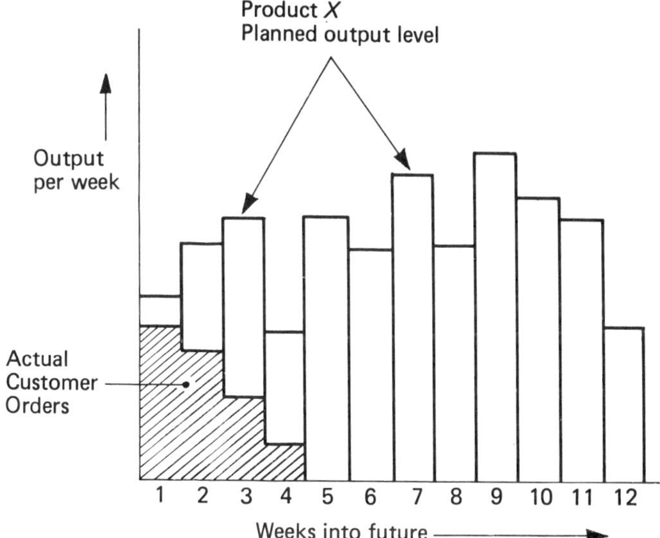

Figure 18.3 *Master Schedule for Product X*

The length of the planning horizon is determined by calculating the longest cumulative lead time for the finished product and adding a period of time to give the purchasing department visibility over future requirements, so that they are able to take advantage of bulk purchasing discounts. The longest cumulative lead time is the sum of all the lead times along the longest route from placing an order for a raw material to completing the finished product (see figure 18.4).

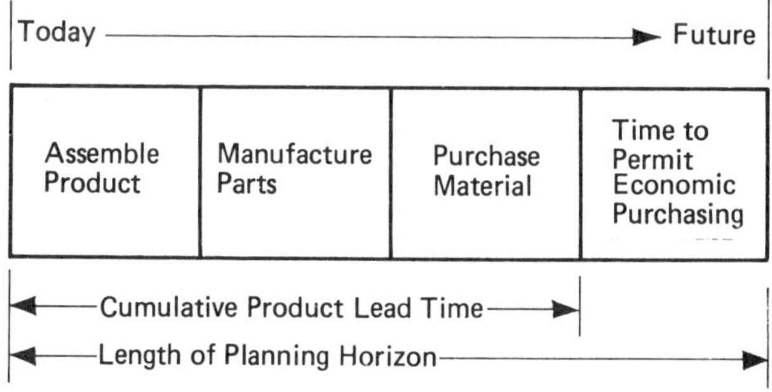

Figure 18.4 *Master Schedule Planning Horizon*

For many companies in practice this will entail using planning horizons of between a year and eighteen months. Since the further ahead a forecast is made, the less accurate it is likely to be, it would be unrealistic to expect that no changes would be allowed to the master schedule, particularly in its later stages. There are, however, increasing difficulties in making changes to the schedule the closer that the beginning or 'front end' of the schedule is approached.

One method of controlling the changes to the master production schedule is to split the planning horizon into time zones, each of which has different constraints on the type of change which can be made (see figure 18.5).

Essentially, that period of the schedule which represents finished products which are currently being assembled should only be changed in emergency situations, since parts and sub-assemblies will have already been manufactured to the original schedule.

In that part of the planning horizon which represents parts currently being manufactured, it may be possible to alter the sequence of the finished products already scheduled, bearing in mind material and capacity availabilities.

In the period which represents orders for materials that have been placed on suppliers, it may be feasible to alter the quantities of finished products on the master schedule if it is possible to make the consequent alterations of material quantities on the open orders with suppliers.

	Today ———	———	———	► Future
Changes Allowed	Emergency only	Alter Sequence of Products Already Scheduled	Alter Volume of Products	Any Changes Allowed
	Assemble Product	Manufacture Parts	Purchase Material	Time to Permit Economic Purchasing

Figure 18.5 *Changes Allowed to the Master Schedule*

In the last section of the planning horizon, or 'back-end' of the schedule, which represents forward information for the purchasing department, it should be possible to make alterations to both the sequence and volume of finished products scheduled, presuming of course, that checks have first been made with the purchasing department regarding any major bulk material purchases which may have been made on the basis of the original information.

Apart from the sales of finished products, a company might also be concerned with the supply of spares in the form of components or sub-assemblies. As described previously, these items have independent demands. However, these independent demands can be incorporated into a MRP system by adding them to the generated dependent demands for the items in the relevant time periods.

As with the master production schedule, the independent spare parts demands could be made up of firm customer orders and sales forecasts as in figure 18.6.

The time periods used in the master schedule will be a result of the degree of control required in the overall production planning and control system and for most companies it is accepted that time periods in excess of one week do not give sufficient control for the setting of priorities for manufactured components and their subsequent progressing.

Some companies have tackled the problem of the choice of time period or time 'bucket' by adopting variable length

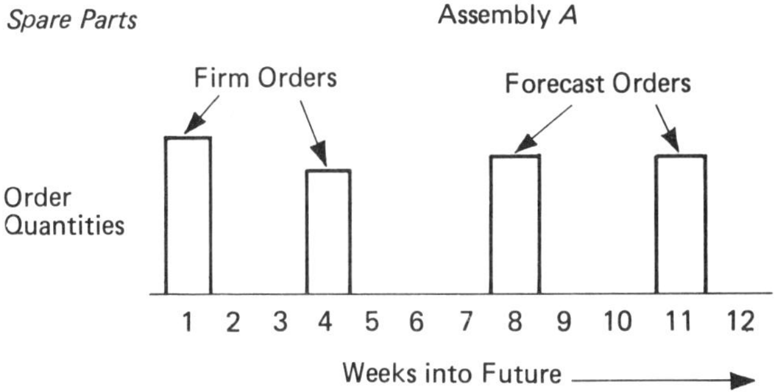

Figure 18.6 *Spares Demand for Assembly A*

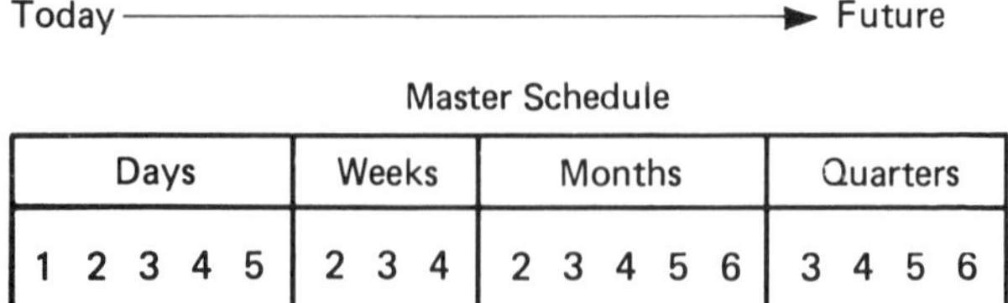

Figure 18.7 *Master Schedule with Variable Length Time Periods*

periods, as in figure 18.7, which give the possibility of greater control of the final assembly operations and less detailed control for the bulk purchasing of materials.

The master production schedule should be, above all, a *realistic* picture of what can be achieved, based on past experience.

It will serve no useful purpose to use 'standard' rates of output or optimistic production targets as the basis for the master production schedule since what will result are excessive inventories, an increasing backlog of unfulfilled requirements and difficulty in setting the correct priorities on jobs.

4 The Bill of Material

The bill of material (BOM) is a file or set of files which basically contain the 'recipe' for each finished product. The 'recipe' in a manufactured goods environment consists of information regarding which materials, components and sub-assemblies go together to make up each finished product, held on what is often known as a Product Structure file; and all the standard information about each item, such as part number, description, unit of measure, lead time for manufacturing or procurement etc., held on what is often known as a Part Master file.

For each finished product a bill of material is originally created from the design and production engineering information. This information will initially be in the form of drawings (see figure 18.8) and assembly charts (see figure 18.9) which together with information on the relevant lead times form the basis of the inputs to the BOM.

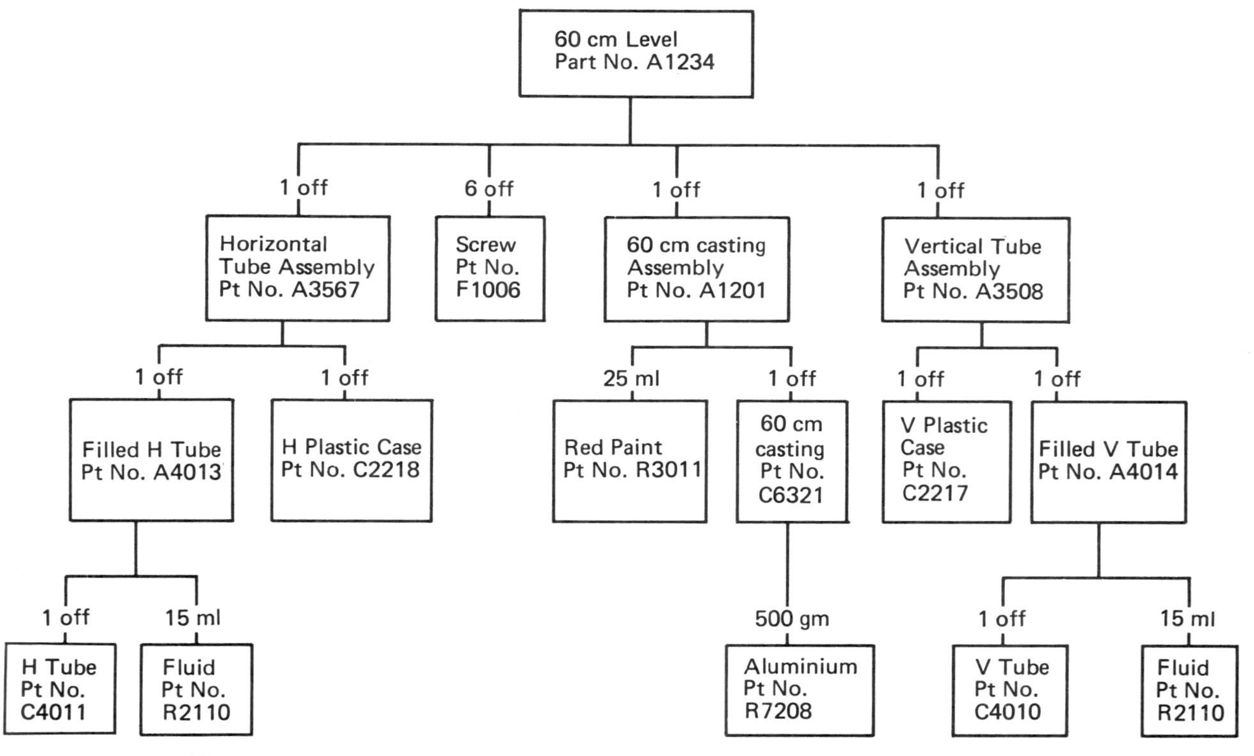

Figure 18.9 *Assembly Chart (simplified) for Part No. A1234 – a 60 cm. Spirit Level*

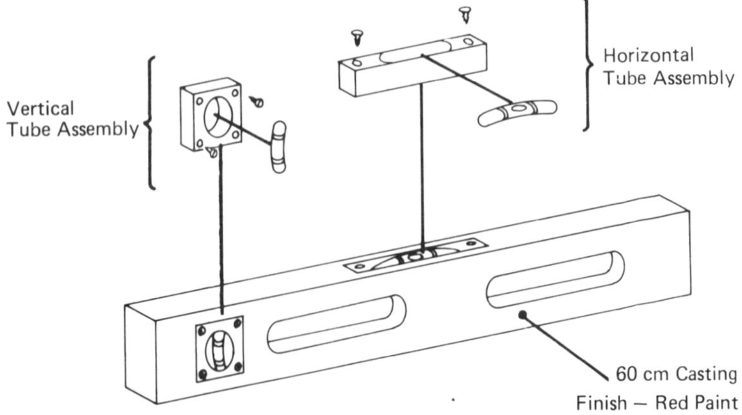

Figure 18.8 *Design Drawing (simplified) of Part No. A1234 – a 60 cm. Spirit Level*

Whilst most MRP systems can cope with part numbers allocated at random, whether they are numeric or alpha-numeric, it is absolutely necessary for all parts or material within the organisation, in whatever form, to be given a unique part number. It may be, therefore, that bulk raw materials and sub-assemblies have to be allocated their own part numbers for the first time, if an MRP system is to be implemented.

It may appear obvious that the information on the BOM needs to be accurate, since inaccuracies can lead to incorrect items or incorrect quantities of items being ordered. However, the problem of file accuracy is complicated by the fact that in many operating environments, there are continual changes to the BOM in the form of product modifications. These modifications may originate from many sources, for example: safety legislation, production process changes, improvements for marketing purposes, value analysis exercises, etc.

The control of the implementation of modifications can be a very time-consuming task for some companies, especially since factors such as the depletion of un-modified stocks and the timing of combined modifications have also to be considered.

One other piece of information that has to be recorded on the BOM is the assembly level at which the item occurs in

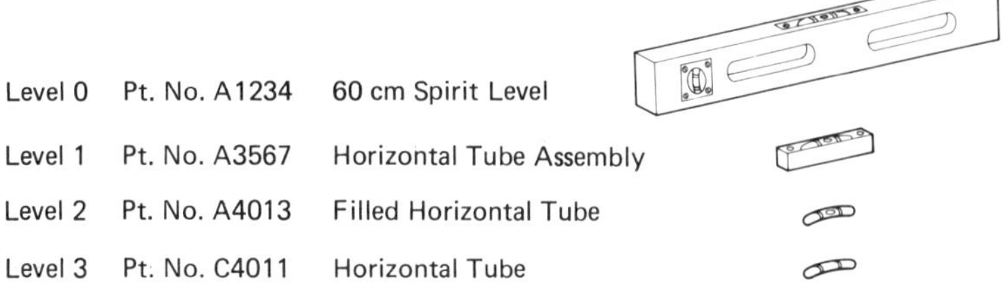

Figure 18.10 *Parts Structure and Assembly Level Numbering*

the product structure. There is an almost universally accepted level numbering system which allocates level 0 to the finished product and increases the level number as the raw material stage is approached, for example see figure 18.10.

The number of levels of assembly breakdown is determined by the complexity of the product and can be as high as twelve for products as complex as aircraft engines.

The key characteristic of a bill of material should be its accuracy, since 'one can never produce mince pies on time using the recipe for sausage rolls!'

5 The Inventory Status File

The inventory status file keeps a record of all transactions and balances of all stock throughout the organisation. The transactions are mainly receipts and issues, starting with the 'On Order' condition and eventually finishing with the issue of the completed product out of the factory. Other transactions may record occurrences such as inspection rejects or stock adjustments as a result of physical stock checks.

Many organisations use the concept of the 'stock condition' to describe the stage which the material has reached, for example: 500 kgs of aluminium part no. R.7208 has been inspected and is in the raw material store ready for issue into Work in Progress. An example of a possible stock condition route is shown in figure 18.11.

If a greater degree of control is required, the work in progress stock condition may itself be split into a number of

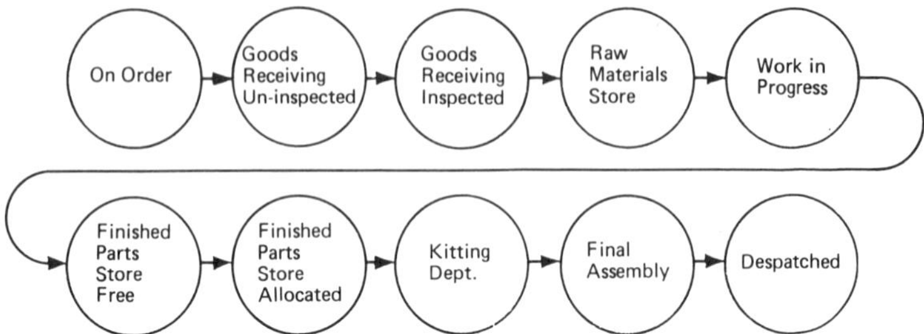

Figure 18.11 *Stock Condition Route for Aluminium Part No. R7208*

separate stock conditions, so that a batch of items may be monitored from one operation to the next (see figure 18.12.).

It should be noted that as material progresses from one stock condition to the next, its part number may also change. For example, when 6 screws (Part No F1006) become part of the spirit level final assembly (Part No. A1234), the balance of Part No. F1006 (screws) in the 'kitting' condition is reduced by 6 and the balance of Part No. A1234 (assembly) in the 'final assembly' condition is increased by 1.

The actual method that is used to input the inventory transactions to the inventory status file may vary considerably. At one extreme, the information may be input on a batch processing basis using punched cards that have been punched from handwritten information.

In the early days of MRP, this method of updating with weekly or bi-weekly processing runs was most common. Unfortunately this led to considerable problems because of the untimeliness of the information.

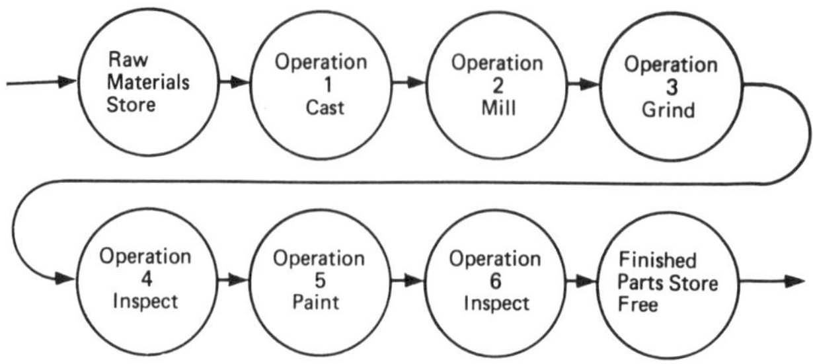

Figure 18.12 *Work in Progress Stock Conditions*

At the other extreme, it is now possible to have automatic monitoring devices on work centres which feed numbers of items completed directly into the computer file.

Most MRP users are currently using either direct 'on-line' inventory updating perhaps using pre-punched cards through computer terminals on the shop-floor, or similarly using pre-punched cards on a nightly batch processing basis.

As with the bill of material, one of the key features of the inventory status file should be its accuracy. The other important feature is the timeliness of the information. Since this accuracy and timeliness will be critical to the running of the MRP system, it is essential that those who will be involved with supplying this information should be thoroughly trained and made aware of the importance of their task.

6 The MRP Package

The MRP package carries out calculations on a level by level basis which convert the master schedule of finished products into suggested orders for all the sub-assemblies, components and raw materials. These calculations or 'requirements generation runs' are likely to be carried out on the computer every one or two weeks so that the situation is kept constantly up-to-date.

At each level of assembly breakdown, the package undertakes three steps in its calculations before continuing to the next lower level. These steps are as follows:

(i) It generates *gross requirements* for the item by 'exploding' the 'planned start' quantities of the next higher level assembly, by reference to the bill of material structure file.
e.g.
A 'planned start' of 200 spirit levels (Pt. No. A1234) in week 15 would be exploded to give gross requirements of 1200 screws (Pt. No. F1006) in week 15. (Refer to figure 18.9 for an assembly chart).

(ii) The gross requirements are amended by the amount of

inventory of that item that is expected to be available in each week i.e. on hand plus scheduled receipts. This information is obtained from the inventory status file and the amended requirements are called the *net requirements.*
e.g.
In week 15 a total of 800 screws are expected to be available, so the gross requirement of 1200 is amended to give a net requirement of 400 screws in week 15.

(iii) The net requirements are then offset by the relevant lead time for the item to give *planned starts* for initiating the manufacture or purchase of the item.
e.g.
If the lead time for the screws (Pt. No. F1006) is 4 weeks, the *net* requirements of 400 screws in week 15 are offset as follows:

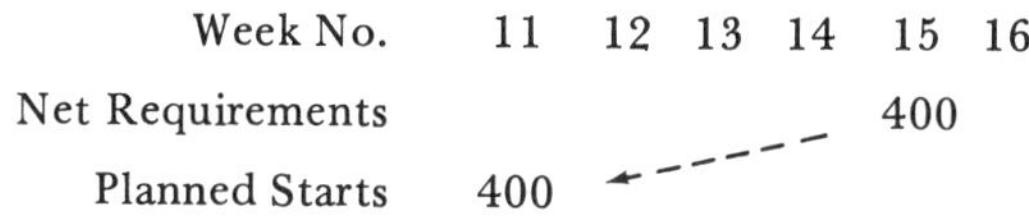

Week No.	11	12	13	14	15	16
Net Requirements					400	
Planned Starts	400					

To summarise, in its simplest form, the MRP package would calculate the requirement of screws for each period of the planning horizon as in figure 18.13.

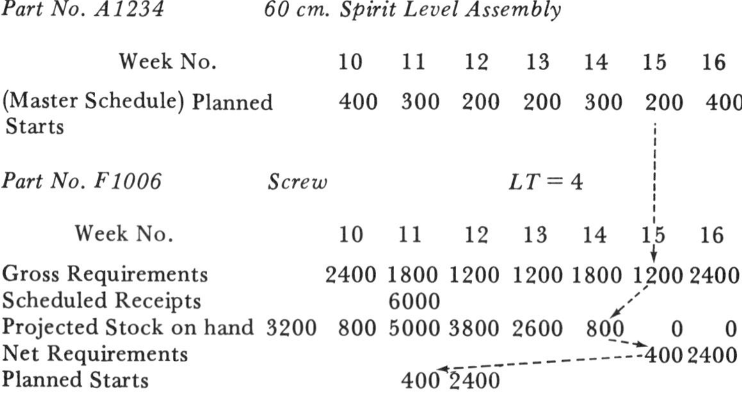

Part No. A1234 *60 cm. Spirit Level Assembly*

Week No.	10	11	12	13	14	15	16
(Master Schedule) Planned Starts	400	300	200	200	300	200	400

Part No. F1006 *Screw* *LT* = 4

Week No.		10	11	12	13	14	15	16
Gross Requirements		2400	1800	1200	1200	1800	1200	2400
Scheduled Receipts			6000					
Projected Stock on hand	3200	800	5000	3800	2600	800	0	0
Net Requirements							400	2400
Planned Starts			400	2400				

Figure 18.13 *MRP Calculation Example*

The calculation above assumes that the only use of the screw (Part No. F1006) is in the assembly of the 60cm spirit level. If this were not the case and if its usage were common to other products assembled by the organisation, for example 40cm and 80cm spirit levels, then the gross requirements for the screw would have been the aggregated requirements generated from the planned starts of all the assemblies using that screw.

7 Batch Sizing in MRP Systems

The simplified approach to the calculation of requirements has, so far, assumed that the net requirements would be translated directly into planned starts, resulting in manufacturing component schedules and purchasing schedules which do not take any account of the cost of machine set-ups or the cost of ordering. In other words, making the requirements as they occur on a week by week basis, otherwise known as the lot-for-lot policy,[2] will certainly reduce overall stockholding costs, but will increase costs incurred through excessive set-up and ordering costs for small batches.

To take account of the *total* costs of managing the materials, that is holding costs *and* ordering or set-up costs, batch sizing rules may need to be applied for the manufacturing or purchasing of items.

There are basically three different methods of batching requirements together; these are fixed quantity batching rules, fixed period coverage batching rules and dynamic batching rules.

(i) Fixed Quantity Batching Rules

The fixed quantity rule essentially states that every time an item is manufactured or bought it is done so in batches of size '*X*' (or multiples of '*X*'). The size of the batch may be determined by a physical constraint of the manufacturing process e.g. furnace size, by considering the quantity that would normally be produced in one shift or in one week, or by some 'economic' calculation.

The calculation that is most likely to be used for an economic fixed batch size is the so-called economic order quantity formula as used in the 'classical' re-order level policy (see page 290) i.e.

$$EOQ = \sqrt{\frac{2A\,C_o}{iC_m}}$$

where A = Demand per time period; C_o = Set Up (or Ordering) Cost; and iC_m = Cost of holding one item for one period; (i being the holding interest rate and C_m the value of the item).

However, it should be noted that in an MRP system, the assumptions upon which the EOQ calculation is based are not valid, that is; a re-order level policy is *not* in operation and there is *not* continuous demand and a gradual depletion of stock of the item. Consequently, although the EOQ may be a guide to the 'best' batch size, it cannot be guaranteed that its implementation will result in minimising total inventory operating costs.

An example of the operation of a fixed quantity batching rule using the EOQ calculation is shown in figure 18.14.

Part No. C6321 *60cm Casting* *LT = 1* *Batch Rule = Fixed Quantity*
Batch Size = 700

Week No.	20	21	22	23	24	25	26	27	28	29
Net Requirements	0	350	100	0	400	0	200	50	100	300
Batched Requirements	–	700	–	–	700	–	–	–	–	700
Planned Starts	700	–	–	700	–	–	–	–	700	–

Figure 18.14 *Example of a Fixed Quantity Batching Rule*

Note: If A, (average demand) = 150 per week
C_s, (set up cost) = £500
iC_m, (holding cost) = £0.30 per item per week

$$\text{Then EOQ} = \sqrt{\frac{2 \times 150 \times 500}{0.3}} = 707$$

$\therefore$ Use Batch Size = 700 items

(ii) Fixed Period Coverage Batching Rules

Fixed period coverage rules calculate a batch size by batching together the net requirements for the next '*y*' periods ahead. The coverage period may be chosen to fit in with a cycle scheduling[3] approach to shop loading where, for example, machined components may be manufactured on a three weekly repeated cycle with one third of components starting in week 1, one third in week 2 and so on. If the choice is not determined by this constraint, an 'economic' coverage period may be calculated by relating the economic order quantity calculation to an equivalent number of time periods' coverage.

An example of the operation of a fixed period coverage rule is shown in figure 18.15.

Part No. C6321 *60cm Casting* *LT = 1 Batch Rule = Fixed Period*
Period = 5

Week No.	20	21	22	23	24	25	26	27	28	29
Net Requirements	0	350	100	0	400	0	200	50	100	300
Batched Requirements	–	850	–	–	–	–	650+	–	–	–
Planned Starts	850	–	–	–	–	650+	–	–	–	–

Figure 18.15 *Example of a Fixed Period Coverage Batching Rule*

Note: Using the same information as in figure 18.14 the Fixed Period would be calculated as follows:

$$\frac{\text{EOQ}}{A} \text{ (average weekly demand)} = \frac{700}{150} \simeq 5 \text{ weeks.}$$

(iii) Dynamic Batching Rules

With dynamic batching rules, the computer uses an algorithm which attempts to arrive at a batching schedule which minimises inventory operating costs. One example of a dynamic rule is the *least total cost* or *part period algorithm*.[2] This algorithm consists of computing the cumulative holding costs and stopping at the batch size just short of the point where cumulative holding costs exceed the set up cost. It makes the cost comparison by first calculating the ratio of the set up cost (C_s) to the holding cost (iC_m) known as the part period value (PPV) i.e. how many parts may be held for how many periods whose holding cost will equate to the set up cost. For example, using the data in figure 18.14, the PPV would be $500/.3 = 1667$ part periods.*

The Part Period Algorithm would calculate the batches as follows:

$PPV = 1667$

Week No.	Net Reqts.	Cumulative Batch Size	Inventory Held	Number of Periods	Cumulative Part Periods
21	350	350	0	0	0
22	100	450	100	1	100
23	0	450	0	2	100
24	400	850	400	3	1300
25	0	850	0	4	1300
26	200	1050	200	5	2300 (>1667)

∴ 1st Batch of 850 required in week 21

continuing

Week No.	Net Reqts.	Cumulative Batch Size	Inventory Held	Number of Periods	Cumulative Part Periods
26	200	200	0	0	0
27	50	250	50	1	50
28	100	350	100	2	250
29	300	650	300	3	1150

Second batch of at least 650 required in week 26
(on the next MRP run the net requirement of Week 30 may be included in the batch).

In this particular example the part period algorithm has produced identical planned starts to those shown in figure 18.15 although, of course, this will not always be the case.

Each type of batching rule has its own advantages and disadvantages. The fixed quantity rule is easily understood and may fit in well with manufacturing process constraints or suppliers' standard order sizes. However, it suffers from the

* *Editor's note*: Similar to the batching algorithm described on p. 371, Chapter 20

drawbacks of generating orders at irregular intervals and, compared to the other methods of batching, it generates higher stock levels.

Since the fixed period coverage rule is directly related to the future periods' requirements, it is more economical in terms of the overall stock levels generated and, as mentioned previously, it may fit in well with the balancing of the workload on the shopfloor. However, it may result in sizes of batches which fluctuate considerably, especially if there are periods with zero net requirements.

Theoretically the dynamic batching rules, especially the part period algorithm, are superior to the other two methods of batch sizing in the reduction of costs. However, they suffer the disadvantages of not being understood as easily and of generating differing batch sizes at uncertain time intervals which, in turn, may lead to difficulties in shop loading.

In general, it should be noted that any batching that takes place at high levels in the assembly structure will affect the requirements for all the constituent items at the lower levels i.e. requirements will be similarly bunched together and required earlier. Therefore, unless set-up or ordering costs are significantly high, it may be advantageous to generate planned starts on a lot-for-lot basis rather than batching, since this will certainly lead to lower holding costs and will keep the relative priorities on manufactured items realistic.

8 Setting Safety Stocks in MRP Systems

Safety stocks are held in any manufacturing system to cater for uncertainty. In an MRP system the major cause of uncertainty, that of the future usage of the item, has been mainly eliminated since items should be produced to meet a plan — *the master schedule.* Therefore, overall, safety stocks in an MRP system should be significantly lower than in a system using classical inventory control policies.

However, safety stocks are still needed because of uncertainties in supply both in terms of the variation of actual lead times and the variation of quantities supplied caused by inspection rejects and material shortages. There will also be changes of demand caused by short-term (emergency) changes to the master schedule and unexpected demands for items such as spares.

The statistical techniques of establishing safety stocks used in classical inventory control systems (described in Chapter 16) are mainly inappropriate to the material requirements planning environment. Alternative methods have therefore been developed for application to MRP which fall into three main categories which are *fixed quantity safety stocks*, *safety times*, and *percentage increases* in requirements.

(i) Fixed Quantity Safety Stocks

Fixed quantity safety stocks are introduced by triggering a net requirement whenever the projected stock on hand reaches a safety stock level rather than zero. Figure 18.16 shows

Part No. C2218 H. Plastic Case *LT = 1* *Safety Quantity = 0*

Week No.		13	14	15	16	17	18
Gross Requirements		200	300	200	400	300	500
Scheduled Receipts		—	—	—	—	—	—
Projected Stock on hand	600	400	100	0	0	0	0
Net Requirements		—	—	100	400	300	500
Planned Starts		—	100	400	300	500	—

a) *Without Safety Stock*

Part No. C2218 H. Plastic Case *LT = 1 Safety Quantity = 150*

Week No.		13	14	15	16	17	18
Gross Requirements		200	300	200	400	300	500
Scheduled Receipts		—	—	—	—	—	—
Projected Stock on hand	600	400	150	150	150	150	150
Net Requirments		—	50	200	400	300	500
Planned Starts		50	200	400	300	500	—

b) *With Safety Stock*

Figure 18.16 *The Effect of a Fixed Quantity Safety Stock*

examples of MRP calculations with and without a fixed quantity safety stock.

The calculation of the size of the fixed quantity stock should be related to the cause of the unexpected usage during the lead time. For example, if the unplanned demand is primarily as a result of unforecasted spares demand for the item, then an historical analysis of this variation may lead towards the setting of a satisfactory safety stock level.

However, since in most cases variations in usage and supply could be the result of many factors and since there are not any 'scientific' methods of setting safety stocks in MRP systems, 'rule of thumb' approximations have been applied. For example, it may be satisfactory to initially set the safety stock level at one week's average requirement or one week's 'maximum' requirement. However, it is essential that the usage of the safety stock is monitored and the level then adjusted accordingly i.e. too frequent use of the safety stock would suggest the need for a higher safety level whereas infrequent use would suggest a lower one.

(ii) Safety Times

The safety time approach for setting safety margins is essentially 'planning to make items available earlier than they are required'. The introduction of safety time is straightforward in that the net requirements are offset by the lead time *and* the safety time to produce planned starts. Figure 18.17 shows examples of MRP calculations with and without a safety time.

Part No. C2218 H. Plastic Case LT = 1 Safety Time = 0

Week No.		13	14	15	16	17	18
Gross Requirements		200	300	200	400	300	500
Scheduled Receipts		–	–	–	–	–	–
Projected Stock on hand	600	400	100	0	0	0	0
Net Requirements		–	–	100	400	300	500
Planned Starts		–	100	400	300	500	–

(a) *Without Safety Time*

Part No. C2218 H. Plastic Case LT = 1 Safety Time = 1

Week No.		13	14	15	16	17	18
Gross Requirements		200	300	200	400	300	500
Scheduled Receipts		–	–	–	–	–	–
Projected Stock on hand	600	400	200	400	300	500	0
Net Requirements		–	–	100	400	300	500
Planned Starts		100	400	300	500	–	–

(b) *With Safety Time*

Figure 18.17 *The Effect of Safety Time*

The choice of the length of the safety time could, perhaps, be related to the variability of the manufacturing or procurement lead time of the item being considered. However, since other factors may influence the use of the safety stock generated by the use of safety time, an arbitrary setting of the safety time and subsequent adjustment based on the monitoring of the usage of the safety stock is satisfactory.

(iii) Percentage Increases in Requirements

The setting of safety margins by the percentage increases in requirements method is particularly suitable for dealing with the variations in supply caused by scrap or process yield losses and are often implemented as 'scrap factors' or 'shrinkage factors'. This type of safety margin is introduced by increasing the net requirements by a factor to produce planned starts. An example is shown in figure 18.18.

Part No. C2218 H. Plastic Case LT = 1 Scrap Factor = 0.05

Week No.		13	14	15	16	17	18
Gross Requirement		200	300	200	400	300	500
Scheduled Receipts		–	–	–	–	–	–
Projected on hand	600	400	100	0	0	0	0
Net Requirements		–	–	100	400	300	500
Planned Starts		–	105	420	315	525	–

Figure 18.18 *The Effect of a Scrap Factor*

The size of the percentage increase in requirement should be directly related to the actual scrap or process yield loss for which it is supposed to be compensating. If this margin is to be used as a buffer against other variations then, again, an arbitrary setting may be made and subsequently modified based on the feedback of the actual use of the safety stock generated.

Safety stocks of finished products to provide a pre-determined customer service level should be set in the traditional fashion by analysing the operation of the sales forecast and translating the resulting requirements into a master schedule for the finished products.

9 Output Reports of MRP Systems

The principal outputs are the executive instructions to make or buy items in the form of requirements reports. Other, more specific reports may be produced such as 'projected on-hand summaries', 'projected shortages', 'expedite lists', 'cancellations' and 'supplier call-off schedules'.

Enquiries may also be made from the various input files, for example, from the bill of material, 'indented parts lists' and 'where used reports' could be obtained and from the inventory status file, 'stock status reports' and 'inventory analyses' could be generated.

In most companies the reports and their formats are specified to fit in with the particular organisational requirements.

10 The Implementation of MRP Systems

The problems that are likely to be encountered in the implementation of an MRP system may fall into many categories but their solutions will be dealt with briefly under two main headings, i.e. analysis of the system task and user involvement and training.

(i) Analysis of the System Task

Before an MRP system is implemented or even proposed, a detailed feasibility study should be undertaken to determine:

(a) How 'standard' are the finished products?
(b) What would be the size and complexity of the bill of material?
(c) What would be the volume of modifications to the bill of material?
(d) How accurate is the current product structure information?
(e) How accurate are the current inventory records?
(f) To what level of detailed control would stock condition records need to be taken?
(g) What length of planning horizon would be necessary?
(h) How easily can finished product demand be forecasted over this planning horizon?
(i) What would be the level of changes to the master schedule?

If the questions above are investigated and answered satisfactorily at the feasibility study stage, then the implementation and eventual running of the system may encounter far fewer problems. Also, before implementation, user involvement and thorough user training are essential.

(ii) User Involvement and Training

The training should include an appreciation of the theory of MRP and more specific instructions for those who are likely to be involved in making particular decisions, for example, covering topics such as:

(a) The effect of changes to the master schedule
(b) The effect of batching
(c) The effect of safety stocks
(d) The importance of BOM accuracy
(e) The importance of stock recording accuracy etc.

Before implementation, it is also essential that the top management of the organisation clearly defines the responsibilities for the creation and maintenance of the data on the various computer files; it is seldom satisfactory to make this the responsibility of the data processing manager!

11 Conclusion

The benefits that can result from the use of a material requirements planning system can be considerable, some companies with successful implementations quoting:[2]

(i) Commonly 30% reduction in component inventories
(ii) Better delivery performance and fewer stockouts
(iii) Up to 5% increases in productivity
(iv) Up to 25% less indirect employees engaged in stores, transport etc.

Apart from these sorts of benefits, MRP may also form the major input to other production planning and control subsystems in the organisation, for example.

(i) *Shop loading* (scheduling), where MRP already supplies the vital information of item quantities and required dates;
(ii) *Capacity planning*, where, with the addition of a routeing file (or bill of operations), detailed loads on departments and work centres can be produced for each period of the planning horizon.

In order to obtain the benefits offered by the use of MRP some organisations may have to change their business methods quite considerably. For instance, instead of accepting orders and quoting delivery dates based, to a large extent, on guesswork and then progressing these orders through the manufacturing departments by the use of 'shortage lists' and 'priority lists' the company may now have to attempt to forecast sales much further into the future, commit themselves to master schedules, commence production based on these schedules and *then* allocate customer orders, as they arrive, to the available unallocated products on the master schedule.

MRP has been used successfully in many different companies since the 1960s in the USA and since the early 1970s in the

UK. It has applications in the manufacture of a wide variety of products ranging from aircraft engines to automobiles, from typewriters to machine tools, from batteries to generators and from lawnmowers to pharmaceuticals.

References and Further Reading

1 Burbidge, J.L., *The Principles of Production Control*, Macdonald and Evans 1968.
2 New, C.C., *Managing Manufacturing Operations*, British Institute of Management Survey Report No. 35, 1976.
3 New, C.C., *Requirements Planning*, Gower Press 1973.
4 Orlicky, J.A., *Material Requirements Planning*, McGraw-Hill 1975.

19
MRP in Pharmaceutical Manufacturing*

STEPHEN J BAUM

Materials Control Manager,
Riker Laboratories

1 Introduction

This case study describes the implementation and subsequent modifications to a material requirements planning (MRP) system in a pharmaceutical manufacturing company.

Prior to 1973, the company's production planning and control activities were mainly manual. Between 1973 and 1976 the initial MRP system was implemented and since 1976 continuing modifications and additions to the system have been made.

(a) Company Background

Riker Laboratories manufactures and markets pharmaceuticals and fine chemicals which are sold both in the UK and overseas.

The pharmaceutical business has three outlets:

Medicines available on prescription.
Proprietary and dermatological preparations sold in a pharmacy.
Contract manufacture.

* Reproduced by kind permission of the author and the British Production and Inventory Control Society.

The Company started manufacture in the UK in 1954 and has grown to a position where it now produces approximately nine million packs per year and exports to over ninety countries throughout the world, many of the markets requiring different packaging due to individual language and legal constraints. Associated Riker Companies overseas are supplied with bulk products for local packaging. Trade chemicals and aerosol components are sold to users, both in the UK and abroad.

Riker Laboratories employs approximately 550 persons of whom 350 work in its manufacturing division. Production includes bulk manufacture of tablets, capsules, aerosols, liquids, subsequently referred to as 'bulk intermediates', and fine chemicals some of which are used in its own products. Due to the stringent laboratory testing procedures, packaging of 850 specifications is completed as a separate operation at a later stage, and on a different site.

2 The Material Requirements Planning System

In view of the Company's rapid development, the manual systems which were in operation into the early 70s gave rise to concern, both in their effectiveness in terms of supply, and increasingly in the value of the inventory that they generated.

In 1973 it was decided to adopt an IBM Requirements Planning Package, using the existing IBM 370/115 computer. The package was modified to our needs by our own systems analysts who worked closely with line management. The changeover was implemented in nine months, but it was a further nine months before the real benefits of the system were felt and the manual systems discontinued. Since that time, the systems have been rewritten and the computer upgraded. Further refinements which include new programmes and changes to print layouts have been made and there are others planned for the future.

The MRP system, its files and a selection of reports are shown in figure 19.1.

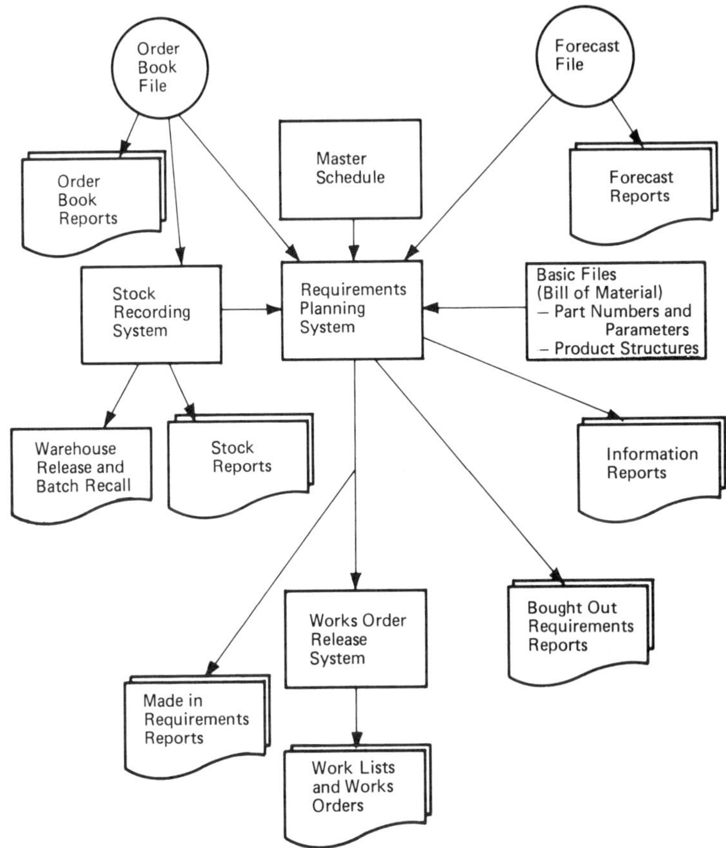

Figure 19.1 *The MRP System*

(a) Inputs to the System

(i) Forecasts

Home trade packs are made to stock. For export orders, the bulk intermediate is made and packaging materials purchased on the basis of a forecasted requirement, with the packaging operation completed on receipt of a firm order.

A unit pack shipment forecast for the forward 15 months,

by month, is prepared and updated quarterly by each of our market managers/customers, where they indicate their expected despatches from the Loughborough site. These are summarised and used as the basis of the projected requirement and input to MRP.

The forecast report form sent to each market shows:

The historical demand over the last 12 months.

The forecasted requirement for the next 12 months as indicated by the customer on the return last quarter.

Columns for the customers to revise/add to their projected needs for the forward 15 months.

Customers can send in amendments to their forecasts at any time and do not have to wait until the next quarterly report. Generally the UK (domestic) requirement can be predicted with a much greater degree of accuracy than many of the overseas markets. Initially, all items were made in advance of the month of forecast, in the expectancy that they could be supplied from stock on receipt of an order.

Due to the forecast inaccuracies, the shortcomings of this approach for servicing export markets were soon realised with increased inventory and redundant packed stock. As a result, the policy for servicing export orders was changed to pack to order.

During the last few years the standard of forecasting in major markets has improved, partly as a result of an educational programme. A manual was prepared to help market managers with their forecasting, and print-outs, monitoring their achievement of orders against forecast, are sent to them with the quarterly report. Regular visits are made to major European customer markets to determine expected requirements. This approach has proved invaluable.

(ii) Master schedule

When MRP was first introduced, the net requirement was planned into a work programme which it dropped out into time buckets. Production departments were expected to manufacture in accord with the programme, smoothing the work load forward as necessary. During the first year of operation it proved exceptionally difficult to organise manufacture in this way, as the requirement did not take account of capacity nor material availability. More and more requirements were appearing in the first time period, masking real priorities. Completion dates were frequently not achieved and a back-log of work developed which needed correction. With hindsight, it was a classic example of a system controlling manufacture.

In 1976 the master scheduling technique was introduced as a plan of what we could realistically expect to produce, taking account of requirements and based on 'historical achievement' rather than 'target' output. Due to the complexity of manufacturing operations, schedules are prepared at all levels. They are a statement of what will be made, how many and when, and are a 'production' plan rather than a 'sales' plan. Based on the net requirement, they are prepared by the planner working closely with production personnel. Regular reviews are carried out, and they are used as a monitor of production at a weekly meeting between production and planning staff.

Recently introduced to the schedules was an 'overplan' to minimise the effect of forecast inaccuracy in a 'make to order' situation. This has proved helpful in providing work for production on the occasions when forecasts have not materialised, or materials are unavailable at the time required, e.g. through a late delivery.

The master schedule is fed back into MRP to provide a net requirement for purchasing – see figure 19.2 – use of MRP.

(iii) The bill of material

Some of the basic files in use were in operation prior to MRP, e.g. the part number master, and product structure files. Obviously this was a distinct advantage in the introduction of the package.

In the pharmaceutical industry, product structure data, i.e. the product formula, is a very strictly controlled body of data, which helps us to maintain accurate specifications.

(iv) Stock records

A computerised stock recording system was in use prior to the implementation of MRP.

Frequency	*Purchasing Department*	*Planning Department*	*Production Department*
Bi-Monthly		MRP print-out (excluding existing Master Schedule – but including stacked lead times). ↓ Used to assess: Net packaging requirement. (Planned Orders). Net manufacturing requirement. ↓ Provides summarised Planned Orders by Work Centre and used to: Smooth requirements against capacity and scheduled on planning charts. ↔ Assess staff levels required. ↓ Charts input to MRP system via new Master Schedule.	Meetings to discuss requirements (labour and capacity). Schedules and manufacturing plans are agreed.
Weekly	Bought out requirement based on current Master Schedule and stacked lead times ↓ Used as basis for placing orders on suppliers.	MRP print-out based on Current Master Schedule but reflecting: Changes to forecasts. New orders. Stock levels etc. ↓ Checked against Master Schedule. ↔ Master Schedule amended only in cases deemed absolutely necessary.	Meeting to check progress against Master Schedule.

Figure 19.2 *Use of MRP*

(b) Operation of the MRP Package

A diagram of the operation of the MRP system is shown as figure 19.3.

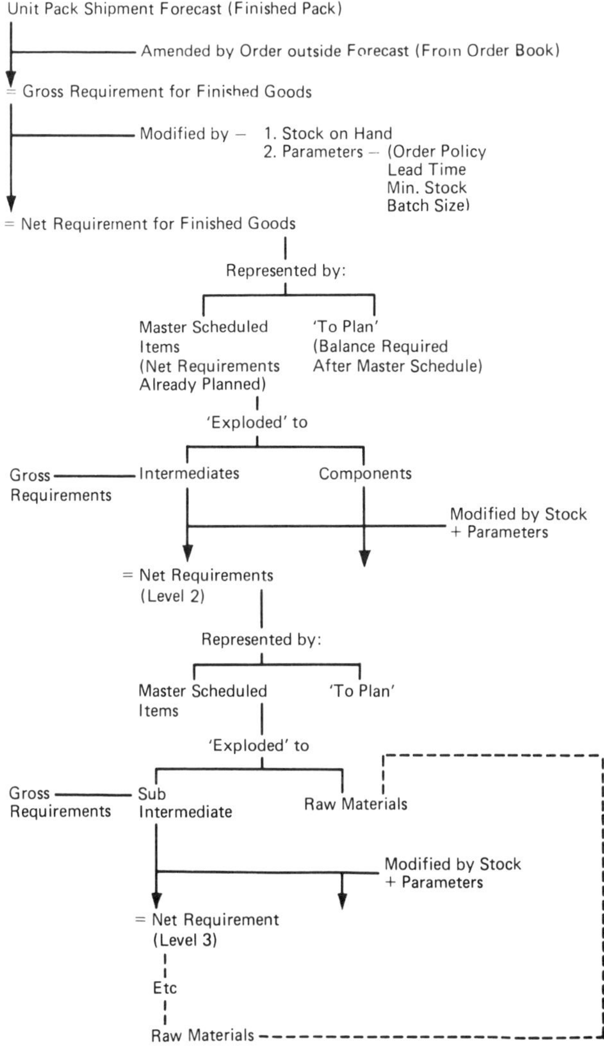

Figure 19.3 *Material Requirements Planning System*

(c) Outputs of the System

(i) MRP print-outs

The original MRP print-out simply showed:

Gross requirements.
Planned orders.
Open orders.
Parameters relating to each part number.

This information provided the 'bones' of the system, but it lacked transparency and frequently led to misunderstanding and cross-reference to additional information by planning staff. Although the relevant data was available to them, it was not presented in an easily and readily understandable form, and when mistakes occurred, it often proved difficult to identify where the error had been made. As a result the print-out was re-designed in 1977, incorporating details of forecasts and orders (see figure 19.4).

Each finished pack specification is reported on a separate sheet and a similar print-out is provided for lower levels. It shows:

Part Number and *Description*

Priority Status – *Action* – requires prompt attention.
Early – product is planned to be made before it is really required.
XMS (excess) – plan to make more than the total 12 months gross requirement.
OK – planned manufacture in line with requirement – no action is required.

History – Total orders/forecast are shown by market for the last 12 months, with the last 3 months by month. The right side of the print-out presents the pack forecast and orders for each market, by month for the next 6 months, with totals for the 3rd and 4th quarter, and for the year.

This information provides the planner

with a full record of the product's recent history, achievement, forecast and orders. There is also a facility for the planner to adjust the requirement, should he deem it necessary. This is shown on the final pair of lines above the '*Totals*' marked '*Production Planning*'.

The parameters used in MRP calculations are given below the '*Totals*' as follows:

Overdue Orders – total outstanding orders which were due for completion by the end of the previous time period.

Total, Allocated and Free Stock.

Safety Stock – a separate print-out, based on past demand variability is available for the planner to determine a desired safety stock.

Lead Time – normal production time from 'material allocation' to 'completion and documentation'.

Order Policy – Discrete, Least Unit Cost (LUC). Fixed Batch Quantity.

Fixed Quantity – batch size.

Cost – Warehouse Cost per unit.

Works Order – last Works Order number issued.

Unit of Issue – K (kilogrammes), L (litres) used, or E (each – used at finished pack level).

The summarised MRP is shown under five headings:

Gross Requirement – calculated from forecast quantity
+ orders above forecast (export)
+ back orders

Note: Orders are compared to forecast. If an order is not received by beginning of month of forecast then the requirement is ignored.

DEPT: TABLET PACKING MISC GROUP – Y

PRODUCT: 3RU106QAA RAUWILOID TABS 60 UK/GEN OVERSEAS PACK

20/11/78 PAGE 741
W/C 20/11/78 W/NO 79/04
PRIORITY – EARLY

	LAST 12 MONTHS	HISTORY AUG 8	SEP 8	OCT 8	NOV 8	DEC 8	JAN 9	FEB 9	FORECAST MAR 9	APR 9	3RD QTR.	4TH QTR.	TOTAL FOR YEAR
	EXPORT – MIDDLE EAST												
FORECAST	3312	60	500		80			80			80	80	320
ORDERS	254	96			96								96
	IRELAND												
FORECAST	600	50	50	50	40	40	40	40	40	40	120	120	480
ORDERS	390				72								72
	EXPORT – AFRICA												
FORECAST	12					12					12		24
ORDERS													
	RIKER JAMAICA												
FORECAST	576		144			144							144
ORDERS	144												
	RIKER PRESC SALES												
FORECAST	23000	2000	1900	1900	2000	1400	1850	1700	2200	1550	5500	5650	21850
ORDERS	22876	1932	1627	1885	1387								1387
FORECAST													
ORDERS													
PRODUCTION PLANNING													
TOTALS	27500	2110	2594	1950	2120	1596	1890	1820	2240	1590	5712	5850	22818
	23664	2028	1627	1885	1555								1555

ODUE ORDERS	TOTAL STOCK	ALLOC. STOCK	FREE STOCK	SAFETY STOCK	LEAD TIME	ORDER POLICY	FIXED QTY.	COST	USAGE	LAST WORKS ORDER	U/I
0	1748	0	1748	0	10	L.U.C.	0	0.XXX	1912	2RU012	E

MONTH & WEEK NO.	NOV 04	NOV 05	DEC 06	DEC 07	DEC 08	DEC 09	JAN 10	JAN 11	JAN 12	JAN 13	FEB 14	FEB 15	FEB 16
GROSS REQUIREMENT	400	596	422	350	350	390	463	463	463	583	425	425	425
WORK IN PROGRESS													
MASTER SCHEDULE	3470												
PROJECTED ON HAND	1348	752	3800	3450	3100	2710	2247	1784	1321	738	313	112–	537–
TO PLAN										4015			

MONTH & NO. OF WEEKS	FEB 1	MAR 5	APR 4	MAY 5	JUN 4	JUL 4	AUG 5	SEP 4	OCT 4	TOTALS
GROSS REQUIREMENT	465	2240	1682	2040	1790	1870	1990	1840	1900	21570
WORK IN PROGRESS										
MASTER SCHEDULE										3470
PROJECTED ON HAND	1002–	3242–	4924–	6964–	8754–	10624–	12614–	14454–	16354–	16354–
TO PLAN			4250		3907		4170			16352

	PART NUMBER	DESCRIPTION	QUANTITY	PARENT EQUIV.	VALUE	OTHER PART No.	PART NUMBER	DESCRIPTION	QUANTITY	PARENT EQUIV.	VALUE	OTHER PART No.
SPECIFIC COMPONENT STOCKS	A1 1001	2 MG RAUWILOID TABS	234.660K	22264		> 2	A34036	LABEL	4000	3478		
	A3 4893	LABEL	7500	6522								

Figure 19.4 *An Example of a MRP Print-out*

WIP – 'work in progress' based on Works Orders for which materials have been issued.

Master Scheduled Items – orders for which manufacturing plans have been made on a Master Schedule, sometimes known as Open Orders or Scheduled Receipts.

Projected on Hand – projected stock, offset by
gross requirement
WIP
Master Scheduled items

To Plan – gross requirement
less WIP
Master Scheduled items
amended by parameters

The forward months 1–3 are shown by week and months 4–12 by month. The first monthly block shows the balance requirement of the month which is not separated into weekly time buckets.

Specific Component Stocks – Details specific, as opposed to common, component stock associated with that product structure.

Future requirements – summaries of future requirements for the quarter and the year ahead, together with their work content (Standard Hours), are printed each month and are used for resource planning, e.g. calculating manpower and capacity levels.

(ii) Works order release

Works Orders are printed by the computer for products required to be started during the next three weeks. Work lists are printed showing the material availability status for those Works Orders.

(iii) Purchasing

The purchasing reports have recently been re-specified incorporating more information on historical data and this has enabled the buyers to identify 'real' requirements, resulting in a further reduction and control of inventory. An on-line enquiry system is now in operation and is proving a most useful aid to identifying stock movements. It is planned to go 'live' in the near future, so that data held by the computer can be updated through the terminals.

3 'Lessons Learned'

(a) Realistic and Accurate Information

(i) Stock recording
Although a computerised system of stock recording was in use before the introduction of MRP, its accuracy left much to be desired. Considerable effort has been given to improving our stock records and educating staff, to good effect, although there is still room for further improvement. For such a system to function, it is imperative that paperwork is not held up or delayed. Constant attention needs to be paid to this aspect as well as to record accuracy.

(ii) Output
Planned output levels must be realistic. Initially we were over optimistic in terms of output expectancy and production regularly failed to meet the plan, which led to back orders. Planning is now based on what can be expected to be made and agreed with production, based on history, rather than target output.

(iii) Product structures
Fortunately accurate product structures (Bills of Materials) were readily available when the system was introduced and this aspect created few problems.

(iv) 'Clean' first time period
Many of the initial inadequacies/deficiencies in the system appeared as an overload/backlog in the first time period. Priority was given to examining the reasons why this was happening and appropriate steps taken to eliminate them.

(b) Systems Development

The initial policy was to work through an internal consultant who specified system requirements. Over a period of time it became clear that working through a third party was unsatisfactory for both planning and DP personnel, and as a result the policy was changed so that now the user clearly defines and writes specifications for the systems analyst to action. This proved beneficial to all concerned, ensuring the user's commitment and has shown in the results.

Another original concept that proved impractical was that any decision made by an individual could be made equally well by the computer, provided that the right parameters had been fed to it. The folly of this approach was realised and the reports redesigned so that the computer now 'crunches the numbers' and prepares information in a readily understood format for the user to make decisions.

(c) Organisation of Planning Department

When the department was set up, it was decided that one group should be responsible for planning the manufacture of bulk product (intermediate) with a second group for planning its packaging. This approach was partly historical, arising from the fact that the operations are carried out at different sites, but had practical limitations in that one group did not have full control and responsibility for fulfilling each product order. In 1976 it was re-organised into two teams, each being responsible for distinct product groups. This includes material requisitioning and planning of both bulk product and its packaging, and has proved a more positive solution.

(d) Training

When MRP was first introduced we did not pay sufficient heed to training and education of staff, resulting in the system often being misunderstood. Later in-company courses using video/audio cassettes were used with benefit to all concerned, and we subscribe to the best external training available for production planning personnel.

4 Benefits

The effect of the introduction of MRP on production was quite dramatic and the following major benefits have been derived:

(a) Staff

Under the manual system, 17 persons were involved in the stock control and planning department. At the commencement it was expected that some of the manual jobs would disappear, but the most optimistic forecast did not predict that the department would reduce to 6 people with improved service and control. Further reductions were also made in the purchasing department, which is currently staffed by 4 people.

(b) Inventory

Total inventory, expressed in months of manufacturing costs, was 7.2 months in October 1974, and this reduced to between 4.0 and 4.5 months in 1979. Its value in 1979 is approximately equal to the 1974 level, while sales have more than doubled during the same period.

(c) Service

To Customers: has improved significantly, particularly in servicing overseas markets.

Home trade items are serviced from stock and a level of 99% is consistently achieved.

Export – the target is to despatch each order within six weeks, allowing four weeks for goods availability and two weeks for export packaging/documentation. 90%–95% of export orders for finished goods are serviced within these target times.

To Production: Production manufacture to a Master Schedule with improved efficiency.

(d) Management Information

The system now in use provides staff with a full picture/status of expected demand and history of each product, intermediate, raw and packaging material. This has provided management with an invaluable aid to decision-making.

5 Conclusions

This case has given an over-view of a system which is in use and fully operational, pointing out some of the difficulties and problems which have been encountered along the road. Many of these were considerable, and the reaction of management and production staff during its formative years was very mixed. Although the programme is still being improved, the results which now have been achieved speak for themselves, and the system has provided a key to both control of production and service to customers, in a business of ever-increasing complexity.

20
Scheduling

C D LEWIS

Professor of Operations Management,
The University of Aston

1 Introduction

Scheduling is a very important area within the field of Operations and Production Management. The problems that can occur are many and varied and unfortunately with any one scheduling problem there are, more often than not, an infinite number of possible solutions. Hence in practice, many scheduling systems are *not* solved using mathematically-based algorithms, but by using simple priority rules such as 'first come, first served'. These rules are usually adopted after a disastrous initial attempt to allocate priorities to individual scheduled items. Such priority ratings start off as 'urgent', proceed to 'very urgent' and finish up such that all items are categorised as 'most urgent'. In such situations, when the English language is unable to produce further superlatives, a numbering system of priority ratings is resorted to.

2 Scheduling Using Conventional Charting Methods

Gantt Charts

Whilst increasingly scheduling problems are being processed by computer, the traditional Gantt chart still remains a useful

Table 20.1 Machine Operation Times for Three Products (minutes)

Products	a	b	c	d	*Total*
	Machines				
A	4	6	3	3	16
B	4	5	2	2	13
C	4	3	4	2	13

tool in presenting scheduling problems in terms of the time duration of operations and the time inter-relationships of those operations. A Gantt chart is simply a specialised form of bar-chart, where the horizontal axis represents time. It is best illustrated by example, rather than by a superfluity of words.

Let us assume that three products, *A, B* & *C* are to be scheduled in the sequence *A–B–C* on to machines **a, b, c** & **d** and that those machines can be operated only in the sequence **a–b–c–d**. Given that the duration of each machining operation for each product is as indicated in table 20.1, what is the overall time that will be needed to complete all machining operations on all products given an inter-machine transfer time of one minute?

Examination of the Gantt chart shown as figure 20.1 confirms that, on the assumption that product *A* starts on machine **a** on time, all the machining operations on product *A* can be

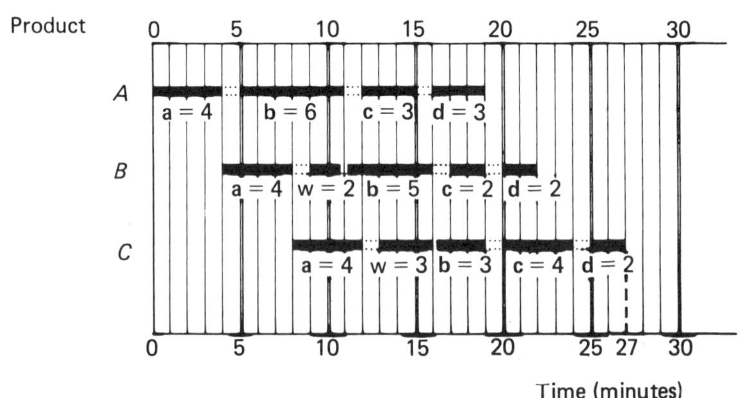

Figure 20.1 *Gantt Chart Showing Loading of Jobs onto Machines* **a, b, c,** *and* **d** (w = waiting time)

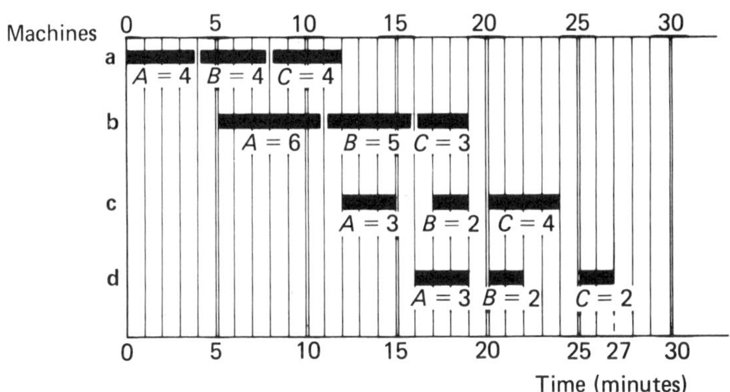

Figure 20.2 *Gantt Chart Showing Machine Utilisation by Products A, B and C*

completed without any waiting, thus giving an overall completion time for product *A* of 19 minutes. This completion time is made up of 16 minutes of machining time and 3 minutes of inter-machine transfer time.

However, product *B* cannot start on machine **a** until the end of minute 4 and completes that operation by minute 8. After transfer to machine **b**, product *B* is required to wait two minutes before product *A* clears that machine. Subsequently, product *C* is also delayed by 3 minutes waiting for product *B* to clear machine **b**. As a result of these delays, caused by machine **b**, the machining of all three products can only be completed in a minimum of 27 minutes.

As well as using a Gantt chart to indicate the loading of products onto machines, a similar chart can also be used to show the loading of machines by products, as is shown in figure 20.2. Here it can be seen that once machining starts, machines **a** and **b** are fully utilised, whereas machines **c** and **d** are utilised only intermittently.

3 Range and Size of Scheduling Problems

The previously considered scheduling problem is just one of many and is usually referred to as an intermittent scheduling problem. That particular problem was only concerned with scheduling 3 jobs on 4 machines. Even in such a simple scheduling situation, where one is able to alter the starting sequence of loading products to minimise overall time to completion, there is as yet no mathematical algorithm which could guarantee to obtain the best result. (Note: As will be shown later in this chapter, optimum solutions are available for loading *n* jobs or products onto 2 machines, and in special circumstances 3 machines, but such solutions are not available for 4 machines or more.)

Thus to find an optimal solution to the 3 product, 4 machine problem one would need to examine all the possible alternatives, which in this case would be 6, namely *A–B–C* (as already considered), *A–C–B, B–A–C, B–C–A, C–A–B* and *C–B–A*. A realistic problem with 20 products would have approximately 2,432,902 billion such alternatives!

Further complications, in practice, could also be caused by such factors as:

(a) rarely are all machines vacant and ready and waiting to be loaded;
(b) machining sequences (in our case **a–b–c–d**) are rarely the same for all products and do not necessarily have to be rigidly adhered to, i.e., machining operation **d** could precede **c**, etc;
(c) estimated machining times are average values which in practice will vary considerably;
(d) machines do not always operate perfectly: breakdowns occur, tools break, etc.

Perhaps by now the reader can begin to appreciate that because of the variety of schedules that could occur in practice and because of the number of complications that could disrupt or invalidate those schedules, optimal solutions are generally impossible. Thus *reasonable* solutions are sought which are most unlikely to be truly optimal, but can be implemented in a practical working environment. Such solutions are usually based on the use of simple priority rules.

4 Priority Sequencing Rules

Some of the priority sequencing rules that are or have been used in scheduling problems are:

(a) First Come – First Served

Although a simple rule and one which appears to be 'fair', because in the real world delivery dates are far more important than the dates when orders were placed, this rule is not particularly effective.

(b) Shortest Processing Time (SPT)

This rule allocates highest priority to products which have the shortest processing times. This rule consistently offers a lower average completion time and also reduces the average number of jobs in the system. Complications with this rule can arise however insofar as new jobs with short processing times can 'leapfrog' old jobs with longer processing times.

(c) Static Slack (SS)

In sequencing rules, slack is defined as the difference in time between the job's due date and the time at which it is available to be scheduled. In the static slack rule, priority is allocated to jobs with the smallest slack, hence jobs arriving well ahead of their due date have a large static slack and are, consequently, given low priority.

(d) Static Slack to Remaining Processing Time (SS/PT)

In this rule highest priority is given to the jobs with the lowest ratio of static slack to remaining processing time. Obviously if this ratio falls below one, the product concerned cannot be completed on time.

Other rules have also been developed but, in general, the shortest processing time (SPT) rule appears to operate better than most and is simple to implement. Its performance is improved by giving high priority to jobs with long processing times – when such jobs have been kept waiting for a specified period of time.

5 Scheduling Algorithms

Whilst it is true that most scheduling situations are not amenable to mathematical solutions, some algorithms have been developed which have gained a reputation for their usefulness for solutions to particular problems in this area and are used within computer scheduling packages. Some of these are described in the remainder of this chapter and should be of interest to the more technically minded reader.

(a) Johnson's Algorithm for Loading n Jobs onto Two Machines

The problem considered is that there are n jobs to be placed on two machines.

The objective is to minimise total elapsed time. There is a restriction that passing of jobs is not allowed, i.e. the same sequence on first machine must prevail on second.

The solution which minimises overall time to completion is found by applying the following rules:

(i) Find the shortest operation which can occur on either machine 1 or machine 2.

(ii) If the shortest operation happens to occur on machine 1, place that job first in the sequence; if on machine 2, place that job last.

(iii) When a job has been sequenced, apply (i) and (ii) to remaining jobs and sequence jobs next-to-first, next-to-last, etc.

(iv) In the event of a tie, priority in sequencing either next-to-first or next-to-last goes to job with shorter operation on the other (i.e., non-tied) machine.

Example (Operation times in hours)

Job	*Machine 1*	*Machine 2*
1	3 second	5
2	4 fourth	8
3	5 fifth	7
4	8 sixth	6
5	7	last 3 (i.e. eighth)
6	6	next to last 4 (i.e. seventh)
7	2 first	8
8	3 third	8

The sequence is 7–1–8–2–3–4–6–5 and is illustrated in figure 20.3.

(b) Johnson's Algorithm for Loading n Jobs onto Three Machines

The *n* jobs–three machine problem can be solved in a similar manner to the two machine problem, subject to *either* of the following conditions being valid:

(i) The minimum operation time on machine 1 is greater than or equal to the maximum operation time on machine 2.
(ii) The minimum operation time on machine 3 is greater or equal to the maximum time on machine 2.

If either of the above are valid, the solution procedure is the same as for the two machine problem, except the sum of operations on machines one and two are compared with the sum of operations on machines two and three.

Example (Operation time in hours)

Job	*Machine 1*	*Machine 2*	*Machine 3*	*Machines 1 & 2*		*Machines 2 & 3*
1	7	3	8	10 first		11
2	6	2	3	8	next-to-last	5
3	8	4	4	12	next-but-two-to-last	8

4	5*	5*	8	10	second	13
5	6	2	2	8	last	4
6	7	4	5	11	next-but-three-to-last	9
7	10	4	2	14	next-but-one-to-last	6
8	11	5*	7	16	next-but-four-to-last	12

* Condition (i) is met

The sequence is 1–4–8–6–3–7–2–5 and is illustrated in figure 20.4.

*(c) Fixed Schedule Problems**

An illustration of such a problem is indicated below, where a supplier of a component has agreed to the six-month schedule shown for an item valued at say £50 for which it is assumed that the holding interest rate is 24% (2% per calendar month) and the cost of setting-up machinery to produce this item is £1,000, irrespective of how many are produced.

For this type of problem it is assumed that the costs to be minimised are only those of holding (or storing) and of setting-up (or ordering). It is assumed that inflation, however rampant, is not likely to affect material and labour costs over a period of a few months, and so, as far as these two costs are concerned, it does not matter when these components are made.

Delivery Schedule

January	400
February	650
March	350
April	450
May	50
June	400
Total	2,300

If the value of the component or item being considered is

* This section is reproduced from Lewis, C.D., *Demand Analysis and Inventory Control*, Saxon House 1975.

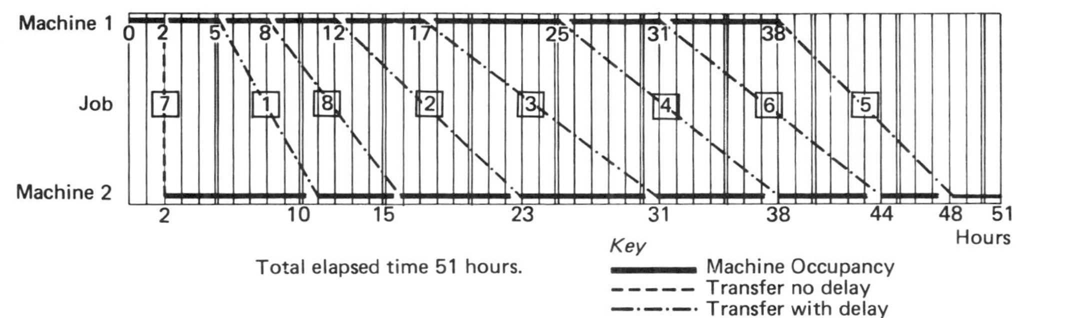

Figure 20.3 *Time Plot of n Job, Two Machine Problem*

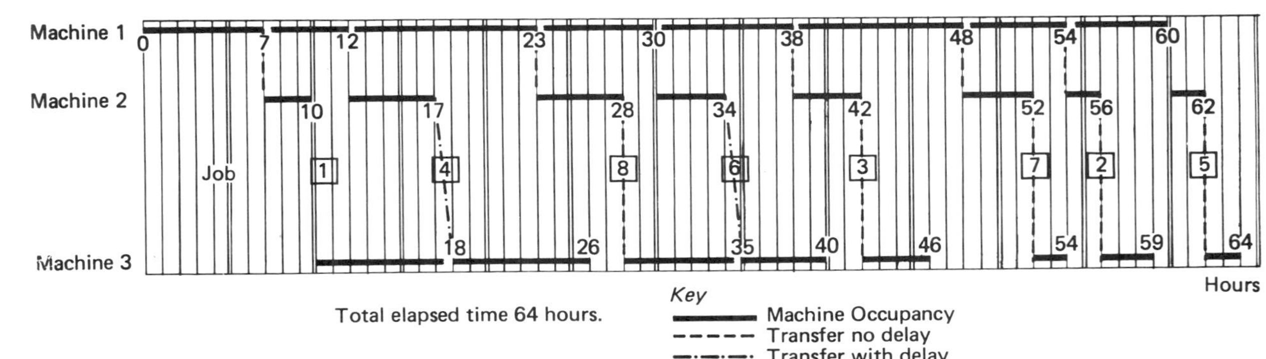

Figure 20.4 *Time Plot of n Job, Three Machine Problem*

£50, at a 2% per month holding interest rate, it follows that it costs £1 per month for each unit stored.

If one considers manufacturing all 2,300 components in January to minimise set-up costs at £1,000 for a single set-up, the cost of storage that will have accrued by the time of the final delivery of 400 units in June will be given by:

$$650 \times £1 + 350 \times £2 + 450 \times £3 + 50 \times £4 + 400 \times £5 = £4{,}900$$

This will give a total cost of £1,000 + £4,900 = £5,900.

If one sets-up every month, and makes exactly the quantity required, no storage costs are incurred and the cost of the policy is that of six set-ups at £1,000 each, i.e. 6 × £1,000 = £6,000.

Thus the costs of these extreme policies are £5,900 and £6,000 and there is, therefore, little to choose between them. However, one can show that the cheapest combination of set-up and storage charges can produce policies costing £4,200 which is about 13.0 per cent less than either of these two extreme policies. Before indicating how one can find this cheapest manufacturing schedule, it should be pointed out that in this class of problem, batch splitting is not allowed – simply because any splitting of batches is bound to increase costs. This occurs because when a batch is split, part of that batch incurs a storage charge whilst the remainder still requires a set-up and its associated full cost.

(i) Dynamic Programming Approach

The dynamic programming approach is based on the principle of optimality which assumes in a time sequence that at each point in time only one of the alternatives under consideration can possibly feature in the overall optimal sequence. In the fixed schedule problem under consideration, for each month the alternatives for that month are evaluated and the cheapest chosen as the optimal sub-policy. To clarify the cost calculations a set-up will be written as 1 × £1,000, a thousand items stored for one month as 1,000 × £1 and an optimal sub-policy carried forward as £1,000. As many optimal sub-policies will not feature in the overall policy, the details of such sub-policies carried forward are not retained, but referred to as 'and *make* more in . . .'

Dynamic Programming Solution to Fixed Schedule Problem

JUNE (Only one alternative)

1 Make 400 in June (1 X £1,000) = £1,000*

MAY (Two alternatives)

1 Make 450 in May (1 X £1,000 + 400 X £1) = £1,400*
2 Make 50 in May and more in June (1 X £1,000 + £1,000) = £2,000

APRIL (Three alternatives)

1 Make 900 in April (1 X £1,000 + 50 X £1 + 400 X £2) = £1,850*
2 Make 450 in April and more in May (1 X £1,000 + £1,400) = £2,400
3 Make 500 in April and more in June (1 X £1,000 + 50 X £1 + £1,000) = £2,050

MARCH (Four alternatives)

1 Make 1,250 in March (1 X £1,000 + 450 X £1 + 50 X £2 + 400 X £3) = £2,750
2 Make 350 in March and more in April (1 X £1,000 + £1,850) = £2,850
3 Make 800 in March and more in May (1 X £1,000 + 450 X £1 + £1,400) = £2,850
4 Make 850 in March and more in June (1 X £1,000 + 450 X £1 + 50 X £2 + £1,000) = £2,550*

FEBRUARY (Five alternatives)

1 Make 1,900 in February (1 X £1,000 + 350 X £1 + 450 X £2 + 50 X £3 + 400 X £4) = £4,000
2 Make 650 in February and more in March (1 X £1,000 + £2,550) = £3,550
3 Make 1,000 in February and more in April (1 X £1,000 + 350 X £1 + £1,850) = £3,200*
4 Make 1,450 in February and more in May (1 X £1,000 + 350 X £1 + 450 X £2 + £1,400) = £3,650
5 Make 1,500 in February and more in June (1 X £1,000 + 350 X £1 + 450 X £2 + 50 X £3 + £1,000) = £3,400

*Optimal sub-policy

JANUARY (Six alternatives)

1 Make 2,300 in January (1 X £1,000 + 650 X £1 + 350 X £2 + 450 X £3 + 50 X £4 + 400 X £5) = £6,000
2 Make 400 in January and more in February (1 X £1,000 + £3,200) = £4,200**
3 Make 1,050 in January and more in March (1 X £1,000 + 650 X £1 + £2,550) = £4,200**
4 Make 1,400 in January and more in April (1 X £1,000 + 650 X £1 + 350 X £2 + £1,850) = £4,200**
5 Make 1,850 in January and more in May (1 X £1,000 + 650 X £1 + 350 X £2 + 450 X £3 + £1,400) = £5,100
6 Make 1,900 in January and more in June (1 X £1,000 + 650 X £1 + 350 X £2 + 450 X £3 + 50 X £4 + £1,000) = £4,900

** Optimal policy

Thus there would appear to be three alternative cheapest policies all at £4,200, which by going back through the various optimal sub-policies can be shown to be those indicated in table 20.2.

It is interesting to note that as early in the analysis as May a 'manufacture every month' policy was already ruled out as the optimal sub-policy for May was to make 450, to cover both May and June.

The great power of the dynamic programming approach is that the larger the problem gets (i.e. the longer the period to be scheduled), the smaller the *proportion* of alternatives that have to be examined. Given an N month scheduling problem, there are 2^{N-1} possible alternative schedules. Using the dyna-

Table 20.2 Manufacturing Schedule

	Deliveries	*Manuf.* (1)	*Manuf.* (2)	*Manuf.* (3)
January	400	400	1,050	1,400
February	650	1,000	–	–
March	350	–	850	–
April	450	900	–	900
May	50	–	–	–
June	400	–	400	–

mic programming approach there are $\sum_{i=1}^{N} i$ alternatives of which only N are full alternatives. Assuming that the combination of part and full alternatives represents only half the computation required for full alternatives we find the following:

Scheduling period (N)	Possible alternative schedules (2^{N-1})	Dynamic programming equivalent Full alternatives $\frac{\sum_{i=1}^{N}}{2}$	% Saving (approx)
6	32	11	66%
9	256	23	91%
12	2,048	39	98.2%

In addition to the power of the DP approach to scheduling being that the larger the problem, the smaller the proportion of alternatives to be examined, the technique also rapidly rejects part alternatives which cannot form part of the overall cheapest policy. This enables the method to be programmed very efficiently. It is apparent from the previous example that if scheduling periods of six or more are to be programmed, a computer package will normally be resorted to in practice and most computer manufacturers and bureaux now offer such DP packages.

(ii) Batching Algorithm Approach

A much simpler algorithm than the DP approach can be used to solve this particular problem, which although it does not always obtain the cheapest solution almost invariably does. On those few occasions that it does not, it selects a solution very nearly as cheap.

To explain this simple approach, consider scheduling a twelve-month period by successfully grouping months together in twos, threes and fours as in table 20.3.

From this table it can be concluded that by batching up from a group of size n to one of size $n + 1$, a saving to the new group of S/n accrues, where S is the set-up cost. This saving is achieved at an increased storage cost caused by the quantity added to the group (D_{n+1}) being stored for n periods

Table 20.3 Possible Manuacturing Groups

Periods												Group size	Set-ups (or groups)	Saving in set-ups per new group
1	2	3	4	5	6	7	8	9	10	11	12			
Ma	Ma	Ma	Ma	Ma	Ma	Ma	Ma	Ma	Ma	Ma	Ma	1	12	–
Ma	St	Ma	St	Ma	St	Ma	St	Ma	St	Ma	St	2	6	1
Ma	St	St	Ma	St	St	Ma	St	St	Ma	St	St	3	4	1/2
Ma	St	St	St	Ma	St	St	St	Ma	St	St	St	4	3	1/3

Ma – Manufacture
St – Store

at a cost of $nD_{n+1}\ iC_m$ (where i is the period holding interest rate and C_m the value of the item stored).

For it to be cheaper to include D_{n+1} in the proposed group of size $n + 1$, the savings accrued must be greater than the storage costs incurred, hence:

$$\frac{S}{n} > nD_{n+1}\ iC_m$$

alternatively

$$n^2\ D_{n+1} < \frac{S}{iC_m}$$

where $\frac{S}{iC_m}$ is a constant, which in the previous example considered was 1,000.

Hence, to apply this technique all that is required to batch up from a group of size n to one of $n + 1$ is an affirmative answer to the question: Is $n^2\ D_{n+1}$ less than a constant $\frac{S}{iC_m}$? If the answer to this question is *No*, a further increase in group size is not economically justified and the group size must be closed at size n and a new group started up with D_{n+1}.

Applying this approach to the previous problem we obtain from table 20.4 a schedule which is the second of the three cheapest found using DP and, of course, costs £4,200.

This simple batching algorithm, invariably does find the

Table 20.4 Possible Cheapest Manufacturing Schedules

Month	*Requirement*	*Group size (n)*	$n^2\ D_{n+1}$	$n^2\ D_{n+1} < 1000$?	*Resulting manufacturing schedule*
January	400	1	650	Yes	1,050
February	650	2	1,400	No	–
March	350	1	450	Yes	850
April	450	2	200	Yes	–
May	50	3	3,600	No	–
June	400	1	–	–	400

optimal solution, but in those few cases where a solution other than the optimum is found, the cost of that solution is only marginally higher. The method is so easy to operate, however, that in practice for the type of deterministic problem just considered it is generally to be preferred to the DP solution. The algorithm can even be programmed on a simple desktop computer with limited storage facilities, such as the TI59 and the print-out from such a programme to the problem considered earlier is shown as figure 20.5.

Silver and Meal[5] have shown that this batching algorithm can be further improved by using the test:

$$n^2\ D_{n+1} < \frac{S}{iC_m} + \sum_{j=2}^{N} (j-1)\ D_j$$

Although this algorithm does not necessarily find the truly optimal solution, it is a slight improvement on the previous method. However, the essential simplicity of the method would seem to recommend its use for all manual applications and also those involving desktop computers.

6 Conclusion

Scheduling is both the most widely encountered area of application in Operations and Production Management and the one that produces the largest number of alternative possibilities. Whilst an analytical approach can offer some guidelines towards more efficient scheduling, very often practical considerations must take priority over theoretical niceties.

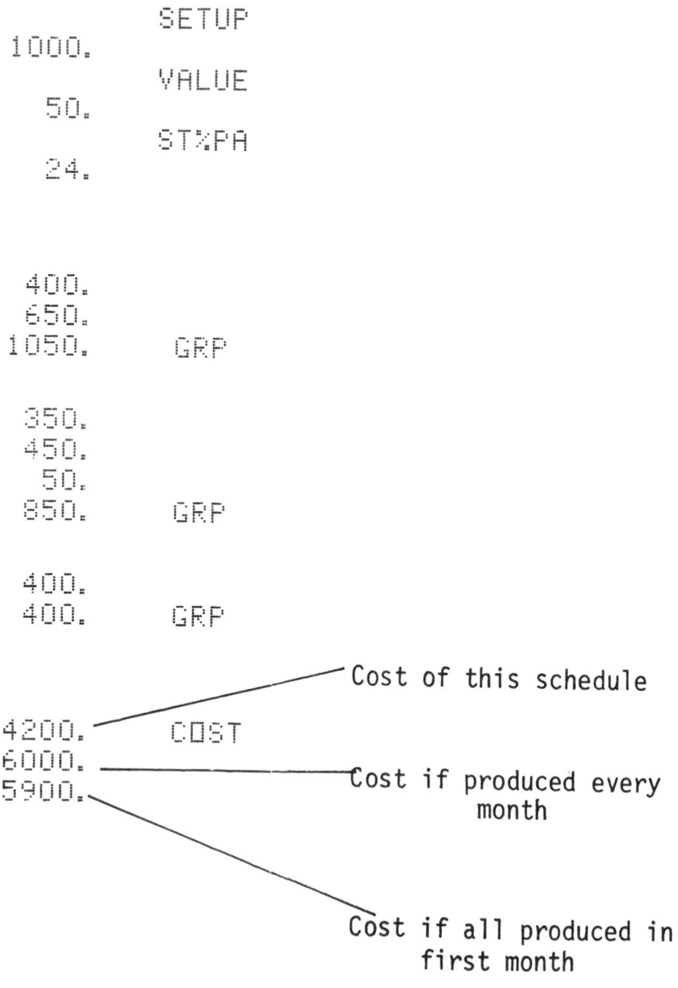

Figure 20.5 *Print-out from TI59 Programme for Batching Algorithm*

With the continuing development of computers, offering larger storage facilities and faster processing times at relatively lower costs and also the experience of several years of using scheduling computer packages, some of these – such as the WASP package referred to in Chapter 13 – are finding increasing acceptance.

For an illustration of the practical problems encountered in scheduling, readers are referred to Chapter 13.

References and Further Reading

1 Churchman, C.W., Ackoff, R.L. and Arnoff, E.L., *Introduction to Operations Research*, Wiley 1957.
2 Conway, R.W., Maxwell, W.L. and Miller, L.W., *Theory of Scheduling*, Addison-Wesley 1967.
3 Hollier, R.H., A simulation study of sequencing in batch production, *Operational Research Quarterly*, Vol. 19, No. 4, 1968, p. 389
4 Johnson, S.M., Optimal two and three stage production schedules, *Naval Logistics Quarterly*, Vol. 1, No. 1, 1954, pp. 61–68.
5 Silver, E.A. and Meal, H.C., A heuristic for selecting lot-size quantities, *Production and Inventory Management*, Vol. 14, 1973, p. 64.

21
Quality and Reliability

D J BENNETT

Senior Lecturer in Operations Management,
The University of Aston

1 Introduction: Specification and Organisation of the Q&R Function

All producers of goods and services are dependent on the quality and reliability of their products. There are many sources of cost associated with poor quality or defective products as summarised in figure 21.1.

Traditionally, companies have tended to concentrate their attention on the 'consequential costs', since legal action was rare and the level of damages relatively low and therefore considered unimportant. More recently however, the emergence of specific laws relating to liability for defective products, together with the awarding of much higher levels of damages, has created a far greater awareness of the 'legal costs'. Although this situation has not fundamentally changed the approach taken to the management of quality and reliability, some associated activities have assumed greater importance. For instance, the ability to recall certain product types or batches has become necessary, particularly in the case of domestic items; while greater emphasis has also been placed on labelling and operating instructions in order to prevent abuse or misuse which could result in personal injury.

Although in most cases the 'legal costs' are met by a third party (insurance company), an approved system of quality

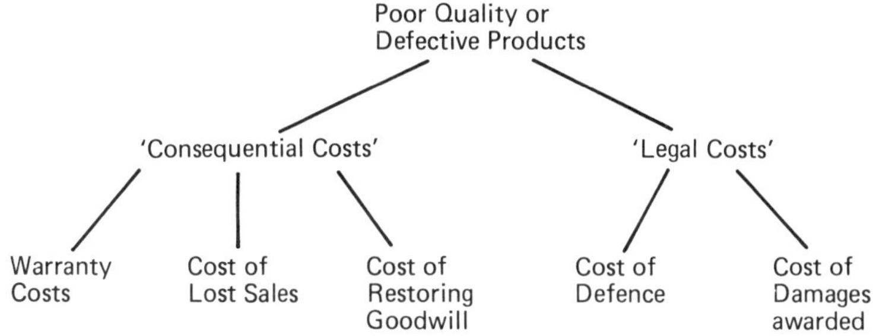

Figure 21.1 *Costs Incurred with Poor Quality*

and reliability management must nevertheless be in operation before the risk will be accepted.

Specifying and Measuring Quality

Quality can be thought of as an asset which may be offered to the potential consumer of a product or service. However, the measurement and assessment of quality is an area where difficulty and confusion can arise due to the often very subjective features of the product from which the impression of good quality is derived.

In this regard it is useful to distinguish between the concept of *quality of design* and *quality of conformance.*

Quality of design refers to the assets which are acquired by the product at the design and development stage. This would be a function of the materials used, tolerances specified, and safety factors allowed, together, of course, with the skill and knowledge of the design team. Quality of design is naturally the fundamental prerequisite for ensuring that the customer is offered a good quality product or service and, although many of the design features can be objectively assessed by the customer, others can only be viewed subjectively. For example, the purchaser of a motor car can readily pass judgment on its fuel consumption or performance, but would have no easy way of measuring overall comfort and paint finish.

The second prerequisite for customer satisfaction is to ensure that the product he is offered follows the design specification as closely as possible and meets the expectations derived as a result of marketing claims. The concept of *quality of conformance* is therefore that of ensuring the design quality of the actual good or service being produced is fully maintained. Individual users can then be satisfied that their expectations will be met.

Although the importance of quality of design cannot be understated, it is outside the scope of this chapter and will form part of the design and development activities described in Chapter 4. However, ensuring quality of conformance is an ongoing activity under the direct day-to-day control of Operations Management and this therefore warrants our greater attention. However, before discussing the problem of managing and controlling quality, the measurement of quality merits some discussion.

In certain cases, a quality parameter can be measured against some numerical scale. For example weight may be expressed in grammes, diameter in millimetres, surface finish in microns etc. Such measures are described as 'variables' and acceptable quality is usually defined by tolerances (upper, lower or both) beyond which items are regarded as defective.

In other cases, however, the use of a scale is not appropriate because the quality measure cannot be expressed numerically, usually only being good or bad (i.e. only two outcomes can occur). Examples of such situations are in the production of metal castings where they are either sound or damaged, or the bottling of beer where bottles are either clean or dirty, labels either straight or crooked etc. Here, quality is said to be measured by 'attributes' and the assessment of good or bad quality in such circumstances is often more difficult than with variables because of the subjective nature of the inspection procedure. This is particularly true in the case of service industries, because here quality is almost always measured by attributes. It would be difficult to employ variables to measure the quality of a restaurant, package holiday or a television programme and often in examples such as these assessment of 'product' quality is left to the consumer. However, the response rate would be slow and therefore there would be some justification in employing some of the procedures used in manufacturing industries.

There are sometimes occasions when a variable is converted to an attribute or *vice versa*. For instance, a diameter could be measured using a go/no go gauge or the quality of newsprint could be evaluated in terms of the number of errors per unit area.

Organisation and Responsibility

A quality system will comprise three main elements, these being:

(a) inspection procedures
(b) quality control
(c) quality audit

Inspection procedures are simply the numerous activities which take place throughout the production system where components, materials, processes etc. are measured and assessed in order to determine whether they conform to design specifications. In themselves they are of only partial use in ensuring good quality finished products and services, because components which are rejected will be prevented from being put into the finished product.

Quality control attempts to go further by using the information gained from Inspection to correct and maintain the production processes and thereby attempts to minimise the number of defective components being produced (or being passed on).

Quality audit is effectively maintaining overall control of the quality system. A number of procedures will be employed in conjunction with quality audit. For example, finished products or services will be selected and tested at random to confirm that the quality control system is achieving the desired results, also gauges and measuring equipment will be regularly checked to ensure that proper inspection decisions are being made.

The relationship between the three elements of the system is shown in figure 21.2.

A question which is often debated but has never been satisfactorily answered relates to responsibility for quality. Of

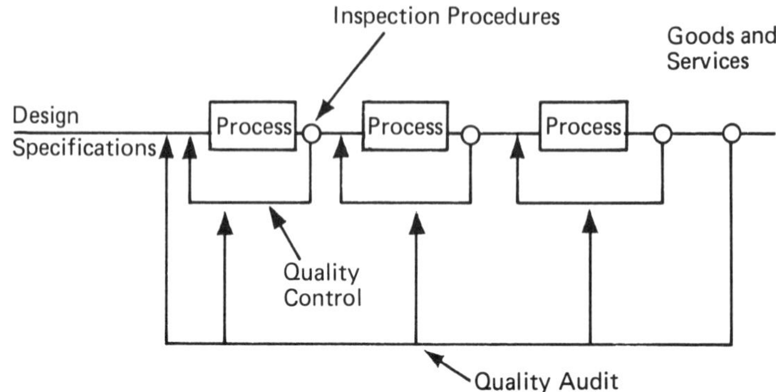

Figure 21.2 *Quality Audit and its Relationship with other Procedures*

course the easy answer is to say that quality is everybody's responsibility and in a sense this is quite true. An organisation which takes a 'total' approach to quality management will ensure that there is an awareness throughout the workforce of the need for quality consciousness. This would apply in all areas from design and production to transport and warehousing because each has a part to play in ensuring that any product is of an acceptable standard.

Zero defects campaigns and quality circles[1] have been used in recent years in an attempt to formalise these motivational aspects of quality management.

The responsibility question, however, more specifically refers to the place of inspection and quality control within the functional organisation of the business.

Often it is found to be a supplementary activity of production under the direction of the production or works manager. However, this situation can be, and quite often is, criticised because it will not generate the impartiality necessary in the quality function. Major influential customers such as motor vehicle manufacturers and defence organisations will rate vendors according to, among other things, the organisation of the quality function and companies who can demonstrate independence from production would be regarded more favourably.

There may be occasions when the quality function assumes enough importance to be the direct responsibility of senior management. A more appropriate arrangement, however, might be to include responsibility for quality within the technical function, which would include design. This would ensure that any decisions made regarding such matters as concessions (allowing the use of items which are outside design specifications) are made by technically competent staff, rather than by personnel for whom meeting delivery requirements is perhaps of greater importance than maintaining quality standards.

The Producer and Consumer Relationship

The discussion so far has centred around the assumption that quality management is of sole interest to producers of goods and services.

Naturally, consumers are equally interested that quality standards are maintained and may wish to have a hand in ensuring that poor quality or defective products are minimised.

This would be particularly true in the case of wholesalers and retailers who are acting as intermediate agents between the producer and the user. To prevent excessive claims against themselves as suppliers and to maintain goodwill with their customers it is in their interest to sell or supply good quality products or services.

Obviously, such agents are not in direct control of the production processes and, as such, cannot directly influence the quality of individual items which they are supplying. A strategy they can adopt however, is to assess the batches of items being received from their suppliers in order to judge whether, overall, their expectations are being met and to return, reject, or correct batches which fall below an acceptable level of quality.

While consumers can often be regarded as the end-users of products, in practice almost everybody in the long chain of suppliers and users can themselves be a consumer of some material, component, product or service being bought from outside. For this reason the approach to quality control just described can even be relevant to producers, who themselves are purchasers of the hundreds of items which go towards the manufacture of their products.

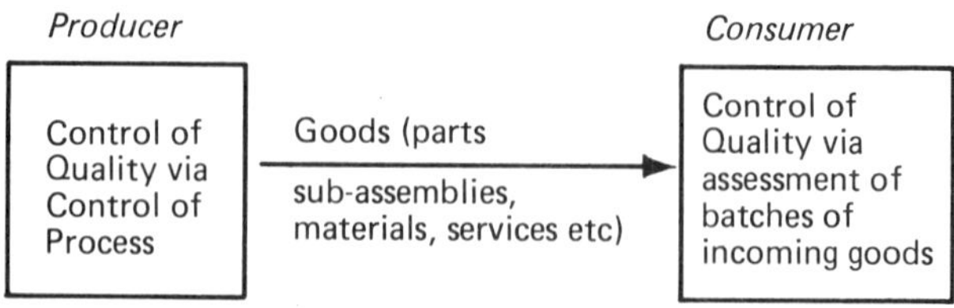

Figure 21.3 *The Producer/Consumer Quality Relationship*

In summary, therefore, there are two basic concepts for the control of quality. First there are the activities of producers who attempt to control the production processes to keep quality of goods within required limits. Secondly there are the activities of consumers who would assess the quality of batches of goods received in order to minimise the probability of putting a defective product into use.

The relationship is shown in figure 21.3.

If in addition to these two concepts we add the idea of measuring quality either by attributes or variables, we have the four basic models employed in statistical quality control and shown in figure 21.4.

2 Statistical Quality Control

The different types of model employed in quality control are usually described as 'statistical quality control techniques'. The reason for this is that they are based on statistical ideas or, more specifically, the area of statistics which relates to tests of significance.

	For Variables	*For Attributes*
Control of Production Processes	Most Common	Less Common
Assessment of Batches of Goods	Least Common	Most Common

Figure 21.4 *The Basic Statistical Quality Control Models (adapted from Jenney and Newton*[2]*)*

Several different types of technique have been developed employing various different theoretical distributions although they may be broadly classified within the categories of model shown in figure 21.4.

Some of the techniques will now be discussed, although only those which have been referred to as the most common will be described in detail.

Process Control Charts for Variables

In 1924 Dr W A Shewhart of the Bell Telephone Laboratories devised a method for controlling product quality which he called the 'control chart'. The use of control charts has progressively gained popularity, until some 60 years later there are few large production units not employing the technique.

The Shewhart model monitors a process to determine whether or not the system is regularly meeting expectations, delivering the specified outcome within the expected range of variation, and achieving management's aim of maintaining a stable process.

The meaning of the term 'control' should be noted when it is used in this context. If disturbances arise that shift the system off its course (they are called assignable causes of variation), something must be done about them. The Shewhart control chart does not indicate what to do, or how to do it, or when and where to do it. It merely indicates that something is changing – that the production system no longer appears to be following an established (stable) pattern. This change must

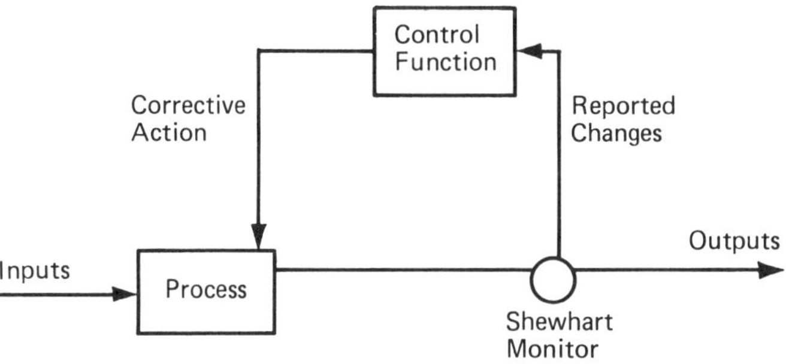

Figure 21.5 *The Shewhart Monitor within a Process Control System*

be reported to some control function which will make the necessary alterations to the process to bring output back within the specified limits. Figure 21.5 locates the Shewhart monitor within the overall process control system.

There are basically two ways in which measurements may drift outside the specified tolerance:

(i) The average may vary with time while the range remains the same. This is illustrated in figure 21.6(a). For example, a cutting tool may wear or a setting may slip.

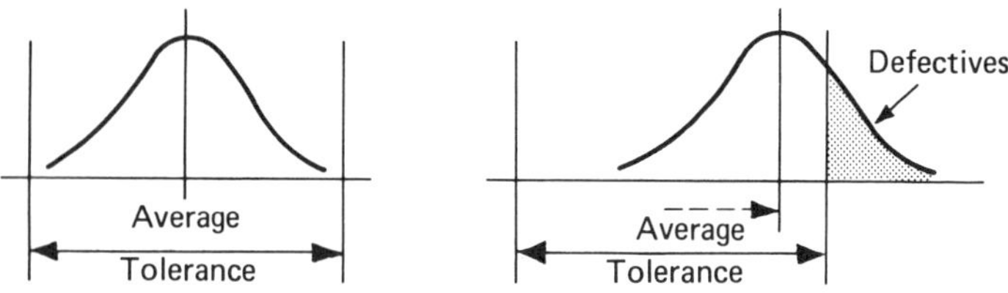

Figure 21.6(a) *Measurement Drift Caused by Shifts of Average*

(ii) The range may vary with time while the average remains the same, as in figure 21.6(b). For example, a machine fixture may wear or slacken.

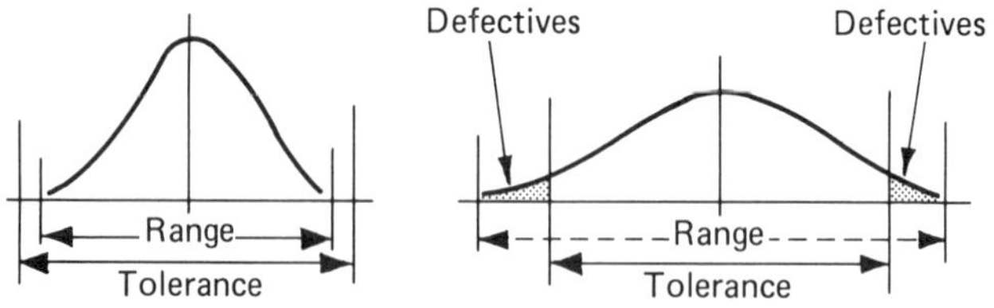

Figure 21.6(b) *Measurement Drift Caused by Variations in Range*

It is therefore necessary to control both the average and the variability of the measurements being monitored.

Averages are usually controlled by $\bar{x}$ (or average) charts, while variability is controlled by R (or range) charts.

Before describing the basis of control charts for variables it is necessary to refer to the idea of the 'Normal Distribution'. This distribution is specified by the arithmetic mean (average) and standard deviation (as a measure of variation) and, since it can be expressed mathematically, its properties can be accurately stated.

In particular,

> 0.025 of the values lie outside +1.96 σ (standard deviation) and –1.96 σ from the mean.
>
> 0.001 of the values lie outside +3.09 σ and –3.09 σ from the mean.

These two relationships are shown in figure 21.7.

To put it another way, if the distribution of measurements was normal, there is a 5% chance of a measurement falling outside the ± 1.96 σ range while still being 'in control'. However, there is only a 0.2% chance that a measurement will fall outside ± 3.09 σ range and still be 'in control'.

However, to use this relationship to control the process it would be necessary, as it now stands, to assume that output from the process followed a normal distribution. In practice, however, this would not necessarily be the case and so in controlling a process we do not tend to plot individual measurements on a control chart, but rather plot values arrived at as a result of taking a sample. This would be done to make use of

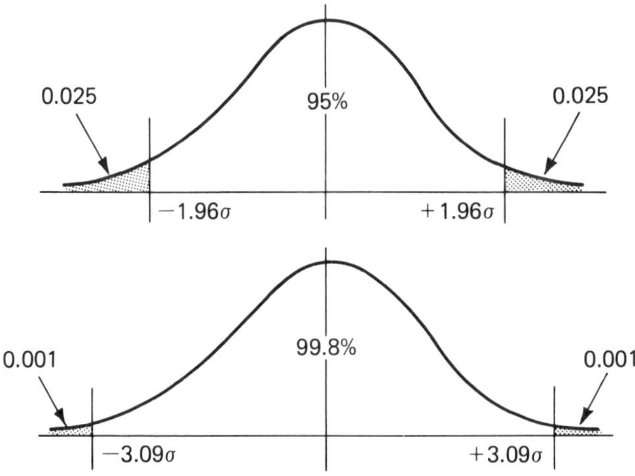

Figure 21.7 *Control Points of Normal Distribution*

the 'central limit theorem' which says:

If n (sample size) is large, the theoretical sampling distribution of $\bar{x}$ can be approximated very closely with the normal distribution.

Moreover in a manufacturing process, where variability is more or less 'normal' to start with, this still holds for relatively small values of n.

Since we are dealing with a new distribution, the theoretical sampling distribution of $\bar{x}$, we must call on another theorem to give us the mean and standard deviation of this distribution.

If random samples of size n are taken from a population which has a mean μ and standard deviation σ, the theoretical sampling distribution of $\bar{x}$ has the mean μ and the standard deviation $\sigma/\sqrt{n}$.

This relationship is illustrated in figure 21.8.

To construct a control chart for averages therefore, the sample number is plotted on the horizontal axis and the quality measure (sample average) on the vertical axis. If the limits to be used are set by reference to the standard deviation, then it is usual to have $\pm 3.09\ \sigma/\sqrt{n}$ as the action limits (i.e. 0.001 level) and possibly $\pm 1.96\ \sigma/\sqrt{n}$ as the warning limits (i.e. 0.025 level), as shown in figure 21.9.

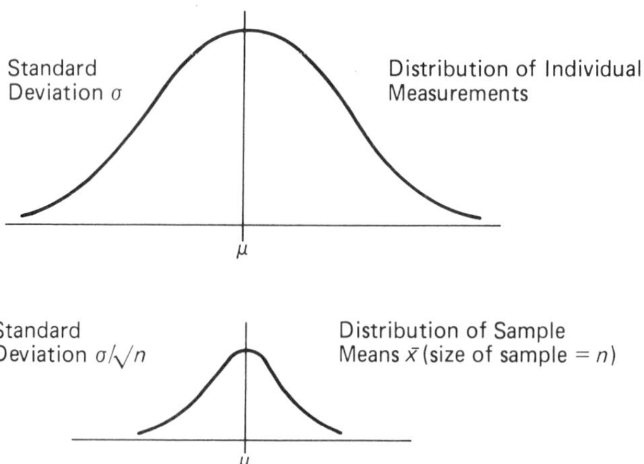

Figure 21.8 *Reduction in Standard Deviation with Sample Size*

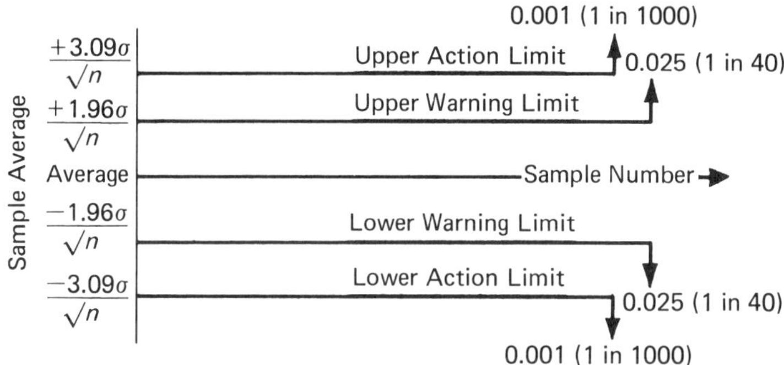

Figure 21.9 *$\bar{x}$ (Average) Chart*

Control charts for ranges are similarly constructed, except that they usually have upper limits only, since a lower limit would only indicate an ever-improving situation, as shown in figure 21.10.

Values of the sample average or range are plotted at specific time intervals. If they go outside the warning limit, no alteration is made, but the process should be maintained more closely. If, however, they go outside the action limit, then necessary alterations should be made.

In theory the chart could be constructed by taking a sample of measurements when the process is in control, calculating the standard deviation, and then calculating the limits from 1.96 $\sigma/\sqrt{n}$ and 3.09 $\sigma/\sqrt{n}$.

To simplify the procedure, however, tables 21.1 and 21.2 may be used, whereby of the range of small samples only ($\bar{w}$) needs to be calculated and multiplied by a constant which has been derived from the approximate relationship between the range and standard deviation.

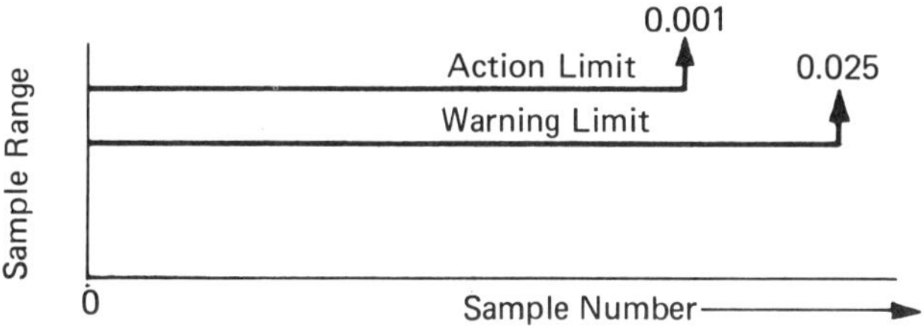

Figure 21.10 *R (Range) Chart*

Table 21.1 Control Chart Constants for Sample Average $\bar{x}$ (adapted from Murdoch and Barnes[3])

Sample Size n	*For Warning Limits* (0.025) C_W	*For Action Limits* (0.001) C_A
2	1.229	1.937
3	0.668	1.054
4	0.476	0.750
5	0.377	0.594
6	0.316	0.498
7	0.274	0.432
8	0.244	0.384
9	0.220	0.347
10	0.202	0.317
11	0.186	0.294
12	0.174	0.274

Note: To obtain limits multiply $\bar{w}$ by the appropriate value of C_W and C_A and then add to and subtract from the average value $\bar{x}$.

Table 21.2 Control Chart Constants for Sample Range R (adapted from Murdoch and Barnes[3])

Sample Size n	*For Warning Limits* (0.025) D_W	*For Action Limits* (0.001) D_A
2	2.81	4.12
3	2.17	2.98
4	1.93	2.57
5	1.81	2.34
6	1.72	2.21
7	1.66	2.11
8	1.62	2.04
9	1.58	1.99
10	1.56	1.93
11	1.53	1.91
12	1.51	1.87

Note: To obtain limits multiply $\bar{w}$ by the appropriate value of D_W and D_A.

Example The following data relate to the weights of boxes of a breakfast cereal being packed by an automatic machine. Figures are one gramme units above or below a nominal weight of 450 grammes.

An average and a range chart are to be constructed for monitoring output from the machine:

Sample No.	1	2	3	4	5	6	7	8	9	10	11	12
	2	1	0	−2	−3	1	−2	2	1	3	2	1
	−1	1	0	1	3	1	1	2	0	−1	0	−2
	0	0	1	2	1	0	3	−1	1	0	0	−2
	0	0	−2	0	2	−1	1	1	2	1	1	1
	1	1	−1	1	0	2	−3	0	−2	−1	1	1
Sample Ave $\bar{x}$	0.4	0.6	−0.4	0.4	0.6	0.6	0	0.8	0.4	0.4	0.8	−0.2
Sample Range w	3	1	3	3	6	3	6	3	4	4	2	3

$$\text{Process average } \bar{\bar{x}} = \frac{\Sigma\bar{x}}{12} = \frac{4.4}{12} = 0.366 \text{ gm}$$

$$\text{Average Range } \bar{w} = \frac{\Sigma w}{12} = \frac{41}{12} = 3.42 \text{ gm}$$

From table 21.1, constants for average chart with sample size $n = 5$ are:

$$C_w = 0.377$$
$$C_A = 0.594$$

Limits are: $\bar{x} \pm C_w\ \bar{w} = \bar{\bar{x}} \pm 0.377 \times 3.42$

and $\bar{x} \pm C_A\ \bar{w} = \bar{\bar{x}} \pm 0.594 \times 3.42$

i.e. 450.366 ± 1.29 (Warning Limits) = 451.656 gms and 449.076 gms

and 450.366 ± 2.03 (Action Limits) = 452.396 gms and 448.336 gms

The control chart for averages is therefore:

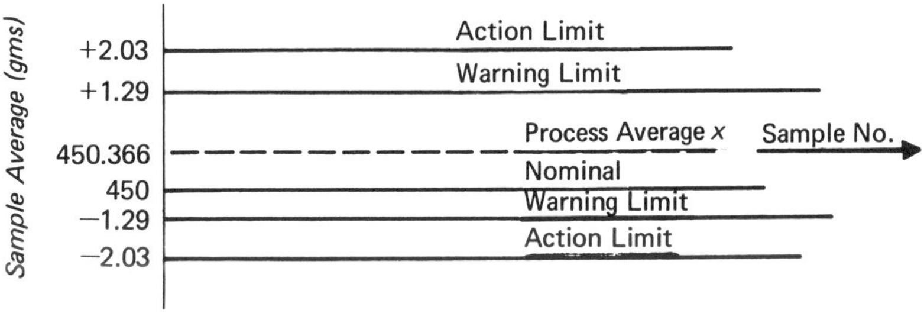

Sample Average (gms)

+2.03 Action Limit

+1.29 Warning Limit

450.366 Process Average x Sample No.

450 Nominal

−1.29 Warning Limit

−2.03 Action Limit

From Table 21.2 constants for the range chart with sample size $n = 5$ are:

$$D_w = 1.81$$
$$D_A = 2.34$$

Therefore, limits are:

$$D_w \, \bar{w} = 6.19$$
$$D_A \, \bar{w} = 8.00$$

The control chart for ranges is therefore:

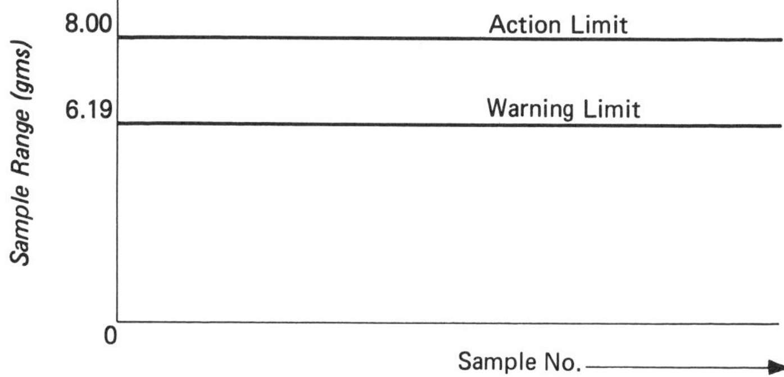

Process Control Charts for Attributes

With this type of chart, the process output is either accepted or rejected by inspection. The process may be controlled by counting and recording the proportion or number of defective items in a sample and comparing this on a chart with a predetermined limit.

The two types of control chart for attributes are therefore:

(i) Proportion defective, p charts
(ii) Number defective, c charts.

They are constructed according to the following theoretical basis: For a sample, size n, where the number of defectives is c*, the proportion defective, $p = c/n$.

* The sample should preferably be large enough to make $n\bar{p} \geqslant 4$, although in most practical examples it will be found that this will produce very little difference in the limits obtained.

For the process the average proportion defective, $\bar{p} = \frac{\Sigma c}{\Sigma n}$.

Standard deviation $\sigma = \sqrt{\frac{\bar{P}(1-\bar{p})}{n}}$ (Standard Deviation of Binomial Distribution)†

And, assuming the normal approximation to the binomial distribution, limits may be given by.

$\bar{p} \pm 3.09\sqrt{\frac{\bar{P}(1-\bar{p})}{n}}$ and $\bar{p} \pm 1.96\sqrt{\frac{\bar{p}(1-\bar{p})}{n}}$

or more simply

$\bar{p} \pm 3\sqrt{\frac{\bar{p}(1-\bar{p})}{n}}$ and $\bar{p} \pm 2\sqrt{\frac{\bar{p}(1-\bar{p})}{n}}$

Example The following data relate to the number of defectives found in samples of 200 glass tumblers taken at regular intervals from the manufacturing process. A control chart is to be constructed to monitor the number of defectives.

Sample	*Sample Size n*	*Number of Defectives c*	*Proportion Defective p*
1	200	6	0.030
2	200	11	0.055
3	200	2	0.010
4	200	20	0.100
5	200	17	0.085
6	200	6	0.030
7	200	15	0.075
8	200	11	0.055
	$= \Sigma n$ 1600	$\Sigma c = 88$	

Average proportion defective $= \frac{\Sigma c}{\Sigma n} = \frac{88}{1600} = 0.055$

† It should be noted that to be statistically 'correct', the above standard deviation formula should only be used where p is greater than 0.05. For smaller values of p, the limits $\bar{c} \pm 2$ or $3\sqrt{\bar{c}}$ should be used (i.e. based on Poisson distribution where $\bar{c} = np$).

On the proportion defective chart the limits are:

$$\bar{p} \pm 2\sqrt{\frac{\bar{p}(1-\bar{p})}{n}} = 0.055 \pm 0.032$$

$$= 0.087 \text{ and } 0.023$$

$$\bar{p} \pm 3\sqrt{\frac{\bar{P}(1-\bar{p})}{n}} = 0.055 \pm 0.048$$

$$= 0.103 \text{ and } 0.007$$

Since only the upper limits in this case indicate a worsening situation we shall only use the 0.087 and 0.103 values.

On the number defective chart the limits are:

$$200 \times 0.087 = 17.4$$

and

$$200 \times 0.103 = 20.6$$

Of course the control chart limits must be whole numbers, so the numbers used here would probably be 17 and 21 (although to err on the side of caution 20 could have been used).

The number defective chart is illustrated:

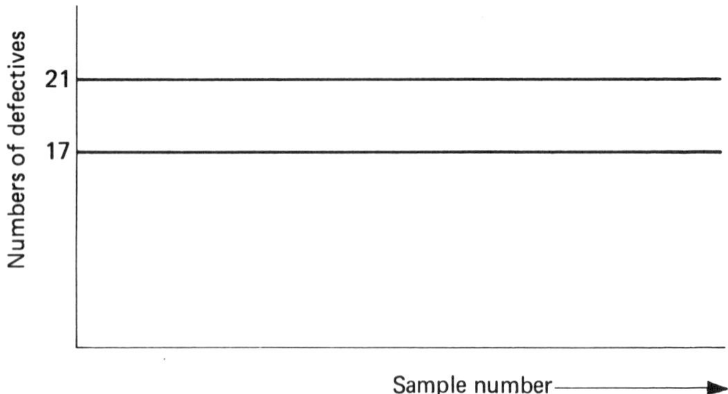

Batch Quality Assessment by Attributes

From the discussion on the producer and consumer relationship it may be seen that the use of process control charts based on the Shewhart model is only appropriate when attempting to control the output from some process. Situations where the process (and therefore the quality) is outside the user's control (for example when material or parts are purchased, work is sub-contracted etc.) make it necessary to establish a procedure whereby it can be ensured with reasonable certainty that the items being used conform to laid down quality standards.

Obviously the only way of ensuring that *no* defective items are used is by 100% inspection. However, in practice, there are several reasons why this may not be a viable proposition, e.g.

(i) Inspection may be an expensive procedure compared with the value and importance of the product;
(ii) Inspection requires destruction of the product (e.g. fuses);
(iii) The inspection process may be tiring, resulting, after a time, in the passing of defective items;
(iv) Handling the product may cause deterioration.

In all the above cases the most appropriate method of ensuring quality standards are met may be sampling inspection or *acceptance sampling*.

The simplest case of acceptance sampling is to draw a random sample from a large incoming batch basing the decision of whether to accept the entire batch on the number of defective components in the sample. If the sample indicates a decision to reject the batch, it may either be subjected to 100% inspection, removing or repairing all the defective parts, or returned to the original suppliers.

This simplest case, because it is only based on taking one sample, is called *single sampling*.

To specify a particular sampling plan it is necessary to indicate the random sample size, n, and the number of defectives, c, permitted in the sample before the entire batch is rejected, (known as the acceptance number). Of course, cases can occur when 'good' batches are rejected or 'bad' batches accepted and for this reason it is necessary to evaluate how well a particular plan discriminates between 'good' and 'bad' batches.

The Binomial probability function (valid when N, the size of the incoming batch, is large compared to n) can be used to calculate the probability of rejecting batches having a certain proportion of defectives, that is P (r or more defectives in sample) = P (rejection of batch).

$$= \sum_{x=r}^{n} {}^{n}C_{x} p^{x} (1-p)^{n-x}$$

where $r = c + 1$ (one more than acceptance number); n = sample size; and p = proportion of defectives in batch.

Note

$${}^{n}C_{r} = \frac{n!}{r!\,(n-r)!}$$

where $n! = n \times (n-1) \times (n-2)$ ——— $\times\ (n(n-1))$

Normally tables of 'Cumulative Binomial Probabilities' would be used to evaluate P (rejection of batch) rather than embarking on a tedious calculation procedure.

An Operating Characteristic (OC) curve may now be drawn for any sampling plan specified by n and c. This is the probability of acceptance (1 – probability of rejection) plotted against the actual percentage of defectives in the batch, as shown in figure 21.11.

The Operating Characteristic curve which discriminates perfectly between good and bad batches would appear as in figure 21.12 but, as previously stated, this can only be achieved using 100% inspection.

OC curves for different values of n and c will have different shapes, some approaching more closely the 'ideal shape'.

Figure 21.13 shows the curves for $n = 50, c = 1$ and $n = 100$, $c = 2$.

It may be seen that increasing the size of the sample increases the ability of the scheme to distinguish between good and bad batches. Furthermore, it should be stressed that the OC curve is defined by a specific size of sample and acceptance number. If the sample is selected on the basis of a proportion of the incoming batch, or if the acceptance number is based on a proportion of the sample, then the discrimination of the plan would vary with the original batch size.

Sampling plans in practice are designed with reference to

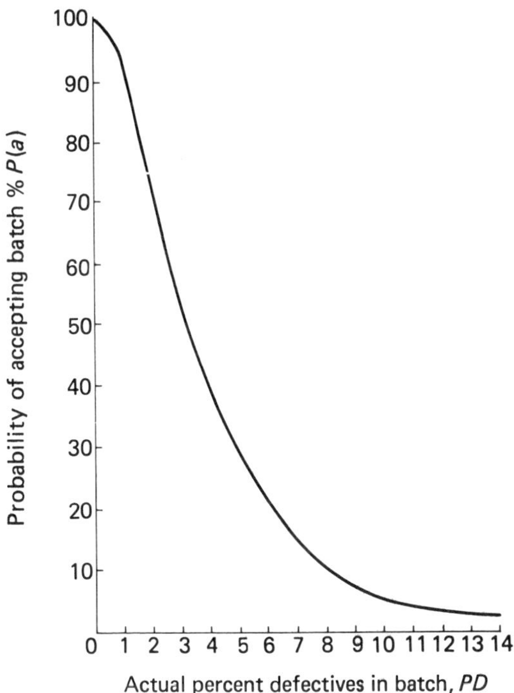

Figure 21.11 *OC Curve for a Sampling Plan with $n = 50$ and $c = 1$*

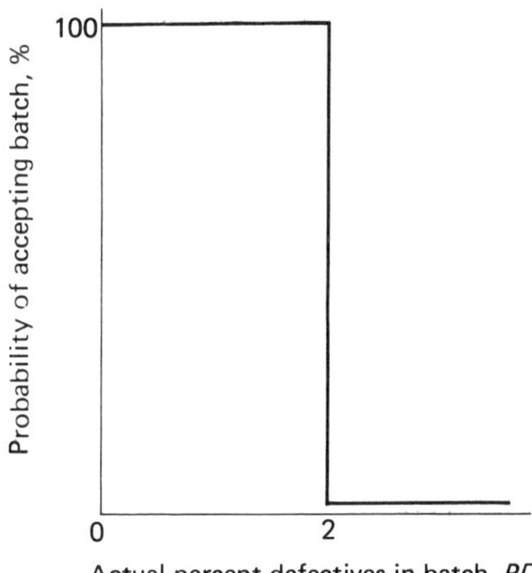

Figure 21.12 *OC Curve Capable of Discriminating Perfectly Between Batches Having More or Less Than 2% Defectives*

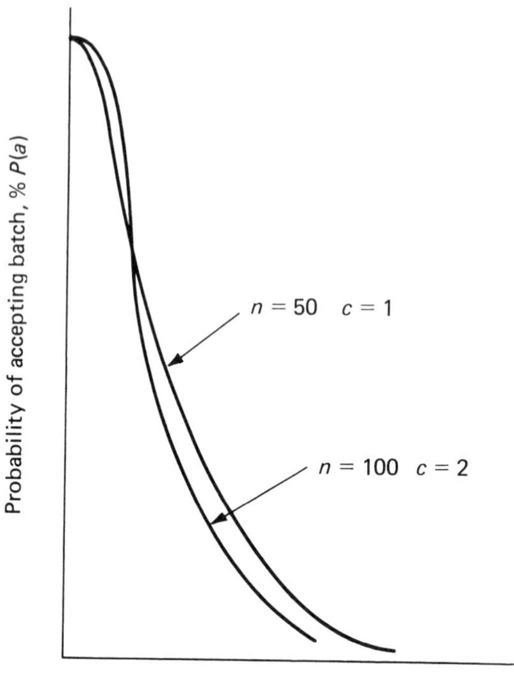

Figure 21.13 *Effect on OC Curve of Increasing Sample Size*

the following four parameters:

AQL = *Acceptable Quality Level.* Batches at this level of quality are regarded as good and we wish to have a high probability of acceptance.

α = *Producer's Risk.* This is the probability that batches of quality level AQL will be *rejected.*

LTPD = *Lot Tolerance per cent Defective* (the Unacceptable Quality Level). Batches below this level of quality are regarded as poor and we wish to have a low probability of their acceptance.

β = *Consumer's Risk.* This is the probability that batches of quality level LTPD will be *accepted.*

When the values of these four parameters have been decided upon, the shape of the OC curve has been defined.

Values of n and c must now be selected which will give an

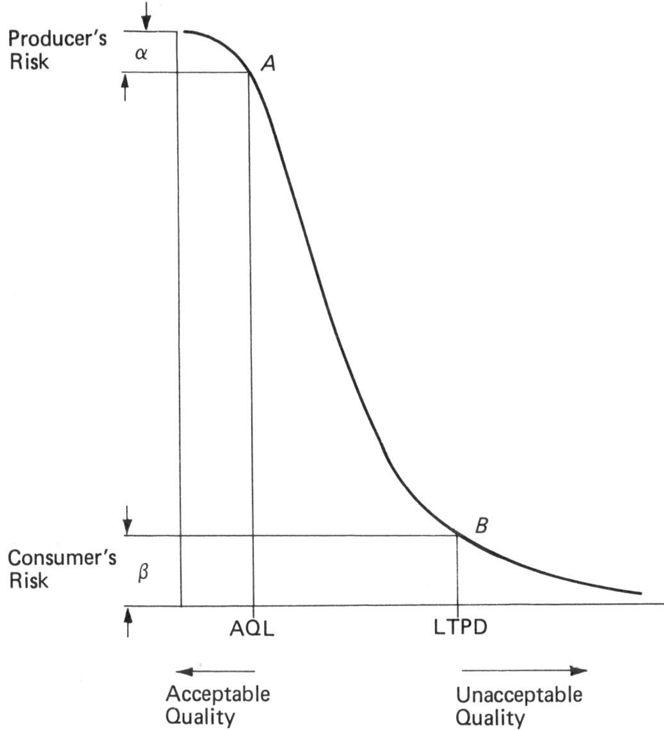

Figure 21.14 *Sampling Parameters and the Subsequent OC Curve*

operating characteristic curve which will pass through the two points A and B shown on figure 21.14.

Table 21.3 may be used for designing single sampling plans to fit certain chosen values of the four parameters.

To construct the plan, find the value of LTPD/AQL in the table which is equal to or greater than the calculated value of the ratio. The sample size is found by dividing the corresponding value of n' by AQL. The acceptance number is the value of c corresponding to the tabular value of the ratio.

Example A builder receives batches of house bricks from a manufacturer. He considers batches containing less than 2% defectives as good and those with more than 5% defectives as bad. He wishes to construct a single sampling plan which will

Table 21.3 Derivation of Single Sampling Plans (adapted from Murdoch & Barnes[3])*

	Values of *LTPD/AQL* for:					Values of *LTPD/AQL* for:			
c	$\alpha = 0.05$ $\beta = 0.10$	$\alpha = 0.05$ $\beta = 0.05$	$\alpha = 0.05$ $\beta = 0.01$	n'	c	$\alpha = 0.01$ $\beta = 0.10$	$\alpha = 0.01$ $\beta = 0.05$	$\alpha = 0.01$ $\beta = 0.01$	n'
0	44.890	58.404	89.781	0.052	0	229.105	298.073	458.210	0.010
1	10.946	13.349	18.681	0.355	1	26.184	31.933	44.686	0.149
2	6.509	7.699	10.280	0.818	2	12.206	14.439	19.278	0.436
3	4.890	5.675	7.352	1.366	3	8.115	9.418	12.202	0.823
4	4.057	4.646	5.890	1.970	4	6.249	7.156	9.072	1.279
5	3.549	4.023	5.017	2.613	5	5.195	5.889	7.343	1.785
6	3.206	3.604	4.435	3.286	6	4.520	5.082	6.253	2.330
7	2.957	3.303	4.019	3.981	7	4.050	4.524	5.506	2.906
8	2.768	3.074	3.707	4.695	8	3.705	4.115	4.962	3.507
9	2.618	2.895	3.462	5.426	9	3.440	3.803	4.548	4.130
10	2.497	2.750	3.265	6.169	10	3.229	3.555	4.222	4.771
11	2.397	2.630	3.104	6.924	11	3.058	3.354	3.959	5.428
12	2.312	2.528	2.968	7.690	12	2.915	3.188	3.742	6.099
13	2.240	2.442	2.852	8.464	13	2.795	3.047	3.559	6.782
14	2.177	2.367	2.752	9.246	14	2.692	2.927	3.403	7.477
15	2.122	2.302	2.665	10.035	15	2.603	2.823	3.269	8.181
16	2.073	2.244	2.588	10.831	16	2.524	2.732	3.151	8.895
17	2.029	2.192	2.520	11.633	17	2.455	2.652	3.048	9.616
18	1.990	2.145	2.458	12.442	18	2.393	2.580	2.956	10.346
19	1.954	2.103	2.403	13.254	19	2.337	2.516	2.874	11.082

20	1.922	2.065	2.352	14.072	20	2.287	2.458	2.799	11.825
21	1.892	2.030	2.307	14.894	21	2.241	2.405	2.733	12.574
22	1.865	1.999	2.265	15.719	22	2.200	2.357	2.671	13.329
23	1.840	1.969	2.223	16.548	23	2.162	2.313	2.615	14.088
24	1.817	1.942	2.191	17.382	24	2.126	2.272	2.564	14.853
25	1.795	1.917	2.158	18.218	25	2.094	2.235	2.516	15.623
26	1.775	1.893	2.127	19.058	26	2.064	2.200	2.472	16.397
27	1.757	1.871	2.098	19.900	27	2.035	2.168	2.431	17.175
28	1.739	1.850	2.071	20.746	28	2.009	2.139	2.393	17.957
29	1.723	1.831	2.046	21.594	29	1.985	2.110	2.358	18.742
30	1.707	1.813	2.023	22.444	30	1.962	2.083	2.324	19.532
31	1.692	1.796	2.001	23.298	31	1.940	2.059	2.293	20.324
32	1.679	1.780	1.980	24.152	32	1.920	2.035	2.264	21.120
33	1.665	1.764	1.960	25.010	33	1.900	2.013	2.236	21.919
34	1.653	1.750	1.941	25.870	34	1.882	1.992	2.210	22.721
35	1.641	1.736	1.923	26.731	35	1.865	1.973	2.185	23.525
36	1.630	1.723	1.906	27.594	36	1.848	1.954	2.162	24.333
37	1.619	1.710	1.890	28.460	37	1.833	1.936	2.139	25.143
38	1.609	1.698	1.875	29.327	38	1.818	1.920	2.118	25.955
39	1.599	1.687	1.860	30.196	39	1.804	1.804	1.903	26.770
40	1.590	1.676	1.846	31.066	40	1.790	1.887	2.079	27.587
41	1.581	1.666	1.833	31.938	41	1.777	1.873	2.060	28.406
42	1.572	1.656	1.820	32.812	42	1.765	1.859	2.043	29.228
43	1.564	1.646	1.807	33.686	43	1.753	1.845	2.026	30.051
44	1.556	1.637	1.796	34.563	44	1.742	1.832	2.010	30.877
45	1.548	1.628	1.784	35.441	45	1.731	1.820	1.994	31.704
46	1.541	1.619	1.773	36.320	46	1.720	1.808	1.980	32.534
47	1.534	1.611	1.763	37.200	47	1.710	1.796	1.965	33.365
48	1.527	1.603	1.752	38.082	48	1.701	1.785	1.952	34.198
49	1.521	1.596	1.743	38.965	49	1.691	1.775	1.938	35.032

* Copyright 1952 American Society for Quality Control Inc. Reprinted by permission.

distinguish between good and bad batches with a producer's risk of 5% and a consumer's risk of 1%.

$$\frac{\text{LTPD}}{\text{AQL}} = \frac{0.05}{0.02} = 2.5$$

Looking at table 21.3 at the column of values for $\alpha = 0.05$, $\beta = 0.01$, the value of LTPD/AQL which is equal to or just greater than 2.5 is 2.570.

The corresponding value of n' is 11.633, therefore the sample size

$$n = \frac{11.633}{0.02} = 582$$

The acceptance number $c = 17$

The *average outgoing quality* for a particular plan is a measure of the percentage of defectives which can be expected to still pass through. It can therefore be regarded as a measure of the scheme's effectiveness.

The expected number of defectives passing through is the product of the proportion of defectives received, the number remaining in the batch (after the sample has been taken) and the probability that the batch will be accepted.

i.e. $$\frac{PD}{100} \times \frac{P(a)}{100} \times (N-n)$$

The average outgoing quality in percentage terms is therefore:

$$\frac{\text{Expected number of defectives}}{\text{Number in original batch}} \times 100 = \frac{P(a) \times PD \times (N-n)}{100N}\%$$

A graph may therefore be constructed giving the Average Outgoing Quality for any proportion of defectives received.

In the case of the previous example, assuming that the number in the incoming batch is 10,000, the graph would appear as figure 21.15.

It may be seen that the Average Outgoing Quality should never exceed a limit, known as the AOQL (Average Outgoing Quality Limit) whatever the actual percentage of defectives in the incoming batch. In our example the AOQL is approximately 1.9%.

In the single sampling example just given, it may be that

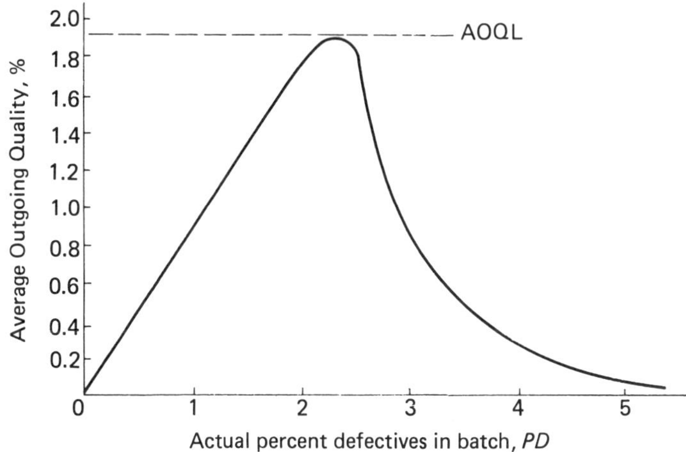

Figure 21.15 *Outgoing Quality % Defectives in Batch for $n = 582, c = 17$*

the cost of inspecting nearly six hundred items was extremely high (and the required sample size might have needed to be even greater). In the case of exceedingly good or bad batches therefore, the cost of acceptance or rejection would be unnecessarily high since a decision could have been taken on the basis of a smaller sample.

Double sampling has therefore been developed in an attempt to economise on the *average* amount of inspection that needs to be done. A double sampling scheme adopts the structure shown in figure 21.16 and operates on the following basis:

(a) An initial sample is taken and the number of defectives found is compared to *two* acceptance numbers c_1 and c_2.
(b) If the number of defectives is less than c_1, the batch is accepted. If it exceeds c_2 it is rejected.
(c) If, however, the number of defectives is between c_1 and c_2 a second sample is taken;
(d) If the *total* number of defectives in the *combined* sample is less than c_2 the batch is accepted. If it exceeds c_2, it is rejected.

Standard tables are available for use in designing double sampling plans for given values of LTPD and AOQL.[4]

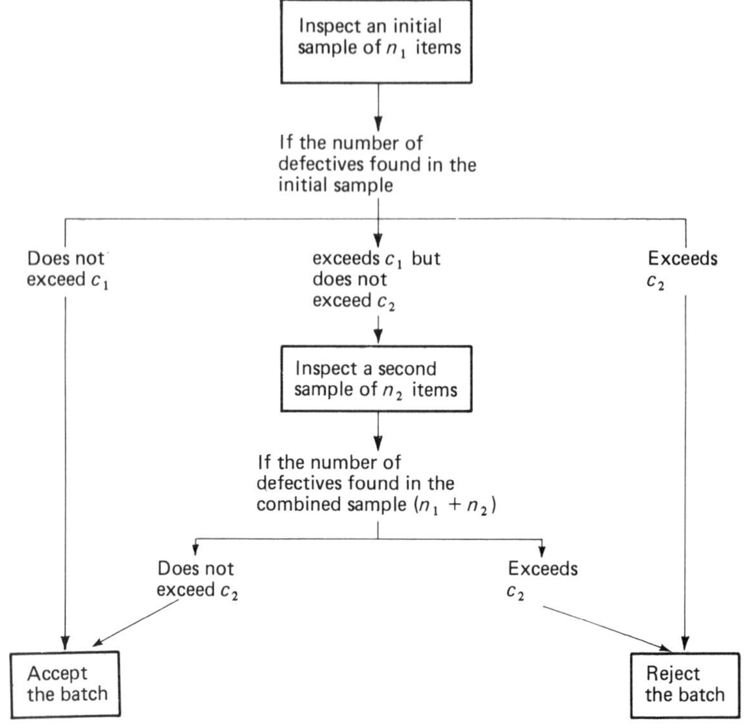

Figure 21.16 *The Structure of a Double Sampling Plan*

It follows that the procedure for double sampling could be extended to triple and multiple sampling where several samples are drawn from a batch with the possibility of acceptance or rejection at each stage. In practice, however, their operation would become laborious and complicated. Eventually it becomes more logical to use an item-by-item or sequential plan based on a sample size of one.

To perform a sequential test, the inspector uses a chart similar to figure 21.17.

On the chart there are two sloping parallel lines being the boundary of the acceptance and rejection regions. As the inspector draws and inspects each item, the cumulative number of defectives found is plotted against the number inspected so far. If the plot crosses the upper line the batch is rejected and if it crosses the lower line the batch is accepted. If it

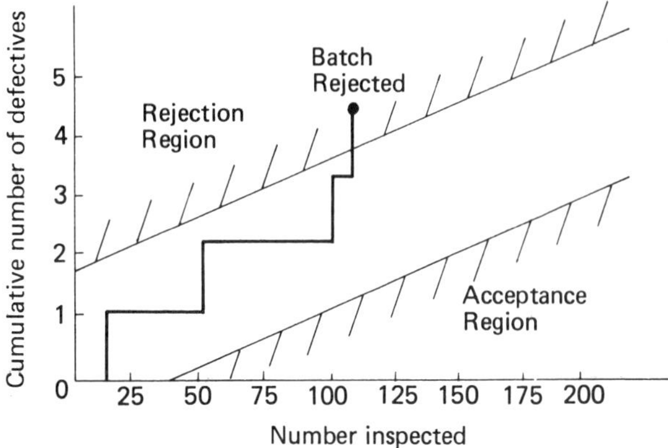

Figure 21.17 *A Sequential Sampling Chart*

remains between the two lines sampling is continued, although a truncated plan may be used to avoid sampling '*ad infinitum*'. It should be noted in the diagram shown that a batch could be rejected almost immediately, on the basis of the first two items drawn both being defective. However, a much larger number must be inspected before the decision to accept is made.

Sequential plans are designed around the same parameters as other sampling schemes and formulae are available which are used to calculate the slope and intercepts of the two parallel lines.[5]

3 Reliability

The reliability theory based on mathematical and statistical techniques was developed much later than that for quality control. Whereas control charts were developed by Shewhart in the early 1920s, reliability was developed during the late 1940s and early 1950s by several American manufacturing and research organisations. However, some specialised areas of engineering and mathematics had been developed earlier which now have become accepted as a part of the overall concept of reliability.

The early approach to reliability involved testing and

improving the life of electronic components, in particular radio valves, used in civilian and military aircraft applications. The reliability of mechanical equipment was probably not investigated to any significant degree until the 1960s when work was carried out in the USSR to study and improve the reliability of cranes, tractors, machine tools etc.

Reliability as a Function of Quality

The words 'quality' and 'reliability' have tended nowadays to be regarded as almost synonymous, despite the fact that as subjects for study they have grown up quite separately.

However, it may be sensible to think of reliability as an asset which contributes, as an inherent factor, to the overall quality of a product. Everyone has his own idea what he means when he uses the term reliability, be he the motorist referring to his car or the NASA scientist speaking of the latest space shot.

Reliability relates to the expectation that a particular item can be trusted to perform its required function and hence, depending on the nature of that item and its requirements, reliability can be a very subjective concept. Disagreement may ensue when a motorist returns to the garage with a one week old car which has developed a slight rattle (. . . 'ignore it sir, it is quite normal for this model to be slightly noisy'), or when a wheel bearing fails after 10,000 miles (. . . 'it is just out of guarantee sir and these things are normal wear and tear'). It becomes necessary, therefore, to attempt to give reliability a definition which, once agreed, might avoid the confusion.

One commonly used definition states:

Reliability is the probability that a system will perform satisfactorily for at least a given period of time when used under stated conditions.

Of course, 'satisfactory performance' and the 'given period of time' would both need to be specified, but at least this simple definition does go some way towards removing the vagueness surrounding reliability. However, this particular definition, although adequate in many cases, by no means covers everyone's concept of reliability and further definitions have therefore been suggested which would give a better picture in various circumstances, e.g.

The *availability* of a system is the probability that it is operating satisfactorily at any point in time when used under stated conditions.

This is different from the first definition, in that it places emphasis on the fact that unsatisfactory performance in itself is perhaps of less consequence than the downtime incurred, i.e. if repairs are effected quickly, availability will remain high.

Another definition looks at reliability in yet another way:

The *operational readiness* of a system is the probability that at any point in time it is ready to be placed in operation on demand when used under stated conditions.

This definition would be of interest to an operator of a piece of irregularly used emergency equipment, e.g. a fire appliance or jet fighter. Many more definitions may be found which have been devised to suit the particular circumstance.

Measuring Reliability

The common feature of all definitions of reliability is the use of the words 'probability' and 'time' and this inevitably leads to consideration of both of these criteria when attempting to measure the reliability of a system.

Take, for example, two pieces of equipment: a guided missile and a motor car. The guided missile functions successfully on the one occasion it is called into service, while the motor car suffers one major breakdown in its 100,000 mile useful life. Does this mean that the missile is 100% reliable and the motor car 0%? This will depend on the unit of time being used as illustrated by table 21.4.

It may be seen, therefore, that consideration of the time factor is of the greatest importance when comparing the reliability of different systems.

How, for example, does an aircraft engine compare with a car engine or a machine tool? Such a comparison is illustrated in table 21.5.

Table 21.4 The Effect of Time Units on Reliability (adapted from Brook[6])

Unit of time	*Missile Failure Rate*	*Car Failure Rate*	*Missile Reliability*	*Car Reliability*
mile	0 per mile	0.00001 per mile	1.0	0.99999 in any one mile
day	0 per day	0.0002 per day	1.0	0.9998 in any one day
journey	0 per journey	0.0001 per journey	1.0	0.9999 in any one journey
owner	0 per owner	0.33 per owner	1.0	0.67 for any one owner
useful life	0 per useful life	1 per useful life	1.0	0 for any one useful life

Note: The car is assumed to travel 20 miles per day, 10 miles per journey, and to have three owners in its useful life.

Table 21.5 Reliability Comparisons for Different Types of Equipment (from Nixon[7])

	Rolls Royce Conway Engine	*Equivalent for Car Engine* (30 mph)	*Equivalent for Machine Tool* (80 hrs per week)
Life between overhauls	10,000 hrs	300,000 miles	125 weeks
Replacement or adjustment of a part	5,000 hrs	150,000 miles	62 weeks
Involuntary stoppage while in use	40,000	1,200,000 miles	10 years

Reliability Assessment and Prediction

Evaluating the reliability behaviour of components and products can only be done by gathering and analysing data relating to failures over an extended period of time.

In the case of items which fail completely, e.g. light bulbs, radio valves etc., such a procedure is referred to as 'life-testing', but the basic principles remain the same for items which may be repaired. In the former, a batch of items are put on test and the time at which each one fails is recorded while, in the latter, the time of each occurrence of failure (breakdown) is noted and the item is repaired and returned to service.

Standard techniques of statistical analysis may then be used to determine the distribution of failures over time.

Example The following data relates to the time to failure of brake sheaves on drilling machines (from Vasil'ev and Babaev[8]).

Traverse interval (*m*)	*No. of breakdowns*
900–1200	2
1200–1500	2
1500–1800	5
1800–2100	5
2100–2400	8
2400–2700	9
2700–3000	12
3000–3300	10
3300–3600	6
3600–3900	1

From these data the *failure probability*, $f(t)$, may be calculated from the number of failures per period expressed as a proportion of the total. It is illustrated in figure 21.18.

The *cumulative failure probability*, $F(t)$, is the cumulative number of failures occurring up to a certain time expressed as a proportion of the total. This is illustrated in figure 21.19.

The converse of this function is the *cumulative survival probability*, $R(t)$ (i.e. $1 - F(t)$), which is the cumulative number of survivors up to a particular time expressed as a proportion of the total. This is shown in figure 21.20.

Of the greatest significance, however, is the *conditional failure rate* (otherwise known as the instantaneous failure rate or hazard rate), $Z(t)$, which is the number of failures in a period expressed as a proportion of the number still surviving.

The shape of the conditional failure rate function provides an indication of any variation in reliability over time. Figure 21.21 shows that for the drilling machine brake sheaves in our example the failure rate is increasing, which indicates an increasing tendency to fail as time goes on. This means that they become less reliable with age.

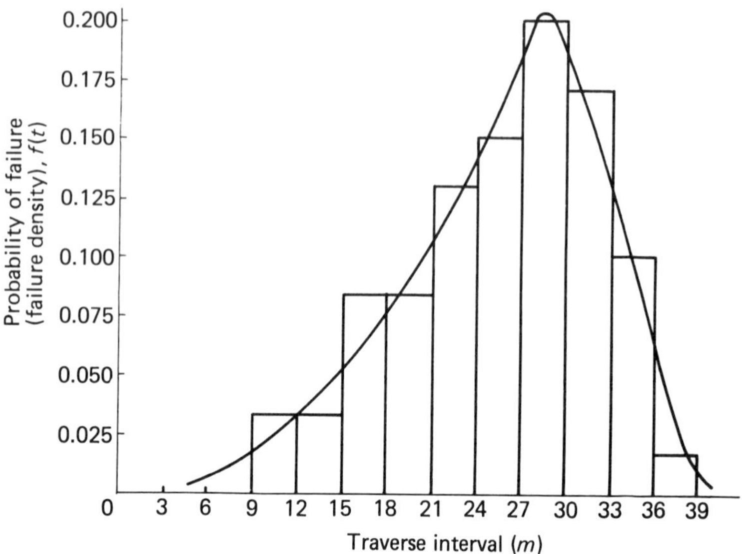

Figure 21.18 *Probability of Failure of Brake Sheaves*

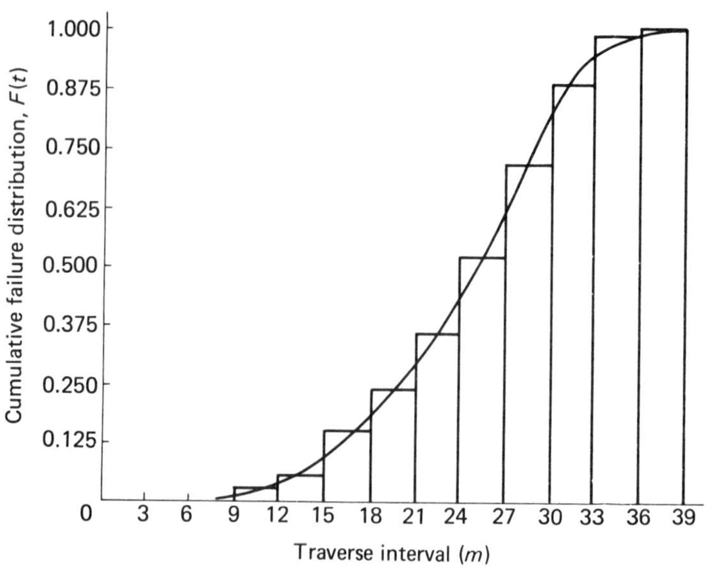

Figure 21.19 *Cumulative Probability of Failure of Brake Sheaves*

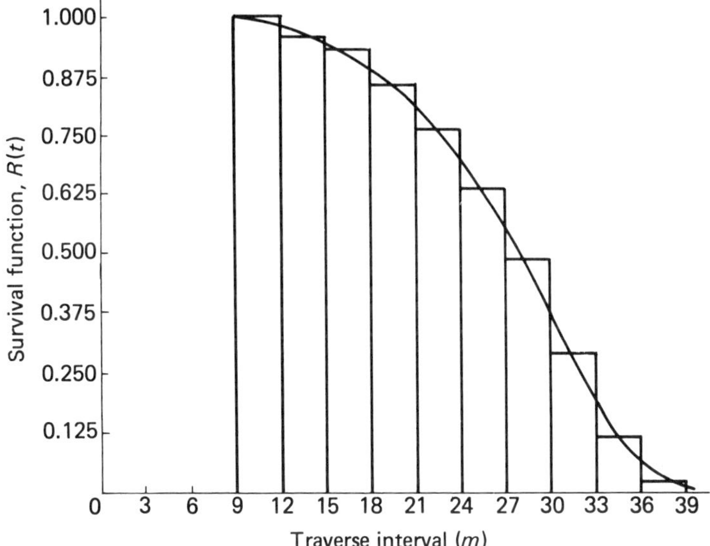

Figure 21.20 *Cumulative Survival Probability of Brake Sheaves*

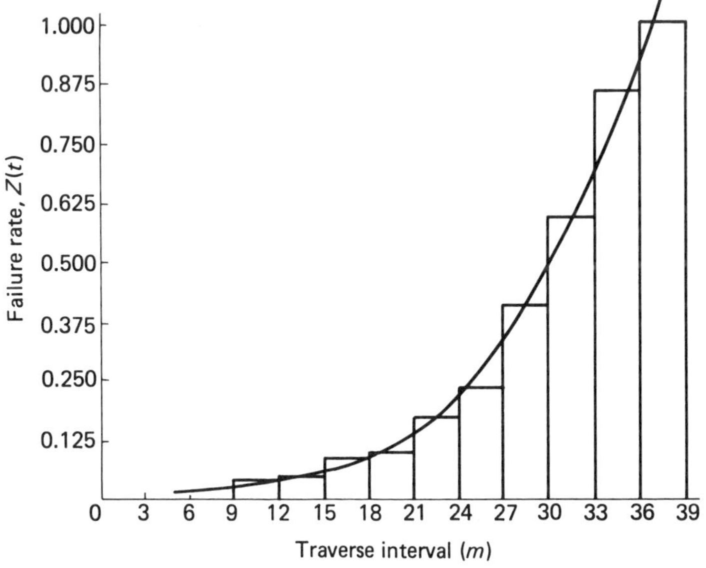

Figure 21.21 *Failure Rate or Hazard Rate of Brake Sheaves*

Had this not been the case and failures occurred completely at random, the failure rate function would have been a straight line as shown in figure 21.22.

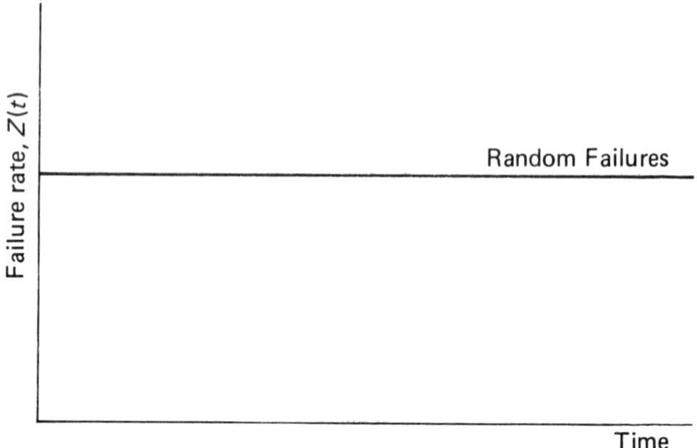

Figure 21.22 *Constant Failure Rate Indicating Random Failures*

Improving reliability would be illustrated by decreasing failure rate as in figure 21.23.

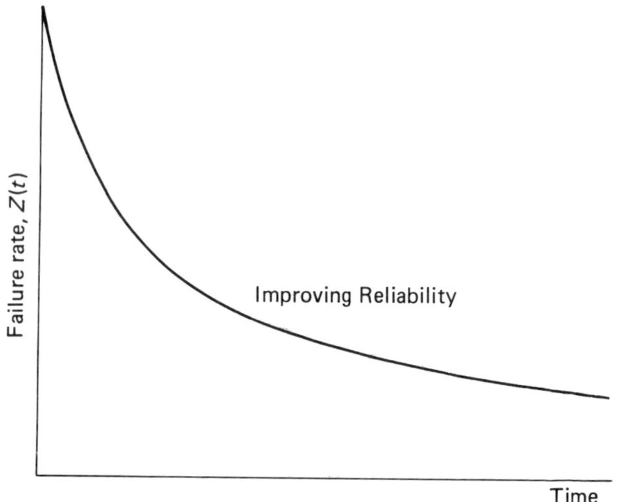

Figure 21.23 *Decreasing Failure Rate Indicating Improved Reliability*

Analysis of human mortality statistics would yield a failure density function as shown in figure 21.24 and failure rate function as shown in figure 21.25.

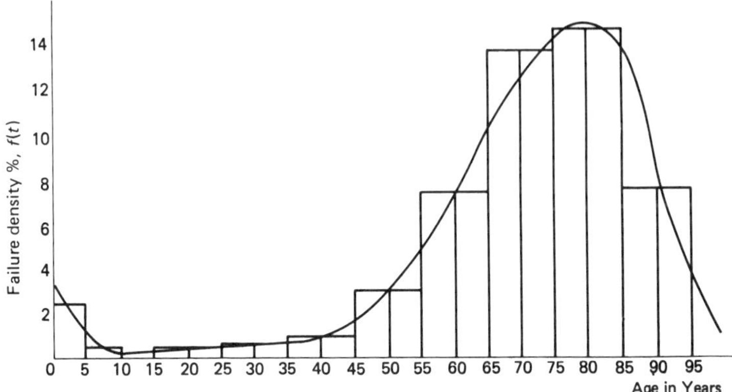

Data Source: Office of Population Censuses and Surveys

Figure 21.24 *Failure Density Functions for Human Mortality*

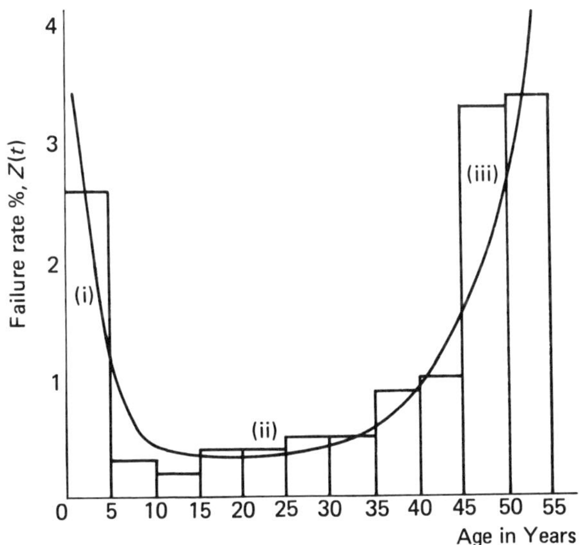

Data Source: Office of Population Censuses and Surveys

Figure 21.25 *Failure Rate Function for Human Mortality*

Here, up to about 5–10 years, the failure rate decreases (i.e. reliability improves), then remains more or less constant up to about 35 years after which time it starts to increase again.

This general pattern is fairly common among certain types of equipment, particularly items of an electronic nature. The graph can be seen as comprising three distinct phases:

(i) Early life or 'burn-in' failures
(ii) Random failures
(iii) Wear out failures

The shape of the failure rate graph in this case gives rise to the popular name 'bath tub curve' which is often used to describe this failure pattern.

Manufacturers of certain items of equipment recognise the existence of burn-in failures and attempt to improve reliability merely by running the equipment through this phase before handing it over to the customer.

Practical Use of Reliability Information

There are many varied aspects of Operations Management where reliability information may prove useful. The two main application areas are design and in the operation and maintenance of machines and equipment. The following areas will therefore be given greater consideration:

Product Design
Investment Appraisal
Costing
Performance Specification
Planned Maintenance
Replacement Policies

Each of these areas requires a knowledge of the long-term reliability of the item in question.

Plant Design

Reliability data from items actually in operation provide a valuable input to the design function.

Diagrammatically the ideal relationship between design,

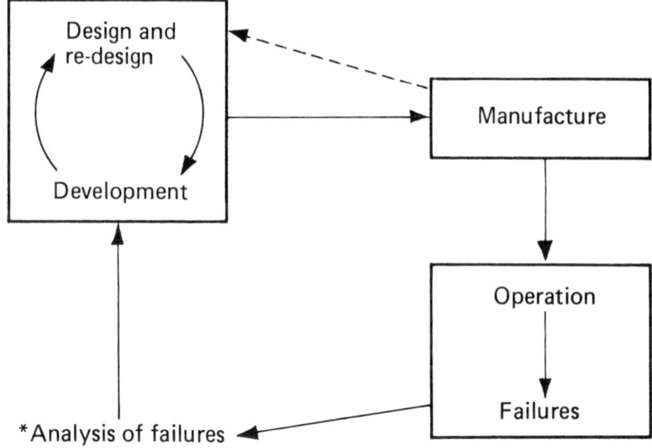

Note: The functions may appear in either the designer or user 'box' depending on circumstances and management dictation.

Figure 21.26 *Relationship between Design Manufacture and Operation of a Product*[9]

manufacture, and operation of a product could be represented as shown in figure 21.26.

It is likely, however, that the 'feedback' both from manufacturer and user is not formalised and, perhaps more significantly, does not relate to the long-term performance of the plant. Failures occurring during warranty are reported to the manufacturer and receive attention, but this is less likely to occur when plant is several years old.

Among the many approaches to improving reliability at the design stage, perhaps the most simple and cost effective is the use of redundancy. The overall reliability of an assembly may be determined from the reliability of each of its constituent parts using the product law of probability. For example, if the reliabilities of three component parts are 0.7, 0.6 and 0.5 (i.e. the probability of satisfactory operation for a given period of time), then the overall system reliability will be 0.21 as shown in figure 21.27. This type of system is termed a 'simplex' system.

Using redundancy is where one or more of the components of the system is repeated or duplicated with the intention of

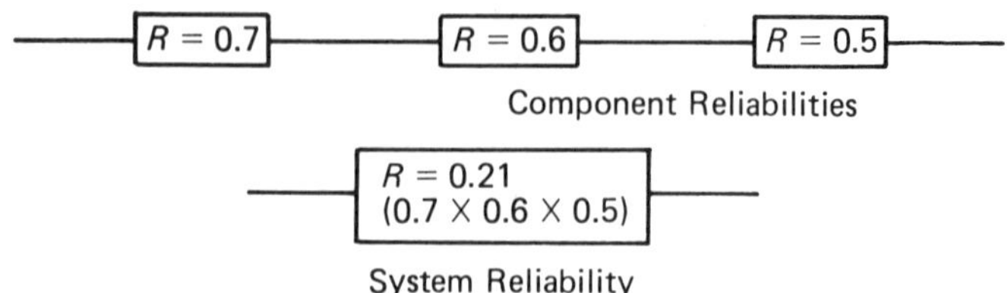

Figure 21.27 *Reliability of a 'Simplex' System*

improving its reliability and hence the availability of the complete system.

In a 'multiplexed' system, all the components will normally operate together so that the system continues to operate in the event of failure of a repeated component. In a 'multiplicated' system only one repeated component operates at a time however and it is necessary to switch to another in the event of failure.

Figure 21.28 shows a component repeated four times in a system, each individual component having a reliability of 0.6. The system reliability is thus increased to 0.97. This represents a factor of improvement of 1.62 for about four times the cost.

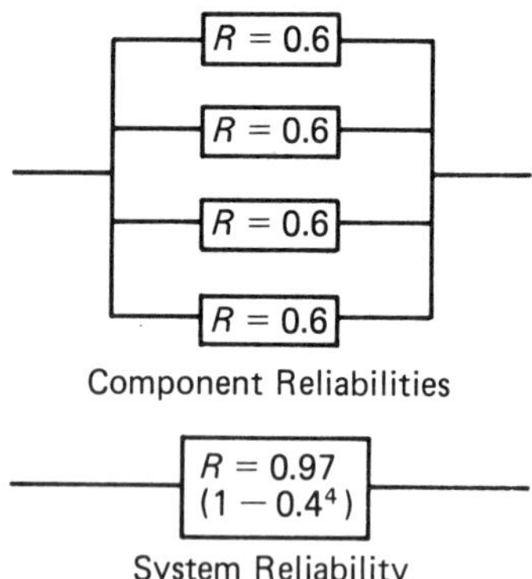

Figure 21.28 *Reliability of a Redundant System*

Figure 21.29 shows how this may compare with the cost of improving the reliability of a single component which follows the law of diminishing returns when volume is insufficiently high to recover the increased design and development costs.

Obviously, duplication is not always a practicable way of

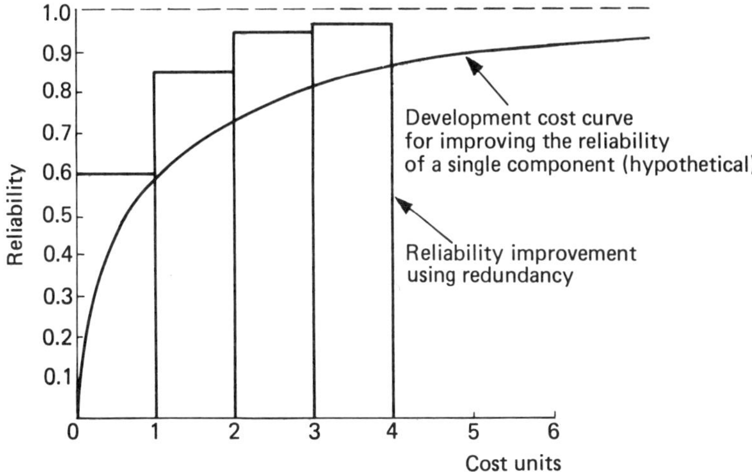

Figure 21.29 *Comparison of Costs of Improving Reliability by Using Redundancy and by Developing Single Components*

improving reliability. Space or weight restrictions often limit its application to areas where 'safety' rather than 'reliability' is of greater importance, e.g. aircraft flight controls or motor vehicle braking systems.

Investment Appraisal

It has already been discussed in Chapter 6 that most methods of investment appraisal, whatever their degree of sophistication, will attempt to compare the cost of a project with the savings or benefits deriving from it. Many organisations, however, still consider the project cost as only the initial capital cost and may disregard the ongoing running costs. More realistic appraisal methods will take into account cash flows throughout the life of a project and such a method would require a knowledge of all the running costs associated with the item throughout its technical life.

Reliability data, and their associated costs, will therefore provide a valuable input to the decision-making processes relating to the financial appraisal of such projects.

Costing

Accurate product costing must be dependent on the total cost of ownership of the manufacturing plant. The concept of 'life-cycle costing' considers all the stages in the life span of a physical asset, i.e.:

Specification, Design, Manufacture or build } or purchase if plant is a standard stock item

Installation

Commissioning and run-up

Running (e.g. power supplies), Maintenance and modification (labour spares etc.), Downtime resulting from failures, Disposal } Operation

Performance Specification

Performance specifications for new products are often limited to 'operating' performance, e.g. capacity, accuracy, etc. There are many measures which may be used to specify the 'reliability' performance of a piece of equipment. Some of these have already been mentioned (reliability, availability, etc.).

Other possible measures are: mean time between failures (MTFB); the average time between successive failures; and mean time to repair (MTTR) – the average time taken to put a failed piece of equipment back into operation (a measure of maintainability).

Planned Maintenance

Planned Maintenance refers to any maintenance work carried out on a piece of equipment as a result of a previous management decision rather than as a direct consequence of that item failing during operation.

One of the most common forms of planned maintenance is 'scheduled maintenance' where work is carried out regularly on a weekly, monthly etc. basis.

The type of work done may vary from simple lubrication of machinery through to more major tasks such as replacement of clutches, bearings, etc. In addition, a schedule may include the inspection of certain items and rectification should their condition be below some prescribed level e.g. tightening-up loose belts etc.

The purpose of scheduled maintenance is, first, to prolong the life of equipment components and, secondly, to replace parts at a convenient time rather than waiting for failure to occur which will interrupt production.

The concept and intentions of scheduled maintenance are sound, but without a good knowledge of the performance of the various machine systems, the maintenance work could be wasteful and expensive. For example, the failure probability of some items might not be time dependent, or their reliability may even be improving with time, in which case maintenance work may be ineffective or even do more harm than good.

An analysis of reliability data for machine components would provide the information necessary to decide which items to inspect and replace and when this work should be carried out.

Replacement Policies

When the running costs of a piece of equipment increase with time, there may eventually come a point when it would be favourable to replace it completely.

Many theoretical procedures have been developed for evaluating when such a replacement should be made (Jardine)[10] and in most cases the objective is to minimise the total costs associated with purchasing and running the plant.

4 Conclusion

There can be no disputing that increasing numbers of purchasers base their choice on 'cost of ownership' rather than 'original cost', often leading to a preference for foreign rather than home-produced items.

The control of quality and reliability of products (and services) is therefore becoming an increasingly important factor for the operations manager in an energy and cost conscious world.

References and Further Reading

1 Hanley, J., Our experience with quality circles, *Quality Progress*, February 1980.
2 Jenney, B.W. and Newton, D., Statistics and quality control, *The Production Engineer*, March 1969.
3 Murdoch, J. and Barnes, J.A., *Statistical Tables for Science, Engineering, Management and Business Studies*, Macmillan 1974.
4 Dodge, H.F. and Romig, H.G., *Sampling Inspection Tables: Single and Double Sampling*, Wiley-Interscience 1959.
5 Crow, E.L., Davis, F.A. & Maxfield, M.W., *Statistics Manual*, Dover 1960.
6 Brook, R.H.W., *Reliability Concepts in Engineering Manufacture*, Butterworths 1972.
7 Nixon, F., *The Joint Responsibilities of Government and Industrial Management*, Institute of Mechanical Engineering Conference on the Reliability of Service Equipment, 21–23 February 1968.
8 Vasil'ev, Y.A. and Babaev, S.G., Nomograms for determining the reliability of products, *Russian Engineering Journal*, Vol. 48, No. 9, 1968.
9 Carter, A.D.S., Achieving quality and reliability, *Proceedings of the Institute of Mechanical Engineering*, Vol. 188, 13/1974.
10 Jardine, A.K.S., *Maintenance, Replacement and Reliability*, Pitman 1973.

22

The Introduction of a Quality Control System for Artificial Legs*

A R ROWLAND

Formerly of J E Hanger & Co Ltd

1 Introduction

Under the National Health Service, every person who has lost a limb and is able to wear a prosthesis (artificial limb) is entitled to be supplied with two identical prostheses for each missing limb and to have them maintained in good order. The Limb Fitting Service has its origins in the centre established at Queen Mary's Hospital, Roehampton, during the 1914–18 war. To-day there are 24 centres in England, Wales and Northern Ireland which see to the needs of 65,000 amputees. The limb industry as a whole has to produce 20,000 new limbs every year and handle 100,000 limbs that need repair.

The history of the artificial leg goes back very far indeed, but little progress was made in its development until the 16th century when new design thoughts coincided with improved amputation techniques. At that time a below-knee limb was made which had a copper socket attached to a wood foot and was suspended on the patient by a leather thigh corset. The limb was hinged at the knee with steel bars.

To-day we make artificial legs from a wide variety of materials for a wide variety of prescriptions which can be

* Reproduced by kind permission of the author and the Institute of Quality Assurance.

grouped as follows:

1. Light metal limbs of traditional design made by craftsmen whose skill and appreciation of the user requirements have established a high reputation for them.
2. Wood limbs mainly for export to countries where the local craftsmen can take a partly prepared limb and shape and finish it for the individual patient. Wood has advantages in warm humid climates and there is an affinity for this natural material.
3. Limbs of modular construction in the sense of having interchangeable sub-assemblies, though there is still the bespoke aspect with the patient/limb interface components.

2 Aspects of the Service

Service is the keyword of the company, a service for the rehabilitation of our patients. This is not a manufacturing company only, because we make the product and carry out the measuring and fitting to the patient. Our prosthetists are, in effect, members of the clinic teams and work with the doctors and nurses who seek to restore their patients to an active life. It is the prosthetist who measures the good leg, takes a cast of the stump, ascertains any particular requirements, and ensures that the completed limb is correctly fitted. Good clinical evaluation is most important.

Each limb is individually made for the patient. This is a bespoke service where the patient's particulars (weight, height, activity, and so on) and limb measurements become the detail specification and the doctor's prescription becomes the order. However, the criterion of success for the limb is not that it is correct according to any drawing or specification (though that is important), but that it is acceptable to the patient.

After the order is placed with the factory the prescription or specification may change. The patient may put on weight or become slimmer, or his stump size may change, or he may even decide upon some change of foot wear because the fashion has changed. Our wood feet are tailor-made to fit the shoe with proper regard to heel height and we dare not assume that it is only the young ladies who follow the trends.

Time is of the essence and we must rehabilitate the patient as soon as practicable. He (or she) has been through a traumatic experience and we must not add to the clinic team's difficulties by failing to provide the limb at the appointed time. Unfortunately, being a bespoke service, time must be allowed to make the limb.

Artificial limbs are sometimes needed by the very young and as children grow into adults and their activities change, they require prostheses of different function, strength, size, and appearance.

The pattern of demand is continuously variable, the range of variation unlimited, but time is limited and acceptance by the individual patient is of paramount importance. This is quite a challenge for quality control, but the British limb industry has achieved high standards and it is company policy to maintain these standards and aim for higher ones to the benefit of patients and the security of our business.

3 Introduction of Quality Control

The organisation for quality control is nothing new because it is predetermined by the management which delegates responsibility for areas of work and it is along the same line that responsibility for quality is channelled. The Quality Department started life about three years ago as an independent service to each area of work, linking together and co-ordinating their efforts for quality achievement. We see it as most important that those sections which provide a service to the design and manufacture groups should also be subject to quality control. These sections include, for example, purchasing, stores, typing, despatch, and progress control.

The introduction of a formal quality control system was recognised by top management as absolutely necessary for two basic reasons. First, there was the need to establish standards in the competitive environment of overseas markets, particularly in the EEC countries where the company had become actively involved in harmonisation programmes. Secondly, there was the technological change in the design and manufacture of artificial legs which now relied less upon the skills of craftsmen and more on those of machine-shop workers. In addition, the need to expand our business in the overseas markets meant that production had to be more cost-effective.

The development of the quality control function was planned on a long-term basis. It was realised that difficulties would be encountered during the transition from the traditional method of working to a system of procedures and controls that would inevitably restrict and in some cases eliminate established practices. The first aim was to gain the confidence of the staff at all levels. Although top management had 'started the ball rolling' it was necessary to show the staff that the decision was right and thus obtain their full support. At shop-floor level the new ways had to be proved beneficial to both employees and patients. Employees had to be assured that management recognised that their knowledge and experience were invaluable. They were consulted at all times and given opportunities to state their problems.

4 Making the Company Quality-Conscious

In the first phase of making the company quality-conscious there were three objectives:

- (i) To establish communications with all departments to enable them to co-ordinate the efforts for quality achievement.
- (ii) To introduce fundamental disciplines of control in those areas which provide a service to production. This initially was confined to drawings and goods inwards.
- (iii) To obtain data on quality achievement.

In the first six months the new inspection department brought under control all incoming goods and prevented faulty materials and components from being placed in stock. Production people soon became aware of the influence this new function was having on them and sometimes there was difficulty in getting parts that accorded with the drawings. The man on the bench who had always made parts fit by hammer or file or by selection would not readily break the habit. And, of course, drawing anomalies came to light and had to be put right.

This led quite naturally to the setting up of a drawing change committee in which representatives from design, production, quality, and production engineering could consider any proposed changes. The committee introduced written procedures for design changes, concessions, and production permits. The same committee now scrutinises new design drawings prior to any pre-production run.

Examination of outgoing legs had always been carried out but was, and still is, a subjective form of inspection. It is in this area that the first data were collected and analysed and led to improved examination techniques. The more efficient inspection was not reflected in the defect analysis because the production foremen were by now wary of submitting sub-standard work.

Investigation into failures and complaints had the benefit of bringing quality control personnel into more direct contact with other departments where they could learn from people with long experience and in return demonstrate in a practical way the quality control approach.

From the experiences and lessons learnt in the first phase, there was further development and implementation of a quality control system in the second.

The introduction of vendor appraisal and surveillance schemes had revealed that our suppliers' standards were not good enough. In fact they were well below our requirements but it was essential to maintain production and also to give our suppliers time to adjust. So it was accepted that sub-standard goods would be considered for use provided that the supplier recognised his responsibilities and could demonstrate that he was progressing towards the required standard.

By now there was a Goods Received Note procedure and a Reject Note System which laid down precise instructions for the identification and segregation of defective goods. It is intended to introduce batch control at the appropriate time and all procedures are designed with this in mind.

On the design side, new drawings are to British Standard

BS308 in metric. It is not possible to change over completely from imperial to metric because legs are maintained for life and some were made over 40 years ago. We do not have obsolete designs.

The investigation work into failures has been formalised and combined with a Defect Report procedure which ensures that all in-use failures on new designs are properly recorded and always investigated with a conclusive report. This work has been carried out by inspectors who have thus extended their knowledge of legs and the function of the components. Their knowledge has been used in the introduction of planning sheets.

5 The Role of the Quality Department

Up till now the Quality Department has been the prime mover in any change or introduction. To begin with, it must lead the campaign against an attitude of indifference that makes many people content to leave things as they are and sceptical of proposed improvements. In the past even known problems were either accepted or passed to the Quality Department with no intention of giving assistance or expectation of the answers. As progress has been made an attitude of co-operation has begun to appear and people sometimes offer to do something in their own departments towards the attainment of quality. Gradually the Quality Department will become less dominant, but it must always play a leading role in order to maintain its influence.

From the inception of quality control it was decided to remain flexible at all times in order to ensure that any system of control was relevant to the particular circumstances and in line with the overall policy. This was felt to be particularly important in the setting up of a new department when it would have been so easy to have followed the examples of previous experience in other industries. All personnel in the Quality Department are encouraged to be forward thinking and to play their part in the development of the quality control function. In line with this policy they are required to carry out any duty within the Department including: goods inwards inspection; writing planning sheets; gauge control; torque wrench calibration; investigation into failures; concession inquiries; and outgoing inspection. The transition from craftsmanship work controlled exclusively by shop foremen to the concept of Total Quality Control with documented controls and procedures is difficult, not only for shop-floor workers but also for the inspectors themselves. Our inspectors, recruited from other industries, were not used to the idea of production that never worked to drawings or specifications. Special appliances for thalidomide victims were created by the craftsman on the bench and not by a designer in his laboratory. It was the foreman who visited the timber merchants to select his wood from tree trunks before any purchase order was raised and years before it was required. It was another foreman who examined the leather skins and approved their use. The inspectors will have to acquire a working knowledge of all these aspects and our policy is to put down in writing, where possible, the parameters which define the requirement and otherwise to transfer the knowledge into agreed standard samples.

It would be very easy to get swamped in the detail of improving quality so that little progress is made in establishing a quality control system. The inadequacies which are revealed each hour of the day all demand attention so it is necessary to keep one's sights on the fundamental issues and resolve the problems of communication and relations between people which affect co-operation and co-ordination. For this reason there are many occasions when a blind eye is turned to design queries, drawing omissions, or certain production practices.

6 Objectives and Controls

To check progress, a list of the broad requirements was made. This list is not static and does not indicate priorities but is to be extended as experience demands.

(i) *Design control*

The objective is to design a limb, or mechanism within a limb, which meets the functional and aesthetic requirements, is safe and reliable, which permits rational production, and is within the stipulated cost.

The need is to produce a new design which will be acceptable to all or to most patients at different levels of amputation. There may also be a problem of interchangeability. Many of our limbs will be maintained for the patient's life so, although designs may be modified and improved, the thousands of limbs in use cannot be made obsolete.

Controls are needed for the following purposes:

(a) To review the design against the performance requirement. This entails carrying out life tests, environmental tests, and ultimately approval tests.
(b) To review the drawings and specifications to ensure their adequacy, clarity, and accuracy for production.
(c) To set down the design disciplines to be observed in order to establish and maintain control of design functions affecting quality achievement.

(ii) *Purchasing control*

The objective is to ensure that the Production Department is given the correct supplies from outside sources at the time needed and at economic cost.

Controls are needed:

(a) To ensure that only suppliers are used who have been approved for their quality capabilities;
(b) To maintain a quality surveillance on each supplier's performance;
(c) To ensure that purchase requirements are adequately specified;
(d) To pass all incoming goods through receiving inspection;
(e) To maintain control of goods and, in particular, the segregation and identification of defective goods;
(f) To ensure proper storage.

(iii) *Production control*

The objective is to control the quality of manufacture and assembly to ensure conformity with the design drawings, the prosthetist's instructions, and any agreed standards. This also applies to repaired and refurbished limbs.

Controls are needed:

(a) To agree and establish standards of workmanship and finish;
(b) To provide facilities and training appropriate to the work being done;
(c) To establish procedures for the control of parts and identification of batches of work;
(d) To control use of drawings;
(e) To investigate any failure to achieve the required level of quality and take corrective actions;
(f) To verify that work conforms to the requirements,
(g) To check tools and measuring equipment regularly;
(h) To feed information back for the improvement of design, manufacture, and quality control.

(iv) *Product support service*

The objective is to provide a limb-fitting service for the rehabilitation of the patient.

Controls are needed:

(a) To give clear, precise, and adequate instructions for the particular limb in accordance with the medical officer's prescription;
(b) To ensure that the limb supplied is acceptable to the patient;
(c) To feed information back for the improvement of design, manufacture, and quality control;
(d) To investigate all complaints;
(e) To provide facilities and training appropriate to the services;
(f) To maintain patients' files.

Today we can tick off many of the items on our list and look forward to the day when we can produce a quality manual setting out the policy, organisation, responsibilities, and procedures which are in being. A review is made of the unticked items to decide priorities, but we have found that there is one fundamental weakness underlying our decisions and that is the lack of quality data. The company has 60 years of experience and knowledge gained and retained by the work force. Many of our employees have been with the company for 40 to 50 years and they tend to recall that standards were better in the past. But no one has recorded any quality data whatever and those memories are often tinged with regret for the good old days and also mellowed by time. At least there is now three years of experience properly set down.

23
Monitoring and Management by Exception

C D LEWIS

*Professor of Operations Management,
The University of Aston*

1 Introduction

With the ever-increasing size and complexity of production and operational systems, the need to 'manage by exception' is becoming more and more important. It is impossible for management to maintain a personal check on all the happenings within such systems, particularly as much of the information defining those happenings no longer appears in a printed form, but is 'buried' in computer storage systems.

Thus exception reporting, whereby happenings that do not accord with previous plans are brought to management's attention, will become an increasing feature of management activity. This will be particularly true of computerised systems where such monitoring or exception reporting will have to be automatic.

Typical exception reporting covers such aspects of operations as:

(i) customers who have not paid bills on time;
(ii) suppliers who have not delivered goods on time;
(iii) suppliers who do not meet the required quality standards;
(iv) clients who overdraw their credit facilities;

(v) subscribers who do not renew insurance cover, licensing fees, etc., on time;
(vi) managers who do not keep within agreed budgets;
(vii) production schedules not being maintained.

One of the first requirements of an exception reporting system must be an exact definition of what is meant by an exception. As an example of this, in Chapter 14 the concept of a monitoring statistic termed the smoothed error tracking signal was introduced. The value that tracking signal took could then be associated with a level of statistical confidence in one's hypothesis that a significant change had occurred (see page 261).

Such a relatively refined measure of the significance of a change is, however, often not required in general exception reporting. It is *consistency* of change identification that is more likely to be the most useful feature of such systems. Thus, if one is prepared to indicate the size of change or deviation from target which is unacceptable, what really is required of an exception reporting system is to ensure that changes or deviations of that size or greater are reliably identified in future.

One numerical approach is to examine the cumulative sum of errors or differences between what is planned and what is achieved. This cumulative sum or CUSUM approach is a very simple technique which has been available to managers for many years. Because, however, it has been largely ignored in the literature, the method is now discussed in some detail using practical management problems as a means of hopefully impressing on readers the power of this simple, but much ignored technique.

2 Cumulative Sums of Errors – CUSUMS

(a) CUSUMS – Interpreted via Golf Scoring Systems

In the game of golf a scoring system has been devised to cope with:

(i) the relatively high numbers involved, i.e., strokes taken;

(ii) the variation in difficulty of each hole, usually three to five strokes per hole; and
(iii) the different stages (i.e. number of holes) of the course that an individual player may have completed.

The scoring system adopted to overcome all these problems establishes a standard and relates every player's performance to that standard. The standard chosen is the number of strokes a professional would be expected to take and this is referred to as 'par'. (Indeed the phrase 'below par' is used in everyday language to indicate one's relative indisposition).

Using this system of referring a player's performance to an established standard, a statement that player *A* is out on the course at two under par and that player *B* is in the clubhouse at one under, indicates that player *A* will beat player *B* if he loses no more strokes to par, irrespective of the fact that it is not specified how much of the course player *A* has completed, or the relative difficulty of the holes he or she has yet to play. An identical situation described in terms of the number of strokes taken would be that player *B* was in the clubhouse on 71 and player *A* had taken 58. This latter description would not be a meaningful indication of the two players' relative performance, even if one were told that player *A* had completed fifteen holes.

Complex though the system of scoring in golf may appear to the non-golfer, in essence all the scoring system does is cumulate the sum of errors or differences from an established standard.

(b) *CUSUMS – the Basic Principle*

This principle of cumulating sums of error (commonly referred to as CUSUMS) is a powerful method of identifying change as can be seen by examining figure 23.1 which represents the performance of a system with an apparent average value of five and a high degree of random variation. What cannot be seen on this diagram is that the average of the first thirty values is indeed 5, but that the average of the last thirty values is 5.3. However, examination of figure 23.2, which shows the cumulative sum of errors referenced to a value of 5 for the same situation, not only identifies the change as occurring at

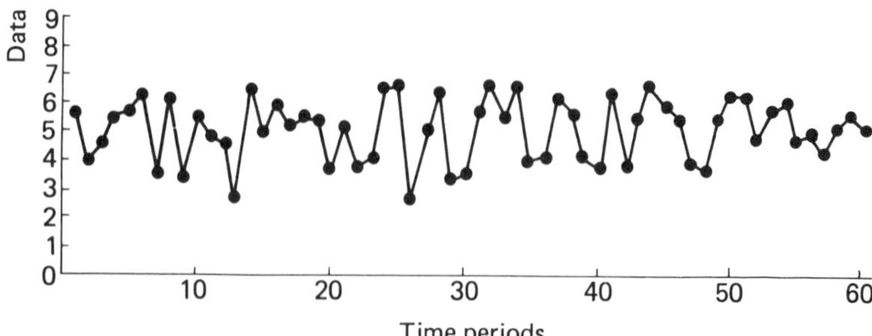

Figure 23.1 *Data with High Degree of Random Variation*

the thirtieth point, when the CUSUM plot no longer remains horizontal (which it has done up to then simply because positive and negative errors cancel out when the true process average is five), but also identifies the size of that change as 0.3, since after the thirtieth value the CUSUM plot rises at an average rate of 0.3 per period.

3 Graphical Use of CUSUMS

The following data (table 23.1) shows a typical budgetary control situation complicated by the fact that not only does

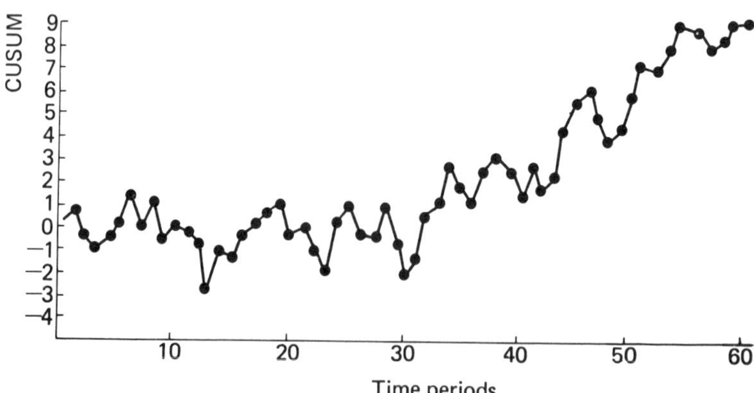

Figure 23.2 *Cumulative Sum of Errors (CUSUM) for Data in Figure 23.1*

Table 23.1 Budgetary Control Data with CUSUM

Month	*Jan*	*Feb*	*Mar*	*Apr*	*May*	*Jun*
Budget	10,000	11,000	9,500	9,500	12,000	10,000
Expenditure	10,000	12,500	11,000	8,300	13,000	9,000
Difference	0	1,500	1,500	–1,200	1,000	–1,000
Cumulative Difference	0	1,500	3,000	1,800	2,800	1,800

Month	*Jul*	*Aug*	*Sep*	*Oct*	*Nov*	*Dec*
Budget	9,000	9,000	11,000	11,000	12,000	10,000
Expenditure	8,000	10,000	10,500	11,500	13,000	11,000
Difference	–1,000	1,000	–500	500	1,000	1,000
Cumulative Difference	800	1,800	1,300	1,800	2,800	3,800

the departmental expenditure vary monthly, but so also does the budget (i.e. the reference is not constant). Presented graphically, without any transformation, this budgetary control data could be presented in four different ways, the usefulness of each of which will be examined individually in terms of indicating expenditure performance against budget.

Graphical Analysis of Budgetary Control Data (Figures 23.3(a), (b), (c) & (d)

(i) *Plot of raw data – Figure 23.3(a)*

This presentation reveals very little of the department's expenditure performance against budget, even though the scale has been enlarged by truncating it at £8,000.

(ii) *Plot of cumulative data – Figure 23.3(b)*

Because, in this form of presentation the cumulative expenditure line is always above the cumulative budget line, it follows that a degree of overspending has occurred. However, the range of the scale has to be large enough to accommodate a full year's expenditure, and it is so large as to make the size of that overspending impossible to measure with any degree of accuracy.

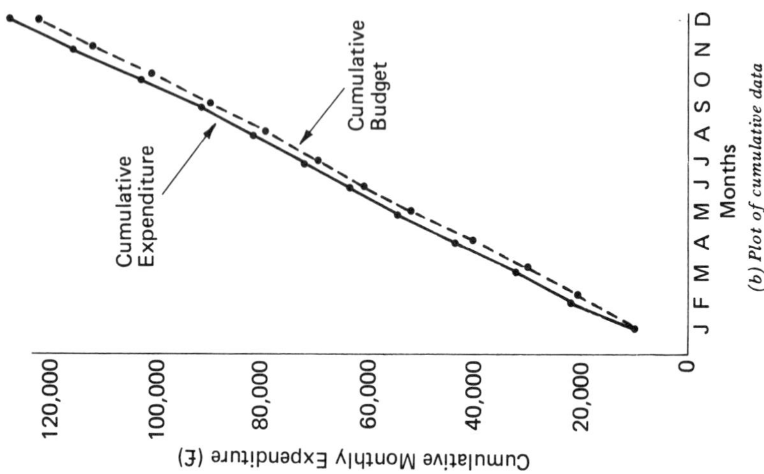

(b) Plot of cumulative data

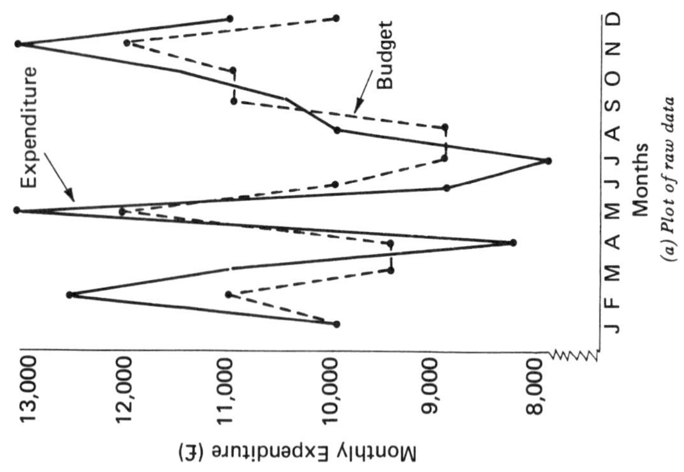

(a) Plot of raw data

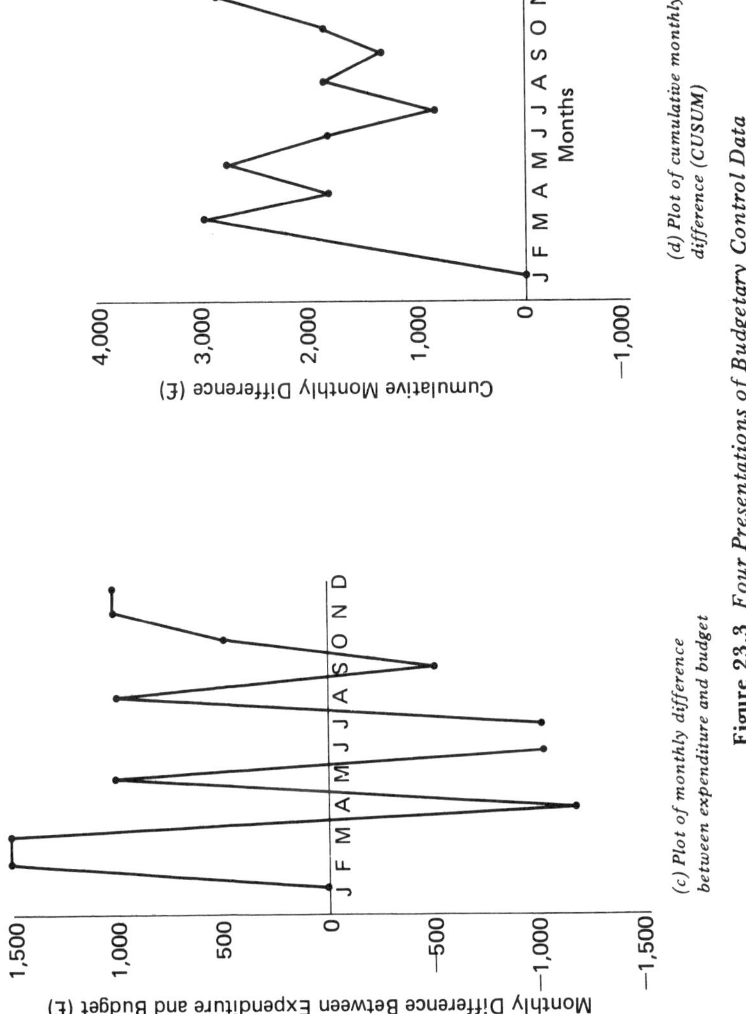

(c) Plot of monthly difference between expenditure and budget

(d) Plot of cumulative monthly difference (CUSUM)

Figure 23.3 *Four Presentations of Budgetary Control Data*

(iii) *Plot of difference between expenditure and budget – Figure 23.3(c)*

This presentation, because of the relatively small range of the scale, can give an accurate indication of the difference between expenditure and budget month by month, but gives little indication of the progressive effect during the year.

(iv) *Plot of cumulative difference between expenditure and budget – Figure 23.3(d)*

With this CUSUM presentation, if the gradient of the plotted values is higher than the horizontal, an excessive expenditure against budget is being incurred. If the gradient is lower than the horizontal, under-expenditure against budget is being achieved and whilst the plotted values remain horizontal, expenditure is roughly equal to the budget over that period of time.

Taking these comments into account, this CUSUM presentation reveals the following. For the first three months of the year expenditure exceeded budget by an average of £1,000 per month such that by the end of March a £3,000 over-spend situation had resulted. Over the next four months, because of a slight degree of under-spending, the over-spend situation has partially recovered by the end of June by which time expenditure exceeded budget by only £800. However, from July onwards, with the exception of one month, excessive over-spending occurred such that at the end of the year a £4,000 over-spend situation was recorded.

It is apparent from the previous discussion that the CUSUM presentation is by far the best method of presenting data graphically when comparing performance between two sets of related figures. A further advantage in the budgetary control type of situation is that if the budget should be altered or re-negotiated the resulting figures can be plotted without changing the scale of the graph, which could be necessary for all the other methods of presentation.

4 Use of CUSUM Technique in Automatic Exception Reporting Systems

Figure 23.4 illustrates some plant performance data whose target value is 90. Below this graph of raw data, is the associated CUSUM plot where 90 was used as the reference value. Superimposed on the CUSUM plot is a V-MASK pivoted b periods ahead of the current point and whose half-angle is controlled by a parameter a; in this case a = 20 and b = 2. The underlying basis of this arrangement is known as a V-MASK/CUSUM test which operates such that the upper limb of the V-MASK cuts the CUSUM plot, and a downward change is detected (as in this case) starting at that point in time, whereas if the lower limb cuts the CUSUM plot an upward change can be inferred.

The V-MASK/CUSUM test is essentially a backwards, sequential test examining the sum of the *i*th most recent

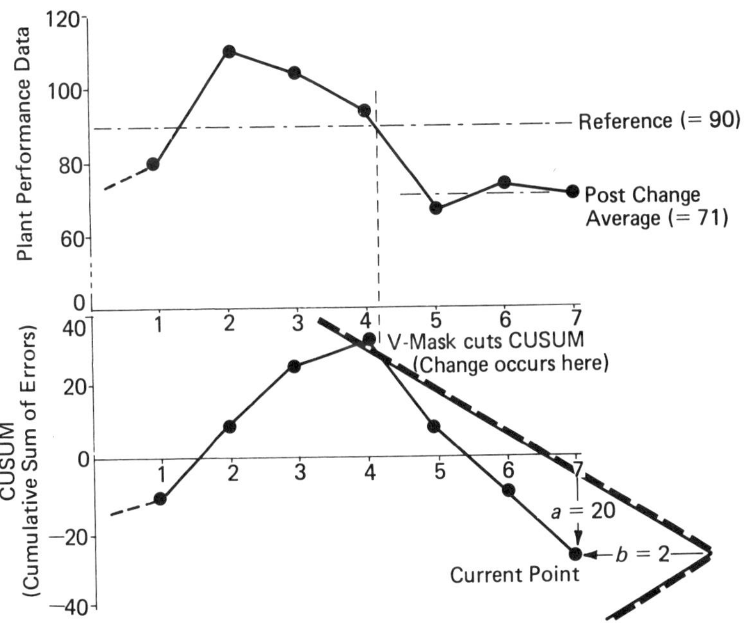

Figure 23.4 *Data with Associated CUSUM with Superimposed V-MASK*

Table 23.2 Tabular Form of V-MASK/CUSUM Analysis Suitable for Computer Implementation

Period (N)	*Demand*	*Forecast*	*Error*	$(a/b - e_N)$	Min $(R_{N-1}; a)$	R_N	$(a/b + e_N)$	Min $(D_{N-1}; a)$	D_N
1	80	90	−10	20	20	40	0	20	20
2	110	90	20	−10	20	10	30	20	50
3	105	90	15	−5	10	5	25	20	45
4	95	90	5	5	5	−10	15	20	35
5	68	90	−22	32	10	42	−12	20	8
6	74	90	−16	26	20	46	−6	8	2
7	71	90	−19	29	20	49	−9	2	−7*

(periods 5–7, bracketed: $D_N < 20$)

V-MASK/CUSUM TEST 1

PERIOD	Print-out		Annotation
		A	
	20.		
		B	
	2.		
		REF	
	90.		
	80.		Demand
	40.		R_n
1	20.		D_n
	110.		
	10.		
2	50.		
	105.		
	5.		
3	45.		
	95.		
	10.		
4	35.		
	68.		
	42.		
5	8.		$D_n < a$
	74.		
	46.		
6	2.		
	71.		
	49.		
7	-7.		$D_n < 0$
	3.	NO	
	71.	$\bar{x}$	

Figure 23.5 *Print-out from TI59 Programme for V-MASK/CUSUM test*

errors against linear limits of the form $L_i = a(i + b)/b$, where a and b are the V-MASK parameters which control the sensitivity of the test. The test was originally proposed by Barnard[1] and made considerably more useful by Harrison and Davies[2] who indicated that the method could be made much more suitable for computer use by representing the test by two equations defining test statistics D_N and R_N where:

$$D_N = \text{Min}(D_{N-1}; a) + (a/b + e_N) \text{ and}$$
$$R_N = \text{Min}(R_{N-1}; a) + (a/b - e_N)$$

In this form a significant downward change can be inferred if D_N goes negative or a significant upward change if R_N goes negative. In either case, the detected change was initiated at that point in time when either test statistic became less than a. Table 23.2 shows the analysis of the data depicted in figure 23.4 using this form of test, and confirms a downward change being detected in period 7 (when $D_N = -7$) and that this change occurred at the start of period 5 (when $D_N = 8$ and was, therefore, less than $a = 20$).

This numerical form of the test obviously replicates the results shown graphically in figure 23.4, but in this form is readily programmed for computer application. This ease of programming of the V-MASK/CUSUM test is verified by figure 23.5 which shows an analysis of the same data, yet again, this time using a programmed version of the test on a TI59 programmable calculator. Note that since the downward change is detected three periods from the end of the data, a post change average value has been evaluated as

$$\bar{x} = 68 + 74 + 71 = 71.$$

5 Conclusion

Managing by exception can only be effective if exceptions are reliably detected. The cumulative sum (CUSUM) method by which errors or differences from a target or programmed level of activity are cumulated over time is a powerful technique in identifying such exceptions. The method can be used either manually by plotting a CUSUM graph, or as an automatic monitoring method when represented by two simple equations.

References and Further Reading

1 Barnard, G.A., Control charts and stochastic processes, *Journal of the Royal Statistical Society*, B, 16, 1959, pp. 151–174.
2 Harrison, P.J., and Davies, O.L., The use of cumulative sum (CUSUM) techniques for the control of routine forecasts by product demand, *Journal of the American Operations Research Society*, 12, 1964, pp. 325–33.
3 Lewis, C.D., Change identification: a necessary prerequisite for management by exception, *Management Decision*, Vol. 14, No. 3, 1976, pp. 3–21.
4 Lewis, C.D., The identification of small changes in process means using a computerized V-MASK, *Quality Assurance*, Vol. 6, No. 1, 1980, pp. 3–8.

24
Analysis of Electrical Rejects in an Electronics Company

C D LEWIS

*Professor of Operations Management,
The University of Aston*

1 Introduction

In this particular study the author acted as a consultant to a company manufacturing electronic guidance equipment for small medium range military rockets. For reasons of security the name of the company must naturally remain secret.

The basic problem of the company was that they were loosing money on this particular contract due to the high proportion of rejects being produced. Because of the encapsulation procedure employed in the production process, finished units rejected for electrical faults could not be corrected and were, therefore, total rejects.

Whilst the company maintained accurate records of rejects as a proportion of total production, these varied considerably from week to week. The company were concerned that such apparently high natural variation in the proportion of weekly rejects would act as a camouflaging factor when attempting to establish whether proposed improvements to the production process would actually reduce the average proportion of rejects.

2 Theoretical Approach

A study of weekly rejects figures as a proportion of weekly production over a period of six months indicated that after an initial learning phase, the proportion of rejects being produced per thousand was of the order of 105, with a range varying from 85 to 125 and a standard deviation of 5. Because of this relatively high variation it was felt that whilst the introduction of improvements in the production process might well produce statistically significant lower average reject proportions, such apparent changes and their causal factors might be difficult to establish positively. An initial study indicated that the size of changes that would be needed to achieve a lowering of the reject proportion to an average sixty per thousand, at which level the contract would be viable, might well *not* be positively detected using classical statistical tests. Because of this it was decided to analyse the reject data using a variable V-MASK/CUSUM test. When a high degree of variation is present in the data under analysis, it was recognised that this test was more sensitive in establishing small changes in process means than more traditional tests such as the Shewhart test. Essentially the variable V-MASK/CUSUM test used was based on the Harrison & Davies version of the classical straight sided V-MASK test (described fully on page 438) where the parameters **a** & **b** controlled the shape of the V-MASK and, hence, the sensitivity of the test. The test was implemented using an interactive computer programme, such that initially a very wide V-MASK was used which was progressively narrowed, thus increasing the sensitivity of the test employed. From the user's point of view, the completed programme allowed data to be searched for a specific number of changes of process means, the significance of which could then be established using a Student '*t*' test – a test for establishing the statistical significance of the difference in sample means.

3 Analysis of Reject Data Using the Variable V-MASK/CUSUM Test

Over a period of forty weeks the company had attempted to reduce the proportion of electrical rejects by introducing two fundamental changes in the production process. Initially, because a high proportion of electrical rejects appeared to be caused by 'dry' electrical joints, a new flux was introduced in the wave soldering process. This certainly appeared to lower the average proportion of weekly rejects, but not to such a level as to make the contract financially viable. Several other changes to the production process were attempted, such as changes in the method of assembly of components etc., but eventually management came to the conclusion that the only way a consistently lower proportion of rejects could be obtained would be through a tightening of the component tolerances. After discussions with the customer negotiating a price increase for the introduction of higher component tolerances, the design specification was altered and this new version of the assembly was introduced. This again appeared to produce a reduction in the proportion of rejects. To confirm that both the introduction of the new flux and the higher component tolerances had produced significant reductions in the average proportion of weekly rejects, the data for the forty weeks covering the period in question was analysed using the variable V-MASK/CUSUM programme. The results of this analysis (depicted in figure 24.1) indicated that having requested the programme to search for up to 4 changes in process meant it subsequently discovered 0, 1, 3 & 2 changes on runs 1, 2, 3 & 4 for which the V-MASK parameter **a** was 79.6, 63.68, 26.4 & 21.1 respectively with **b** kept equal to 2. Ignoring run no. 1 which identifies no changes and run no. 3 which identifies a spurious, insignificant change at period 40, run no. 4 of this analysis confirms that the introduction of higher component specifications in period 32 brought about a significant decrease in average rejects per week from 81 to 62 and the earlier introduction of the new flux in the wave soldering process in period 7 reduced the average rejects per week from 105 to 81. Both these changes are confirmed at a very high level of statistical confidence in excess of 99%.

```
DISTAT


WHAT IS THE NAME OF THE FILE WHERE YOUR DATA IS STORED?ART

HOW MANY OBSERVATIONS (1 TO N) DO YOU WISH TO USE,N?48

DO YOU REQUIRE A SINGLE RUN,FOR WHICH YOU  SPECIFY A&B?N

UP TO HOW MANY CHANGES DO YOU WISH TO DETECT, MAX 8?4


SUMMARY
=======

RUN   CHANGES   A FOR        *** STATISTICAL INFO ***
NO    DETECTED  V-MASK       MSE         MAPE       BIAS
===   ========  ======       ===========================

 1        0      79.6        417.818     24.2637     0
 2        1      63.68       294.068     18.0769     1.43051E-06
 3        3      26.4094     254.233     16.171      2.22524E-06
 4        2      21.1275     238.775     16.0217    -1.74840E-06
B FOR V-MASK = 2    FOR ALL RUNS


DETAILED SUMMARY
================

RUN    CHANGE     BEGINS-     MEAN OR     SIZE OF      CONFIDENCE
NO     NUMBER     DATA PT     REFERENCE   CHANGE       LEVEL %
===    ======     =======     =========   ======       =========

 1      ****       START       77.375      ****
 2      ****       START       85.6129     ****
         1         32          62.3529     23.26        99.981
 3      ****       START       96.9091     ****
         1         12          77.7727     19.1364      99.7757
         2         34          56.8333     20.9394      98.867
         3         40          66.2222     9.38889      38.1731
 4      ****       START       104.5       ****
         1         7           81.08       23.42        99.8289
         2         32          62.3529     18.7271      99.8815
```

Figure 24.1 *Summary Output of Change Identification Analysis*

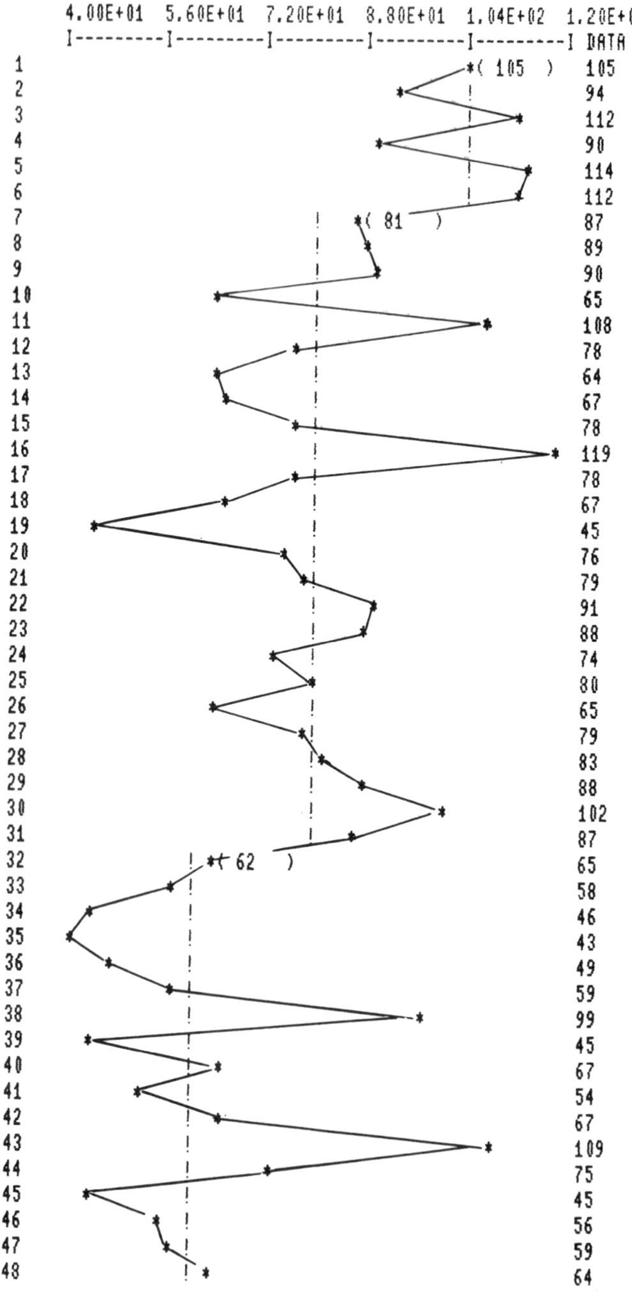

Figure 24.2 *Computer Print-out Indicating Fall in Reject Level per Thousand from a Level of 105 to 81 to 62*

A graphical interpretation of this analysis, also available from the computer programme, is shown in figure 24.2.

4 Conclusion

Having identified and confirmed the changes in weekly reject levels, the company were concerned that, with such a highly variable production process, any deterioration in reject levels should be identified quickly. Having ascertained that the previous changes had been identified using a V-MASK/CUSUM test with V-MASK parameters a = 21.1275 and b = 2, weekly reject figures were continuously monitored using the test with those parameters.

Author Index

Subject Index